Autonomy, Consciousness, and Personhood

Autonomy, Consciousness, and Personhood

A Primer for the Public Dialogue on Abortion

STEPHEN BUJNO

WIPF & STOCK · Eugene, Oregon

AUTONOMY, CONSCIOUSNESS, AND PERSONHOOD
A Primer for the Public Dialogue on Abortion

Wipf & Stock
An Imprint of Wipf and Stock Publishers
199 W. 8th Ave., Suite 3
Eugene, OR 97401

www.wipfandstock.com

PAPERBACK ISBN: 979-8-3852-6114-7
HARDCOVER ISBN: 979-8-3852-6115-4
EBOOK ISBN: 979-8-3852-6116-1

VERSION NUMBER 03/20/26

To my grandchildren
Hannah, Aubrey, Max, Savannah, Joseph, and Chloe

May their world find public dialogue reverenced
by the mind and heart.
Prevailing in charity, may the idea of personhood find its summit.

The fool tries to convince me with his reasons; the wise man persuades me with my own.

—Anonymous

Contents

Author's Preface | *ix*

Acknowledgments | *xv*

1 The State of Things | 1

2 Foundations of a Dialogue | 14

3 Reorienting the Discussion | 38

4 Human and Life as Quantifiable? | 73

5 Personhood as Qualifiable? | 98

6 The Death of Pro-life and Abolition of Pro-choice | 182

7 The Arguments Ahead | 228

8 For Consideration | 291

Bibliography | 303

Author's Preface

Half of what I say is meaningless; but I say it so that the other half may reach you. —Kahlil Gibran

We are not happy unless our acts of passion can be made to look as though they were dictated by reason. —Aldous Huxley

I am convinced that men hate each other because they fear each other. They fear each other because they don't know each other, and they don't know each other because they don't communicate with each other.
—Martin Luther King Jr.

I HAVE BEEN TEACHING ethics and social justice as they relate to the public abortion issue for over twenty years. That instructional experience has ranged from seminar groups to high school and undergraduate students, as well as postgraduate scholars stepping into doctoral programs. Among their ranks are nurses, physicians, scores of nursing and pre-med students, those studying biomedical engineering, hospital chaplains, priests and ministers, and members of religious communities, along with budding ethicists. They are what might be called members of the *informed public*. Their views on abortion have included the full gamut of nuanced positions. Few have claimed to be simply pro-choice or pro-life without some qualifications. But in the course of class or forum dialogue, eventually their position leaned to favor either the preservation of female bodily autonomy or that of fetal life. Most importantly, they have been on the whole willing to engage in dialogue. I have found them amenable to respectful discourse, even though at some point the conversation with myself and with their peers became muddled and wearisome. This impasse was rarely due to obstinacy. Typically, my experience holds that frustration arose for identifiable, although lamentable, reasons. The degree to which they lacked confidence in aspects of their arguments was a factor. More often, if contrary points introduced were novel to them, the required reflection wisely called for a pause. Other times, by their evaluation, they deemed those in the exchange unwilling to agree with the conclusion they accepted as true. In some unfortunate cases, particularly with the latter, they withdrew once their stance, assumed uncontestable, was not being considered and accepted.

I teach ethics as it relates to issues and moral problems in society and, more often, ethics as it specifically applies to medical professionals. In these various courses, the first week introduces logic and critical thinking, and the following two weeks are dedicated to philosophical anthropology. That field delves into inquiring what the fundamental aspects of the human person are. To study *what a thing is* is known as ontology. Ontology then is the study of *being*, where specifically students in my courses are exposed to a variety of approaches questioning what *is* this *being* referred to as the *human person*. At first, it appears odd to cover something thought so familiar. But it is not uncommon for students, at the conclusion of the course, to remark they never realized the myriad of perspectives that have developed over the course of history concerning this unique species they count themselves among. The point they are to glean, though, is why this consideration of personhood matters. One exercise I use to demonstrate the centrality of *being* for ethics is to ask what questions they might have if I were to seek their permission to kill a living thing, out of sight, on the floor behind the podium. Within a few questions, at least one student will ask, "What *is* it?" That is the correct question. If I tell them, "It *is* an insect," no student typically objects. If I say, "It *is* a rabbit," nearly all become uncomfortable about killing an animal many have as a pet. There is an aesthetic element involved there, which will be brought up later in the text. Finally, if I say, "It *is* a human baby," their facial expressions reveal understandable disgust of a thought experiment where a living human baby is cavalierly killed. The point is that until one determines what a thing *is*, it is impossible to evaluate any ethical stance involving that thing; and further, our evaluation is influenced by others and culture. Thus, any ethical evaluation is tethered to *being*.

This ontological lesson then segues into how dignity is ascribed to those *beings* who are not just living humans, but persons. From that, the students are asked to consider if dignity pinned to living human persons is recognized (discovered) or constructed (assigned). They are asked to consider if there is a discovered human nature all share as persons, or if the dignity of living humans as persons is assigned by some capacity or value. What is the sampling of responses? Some students initially confuse personhood with personality, something that is partly inherited and partly developed. There are those who think personhood as applied to living humans is on a gradient, while others think that not only can personhood be gained but, along the same scale, it can also be lost. Then, an idea quite relational is that one's own personhood can be sustained by others if an individual's consciousness, and thus personhood, is lost. This evaluation perhaps connects with those students who think only the female determines the personhood of the unborn living human. The most common response is that any living human is only a person when they are self-aware, though that term is left rather vague. Many think that the *is* of personhood is *inside* the body, which they realize treats the body like the cover of a book. That of course does not account for the role of the body, but it supports their view that what *is* important, concerning the human person, *is* inside. Others bemoan the hopelessness of this venture to determine personhood and simply admit that it cannot be defined. Eventually, admitting it or not, the students realize the impact of personhood not just for the ethical evaluation, but for the legal issues formed from and influencing the ethical considerations. They also recognize how a view of personhood affects concerns of power (who decides personhood) and natural rights (what is the origin of dignity pinned to personhood).

On that last note, depending on the specific course, throughout the semester these questions arise on human nature, capacity, or value. However, the question as to *why* personhood is important remains. The *why* they learn is that this recognition of dignity tethered to personhood is associated with medical consent, capacity, privacy and confidentiality, testing and research, maternal and fetal care, end-of-life issues and the forgoing of treatment, along with immigration, racial issues, and the impact of climate on vulnerable populations. And, of course, it is central to the dialogue on abortion.

Students at all levels typically have some articulated stance on each of those topics. More often than not, they find it problematic that an ethical judgment in one application reveals an ethical inconsistency when applied to other topics regarding human dignity. For the most part, their position on personhood is not foundational, but gleaned backwards from adopted or ideological positions. This logically exposes ethical inconsistencies and thus forms an injustice, which here is the application of two differing standards to two like cases of the same kind.

The foundational premise that *either some living humans are persons or all living humans are persons* presents a conundrum worth pursuing. If one holds to *all living humans are persons*, that has ethical ramifications and constrains perceived dignity in terms of autonomy. If the judgment is that *some living humans are persons*, that has ethical ramifications as to who are persons and who decides. This *either some or all* axiom rationally presents itself as the necessary fulcrum in addressing the abortion issue stalemate, moving the ethical evaluation to moral value.

What follows in this project is a rational argument formed from the distillation of those experiences. Through candor and transparency, this text offers strategies for entering into and remaining in dialogue. The goal is to facilitate public discourse on the enduring social justice issue of abortion. That is a work of public philosophy. Consider it a plea in dialectic form clarified by humility. Today, the public discourse on the topic of abortion has been shaped by partisan positions and ideological endeavors. It is not much better in academia, where often the scholarly tone simply adds a level of condescending arrogance. Those in the scholarly world engage in the topic of abortion primarily formed by arguing the dogmatic correctness of their position, while attempting to dissect opposing points of view. In the community and on social media, the exchanges consist primarily of memes and slogans, signs and protests, and verbal bullying. In all venues sides have formed, and allegiance to one's position is a loyalty often expressed by refusing to listen to an adversarial position. The other "side" is not thought of as an alternative position to consider, but as threatening, intractable, or both. What is presently needed is a type of discourse that would lead to an analytical consideration of various positions with openness to the clarification, strengthening, and possible reform of one's own argument. That is not a compromise but a win for any position.

Aligning with that goal and tone, this text is designed to be argued *with* rather than argued *against*. No position on abortion will be affirmed, but arguments for consideration will be offered. Arguments, as will be explained, are not the same as quarrels but are intended to lead individuals to express their truth clearly and rationally. Passion is both necessary and expected for the abortion topic, but mere outrage is a poor evaluator of any argument. The goal cannot be to silence or subdue the opponent and declare a win. Any rhetoric or expertise must be oriented to the pursuit of expressing truths clearly in charity. That requires guided engagement, where perhaps the classroom exchange can spill out into the public sphere. The Latin maxim *audi alteram partem* translates as *listen to the other side.* To listen does not mean to agree, neither should listening be thought granting a voice to the opposition. Listening requires dialogue, where the probing of truth cannot remain a solitary venture. It is my humble hope and steadfast desire that *Autonomy, Consciousness, and Personhood: A Primer for the Public Dialogue on Abortion* sufficiently presents the necessary elements to become a primer capable of cultivating respectful dialogue in the public sphere.

Acknowledgments

This work serves as a primer yet makes no pretense to be exhaustive. Nonetheless, recognition must be given to the multitude of friends, relatives, students, colleagues, medical professionals, and willing public audiences whose prodding and picking I have perhaps exhausted.

It is not a palatable trait for relationships to constantly question premises and rapid-fire inferences that logically derive from spoken propositions. My wife Tina has suffered perhaps more than others on that account. But I am sincerely grateful. To my longtime childhood friend Douglas Kelchner and high school classmate Debbie Dunn Fish, sincere thanks for their critical reading of and suggested edits to early drafts. Such feedback helped frame the chapters and section sequences. Per their observation I added a standalone chapter on critical thinking and logic. Too, a particular acknowldgment is warranted to Jason and Carolyn Lesher at Ensinger's Printing, who gratefully provided pro bono bound drafts for me to edit as hard copies. Being among the last of the Boomers, I still find the printed page preferable to the computer screen.

From years of teaching at varied institutions at both the undergraduate and graduate level, I wish to recognize those many philosophy, ethics, nursing, pre-med, engineering, and medical professional students who have molded my thoughts. Though left unnamed, they offered stories and experiences that have caused me to hone the arguments. Respect for them has enforced a mutual respect for developing a dialogue style. They have spontaneously demonstrated with their aha moments in the classroom those insightful points that seem to have hit their mark. Many of those strategic claims now appear as elements in this printed text. Further, since nearly every course I teach begins with a section on syllogistic logic, the many arguments I developed to demonstrate various points in the classroom have found their way into this manuscript. The student's inherent inquisitiveness and acumen for ferreting out false premises coupled with respectful interaction has symmetrically appropriated my thinking and form of expression. It is worth mentioning my appreciation to all the folks in Cheyenne, Wyoming, who hosted me as a keynote speaker where the contents of this book were given the first light of day. It will remain my boast that the hundreds there offered the initial public sounding board and proving ground for my approach to the public abortion dialogue.

As an acknowledgment of note, I can hardly express my appreciation—nay, my admiration—for the unparalleled editing skills of Linda Singerle. To wade through this manuscript in its preparation for final submission, she completed tasks ultimately foreign to me. I am indebted. This collaboration is only sweetened by the fact that Linda was a bridesmaid in my wedding to my good wife Tina some 36-plus years ago. I would turn to her again without reservation. On that note, allow me to once again express gratitude for my wife, Tina, who over the course of my academic career while I juggled teaching, course design, thesis and doctoral direction, and typically three books at various stages of adoption, has shouldered a disproportionate amount of the necessary family duties, while running her own studio pottery production enterprise. I recognize that, in many ways, she has chosen the first things in this life. Her evening hours watching Brit Box likely serves as therapy. For myself, I have found that as a lifelong artist, malcontent, and resident cynic, the ideas flow faster than the ability to form them into concrete expressions. Yet, my sardonic rumblings too often become rants that misdirect my energies. Tina has a civilizing effect in that regard and mention of it here seems a paltry homage. There is a price for passion.

Finally, I wish to mention my parents, Rose Marie and Charlie, who are but with me in spirit. My good mother would not understand much of what I write, but she would be impressed that Stevie wrote another book. Her Italian recipes, which I prepare daily, sustain me, as do the many memories. As to my father, Chup never finished tenth grade as he lied about his age to enlist and serve in the European theater of World War II. Of my modest accomplishments, he would simply be proud. This type of writing would not have flowed from his education at the "school of hard knocks," as he would put it, but to see another book with his family name on it would cause him to smile. Such are the formative years that stealthily have set me upon unfamiliar paths, fostering in me a reverence for the roles others have taken on this pilgrimage of life, of which this book is but one minor step.

I

The State of Things

Because a thing seems difficult for you, do not think it impossible for anyone to accomplish. —Marcus Aurelius

Most of the greatest evils that man has inflicted upon man have come through people feeling quite certain about something which, in fact, was false. —Betrand Russell

Hope sees the invisible, feels the intangible, and achieves the impossible. —Helen Keller

THE ABORTION DIALOGUE IS in crisis. It is not that the requisite dispositions and acumen required for dialogue are exceptional, but the experience is rarely positive and even less so satisfying. To a greater degree, regardless of positions, dialoguing in the present state of things is found to be both disheartening and ineffectual. Those who hold a female's bodily autonomy as the paramount metric recognize that any concession to the primacy of fetal life reduces that autonomy. Those who hold fetal life as the paramount metric similarly recognize that any concession to the primacy of a female's bodily autonomy comes at the expense of the life of the fetus. Those who remove themselves from the present onerous conditions are resigned to the fact that the inevitable frustration of trying to convince the "other side" of the probity of their own position and subsequent injustice of opposing it is not worth the effort. Others circumvent that impediment by reserving any exchange to the company of affirming minds where agreement is assured. Thus, for both the resolute and receptive, any attempt to engage in a public exchange concerning abortion is judged futile. There are no common ideas, save what constitutes social justice, to enter into dialogue. Experience has demonstrated that participating in any discussion on this important topic comes at the cost of personal frustration and relational discord. Though regrettably accepted, it seems in the presence of stubborn opposition, feigned indifference or claims of obscure complexity are strategies for avoiding the issue publicly and the preferred path for maintaining personal peace and friendships. Unfortunately, all these scenarios form echo chambers fostering unchallenged opinions and thus creating deep ideological chasms. This is equally true for discussions encountered in the sphere of social media, and disappointingly so with any exchange on entertainment news programs, where adversarial language is designed to snag and ensnare the minority position.

When the public is exposed to news stories, the lineups are purposefully arranged as an arena to pit opposing views against each other. It becomes quite easy for any supporter of a position to champion their own verbal gladiator, while swelling in disdain for the opposition. Or when the public encounters printed diatribes on the abortion topic, the opinionated rhetoric calculates how to reach those who subscribe to their position, while simultaneously being acerbic and antagonistic toward any opposing viewpoint. Whichever side the think-piece aligns with, it is eagerly passed on to serve as ammunition proving the veracity of one's own position. When shared with like minds, it is meant to be affirming. When shared with adversaries, it is hoped to more clearly articulate the social justice transgression that someone did not or could not make convincingly themselves.

It is not much different on social platforms where opposing views, presented with extreme language and contentious claims, are designed not for interaction but to bait a reaction. It appears those who engage in social media have absorbed the irrational exchange manner of journalists and public intellectuals. That online domain of social platforms simply mimics the combative posturing and polemic style of the so-called public intellectuals. Perhaps from the position of a mere spectator, the tradeoff is that personal frustration can be more readily channeled as indignation and scornful sarcasm at the disagreeable "side." But that psychological buffer is not present while in face-to-face conversations. The personal venue can be intimidating, as abortion remains overtly charged with controversy. Like all things of religion and politics, in which the topic of abortion is inherently embedded, personal viewpoints assumed to invite hostility are thought to be better left undiscussed for the sake of maintaining civility. Thus they retain little more than a peaceful façade, the negative peace that Martin Luther King Jr. warned stems from complacency and elevated civil order over justice.

But whether in print or in person, any public exchange on abortion tends to devolve into two general forms. The first takes the stance of an appeal solely to maintain a fixed position. There is a side that is to be defended. This type of adversarial exchange is designed for those who champion their rigid views. But this unfortunately appeals only to others who share the position with an equally fixed mind. This does little to increase understanding, for when an alternative point is offered it utilizes an extreme position few may hold, but hopefully makes the other person seem ignorant and therefore in error. If a reply is permitted, it is not intended to pursue the truth but is phrased as a rebuttal better suited as a headline than a respectful response. This is not the realm for an authentic encounter between persons willing to listen in order to understand, but only for those willing to listen, waiting for a pause so that they can make the other person understand. The required respectful dialogue in pursuit of truth, where one is willing to have their position examined, is absent. But fostering a willingness to listen and understand demonstrates a respect for the other person or persons. And further, such willingness demonstrates a respect for the truth. The privation of these conditions is the breeding ground for a rhetorical diatribe.

Here is a way this can be described. The interlocutor, as the person who asserts a position, begins with the presumption that the other person's position is in obvious error. Further, though, the interlocutor also thinks that their own position is irreformable. And though it is expected for anyone to assert what they understand to be true, to think one holds an immutable truth risks being cerebrally arrogant, and such immunity from reform perpetuates erroneous thinking. If one's position is true, based on a valid and sound argument, it will withstand logical inquiry. Anything less lacks intellectual humility and risks perpetuating falsehood. Under these conditions, the questioner—the person who should test the claim of the interlocutor—finds little opportunity to engage in rational dialogue. But regardless of the motivation, if the rhetorical tactic of the interlocutor is to win the argument through a mixture of verbal bullying and imposed guilt, then what forms is but a monologue in the presence of a bystander. Sensing this manipulative strategy is not ordered to truth, rather than suffer continued disrespect and the perceived waste of personal time, the questioner disengages. The interlocutor does not win, but truth does lose.

Anticipating those circumstances in the public climate, many see no reason to pursue a public dialogue on abortion. And those yet willing to pursue such a dialogue see no rational way to initiate, let alone sustain, such an exchange. Others, in growing numbers, preemptively dismiss the utility of any attempted dialogue with people they think incapable of accepting their stance, which is obviously correct in their mind. Or perhaps because the other side is thought to be based entirely on some impenetrable ideology, it is best to employ nonrational tactics and settle for silencing the other, which gives the impression of victory. In short, if the task is thought futile, why invite certain frustration without the possible means of winning the other over? Yet, some do periodically engage in personal exchanges, and others post or respond occasionally within a social media thread when the abortion topic arises. And even those who would never themselves personally engage or post are glad when others do take up their mantle. There is good reason for that; it is the same reason journalists and public intellectuals engage in this topic. It is appropriate and noteworthy that many in the public are passionate about the issue of abortion, as it affects central aspects of the human person and should remain nothing other than a fundamental social justice concern. But positioning on the topic has consequences. The public compares the present abortion issue to other historical movements where those who did not support the reform are now looked back on with indignation. It is comfortable to think that if one were alive at the time, they would have aligned their views with what currently seems to be the correct side of history. Few care to be among those whom the future will declare to have supported a social justice atrocity. This comes immediately to mind concerning the abortion issue. So, the centrality of the various elements of bodily autonomy, human consciousness, and the notion of personhood will inevitably keep the abortion issue relevant. Because those central ideas of humanity are not solvable, the abortion issue while remaining relevant will also remain perennially contentious. The future will inevitably weigh in on the present abortion issue, if even the future itself will be another period's past history requiring continued evaluation and thus improvement. Yet, as truthful gains are made, each side will continue to define its position by what human right or personal interest is ultimately being supported or suppressed.

This then presents a very important point in the public debate. Though in reality there are not merely two "sides" to the abortion issue, whatever one's nuanced position may be, when distilled down it is conveniently corralled into either the "for" or "against" abortion binary. The reasoning is that regardless of the nuanced position, ultimately that position results in either depriving the female of bodily autonomy or terminating the life of the unborn. That is why the monikers of pro-choice and pro-life have developed with little resistance and stubbornly persist as sloganized positions. They will be used here for rhetorical convenience, not as a fallacious straw man dichotomy. In the public dialogue, if any nuanced position develops or is expressed, it is interpreted as essentially supporting either the female's autonomy or the unborn's life. Does not being pro-choice with exceptions necessarily limit some females' bodily autonomy? Would not a pro-life stance that allows exceptions necessarily concede it is acceptable to terminate the life of some unborns if the circumstances warrant it? Perhaps these "sides" may have something to do with the human mind seeking understanding through categories. Or perhaps the general agreement allows support through affiliation of like-minded premises. But one person's ethical exception is another person's ethical concession. To the mind of some, the acceptance of any nuance is conceding ground thought to result in incremental deterioration of their advocated social justice position. Also, the exceptions are not always clear-cut, nor are they easily agreed upon. For example, who determines when a female's reproductive freedom *may* be controlled by others, and under what conditions? Likewise, *why* should the preservation of an innocent fetal life be contingent on the subjective values or personal goals of others? On the basis of these points, and others too many to list, the abortion dialogue is in crisis.

REASONING AND CONFUSION

The status quo of the abortion dialogue is one of confusion. The preceding scenarios offered were but a brief observation of the present state of things concerning the dialogue on abortion. A significant portion of the remedy is to employ critical reasoning. That may seem obvious, as would the precept that one must not merely reason, but reason well. However, reasoning is more easily defeated not by dismissing its power for both understanding and truth, but by thinking it is done well when in fact it has been done poorly. This then is the first concern, that if reasoning is held as the surest path to an agreed-upon truth, how does one appeal to reason with another who does not recognize they are being irrational? The second concern flows from the first, in that they assume they have a well-reasoned position, but they tragically do not know what they do not know. The first condition is presumption that results in a dogmatic position. The second condition is ignorance that persists in a state of confidence. And the result of such a predicament is that overly confident positions have fallen prey to those binaries that offer no common thread to initiate dialogue.

To address the first concern if one has not arrived at their position via reason, they will not likely be moved from confusion to truth using the rational method, when unbeknownst to them they never used reason to initially form their thoughts. They may, and certainly can be persuaded to do so, but not initially and certainly not easily. An isolated mind is a difficult barrier. Moving from ignorance to knowledge, dullness of mind to understanding, and foolishness to wisdom is not accomplished by individuals in isolation. Ignorance, dullness of mind, and foolishness are the enemies of an enlightened mind. They require another to aid to formation, to prod, and even to drag one out of such conditions.

A philosophical way to explain that process can be found in Plato's allegory of the cave, which has found its way into popular culture. Even if the epistemological point is not popularly known, it can serve as an illustration here. In this allegory, prisoners are fastened by chains to the wall within a cave. They are aware of each other only by sound and the sight of shadows in dim light. Since childhood, they have known no other existence, so this is nothing other than their unquestioned reality. Behind them is an elevated walkway. On the other side of the walkway opposite the prisoners is a fire, situated so as to cast a shadow on the wall directly in front of them of anything or anyone that appears on the raised walkway. Various people and objects are paraded across this walkway, casting shadows onto the wall the prisoners are facing. These shadows remain all they know. But when one of the prisoners is released, the "new reality" would be now knowing the genuine cause of the shadows. The light of the fire hurts the eyes of the released prisoner and, as with anyone who discovers their present reality was entirely fabricated, this creates a state of confusion and anxiety. It may be more comfortable for the prisoner to return to face the wall in the same way that ignorance can be willfully held and protects one from uncomfortable truths. But Socrates, whose allegory Plato is retelling, goes further and suggests that the prisoner is dragged entirely out of the cave. There the light of the sun cannot compare to the light of the fire. It takes even longer for the prisoner's eyes to adjust. But now the prisoner sees reality not as it was thought to be but as it really is. The sky, the trees, and all that is experienced in ways not previously known understandably overwhelms the prisoner who is now free from the cave. Knowledge, understanding, and wisdom came at the price of confusion and pain. This is not unlike how being open to new realities is always a risky condition for any isolated mind. The same is true for entering any exchange on the topic of abortion, as one may face the hazard of seeing things differently—one might even say perhaps in a new light.

But that painful adjustment is not the end of the allegory. It is natural for anyone who has become enlightened to share their discovered insights. The prisoner then, returning inside the cave to relate his experience, is like one with newfound knowledge, understanding, and wisdom thinking they can return to ignorance, dullness of mind, and foolishness. It is not possible to un-know what one now knows. But those who have not yet shared the discovery of insights will hold the enlightened individual in contempt. Or, as in the allegory, the prisoners conclude upon hearing their previous companion's expression of true reality that this search for things as they really are is just too painful. They prefer remaining content with the comfort they can find in the shadows of the cave.

This allegory is used here to express the journey to enlightenment, but one cannot be enlightened if they think their position is irreformable. Too often when one's own ignorance is not realized, it becomes easier to project that ignorance onto those who disagree, thinking it is they who by default are the ones in the dark. That itself is intellectual arrogance, and knowingly or not, it is akin to preferring the shadows of the cave. So, perhaps the first test of a necessary predisposition for critical thinking is to not assume the other person or opposing position is the one still "in the cave" simply because they contest a dogmatically held position. An open mind is needed, but an open mind cannot be open to everything; more on that shortly.

There is always potential for intellectual growth in considering alternative positions, for no one knows everything necessary, and even fewer know those necessary things sufficiently well. That then sets up the condition to address the second concern, that those who tragically do not know what they do not know are ignorant in a state of confidence. Intellectual humility is the sole antidote. To address that, Socrates offers a paradox, stating that of those things he does not know, provided he knows that he does not know them, then in that little regard he is wise knowing himself foolish. That is to say, at least he was not a fool who thought he knew something when he did not know it. So, the second condition (ignorance that persists in a state of confidence) is not only that the interlocutor has not arrived at their position by reason, but that they are unaware of what they do not know. This is the condition of the chained prisoners prior to being aware that the shadows are not reality. It would be analogous to the many aspects of certain positions on the abortion topic where errors are held not willfully, but from an unknown ignorance that remains unopen to reform. Some people are comfortable wearing blinders, but that relates to those who are willingly being irrational. What is meant here is more analogous to a self-guided individual, who may be doing their best to employ rational thought but who remains unaware of facts and ideas that may necessarily alter their position. Without someone to direct them to the full breadth of knowledge required for a rational judgment, they falsely assume that their position is sufficiently informed. Recognized foolishness is the beginning of wisdom, and it requires intellectual humility. It is better to know if one is in error and to allow oneself to be enlightened, than to not know and remain in ignorance due to pride. The obstinate mind is unteachable, and the willingness to engage alternative positions tests the presence of that condition and demonstrates intellectual maturity.

REFLECTION AND HOPE

If the abortion dialogue is in crisis, and the status quo is one of confusion, then what is the point of dialoguing on this important topic? Early twentieth-century writer G. K. Chesterton (d. 1936) remarked in *What's Wrong with the World* that something worth doing is worth doing badly.[1] The idea is offered here not to suggest anyone should accept being bad at reasoning. Rather, despite personal inadequacies, the topic discussed in good faith must be tried even if ability and circumstances are not ideal.

1. Chesterton, *What's Wrong with the World*, 175.

In short, abortion is too important a topic to leave to the so-called experts, or for the amateur to think it requires suspending judgment until some things are known expertly.

But for both the so-called expert and the so-called amateur person in dialogue, what then might be the first step to overcome such a crisis that animates much confusion? In a nutshell, it is self-reform. And though it is appropriate to use the term self-reform, it will be clearer to speak of the self becoming *intentionally reflective*. Forming an intentional stance is not sufficient on its own, as one's intention can be shrouded by a benevolent goal. In the abortion dialogue, toxic language is often unethically rationalized to influence the thought of others and their subsequent action. It is not uncommon to witness gaslighting as a means to induce uncertainty, and with this uncertainty to fester fear by hurling extreme scenarios and threats of the perceived eroding control of one's own position. Such manipulative *gaslighting*, a term from the 1944 eponymous movie, can in the abortion dialogue take the form of the prolifer inducing fear by portraying unsympathetic mothers ripping babies from their wombs, or the pro-choicer fostering images of females once again dying in droves from back-alley abortions. In the public dialogue on abortion where much is at stake, it is not uncommon to excuse such irrational coercion and emotional manipulation, perhaps even finding it a necessary tactic. But this machination of using such utilitarian tactics to win the other over to a position deemed worthy will come at the cost of embroiling all involved in nothing but continual frustration and fruitless exchange.

Though easy to understand why this occurs, it must remain unacceptable to give in to such a strategy. It remains tempting, when championing the preservation of female bodily autonomy or the saving of unborn lives, to not question the means for attaining those goals. After all, it would seem on the surface that any *good* held as inviolable would ethically require uncompromising methods of preservation. With something held as sacrosanct, the rhetorical gaslighting justifies a proportionate course of action to establish what each side invokes as necessary to attain social justice. It is thought better to stop others from controlling the female body or to stop innocent babies from being killed in the womb than to wait for someone to come around by recognizing the truth incrementally. It is an accepted gambit that for the good of society, the end justifies the means. But a reflective disposition does not dispose of the goal, only the illicit means to achieve that goal. And to be clear, by contrast the goal of being intentionally reflective is to first scrutinize one's own disposition before engaging with another. And even then, one must always be keen not to impose unexamined views on the world, but rather to have one's own position tested and refined. This is expressed by the oft-repeated aphorism that one must first *know thyself*. To *know thyself* is the first functional order of knowledge. This ancient maxim can be found from the fifth century BC, whether in the Judeo-Christian scriptures of Lamentations or adorned above the Greek temple of Apollo with the Oracle of Delphi. To be clear, though, to *know thyself* offered here as a reflective intentionality cannot be confused with self-affirmation or confidence. Simply holding a belief and then being true to that belief, as in taking a stance, is not knowing thyself. That disordered notion of being true in one's belief is what many unwittingly consider authenticity. It may demonstrate one is consistent and even sincere, but being true to one's belief is not authentically reflective if the intentionality is not mediated. In other words, the self-reflective concept to *know thyself* is essentially interdependent with others who strive for such intentionality themselves. Knowledge of thyself is not possible isolated from other positions, for others equally hold the duty and role to reciprocally sharpen thought and correct fallacious thinking.

Here is that notion explained. In *The Doctrine of Virtue*, the late eighteenth-century philosopher Immanuel Kant spoke of knowing thyself as an imperative to searching one's own heart,[2] for the purpose of discovering intentions behind a desired action or position. This intention cannot be reduced to conviction. Therefore, this intentionality can be neither self-satisfaction nor confidence in one's stance. The reflective quality rather humbly adapts the self-reflection to make necessary changes due to invalid arguments or fallacious thinking. This reflective intentionality aids in composing oneself in a way that brings all the necessary conditions for respectful dialogue to a requisite level. Although no small task, it is in fact possible. Possibility is the maidservant of hope, and courage is the vehicle that pursues such possibility. For a historical and cultural illustration of that courage and hope, consider twentieth-century Russian dissident Aleksandr Solzhenitsyn, who served eight years in a gulag under Stalin's regime for charges of malicious agitation. Once eventually exiled, Solzhenitsyn criticized those who lacked civic courage as possessing the first symptom of the end. The end he was addressing was

2. Kant, *Doctrine of Virtue*, §14, 107.

weakness in the face of political resistance. His criticism was sharply directed at Western elites and intellectuals who sadly thought courage to be obstinacy and boldness against opposing powers and ideas. But it can be argued in his stead, this courage is not reserved for enduring imprisonment and forced labor, but must surface against the festering antagonists that stifle the willingness to articulate and thus defend a reflective intentionality. In the abortion debates, is not boldness in one's stance, by virtue of that boldness, thought to be a demonstration of courage? And do not many confuse obstinacy with the unwavering dedication to one's position? Rather, resolute courage is needed for one's intellectual autonomy and boldness to express the related ethical freedom. Therein lies the hope. It is the individual human being, thought unexceptional, who must overcome the trap of vacant courage, hidden under the guise of allegiance to a presently held position. Solzhenitsyn thought too many placed the mantle of hope on political or social reform as a proxy for this individual transformation. But reform from the top down can only be imposed and thus enforced by law and ideology. Reform from the bottom up, from self-reflection, has the potential to shift minds and persuade society in ways that laws and restrictions cannot achieve. In terms of personal reform then, the first functional order of self-knowledge requires intentional reflection. That is possible and offers hope for a fruitful and respectful dialogue on the topic of abortion.

Courage as a moral freedom is a welcomed virtue whether or not the goal is attainable. When the goal is possible, courage stands as a prerequisite for the notion of hope. But the notion of hope is not self-evident. People often use familiar terms without knowledge of the essential definition. In the next chapter, one of Plato's dialogues that considers the definition of justice will illustrate that point. But for now, perhaps accept that the term *hope* is another good example. Hope is frequently misunderstood to be a wish. But a proper definition of hope cannot sustain false expectations. Both hope and a wish may be future-oriented, but to *wish* holds the connotation that one's desire may be for something impossible. More importantly, a wish also concedes that what is desired can be granted by others, removing it from within one's own power and agency. In contrast, hope is grounded in reality and is self-sustainable; hope does not originate from the desire of others. For example, another's unwillingness to be rational does not preclude anyone from engaging them; it only makes the task more arduous. Even entering into a conversation on abortion with someone who is irrational can affirm hope as the firm expectation in a future possible good. The expectation of dialogue is firm, not certain. No one needs to hope for something that is assured. And hope must be directed toward something future-oriented—here, possible reform and respect. So it excludes both the present and the past, which may seem steeped in ignorance and obstinacy. But this hoped-for future must also be possible. Unlike a wish, hope is irreconcilable with holding out for any exchange until others agree with one's viewpoint. Finally, one hopes only for what is good, which, to the point here, must be one's own position on abortion rationally established prior to being asserted. Understood this way, hope shields the patronizing of other positions and preserves oneself from others' delusional ambitions of shallow victories. That establishes bidirectional respect and makes dialogue not merely possible, but a noble goal.

Returning to Solzhenitsyn, his captivity and counterrevolutionary charge was not because he participated in espionage or organized resistance. He disparaged Joseph Stalin in a private letter to a friend. It was reported that he referred to Stalin as "the man with the mustache," which is enough where dissent is not allowed. The courage spoken of here carries no comparable retribution, yet people seem to self-impose a mental internment and consequently remain rationally unengaged. It is easy to maintain the façade that only those who disagree are considered irrational. For example, the pro-life position is claimed to be anti-choice by the pro-choice group, and the pro-choice position is portrayed as anti-life by the pro-life group. Each group's identity forms relative to the negative position of the opposition. Philosophically this is known as *ressentiment* (from the French), where spite arises toward the perceived opposition and forms the position by what is obstructed. On the topic of abortion, it could be understood as the opposition becoming a surrogate for one's own frustration. The pro-lifer sees the *other* only as anti-life, just as the pro-choicer sees that *other* only as anti-choice. This arises because each has not developed the ability to defend their position rationally, so the "other" is categorized as the irrational impediment to their goal. It is an emotional ethic formed by cultural pressures, articulated both by philosopher Friedrich Nietzsche and the early twentieth-century phenomenologist and ethicist Max Scheler. Scheler spoke of this as an impulse to orient oneself in terms of the detraction from another's position, where indignation surfaces and the other is perceived as an enemy. It would be oversimplified to think that is the whole of it, but it is a significant part of why the abortion dialogue is in crisis. The subsequent confusion and crisis in dialogue must yield to the intellectual growth demonstrated by considering alternative positions, rather than dismissing them outright as morally inferior. Nietzsche, in his *On the Genealogy of Morals*, addressed this notion of helplessness against those in positions of power and domination. He argued that it can easily result in some compensation as an *imaginary revenge*,[3] where framing the other opposed to one's own values offers a sense of moral superiority. There is more to that idea, but an aspect of it can be applied here. Framing the other in terms of an enemy is not productive to dialogue, and conviction does not ensure certitude. If one can listen, seeking to understand while remaining humble to *know what one does not know*, then no expertise is necessary to become *intentionally reflective*. This remains the hope to mitigate frustration, to appease relational discord, and to engender public dialogue on the abortion topic. To pursue this further, though, the elements that constitute the foundations of a dialogue need to be further explored.

3. Nietzsche, *Genealogy of Morals*, §10, 36.

2

Foundations of a Dialogue

In true dialogue, both sides are willing to change. —Thích Nhât Hạnh

Only free men can change their minds and be surprised; and while no men are completely free, some are freer than others. —Ivan Illich

"But where shall I find courage?" asked Frodo. "That is what I chiefly need." "Courage is found in unlikely places," said Gildor. "Be of good hope!" —J. R. R. Tolkien, *The Lord of the Rings*

A DIALOGUE AND A conversation both involve the exchange of thoughts. The term *conversation* is more common and considered less formal than a dialogue. A conversation is typically spontaneous and more likely used to describe interactions that can range from chatting about the weather to who will be the next president. To converse literally means "turning ideas about with another," and conversing can both initiate and sustain one's interests—e.g., what is the weather and who will be the next president? Something more is needed with the abortion topic, so by contrast the term *dialogue* is more aptly suited. The term *dialogue* is formed from the Greek root *logos*, which connotes a reasoned thought, and the prefix *dia-*, which carries the notion of "through the point." So, in contrast to a conversation and turning ideas about, those in dialogue are expected to precisely reason through the point. For most in society, the meaning of what constitutes an exchange has undergone some modifications as society adjusts to the purpose of the interaction, the technology used for communication, and the forum in which the exchanges take place. Sometimes this change is useful, providing people with the means to adapt ideas and develop expressions relative to the culture and time in which they live, and in ways in which they can be more conveniently accepted. But in contrast with holding a conversation, when engaging in a dialogue a necessary skill set is lacking for *reasoning through the point* with issues and important topics in the public sphere. The present style of discourse surrounding the abortion issue is a prime example. This text will examine that problematic discourse later, but first it is necessary to pinpoint the characteristics of what constitutes a dialogue. This will provide essential contrast with many of the mainstream exchanges that prove incapable of engaging others respectfully, which, in the process of making a point, do not pursue truth as the goal.

ENTERING INTO A DIALOGUE

It is not uncommon for someone to begin a discussion by trying to ensnare the other person with a catchphrase. This is colloquially known as a "gotcha" moment. In the public abortion discussion, the use of witty epigrams is ubiquitous. For example, a person might lead with one of the following.

> "I'm not choosing to not have a child; I am only choosing when to have a child."
>
> "Life begins at conception, and life is the most fundamental right for all humans."
>
> "Abortion is about power and control, not about what happens to the unborn."
>
> "I am for the death penalty because they're guilty, and I am pro-life because the unborn are innocent."
>
> "Embryos are not babies. You can freeze and restore an embryo, but you cannot do that with a baby."
>
> "One of the aborted children might very well have been the scientist who cures cancer."

The single goal of each buzz line is to defeat the other person's position with what is thought an unanswerable affirmation. However, a skilled logician, regardless of stance, could and would logically parse out the equivocation or errors in judgment of each phrase. It would take time, clearly presented definitions, rephrasing of those lines into arguments, and so on. It is likely that anyone attempting to do so would be accused of not getting the point, overthinking the claim, or simply being opposed to the side that the person proffering the catchphrase sees as correct. People have discussions so often that it is assumed that merely asserting a point is sufficient to settle the issue.

But as experience bears out, it is not uncommon to think of something done ordinarily as unexceptional and therefore not requiring any specific skillset. So, if the formal distinction between a conversation and a dialogue can be temporarily set aside for the following analogy to be relatable, it will be helpful to speak more generally about having discussions. Being in a discussion is both ordinary and unexceptional, but only dialogue can test to what extent the requisite skills are present. Otherwise, familiarity breeds complacency; and, as having a discussion is routine, the necessary competency seems more intuitive than a honed craft. For example, here are two analogies. It would be notable for someone to first question *how* to read a book prior to *reading* a book. But doing so would reveal that there is a great distinction between mentally reciting the words and actively reading the text. There are many literate people who struggle to comprehend what they read but would be indignant to have their reading ability questioned. Yet, analyzing what is read for meaning at various levels is a skill that involves far more than interpreting the symbols on a page. The same is true for the skill of thinking and thus claiming to know. Knowing comprises far more than interacting with and forming an opinion on the information presented. It involves comprehending the terms, critically analyzing the claims of truth to form judgments, and, most importantly, while separating irrelevancies and fallacies, being able to articulate the argument prior to any acceptance or criticism. Here too there are many competent people who struggle to articulate their thinking but would resist any claim that they do not know and thus are not thinking well.

It is the same for *entering into a discussion*. Many may be keen to discuss, but few do so well. That may sound obvious to some, but many in the prior group think of themselves in the latter. That is a hazard for any topic of a dialogue, particularly abortion as the matter under consideration. But as stated, once the skill is thought intuitive, intentionally directed effort is not recognized as necessary for such an unexceptional task. Like active reading, there is such a thing as active listening, which must exceed the mental interpretation of what was heard. And like thinking critically, there is such a thing as critically listening, which must surpass interacting with and forming an opinion on the received information. Both active listening to understand what is being communicated and critical listening prior to forming a response to the presented truth claim are fundamental for any fruitful exchange. Even if this is accepted as true or obvious, like many things it can be known and yet not commonly practiced. Further, the necessity of such a recognized skill, or the lack thereof, is only amplified when the exchange ramps up from casual conversation to a pointed dialogue whose topic is a hot button issue based on strong convictions.

To extend the analogy, it can further be argued that one is in dialogue when thoughtfully engaging with a written text. If a dialogue is between two or more people who engage a thought outside of one's original position, then logically readers enter into a dialogue with the text as they engage the presented thoughts. Therefore, a reader must *actively listen* to the claims of truth made within the text and *critically think* prior to forming a response to those claims. The necessity of these skills is more acute if the reader intends to rise above the baneful level of the present public discourse on abortion. Active listening, active reading, critical thinking, and engagement are requisite skills that must be honed.

This proposed method of dialogue, when applied to the topic of abortion, is in contrast with modern sensibilities. Many attempt to quickly assess the "side" of the other position and then retort with a prepared buzz phrase or ready-made rebuttal. Too often with such shallow engagement, there is little to no intention of listening first to critically judge the claims of truth or to thoughtfully analyze the nuance of the position. Rarely is the goal to first understand the presented contrary position more clearly. Typically, once the "side" of the other person, group, or text is determined, any attempt to dialogue ends because the other party is then cast into a predetermined stance understood by previously absorbed opinions. For the unskilled reader, listener, and thinker, this is the end of the analysis; the other person, group, or text has been adequately categorized and the exchange is thought futile.

This is clearly demonstrated by the assessment of American political parties where individual positions are swiftly categorized relative to the polarized stances of the left and right sides. In political discourse, when a person offers a position on some economic or social justice issue, the attempt to align it with one of the partisan positions is almost reflexive. It becomes very difficult to overcome that initial impasse, and thus any position offered appears suspect, if not summarily dismissed.

The abortion issue, with sides that have ironically fallen into those partisan political platforms, suffers from the same divisive arrangement. When a person tries to articulate a position on this topic, once it is detected to ultimately support or oppose an abortion, a mental curtain is drawn, stifling both critical thinking and listening. Then, like those partisan positions, once it is suspected to be in agreement with the other side, it is in similar fashion summarily dismissed and the dialogue deteriorates.

It is important at this point to reiterate that even respectful exchanges may not result in fruitful dialogue—thus the necessity of hope. The difference here is how such a quest for truth is conducted. To explain that, a contrast is useful. Both a debate and a dialectic have a respect for truth, but they differ in how that truth is pursued and determined. The one that often occurs in public discourse, particularly on the topic of abortion, is *debate*. In a debate, each side remains firm in their position and uses sincere, or sometimes unfairly misleading, rhetoric in an attempt to win the other side to their perspective. In a debate, there is a winner and a loser. The winner is thought to be determined when one party insufficiently responds to the facts or rhetorical points presented. This insufficient response is held to be "losing," and it is presumed in a debate that the party that succumbs to a better argument should be compelled to agree with the opponent's position. The "truth" is presumed to be the position of the winner. The debating sides make no attempt to assist one another, clarify the other's argument, or to concede their own areas of weakness. In debate, the goal is winning, with each assuming the other position is in some fashion unsatisfactory.

But another type of discourse is *dialogue*. The type specifically proposed in this text is known as the *dialectic* method. The goal of this method is not to win (in the sense of a debate) but rather to find the truth of a matter, at least to the degree it can be attained. The use of dialectic is ancient; indeed, it is often referred to as the Socratic Method and fills the pages of Plato's dialogues. The only way to "win" in a dialectic is for all involved to reach the truth they are dialoguing about. In dialectic, this truth cannot be reached by deception or crafty emotive language, but by means of logical argumentation based on critical thinking. Again, such engagement is not without passion. As rhetoric is the art of persuasion, it is useful to both know and adapt the speech and style to the intended audience who, it is hoped, will be persuaded by the logical argument presented. Aristotle would understand rhetoric used that way and would see it as an ample tool allowing dialectic to reach a truth and therefore maintain respect in the exchange. Plato was suspect of any use of rhetoric, as for him it was an emotional tool used to persuade another unwittingly by circumventing reason and was thus disrespectful to the questioner. Perhaps for simplicity's sake, both Plato's caution of deceptive manipulation and Aristotle's insights as a useful pathos are valuable in applying rhetoric to any dialectic. But regardless, in all dialectics each side permits the other to reform or even correct their points as both work toward the goal of determining truth.

The difference between debate and dialectic can be described as the difference between two people wanting to know the best route to a restaurant rather than two people debating their usual route is better. With the latter, "winning" is attempting to make the other person agree that their current position is the correct one. In the former, the goal (which in reality is not "winning") is attempting to agree together on the best route to the restaurant regardless of personal preference. With that stated, returning then to applying the dialectic method to reading a text, scrolling through the news, or engaging in dialogue, it benefits all involved when the goal is a shared path and not a perceived irreformable truth. It is far better for all, and for the abortion topic at hand, to accept correction than to champion one's dogmatic stance that seems correct because it remains untested. Remaining within the familiar and seeking intellectual comfort are stubborn foes of any truth seeking.

Another point about the dialogue on abortion that should be understood is that neither critical listening nor critical thinking need begin from a neutral position. There are likely not many, if any, neutral positions on abortion. It is an important topic to human society, and sincerely held positions are appropriate. It is also expected that one would want to defend these sincerely held positions; however, positions are not true simply because they are sincerely held. Sincerity is a noble trait, but it cannot be held as an absolute. Sincerity does not signal the correct position any more than emotional outrage determines truth. In fact, thought of in that way, a claim to sincerity can actually mask one's own insecurity of having a position questioned. In other words, it is thought that others questioning one's sincerity is ample reason to disengage. It can be played as being thought to be personally ingenuous and, as a defensive tactic, allows one to assume the moral high ground. That is but a mask for the truth. These, and any similar scenarios, appear in discussions as conversation stoppers that will logically devolve into a diatribe. Though more subtle, a diatribe colloquially known as a rant allows the competitiveness of a debate to enter the discussion without any intent of interaction. It forms a no-debate zone. So, even in the absence of a neutral position on abortion, one should be careful not to attempt to neutralize the discussion by initiating a one-way debate. The dialectical method allows the balance of reason and rhetoric in any exchange.

It is worthwhile reiterating the roles of those partaking in a dialectic, along with expanding on the method involved. The dialectical method begins with a position or claim that philosophers call a thesis. The person who puts forth the thesis is the *interlocutor.* The cross-examining of the thesis is known as the *antithesis*, or the questioning of the premises, and the person who proposes the antithesis is the *questioner*. Perhaps in simple terms, the interlocutor proposes something as true, and the questioner tests the proposed claim. The dialectical method will then permit the questioner to investigate the premises supporting the interlocutor's argument. Both then, the questioner in tandem with the interlocutor, will clarify the terms, determine the truth of the premises, and ferret out any errors in how the argument was formed. Plato's dialogues of Socrates provide many examples of this dialectical method, employing multiple interlocutors while Socrates is always the questioner. Most importantly, Socrates does not question the integrity of the person, only the veracity of the thesis or the truth of the premise set forth by the interlocutor, because there is only one goal: to arrive at *a* truth. The following paraphrase from Book I of Plato's *Republic* will demonstrate the use of this dialectic method.

In this exchange, the topic of the dialogue is justice—specifically, what justice means. The interlocutor is the wealthy merchant Cephalus, who claims that justice means holding to the truth of a thing while also being responsible for one's own debts. The questioner is Socrates, who is not so certain as to that premise, which here is expressed as a definition of justice. Following the idea of being responsible for one's own debts, Cephalus's example proposes a thesis that it is justice when one responsibly returns a borrowed item rightfully to the owner. Socrates offers an antithesis by questioning whether that would still be justice if one should return a borrowed weapon to the owner who was not mentally stable and likely to do harm to others. Because of that potential predicament, Cephalus sees the possible danger in his definition of justice. He realizes it needs to be reformed, as it cannot be *true* that repaying one's debt will always lead to justice.[1] Notice that the original position was abandoned once it was demonstrated to be in error. It is evident that Cephalus escaped the temptation to do what is now commonly referred to as *doubling down*, that is, sticking to an erroneous claim to avoid admitting error and appearing to have lost the argument. Accepting reform is honorable and is counted to his credit. Still uncertain as to the true definition of justice and not feeling equal to the task, as often happens when an error is rationally unmasked, Cephalus abandons the dialogue. Socrates solicits another interlocutor named Polemarchus to continue the dialectic in Cephalus's stead. With Polemarchus, through a series of analogies, Socrates further distills the definition of justice through the process of eliminating errors. This is done by whittling down problematic definitions in an effort to flesh out the truth. After Polemarchus, yet another interlocutor named Thrasymachus enters the dialectic, but he will only continue if his fee is satisfied. Thrasymachus, like his fellow Sophists, considered himself an expert arguer and made his living by winning arguments or teaching others to do so. Socrates despised the Sophists, finding their interest in winning and demand for compensation contemptible and diametrically opposed to the search for wisdom and truth. This time, rather than leaving the dialogue, Thrasymachus chooses diversion by switching the point. He prefers to seek the definition of justice in terms of what is required of rulers and their use of justice connected to power. Thrasymachus too eventually leaves the dialogue, and Socrates then engages others in dialectic. Socrates ultimately holds that justice is a quality of the soul and, to the extent that one can do good, it is justice for one's own desires and reason to both be in harmony.[2] That may appear disappointing, and perhaps even unresolved. But as with most things philosophical, a single definitive answer is not reached. That is not a flaw of the dialectical method or its application of logical reasoning, but the realization that some ideas such as justice resist universal definitions that satisfy all applications. Such ideas are like persons themselves; they are not solvable in some finite way but are to be perpetually pondered, unveiling deeper understanding without exhausting room for further inquiry.

This predicament applies to the abortion dialogue. Some aspects of the terms *human*, *life*, *autonomy*, *consciousness*, and *personhood* are

1. Plato, *Republic*, §331, 595.
2. Plato, *Republic*, §331, 595–610.

known well, and other aspects of them remain challenging to know better. Toward this end of knowing better, the dialectical method affords a viable process of reasoning, oriented toward respect for both truth and person. One could only imagine how Socrates would engage interlocutors today on the topic of abortion. Socrates perhaps would consider those championing their rigid positions on consciousness or autonomy in the media as Sophists, only intent on winning, with the desire to be compensated by recognition of their skills or by gaining celebrity status as a defender of their side. He would find the contemporary tactic of offering rare or extreme examples, like playing "gotcha," to be lacking harmony between what one desires and the use of reason to achieve it . . . thus making the pursuit unjust. Socrates would be vigilant to uncover errors in the definitions of *human* and *life*—not as a means to corner the opponent and give the appearance of winning the argument, but to flesh out what can be known. Socrates did not celebrate Cephalus's or Thrasymachus's walking away as shallow victories. Neither should someone think themselves wise because they have stumped the opponent.

Imagine interactions on abortion where each position would have the opportunity to respectfully express their position and then invite open interrogation in accord with logic and critical thinking. Further, it would be much better if each would respectfully state they will reflect on the points, in hopes of reengaging at a later time. The dialectical method serves these purposes and maintains respect for the interlocutor. Respect for persons and for a discoverable truth is nearly always found wanting in the public forum, news outlets, and social media platforms. Each of those more closely aligns with the format of a diatribe. Those venues are set up for confrontation, where more often than not the spectacle of flurried outbursts is just emotive deflection appealing to the targeted group who already accepts the premise as unquestionable. The diversion of walking away or changing the topic, as in Plato's dialogue, conceals underdeveloped or weak points that are held dogmatically. When these are paired with fragile dispositions, neither respect for persons nor truth is possible. These forms of interaction are performative, and this theater spills out into the public dialogue on abortion. To disagree is merely thought to be incapable of getting the point. Then, not getting the point is thought of as ignorance. And finally, the ignorant are bullied into getting the point they appear incapable of defending against. Often, in these exchanges, the winner is thought to be determined by the level of emotional indignation. Emotional outrage may gratify one's ego; but without the logical underpinnings, the resultant indignation untethered to truth results in a diatribe.

The catchphrases listed at the beginning of this section are, in fact, just diatribes. Understood as irreformable truths, they make the interlocutor feel a sense of accomplishment in how they often cause the questioner to scramble into an explanation. A couple of those examples formed into a dialectic might be illustrative of how such unease is easily remedied by determining the underlying premise, questioning it, and redirecting the discussion. In these examples, the interlocutor is Follis, and the questioner is Sophia. Here is one to consider.

> *Follis:* I am for the death penalty because they're guilty, and I am pro-life because the unborn are innocent.
>
> *Sophia:* Good Follis, can you tell me why you chose guilt as the determiner for life and death?
>
> *Follis:* Because, Sophia, guilt determines the penalty.
>
> *Sophia:* Very good. So, if a person poses a threat to another, say a communicable disease that they themselves did not get through poor judgment, would you say they are guilty?
>
> *Follis:* No, in that case I would not.
>
> *Sophia:* So though guilt fits to impose the punishment of the death penalty by your standard, the threat of the unborn on the female may stand regardless of the unborn's innocence.
>
> *Follis:* It would appear so.
>
> *Sophia:* Then are you not inconsistent, Follis?
>
> *Follis:* I see what you did there. The unborn may pose a risk to the female, and it is not their guilt but the threat that is of concern.
>
> *Sophia:* It is a step further from folly to consider such a clear insight.
>
> *Follis:* I might then defer to the medical community on that.
>
> *Sophia:* But the medical community does not claim it is doing harm by saving the female's life, yet it is doing harm to execute a criminal.
>
> *Follis:* I think then, the medical community is inconsistent too.

Here is one other put into dialectic form.

Follis: I hold, as the Sophists do, that embryos are not babies. You can freeze and restore an embryo, but you cannot do that with a baby.

Sophia: That is an interesting term you use, Follis, referring to the embryo or unborn as a baby.

Follis: It is merely a slip of tongue. I realize the term *baby* is typically used for desired unborn children or infants. I would rather not focus on that term.

Sophia: That is fair enough. But no one has tried to freeze and restore babies, however you use that term. Is that correct?

Follis: Yes, to the best of my knowledge that has not ever been attempted.

Sophia: If someone did try it, by Zeus, and were successful, would that mean that embryos are indeed like babies?

Follis: No, in fact, many other characteristics distinguish embryos from babies, which is why I want to withdraw from using that term.

Sophia: But your argument about what could or could not be frozen would no longer be valid if a fetus, assuming that it is a more suitable term, could be frozen and restored.

Follis: That is true, I admit it, and I do prefer the term *fetus*.

Sophia: Then why persist in an argument that has a shelf life? Also, are not full-grown humans presently frozen in the hope of being restored?

Follis: In spite of your pun, I will use my original argument until they are successful freezing and restoring a fetus, or thawing out a full-grown human, as you have pointed out. Then after that, I will accept that I cannot.

Sophia: Follis, you are only postponing your folly.

Follis: Perhaps, but it presently remains effective for my cause.

Sophia: Then, on that, my good friend, we differ as to what may be called a good cause.

Those brief examples were not meant to appear clever and certainly were not exhaustive to the point of attempting to solve the issue with each claim. They are provided only to demonstrate that a dialectic, and not a diatribe, has some power to ferret out inconsistencies in reasoning for those with an open mind.

Prior to addressing more directly the goals of a dialogue, a brief mention about the concept of having an open mind regarding any weighty topic such as abortion is warranted. The importance is twofold. Firstly, obstinacy and prejudice form from not being receptive to alternative positions, where in a pluralistic society tolerance is a civic value. Secondly, up-to-date information and evolving circumstances must be permitted to adapt to, and even challenge, present ethical judgments. To the first point, all dialogue requires that two or more are engaged in the discussion and, particularly concerning a dialectic, that the rules of logic are to determine the truth. If the interlocutor will not engage due to an obstinate closed mind, it is not a dialogue. If the interlocutor will not submit to the principles of critical thinking, they are only interested in offering a diatribe. Then to the second point, though ethical principles can remain constant, their applications are usually dynamic and are not always self-evident. If the interlocutor is not open-minded to that understanding, then both the lack of dialogue and critical thinking will become evident.

It would appear then that being open-minded is a sign of intellectual maturity and exhibits a willingness to dialogue and think critically. That is true, but only under certain conditions. Here are two unequal conditions to consider. Firstly, there is the open-mindedness that leads to *withholding judgment* only until the interlocutor's position is understood more fully and thus able to be judged by its own merit. Secondly, there is the open-mindedness that leads to being unduly *influenced by cultural whims,* resulting in ethical inconsistencies and dogmatically held ideologies. Only the first instance of open-mindedness can convey intellectual maturity, where one is in a dialogue and the judgment is governed by critical thinking. It is not found with the second instance, where proposing to be open-minded is in reality accepting cultural influences uncritically. This only results in impoverished critical thinking that ironically mirrors being unwittingly closed-minded. But there is yet one more essential criterion to consider for open-mindedness. If being open-minded can indiscriminately result in being influenced by cultural whims, then it follows that with particular aspects of the issue of abortion, it is the mind settled to certain truthful judgments that demonstrates critical thinking, resulting in a respectful dialogue. In such a case, the openness is how the settled truth is interpreted and applied.

For example, in the abortion dialogue one may be settled on judging that respect for bodily autonomy is a just and proper judgment, and similarly the termination of an innocent person's life is an unjust and improper judgment. But the open-mindedness must examine if there is *any* limit to respecting bodily autonomy with oneself, or in relation to another. Likewise, the open-mindedness must examine if there is *any* scenario where preserving an innocent life is disproportionate to the potential goal, or if the innocent life is threatening that of another. Without working out the particulars for each at this point, it is enough to hold that some truthful judgments of the dialogue may be settled, while evolving circumstances and the applications require an open mind. Trying to preserve an invested position by not considering valid and sound arguments in this regard is the mark of a closed mind and exhibits intellectual immaturity. As Chesterton put it, an open mind is like an open mouth; it should remain open, but shut once it has found something solid to close upon. Having an open mind need not be about the truthful judgment of the settled ethical idea or principle, but the assessment of the concrete application. Applying ethical ideas and principles requires prudence, which is the virtue of rightly acting in a particular situation. This then aligns with the settled, truthful judgment. Again, dialectic is uniquely suited to this task as the means to the respectful exchange necessary for any abortion dialogue.

THE ELEMENTS OF AN ARGUMENT

A dialogue is the trading of ideas. This implies more than a willingness to interact if that trading of ideas is to result in a fruitful exchange and be oriented to truth. To that end, the two parameters offered here as consideration for constructive dialogue will be *the elements of an argument*, to determine truth and validity, and *the necessary dispositions* as conditions for such truth and validity to develop. The first, concerning the elements, aids in understanding what specifically constitutes an existent philosophical argument. Though most equate an argument with disagreeable quarrelling, that requires neither skill nor dialogue. In critical thinking, an argument is a structured rational proposal of premises that logically supports the conclusion. According to Aristotle, those premises, the terms used in them, and the conclusion form the argument. This trio of elements, known as *the three acts of the mind*, is established in sequence, much like building blocks: terms are used to build premises, and the premises build to a conclusion. Each act of the mind will be briefly explained in simple, straightforward terms with accompanying examples. Though doing so will not be an attempt to offer a mini-course in syllogistic logic and critical thinking, such a survey of these elementary principles will help in sorting through the various proposals as to the strongest arguments for autonomy, consciousness, and personhood. Without being exhaustive, the other parameter will be offered as a series of dispositions that, even with true premises that logically support the conclusion, will not have the sufficient conditions offering a suitable arena for a respectful exchange in the abortion dialogue.

To grasp the elements of a logical argument, it is crucial to realize that each subsequent act of the mind is contingent on the previous ones. That is to say, each act is ordered to the next and all three are interdependent. These acts are the basic principles and building blocks of rational thought. They are directed toward the pursuit of truth and thus must be used foundationally for one's position on abortion. It is likely to appear rather systematic and perhaps too structured to employ in an informal discussion. But as explained in the opening of the previous section, in the same way few question *how* to read a book prior to *reading* a book, perhaps even fewer set out to determine *how* to think prior to engaging in *thinking*. What follows is intended to improve how one thinks so that this approach to thinking may be applicable to a respectful dialogue on abortion. It is simply important to know *how* to think prior to being concerned about *what* to think.

The first act of the mind is *simple apprehension* that results in a *term*. It is the first step on the ladder of an argument. This first act involves terms that form the understanding, apprehension, and meaning of the words used. A term is a word or group of words that forms the subject or the predicate of a proposition. A term need not be a single word, as the idea represented by multiple words such as *bodily autonomy* and *conscious person* are each single terms. The concern of this act of the mind is that the term must be clear (it can be comprehended), unambiguous (it is not confused with another term), and exact (it is specific and accurate). If the term is unclear, ambiguous, or vague, then the disagreement is likely over needless confusion. For example, *bodily autonomy* is more exact a term than *free to do what one wants* with one's own body, since one cannot ethically self-harm and cite respect for bodily autonomy in defense. That leads to the next point that *bodily autonomy* is only a clear term if it is understood as *respect for bodily autonomy*, which is to represent the rational and intentional exercise of personal autonomy. And as to ambiguity, bodily autonomy is not the same as bodily freedom, which connotes no existing restraint toward a goal with the body, whereas bodily autonomy concerns itself with a freedom that is directed to bodily health and wellness. So to this last point, an example would be that in terms of respect for bodily autonomy, one may ethically decline disproportionate medical intervention, when by contrast bodily freedom speaks more to taking risks that may cause harm to the body. That is only one example; but ultimately, with the first act of the mind, unless the term is understood exactly, clearly, and unambiguously, the *what* that one is referring to cannot properly be communicated and thus deforms *how* one thinks.

The second act of the mind is when those terms are combined into phrases known as propositions, also referred to as premises. A proposition forms a judgment and can only be true or false in deductive logic. It consists of a *subject* (what is being addressed) preceded by a *quantifier* (how many are being addressed). The proposition ends in a *predicate* (what is being said of the subject), connected by a *copula* (affirming or denying the predicate of the subject). Here is an example of a proposition: "Consciousness is a necessary condition for personhood." And though every proposition has four parts, it is better explained by rephrasing the proposition from conversational form into what is known as its *logical form*. The logical form may be awkward to read but makes it easier to illustrate the parts. As a side note, rearranging the premise into logical form also aids in paraphrasing, as the meaning becomes more apparent.

Here is the conversational form placed above the logical form for comparative purposes. Then with each part appropriately labeled with a superscript, the rephrasing will be explained.

> *Consciousness is a necessary condition for personhood.*
> *All*^{Q} *[those who are persons]*^{S} *are*^{C} *[those with the condition of consciousness]*^{P}.

Notice the premise in conversational form does not explicitly state whether this consciousness refers to *all*, *none*, or *some*. But as consciousness is necessary, by implication it refers to *all*^{Q} of the subject as persons. Since propositions in deductive logic are in the order of (1) quantifier, (2) subject, (3) copula, and (4) predicate, here the subject *personhood*^{S} was moved to the second position immediately following the quantifier. This also is to make it clear what the quantifier *all* is referring to. Keep in mind that the added phrases, *those who are* or *those with,* are only used to resemble natural speech and have no bearing on the structure or understanding. Now the predicate is *consciousness*^{P}, which is what is being said of the subject and has been moved to the last position in the premise. Finally, the copula in that premise is *are*^{C}, which can now *affirm* that the predicate consciousness is to be said of all the subject, which is persons.

Here is another example. In conversational speech, one can argue as true that "Bodily autonomy is not recognized for all females." In logical form, this would appear as "Some^{Q} [females]^{S} are^{C} [those who have been denied bodily autonomy]^{P}." Notice again that the quantifier was not explicit as to how many, but the assertion of *not recognized for all* implicitly holds that the subject was referring to only *some*. The subject, which may seem obvious, is *females*. The predicate as *those who have been denied bodily autonomy* is that which is said of the quantifier and subject together as *some females*. And finally, the copula *are* is affirming that this autonomy, which is being denied, is being denied not for all or none, but for *some* females. Take note that each of those propositions is either true or false. They are making a judgment, which is the purposeful outcome of Aristotle's second act of the mind. But what each of those terms actually is intended to mean remains the object of the first act of the mind. The meaning is in the terms, and the judgment is in the proposition or premise.

Prior to explaining the third act of the mind, notice that this method of determining truth through logical reasoning is not intuitive. It requires skill and intentional effort; even when presented systematically, it may still remain difficult for some to grasp. If that is true to any degree, then the various claims to truth and unintended interpretation of terms during any discussion on abortion can equally remain difficult for some to grasp and thus resolve. If the thinking process itself is found difficult, then so too will thinking through the application of the process be found difficult. Such difficulty will inevitably leave the premised truth in question if the interlocutor cannot logically defend the judgments.

Finally then, the third act of the mind is discursive reasoning, and it results in a syllogism. A syllogism is a deductive argument; it uses the judgments of two premises to logically result in an expressed conclusion. If both of the premises are true and the logical form is valid (validity is the correct arrangement of a syllogism), then the interlocutor must rationally accept the conclusion as also true. Returning to the first example of a proposition, here is one way it may be the true conclusion in a syllogism.

P1 All [those who can assert bodily autonomy] are [those with the condition of consciousness].

P2 All [those who are persons] are [those who can assert bodily autonomy].

C Therefore, all [those who are persons] are [those with the condition of consciousness].

Notice that the subject in the second premise (minor premise) has become the subject in the conclusion, whereas the predicate in the first premise (major premise) is the predicate in the conclusion. Also notice that what is known as the middle term *[those who can assert bodily autonomy]* appears in both the major and minor premise. The middle term is the shared element for each premise and does not appear in the conclusion. The conclusion is made up of the subject from the minor premise and the predicate from the major premise. The position of the subjects and predicates determines what is known as the *mood*, while the position of the middle terms in the premises is known as the *figure*. It is beyond the scope of this brief synopsis to explain that further, but the mood and figure are important as they determine whether the syllogism is valid. That stated then, if the terms are clear (no equivocation), the premises are sound (each is true), and the syllogism is valid (correct mood and figure), then the interlocutor must rationally accept the conclusion regardless of whether it is agreeable to their position. That does not mean they will assent to the conclusion's judgment, which is often expressed as belief, but it does compel them to engage the premises and thus dialogue.

Returning to the example, now restated in conversational form, it reads as *consciousness is a necessary condition for personhood*. That is the conclusion of a logical argument. This use of syllogistic logic does not discount passion or sympathies, but it also does not recognize either of those as the means to determining truth or validity. These rules of syllogistic logic, though only briefly presented, are required as the tools for critical thinking. They are not rules intended to restrain a person from expressing passion, but they are designed to restrain arriving at false conclusions passionately. They are the rules of engagement in any rational dialogue. Without such a standard, one is no longer in a logical argument but an ideological quarrel or emotional exchange. For those who experience such, it is anarchic. A person's claim is not "correct" because they claim it to be so, but rather it is true only if they have demonstrated it to be so. An argument is not "won" because a person is outraged about the topic; an argument is demonstrated to be valid by the rules of syllogistic logic and, with true premises, to confer a true conclusion. The elements of an argument, properly understood and adopted, are rationally required for a fruitful exchange, respectful considerations, and a constructive dialogue concerning the issue of abortion.

THE NECESSARY DISPOSITIONS OF A DIALOGUE

This last section serves as further investigation into the required foundations of a dialogue introduced at the beginning of this chapter. Some foundations, mentioned previously, reappear as conditions, which here will be referred to as dispositions. Yet prior to that, additional elements require introduction. First, the term *disposition* comes from the Latin *disponere*—an action of putting things in order. Disposition is commonly understood as a frame of mind, and that works fine in this application since reasoning in dialogue calls for the orderly framing of one's mind. In the public abortion dialogue, each should be working to put things in order. Yet in reality, many forces work against these dispositions and that rational ordering. Such a reality must recognize that even rational argumentation, while adhering to logical rules governed by the three acts of the mind, will not by itself be sufficient for a fruitful exchange and a constructive dialogue. The human person needs more than logical rules. It must be admitted that human persons are not logic-processors, responding to rational arguments the same way one reacts instinctively to a stimuli. This does not refer to the value of rhetoric, which is useful to persuade the interlocutor to truth.

The point here is that logic is not reasoning proper; it is the *tool* of reasoning, and this tool only works under certain conditions. Rational dialogue, then, requires certain conditions of necessary dispositions that can allow the tool of reasoning to progress those in dialogue toward truth. This section will address that claim and those dispositions. In this pursuit, the terms *necessary* and *sufficient* will be used. Allow an analogy for the explanation. Every recipe requires necessary ingredients, but it is only those necessary ingredients *in toto* that allow the recipe sufficiency to complete the task. That is, all are necessary, but the absence of one will result in a lack of sufficiency. In dialogue, the logical progression through the three acts of the mind is necessary, and perhaps constitutes a primary ingredient of any rational exchange. But as stated at the beginning of the previous section, truth and validity necessitate particular dispositions for any dialogue, particularly one on abortion. What follows is a consideration of some necessary dispositions.

The first necessary disposition to consider is the *reciprocal engagement* of ideas, which must exceed simply the sharing of opinions. That may appear obvious, but what is obvious at first blush often remains undetected unless intentionally examined. A dialogue is performance art. It is a performance as in being "an artful dialogue," not in the sense of being staged or acted out, but still one whose success is pinned to the reciprocal and willful participation of all involved in the exchange. And this exchange must exhibit openness while being forthright, which in dialogue comprises the second disposition of *mutual respect*. This mutual respect is where one must permit another to examine the logic of their own position. Otherwise, in the absence of this subsequent respect and reciprocity, an asymmetry arises between professor and student, expert and novice, cleric and laity, member of the affected group and advocate. That inevitably devolves the exchange into a diatribe, where likely any disagreement will be interpreted as disrespect rather than sincere inquiry. Here what appears to be obviously true to the interlocutor, which in reality may or may not be true, is not obviously true to the questioner. But if the questioner's passivity is imposed by some forced silence, any psychological manipulation or verbal bullying can ironically be thought a substitute for respectful agreement by the interlocutor. With no opportunity to reply, suffering such cosmetic silence is undeniably patronizing, and the submission is thought to be confirmation of agreement.

Yet even when all involved respectfully reciprocate, there must be present the integrity of one's claim or stance. This means that mutual respect warrants, as the third disposition, a previously thought-out and *reflective position* on the part of the interlocutor. Recall that sincerity cannot replace rational reflection; the proposed truth is to be interiorly interrogated prior to any engagement with another. From this, each party is beholden to ferret out their own questionable premises, flaws in logical form, and fallacious thinking to the best of their ability. Claiming sincerity or authenticity, and in this case even ethical consistency, is no substitute for attentive consideration and rational deliberation of the points offered. But people are not often reflective in this way, or they lack the requisite competency; and from those deficiencies, ideological mantras or talking points involuntarily surface. For the questioner, this leads to predictable mental fatigue because peripheral points must be laboriously addressed, and ideologies exhaustively challenged, often with another who either does not understand or will not accept rational correction. This frequent predicament then requires fortitude that, as the fourth disposition, manifests as the *habit of persistence*. This persistence serves as the vehicle to reorient the dialogue back to the main premises to whittle down logical diversions. Such persistence serves both as endurance while in a difficult topic, and also as stamina for the questioner who must moderate their own passions that would equally prove inhospitable to pursuing the truth.

Even with appropriate persistence, such difficult and complex ethical analysis should not be left untried. From those third and fourth dispositions, two more surface. The first of those two is that such dialogue must have *adequate time* to unfold. This would entail not simply the willingness but also the time-laden space that may afford patient listening and requisite exchange. The questioner must digest what is proposed and then respectfully probe the premises of the interlocutor. Finally, the sixth disposition that unfortunately is found in scant supply in contemporary society is the *proper environment* so that all the other dispositions may adequately form. This proper environment is the ecosystem for any dialogue. Both adequate time and the physical opportunity used to be nurtured in neighborhood encounters, social clubs, church halls, and company get-togethers. But those opportunities have waned. Even where or when there may be the minimal opportunity to engage in dialogue, present social norms dissuade the open discussion of hot button issues, abortion chief among them. As opportunities and social norms have decreased, so too have those dispositions decreased, and with them the skill of respectful dialogue. The use of virtual spaces and social media platforms has proved far less conducive to shaping these dispositions. The lack of intimacy and asynchronous interaction cannot provide an adequate structure; and more often than not, they deepen the adversarial tenor through algorithm-created echo chambers. The sad reality is those forums and platforms have become the default ersatz "public square," and their inherent inadequacy has only proven to complicate dialogue and frustrate fruitful exchange. Though this hints that the art of public dialectic is near extinction, the remedy ironically holds that developing or nurturing the skills of dialogue remains within personal competencies and thus is freely chosen or rejected. That means that willfully adhering to rational principles and being conscious of the necessary dispositions places all the elements of sufficiency for dialogue within the grasp of the questioner. The interlocutor(s) must cooperate, but as that cooperation is in the control of that individual also, all in dialogue must remain vigilant and are ultimately responsible for engaging the topic of abortion.

It is important to consider then what connects each condition to personal responsibility in terms of the manner and form of engagement. To be clear, this obstacle too is one under personal control. Though not a disposition itself, as was mentioned prior, this personal obstacle is *fear.* It is a disabling disposition. The meaning of this term fear is not to be understood as the lack of confidence, which more closely aligns with low self-esteem. In the dialogue on abortion, this fear is directed to a specific object that, when undiagnosed, stifles dialogue. Psychology refers to this type of fear as *atelophobia*. It is a fear of taking a firm public stance on what may turn out to be a flawed premise. Derived from the Greek *atelès,* which connotes imperfection, it is the fear of apprehension from potentially reversing one's invested position. Personal honesty will admit that reality, if only in the quiet of one's own mind. To state it colloquially, one fears "losing face" by appearing wrong, thinking that being corrected is a sign of lack of intelligence.

The interlocutor's sole alternative to a change of mind is obstinacy. Here is an example of what is meant by this fear in terms of a dialogue. It is not uncommon in the media, on social platforms, or in the public square for individuals to struggle to defend a particular point on abortion they hold militarily, such as "there are no elective late-term abortions" or "there is never moral certainty that an abortion is necessary for the physical life of the mother." The case might even be that they are repeating a rebuttal they did not form by themselves, one they adopted from a trusted source. A common scenario is the sharing of an advocacy article or video in the hope that it will be just as convincing to the questioner as it appeared to their own mind. Not all arguments must be original, and articulating the points formed from another is reasonable. But without familiarity of the argument's context or personally being able to verify the truth of the premises, the argument is only acceptable to those who would agree in spite of the veracity of the claim. The interlocutor, feeling inadequate to defend their advocacy by this postured response, shields themselves against critical interrogation by defending their own integrity and questioning the other's integrity. If intellectually cornered, a fallacious diversion such as an *ad hominem* (an attack against the person) or red herring (irrelevant to the topic) appears to be the only perceptible means to "save face," maintain credibility, and remain secure in their original stance. Therefore, being unable to respond to reasonable questioning, such a fear leaves an individual susceptible to having their premises dislodged, abandoning the now vulnerable claim at the crossroads of reason and ideology.

At this juncture, the original argument may require *minimal* reform due to ambiguity or equivocation, or *substantial* reform due to flawed logic or errors of truth. In other words, they would need to rationally determine what other aspects of their abortion position have been affected (conditions are not isolated) and accept rational rehabilitation. It stands to reason that the more foundational the erroneous premise, the greater the level of fear of reform. Quite possibly, a person may be required to fall into an agnostic position (it is wise to admit one does not know) if not rationally "flip their stance" (it is wise to admit one was in error). That is the risk of allowing one's position to be rationally interrogated. To the point, then, a dialectic goes where the truth goes, so entering into a dialectic is assuming a risk to both one's ego and one's position on abortion. But the dialectical method is designed to pursue and discover truth; and that risk *for* truth, to the extent it can be discovered, has the potential to demonstrate rational integrity by admitting errors and accepting the reform of one's argument. Nothing is lost, save pride, if the dialectic reorients even the entire position. The ultimate goal is to be correct in one's position, not to simply appear correct to a sympathetic audience. Such ethical maturity, though found in scant supply, is to be lauded. It is an understatement to suggest it as anything other than much needed in the current public dialogue on abortion.

But further, a clear and sufficiently proposed argument must also be transparent in the path toward its identified goal. It is not uncommon when one is asked a series of questions that a legitimate concern emerges of being coaxed along a path to a disagreeable conclusion. This is often thought of as being set up or tricked. But critical thinking's use of logic cannot be derailed by deception; in fact, logic exposes such craftiness. Logic is governed by rules or, better stated, by laws that when properly followed reveal the argument's illogical components and thus the thinking as uncritical. Skilled deception is the antithesis of logic; such was Socrates' view of the Sophists. Understanding properly what an argument is and how it is formed deflates such duplicity. If the series of questions asked do in fact express true premises, and the argument's form is valid, then reason dictates that the sound truth of the conclusion must be accepted. Hence, if done properly, those proposed questions can guide one to the truth. But if the series of questions does not fit those parameters, then the deception can be exposed by simply questioning any equivocation, a false premise, or the argument's validity. The example of Socrates questioning the definition of justice is a clear example. The matter here is that no one should fear being walked into a conclusion by deception. Either the conclusion should be accepted as demonstrated true by reason and logic, or the conclusion should not be accepted as true because the same reason and logic have demonstrated it false. The questioner either is correct or needs to be corrected; similarly, the interlocutor either is correct or needs to be corrected. In either case, when someone or something requires correction, it is not the *appearance* of truth but truth itself that wins. To be demonstrated wrong is to be shed of ignorance. And one should not fear to be wrong. One does not even cease to be an expert if demonstrated wrong; they simply are experts who were wrong on a particular point. With logical and critical thinking, the only fear should be either to not recognize the error, *which is ignorance*, or to recognize the error and not capitulate, *which is obstinacy*. If everyone's goal is truth, regardless of the initial position, then making an error just brings one a step closer to knowledge founded on that determined truth. One's fear should not be to make an error in logic, but only to resist reform and repeatedly make the same error.

With that being the case, it should be evident (but also may be disappointing to discover) that the goal of a dialectical conversation is not to have the other person switch sides, as the Sophists aimed to do. The positive effect of improving one's knowledge of logic and critical thinking as applied to the dialectical method is not simply to avoid making mistakes but to ferret out others' fallacies and errors so as to not fall prey to manipulation, intentional or not. Here is that expressed as a syllogistic argument.

P1 People who understand the dialectical method of dialoguing are less likely to fall prey to manipulative rhetoric.

P2 People who try to reason out the argument with logic and critical thinking are people who understand the dialectical method of dialoguing.

C Therefore, people who try to reason out the argument with logic and critical thinking are less likely to fall prey to manipulative rhetoric.

Understanding the dialectical method is key. With the dialectical method, one does not fear being corrected, but rather invites it as necessary reform on the path to truth. The fear of being manipulated is also reduced because the necessary premises are identified and interrogated. A dialectic is a type of dialogue that involves the exchange of well-reasoned thought, pursuing, acknowledging, and thus preserving both truth and respect.

3

Reorienting the Discussion

The ultimate measure of a man is not where he stands in moments of comfort and convenience, but where he stands at times of challenge and controversy. —Martin Luther King Jr.

In reality the monk abandons the world only in order to listen more intently to the deepest and most neglected voices that proceed from its inner depth. —Thomas Merton

There are many men of principle in both parties in America, but there is no party of principle. —Alexis de Tocqueville

IT IS COMMON TO experience discussions surrounding the abortion issue as wasting personal time and draining intellectual energy. The tragic irony is that any dialogue on this topic requires both time and energy. The concern becomes how to direct the effort so that each is properly used. As previously stated, the art of dialogue requires intentional effort. It is not merely intuitive, nor is it a sought-after skill in contemporary society. That forms a double danger. In truth, those without formal education may have developed pedestrian dialogue skills that prove no worse than those formed through higher education. Neither logic skills nor critical thinking requires formal training, although such training is preferable. And for those with academic degrees, such classes seldom occupy a spot on academic schedules already bloated with required courses. So if it may be assumed that such skills are in need regardless of position, then both the lack of time and appropriate venue have a deleterious effect on the public dialogue of abortion. The concern addressed here then is to how this topic can be reoriented to better direct such limited energy, time, and skill. It is not as though the opportunities are not plentiful. This social justice issue rightly incites passion, and the topic perpetually occupies space in politics and the media, resurfacing nearly every election cycle. But those who do engage, or who witness others doing so, recognize that eventually an impasse is met, at which juncture two sides rationally form. That is not a false binary, nor does it create a straw man argument easily defeated by arguing exceptions and alternative postures. Yet, it is in fact *the problem*, and should make evident that recognizing this polarity does not rationally necessitate arguing from one of those sides. It is *the approach* that requires reformation.

There is admittedly more to this dichotomy than "choice" and "life," but the point that there remains some demarcation where one idea ends and the other begins is important to grasp if one is to understand the present source of frustration. The argument that lies ahead in this text requires comprehending that dilemma, so as to find value in reorienting both the approach and the focus. Even if, in the public sphere, admittedly few may fit neatly into either of those sides, the gradation at some point tilts the judgment favoring the pro-choice or pro-life position. The pro-choicer may be amenable to some concessions, but at some point, the reduction of a female's choice will begin to favor the pro-life position. Likewise, the pro-lifer may be receptive to a female's autonomy, but at some point, favoring choice over that of the fetal human life will appear to be pro-choice. So then, even within the nuances, it appears that when one side ebbs, the other side wanes.

There are many nuanced stances between the two poles. But people will have to logically agree that ultimately their nuanced stance will result in one of two consequences. Either the female's autonomy will be upheld, or the fetal life will be preserved. Here is that point expressed in the form of a logical inference known as a *modus ponens*, where an antecedent claim (P) conditionally implies a consequent claim (Q). In formulaic construct, it reads, "If P, then Q. If P, therefore Q." Here is the logically inferred position of the pro-choice side.

> If a person affirms a female has the final decision of what to do with her own body (P = bodily autonomy), then the choice whether to carry a fetus to term is ultimately up to the female (Q

> = support for choice). Because a person affirms the female has (P) bodily autonomy, therefore the person supports (Q) choice.

The following *modus ponens* illustrates the logical inference in support of the pro-life position.

> If a person affirms the life of the fetus is primary (P = primacy of fetus), then the choice whether to carry a fetus to term is determined by preserving fetal life (Q = support for life). Because a person affirms (P) the primacy of the fetus, therefore the person (Q) supports life.

This predicament may be imagined as each "side" standing on a narrow mantel of either "choice" or "life." There is sufficient lateral movement to accommodate the nuances, circumstances, and exceptions, which allows one to remain on either of those two ledges. But at some fulcrum point, the distance from the polar stance of choice or life causes the position to tip over. Wherever that point may be, it will result in one abandoning their original binary stance to the adoption of another. The resulting perception is that the opponent has been "won over." To "win" is to knock the other off of the ledge. Thus, society has recognized the logic of two "sides." From this, a concern arises (the topic of the following section): it is not clear if personal values and beliefs have formed the stance, or if the stance was adopted and then the values and beliefs conformed to fit.

Engaging in a dialogue on the abortion issue requires muddling through much irrational silt. The goal is to reframe the abortion issue while respecting the ideas of choice and life, but navigating the dialogue in such a way that personal time and intellectual energy can be directed to mutual understanding and respect for truth. The binary is not dissolved by illogically dismissing the two sides but by recognizing neither side is a point of entry into rational dialogue, nor is either side worth the investment.

DISCERNING POSITIONS ON VALUE AND BELIEF

The argument of this text is to make clear that neither sloganized stance claiming the position of pro-choice or pro-life is useful. In fact, it is quite the opposite. Though the "sides" retain a logical inference, both as positions and as slogans they should be abandoned. This is true regardless of whether they act as a mere placeholder for the positions, and it does not suggest that new slogans should be sought. Nonetheless, neither expression is properly disposed to speak for the central premises that extend to the judgments. Again, the reason is not the absence of ultimate binary ends, but the fact that those ends proposed as slogans cannot be the logical determinants of an ethical judgment on the abortion issue. If personal time and intellectual energy are factors to be conserved for essential components of the dialogue on abortion, then it is quite necessary for any dialectical conversation on abortion to engage in anything but the strongest arguments. Those must be reached by the dialectical method, of course; but ultimately when concluded as the final distillation of divergence between the values and beliefs attached to choice and life, such alone will prove worthy for a reflective engagement.

There remains a concern to consider, and the veracity of it as a supposition will have to be weighed. In the public dialogue on abortion, people are more likely to align with a position based on autonomy or life, and then work backwards seeking ways to defend that stance. There remains something foundational that is left unexpressed. That claim may appear easy to dismiss, but it is likely that anyone who has engaged another on the topic of abortion has found adherence to a position to be stronger than the explanation. What that evokes is a conclusion accepted as self-evident. This assertion eventually leads to a rational impasse, perhaps expressed by the idiom, "There is no reasoning with you." The frustrated interlocutor need not entirely have arrived at the judgment uncritically, but the values and beliefs aligning with the identities of pro-choice or pro-life are in a symbiotic relation. The focus determines the values assigned to either *choice* or *life*, which then forms a belief determined by the hierarchy of any value assigned. Even if it is reversed—where a belief forms the value, such as with dogmatic stances—that priority does not alter the point of the argument that the position nourishes the values and beliefs, or vice versa. Here is how that could be understood. One's *values* and *beliefs* attribute ethical worth to the ideas of choice and life, which then are used to form the premises, which themselves are attached to the abortion issue as being pro-choice or pro-life. Those *premises* express the judgments. The *judgments* as the logical result of the premises then affirm the conclusion expressed as an expressed *position*. The logical progression should be from *values and beliefs*, to developed *premises*, to an affirmed *position*, but there is an unarticulated aspect of each premise that has left a gap.

There should be nothing controversial in that claim, and to some it likely appears obvious. But the values and beliefs connected to the ideas of autonomy and life require a middle term that is not expressed. This middle term must appear in both of the premises to an argument, but it does not appear in the conclusion that functions as the logical judgment being asserted. Here are those syllogistic arguments with the *middle term in italics*, the **major terms in bold**, and the minor terms underlined; each will be referenced shortly. But in order to understand the point, consider dialoguing with someone who merely asserts each conclusion.

P1 To align with the *preservation of human dignity*, a female requires **bodily autonomy**.

P2 The pro-choice stance is a position that aligns with the *preservation of human dignity*.

C1 Therefore, the pro-choice stance is a position requiring **bodily autonomy**.

This is how it would appear for the pro-life position.

P3 To align with the *preservation of human dignity*, a fetus requires the **protection of life**.

P4 The pro-life stance is a position that aligns with the *preservation of human dignity*.

C2 Therefore, the pro-life stance is a position requiring a fetus the **protection of life**.

It should be clear at this juncture, though there are other ways to express it, that both positions are in pursuit of the same idea, which is the *preservation of human dignity*.

The preservation of human dignity was chosen for illustrative purposes, but also because it can logically function as the foundational concern. When someone seeks a goal (foundational concern), they pursue it by achieving objectives. For example, a person may have the objective of eating in order to satisfy hunger pangs. An objective and a goal do not swap positions, as a person would not think that hunger pangs could be the goal of eating. If a full stomach is achieved, the objective of eating would no longer be sought. So, in the syllogism example, both autonomy and life are objectives sought for the sake of human dignity, and not human dignity as the objective to achieve autonomy and life. Rather, each is considered the means to preserve human dignity. If the preservation of human dignity could be achieved without them, they would not be sought. The point is that they are objectives to attain a goal, for without the objectives of autonomy and life, the goal of human dignity would not be preserved. If, at this point, a question arises that both "sides" seem to each have one aspect of what is needed together to preserve human dignity, then it should be evident that there is something amiss in each argument. But the point at this juncture is to illustrate the claim that when the objective is misunderstood as the final goal, confusion arises and confounds dialogue. So, regardless then of how the argument (syllogism) is constructed, the middle term that is shared by each position is left unexpressed in the conclusion used to illustrate the position. In short, both sides seek the fulfillment of human dignity but have left it unexpressed. If the unexpressed goal is not rationally arrived at, it cannot be engaged. If the unexpressed goal is assumed to be opposed by the other position, then it is considered an affront to one's foundational human dignity. The judgments of autonomy and life are tethered to the premises that form those judgments, but the judgment (the conclusion of the argument in those examples) remains by and large unstated and uncritically upheld by the values and beliefs attached to the middle term. This means that the support for autonomy or life may be ideologically held as the only way to achieve the unexpressed preservation of human dignity. But nonetheless, adherence to the values and beliefs compels support for the positions, which for that reason stand in clear and unresolvable opposition to each other. This is a stalemate.

This line of thinking then forms a judgment, giving the stance holder the impression that any sensible person who desires human dignity would favor autonomy over control or, to the other perspective, would favor life over death. Therefore, the values and beliefs to support autonomy without the stated premises, to be consistent, accept the judgment of autonomy over compulsion and then the position of *pro-choice*. To the other stance, the values and beliefs to support life, without the stated premise, accept the judgment of life over death and then the position of *pro-life*. And as previously stated, it is not clear if those intuitively held values and beliefs seek alignment with the affirmed position or if the affirmed position seeks alignment with the held values and beliefs. The stalemate arises because there is no opportunity in the conversation to engage the unarticulated premises (preservation of human dignity) and then the corresponding logical judgment. The identity that resides in the affirmed position of pro-choice or pro-life is forced to carry the ethical weight, which it cannot. Each position ultimately becomes an identity; and one cannot argue with an identity, which, when internalized, inevitably becomes interpreted as a personal offense. Only the expressed terms of premises (autonomy, life, pro-choice, pro-life) that form the identity are thought fair game in any dialogue. But if they are not explicitly stating the middle term (preservation of human dignity), or indeed why they are diametrically opposed and forming those polar stances, they become difficult to engage. The following two chapters will be devoted to a more thorough explanation of the terms *autonomy* and *life*.

But if at this point further explanation may be temporarily set aside, consider that if someone holds an assumption based on unarticulated terms within a premise, the degree to which the stance has been rationally or intentionally chosen is questionable. Since the identity conceivably resides in the affirmed *position* based on the *values and beliefs* held, if it is not clear which seeks alignment with the other, the position of pro-choice or pro-life may be adopted stances but cannot authentically said to be rationally chosen. The concept of pro-choice or pro-life is the minor term in each premise. Those, expressing the values and beliefs, preceded the formed judgments with the unarticulated middle term as the preservation of human dignity. This then gave rise to the positions expressed as the major terms of *bodily autonomy* and *preservation of life*. Here is that point restated in simple sentence form. The pro-choicer intuits the value of autonomy over exterior control, judges *autonomy is primary* as necessary for human dignity, and adopts the position of pro-choice. The pro-lifer intuits the value of life over death, expresses the judgment *life is primary* as necessary for human dignity, and adopts the position of pro-life. Why is this crucial to grasp in an abortion conversation? If the path to a stance is understood as judgments giving rise to the position (minor terms), when the judgments themselves were formed by premises based on personal values and beliefs, then not being able to address why each is essential for human dignity (middle term) will result in fruitless conversation. Attacking the identity of pro-choice or pro-life, each formed by personal values or beliefs, will only result in a reaffirmation of the positions to preserve those values or beliefs. The ostensible position (minor term as evident) is a presupposition that simply foments a quarrel and instigates one to "double down," shielding personal values and beliefs from a perceived attack on the position one intimately identifies with.

To state the experience plainly, perceived indignation forms the rational impasse. The pro-choicer is bewildered and frustrated that the pro-lifer could hold a judgment of exterior control over female autonomy, as the latter (female autonomy) is thought to be the major term to uphold human dignity. Likewise, the pro-lifer is bewildered and frustrated that the pro-choicer could hold a judgment of death over life, as for them it is thought that life is the major term to uphold human dignity. By that reasoning, those of either "side" can rightly be incensed that their own beliefs and values as undermined by the opposing position, represented by the major term, have been rejected. And in the absence of common grounds for dialogue on the major term of those premises that formed the judgments, each person retreats to their position's sloganized stance. Then the conversation is reduced to each side speaking over the other side to champion their own position expressed by their premiseless judgment. The winner is declared not based on critical thinking or logical argumentation, because the correct major premises cannot be engaged. Advocates on each side are prepared to echo support for their championed position, and any potential dialectic is thwarted. If there is an actual engagement, which understandably arises from the passion to uphold one's beliefs and values tied to female autonomy or fetal life, it surfaces as a tenuously tied pretext developed to espouse the stance. Again, this is true for whatever that middle term may be, but upholding human dignity is a likely common goal.

Perhaps the average individual would not express the experience as it was just articulated, but one need not venture too far into a discussion on this topic of abortion before the same frustrating reality surfaces. The problematic issue and the lack of critical thinking is accepting that those slogans encapsulate an argument. Individuals who support a side may contest that as a simplification, but they will, at some tipping point, find one of the two stances to evidently express their position more closely than the alternative. At that point, the slogans undeniably become a logical fallacy. Both sides on the abortion debate have deployed this fallacy, and slogan-based arguments by their nature foment factions and become weaponized tools to flatten an issue where the measurable goal is to bulldoze the opponent. Whether admitted or not, this unwittingly reveals intellectual laziness in the inability to form one's own argument, or clumsiness in developing a proper counterargument, so that an *ad hominem* attack becomes the default response. In fact, both (laziness and clumsiness) might be in play. As the opposing side then becomes reduced to the extreme determined by their tipping point, villainizing the opponent is the substitute for engaging in dialogue. This may not be out of spite, but it does gratifyingly appease the ego. The pro-choicers accuse the pro-life side of prioritizing the life of the unborn over that of the female and imposing their own values and beliefs on females who are advocating their bodily autonomy for the preservation of human dignity. Then the pro-lifers accuse the pro-choice side of prioritizing the female's autonomy over that of the innocent unborn life, imposing their own values and beliefs over that of the unborn and thus over the preservation of human dignity.

Plainly stated, the pro-choicer asserts that the female is being forced to carry an unwanted pregnancy, while the pro-lifer asserts the female is killing an innocent unborn life. Each presents the other side not simply as an antagonist to their chosen and expressed position, but an enemy that frustrates their values and beliefs which are to uphold human dignity. Each expressed position ultimately becomes antithetical to the *other*, but the *other* is seen merely as one whose contrary stance is assumed to logically block the values and beliefs necessary for their expression of human dignity. There can be no resolution as to the merit of the values and beliefs, and the premises that led to the judgment are not up for discussion. Each side conjures a reaction, asking only in the end if the woman will be forced to carry the unwanted fetus, or if the unborn fetus will die. And it must be kept in mind that given the evidential ebb and flow of how culture and society leans, those judgments appear to result in some zero-sum assumption. So then, to not lose ground, each side remains entrenched. Thus, the abortion debate perpetuates an adversarial atmosphere where one side asserts the horror of the other's judgments, whether it is controlling the woman's body or killing the unborn baby. Because the shock value of those assertions is reduced in effectiveness after continual reuse, the *ad hominem* rhetoric becomes increasingly aggressive, and false equivalencies such as dystopian nightmares or images of a holocaust are hurled into the public sphere. As the interactions become more hostile, the analogies become more fanatical, and the examples to solicit a reaction must themselves become more extreme. Each side postures for the moral high ground, with visions of vindication by some future time period's appraisal of them in the present as having chosen the right side of history. Any favorable nod to a reasonable point outside one's own position, upon this rationale, is framed as betrayal to the cause of preserving human dignity. If someone converts, they are lauded by the "winning" side as finally having succumbed to reason. But if there is any truth that there may be a disconnect between one's values and beliefs as attached to a stance, the tragedy may be that the convert's newfound values and beliefs likewise were not ascended to by critical thinking. This individual, then conforming to their newly adopted stance, will equally find their newly held stance to be as rationally indefensible as the previous position. The new values and beliefs simply become dogmatically aligned with their new, reformed identity, and the stalemate remains.

There are two common ways to address such conflicting and seemingly impenetrable positions. One is always worthwhile and effective, while the other is a stop-gap strategy that can be ethically problematic. The first is listening to the other side, and the second is seeking compromise. In opposition to the first point, the pro-choicer will wonder why enter into an argument with someone who is intent on controlling a female's body. Likewise, the pro-lifer will wonder the purpose of engaging a person who advocates for the killing of unborn babies. For either side, such an enterprise is thought futile, or patronizing, or perhaps even lending credence to a non-negotiable claim. Opposition to the second, that of seeking some compromise, would question if there can be any middle ethical course between killing an unborn fetus and controlling a female's body. Considerations have been put forth—for example, the pro-choicer might concede to a compromise confining abortions to the first gestational trimester. But the pro-choicer would necessarily have to contend with the contradiction of tolerating the control of a female's body for the last six months as an ethical concession. The toleration would only be temporary. To the other side, the pro-lifer might concede to the same compromise, accepting a position that permits abortions within the first gestational trimester. But the pro-lifer would have to rationalize the contradiction of tolerating the termination of a fetal life in the first three months as an ethical concession. This toleration, too, would only be temporary. In a pluralistic society, as stated earlier, tolerance may be a necessity. But tolerance is not acceptance. Philosophically it can be explained as enduring an evil one cannot, or is unwilling to, overcome. Think of tolerating an unpleasant therapy in pursuit of health. It is accepted grudgingly, but with a goal of dispensing with the unwelcomed concession once health is restored. In the abortion debate, toleration may be employed as a compromise or temporary concession, if the logic is to lessen the perceived illicit act as a stop-gap measure. It would be acceptable perhaps to use toleration as a rationale in political maneuvering. But psychologically, any compromise can be nothing more than an ethical pause, accepted as an ill-received incremental loss or gain relative to one's perspective. This is easily demonstrated by a public ebb and flow within the debate, whereas when one side gains ground, it is perceived to be at the expense of the other side.

This dichotomy can hardly be seen as anything less than one position threatening the other. Once more, this is by definition a zero-sum schema. Though there are many ways to address this, one origin of a solution is situated within Socrates' view of justice. Recall in Plato's dialectic, he surmised justice as harmonizing desire and reason. Even with no static compromise remaining ethically acceptable between autonomy and life, the desires expressed as values and beliefs supposedly to support human dignity can aptly be investigated by reason. This is only possible when the desire to uphold human dignity is untethered from the position, so that it can be examined to what degree it retains one's values and beliefs. In short, the examination of values held and of beliefs ascribed can be rationally accounted for only when detached from the dichotomies of autonomy and life, which are thought to retain the unarticulated goal of human dignity. This is impossible without *listening to the other side*. The contention to listening was to the position, which is perceived as non-negotiable and thus considered futile. But listening remains worthwhile and effective in terms of disclosing the underlying values and beliefs as they form one's goal. It is in this way that the maxim, expressed in Latin as *audi alteram partem*, has the potency to harmonize desires and reason and thus be just. It would operate in Socratic fashion with each party first expressing their position, while allowing interrogation to rationally whittle down the errors as to how those positions align with values and beliefs that claim to support the goal. This is not the solution, but rather than seeking a compromise on the positions, it serves as the point of entry where dialogue can take initiative. Listening to the other side affords that opportunity. This unveils the ethical consistency (or inconsistency) of each position comparative to one's core values and expressed beliefs. The position of a person may be clear, but even considering the nuance of each position, people publicly lean pro-choice or pro-life based on the weight they grant either autonomy or life to support human dignity. Some may rebuke that, but in honest reflection it must be admitted that one's nuance favors a particular side. Restated another way, the position is not the belief or value; it is the judgment expressed as the position that forms an allegiance that need not be necessarily tethered to the goal of human dignity.

If people tend to value autonomy and life as not ultimate ends, they then exist as a means to the preservation of human dignity. The values and beliefs ascribed to those ideas of both autonomy and life can be explicitly expressed. Then if the values and beliefs can be expressed, they can be listened to. If they can be listened to, then it can be determined by assessment to what degree they uphold the goal of human dignity. This requires dialogue. If one listens, and that listening is reciprocal, then the anchoring of those values and beliefs can be rationally questioned. The last two sections of this chapter will deal with that directly; but for now, to scaffold the point, here is another expression of a nuanced example. Assuming both sides once again have a goal of upholding human dignity, the pro-choicer may value certain liberties that autonomy maintains, but perhaps nuance their stance to not believe terminating a fetal life for birth control is a legitimate reason to support abortion. Likewise, a pro-lifer may value certain expressions that physical life affords, but nuance their stance to not believe the intentional termination of a fetal life to save the physical life of a female is comparable to an elective abortion. If the "end result" of restricting a female's autonomy (pro-choice) or terminating a fetal life (pro-life) is repugnant, arguing over those judgments is fruitless. This is because they are preserved by values and beliefs of autonomy and life thought to sustain the unarticulated aim of preserving human dignity. This is amplified if one's values and beliefs have been found to be ideologically formed—for example, under the umbrella of women's rights or a theistic affiliation.

This schema, then, as with most prevailing perspectives on contentious public topics, seems to offer the observation that no resolution can be sought outside of compromise or conversion. That is ultimately not true. But there is just enough truth within such a claim to make it seem rationally sensible. So, where to begin? The first logical question to ask must be critically reflective if the public presentation of the abortion issue is the source of irreconcilability. The second requires critical listening to determine both the truth and validity in the public arguments presented. With the first, critical thinking must be brought to bear in the present discourse where those premises are investigating the underlying values and beliefs as connected to ultimate goals. And with the second, logic will be brought to bear to determine the extent of truth of those premises and to what degree the arguments then remain valid. With the first point, if any disconnect between values/beliefs and goals can be revealed and reformed, there remains hope to penetrate the impasse. That speaks to the futility of being inattentive and to the effectiveness of reconcilability. With the second point, it provides insight into where to begin the discussion, meaning that any existing merit will reveal its truth and validity. That speaks to the futility of peremptory rationales and to the effectiveness of listening.

Varied positions do exist within each side, and the majority of positions on each side do accept some nuanced form of the argument. But even though there are varied positions within those sides, they are based on values and beliefs attached to goals not purposely formed or explicitly stated. It is those unspoken premises that ferment division, remaining under the radar of each side. The sides then form as ideologies. Here one can understand ideology as a stance not reached by critical thinking or logic, but held because of a particular identity with a political affiliation, religious principle, or cultural creed. To explain the point, if someone senses there are logical problems with their side but will not critically reflect on their own position, the tendency is to remain attached to the group because the affirmed identity provides comfort and cover. If the identification is so tightly tied to their camp that changing one's mind can bring high cultural and personal costs, then rather than critically listening, the goal becomes to protect the ideology regardless of any discovered truth. Such ideological underpinning imprisons one in false premises and a fallacious argument. It creates an identity with a side that offers comfort that is threatened by critical reflection or critical listening. Identities are important as they do offer a sense of solidarity and assurance; but without rational roots, identity becomes a wall impenetrable by logic and critical thinking. At that point, the foundational goal of preserving human dignity is severed from the ethical judgment that either side is affirming as a value and belief. Group identity and cultural ideology provide the solace for upholding positions that offer comfort over truth seeking. It becomes no longer about judging the ethics of abortion by truthful premises, but about standing up for one's ideology formed by an identity. Yet it is precisely within this irrational schema that listening to the other side engages the premises and, by that type of engagement, can unmoor such errors from one's own judgments.

The argument thus far is principally that even with much nuance, the abortion issue is framed as the dichotomy between those who ultimately support autonomy or life. Both of those ideas are rightly central to human dignity, as autonomy is fundamental to one's psychological being and expression of personal agency, while life is the source of one's physical being and primary to personal agency. That is also why those on each side properly evoke strong emotive responses. Further, it is why the objectives of each side are resolutely defended and championed as non-negotiable causes. Rather than the preservation of human dignity, autonomy formed as the position of the pro-choicers and life formed as the position of the pro-lifers have unwittingly become the goals of non-negotiable sides. Either position gaining the upper hand in the public dialogue is thought to clearly come at the expense of the other side. It is held that when the life of the unborn is preserved, female bodily autonomy is conceded; or, otherwise, when female bodily autonomy is preserved, the life of the unborn is conceded. That is a stalemate. It should be clear that this polarization stems from the controversy over the judgments from which those positions were affirmed, but what is left unarticulated is how they underpin human dignity. Listening to the underlying values and beliefs as aligned to the premises is the only means to breach what appears, by that logic, to be a zero-sum game where every concession is considered a loss. As stated at the onset of this section, if personal time and intellectual energy are factors to be conserved for essential components of the dialogue on abortion, then it is quite necessary for any dialectical conversation on abortion to engage in only the strongest arguments. Understanding what preserves human dignity (better stated as the determination of personhood) is essential. Though much more on that will be addressed in this text, the present point is that the sides of the abortion issue in the public forum must first be dismantled.

THE VALUE OF BODILY AUTONOMY

There is the often unstated, and unrecognized, reality that both the pro-choice and pro-life camps essentially support the value of female bodily autonomy. The same of course is also true of valuing life, though treatment of that topic will occupy the following section. The differing of value with autonomy is not so much a matter of degree, except as understood in assigning the tipping point as to where the priority of one succumbs to the other. This is not an attempt to state what might appear to be obvious, but to press the notion that the valuing emphasized here is in contrast to ethical indifference. The pro-lifer is no more indifferent to the bodily autonomy of the female than the pro-choicer could be said to be indifferent to the life of the fetus. So, to rephrase it, beyond rare is the individual who is ethically indifferent to the preservation of a female's bodily autonomy, simply because there is thought to be no ethical claim to that value. That fact alone immediately reorients the initiation of a discussion, that there exists the valuing of bodily autonomy, antecedent to the exercise of that value when applied to the abortion topic. When one speaks of valuing an idea like bodily autonomy, the concept is not one that is entirely accepted or declined relative to one's stance; rather, it is the divergence as to how the concept is applied, and specifically under what conditions, that matters (and that often goes unvoiced). Staging this claim is not an attempt to seek common ground between stances, but to recognize bodily autonomy as a common interest so as to establish the extent to which it can be exercised. The aim is to remove any facets of the application of bodily autonomy that cause unnecessary division. Prior to exploring those facets, consider the following syllogistic arguments, as to whether each fairly represents an exchange between stances on autonomy relative to the abortion topic. The pro-choicer would argue to the pro-lifer that—

P1 If you value bodily autonomy, you will support a female's access to abortion.

P2 If you support a female expressing bodily autonomy, then you value bodily autonomy.

C1 Therefore, if you support a female expressing bodily autonomy, then you will support a female's access to abortion.

And in reply, the pro-lifer would respond in like manner to the pro-choicer that—

P3 I do value bodily autonomy, but not a female's access to abortion under any condition.

P4 I support a female expressing bodily autonomy, because I do value bodily autonomy.

C2 Therefore, I support a female expressing bodily autonomy, but not a female's access to abortion under any condition.

In either syllogism, the valuing of bodily autonomy was the middle term. Recall that this middle term is the shared term of both the premises that form the logical progression to the conclusion. Recall also that in the conclusion, which is typically thought of as the result of the argument, the middle term "I do value bodily autonomy" is not articulated explicitly and therefore neglected.

That provides a synopsis of the mutual valuing of bodily autonomy. Even the pro-lifer is not ethically indifferent to the expression of bodily autonomy, but will differ in terms of how such autonomy is applied and under what conditions. And in truth, even within the pro-choice camp, the tipping point is very dynamic, as nuances may set limits on the expression of bodily autonomy even when the claim of valuing it is upheld. As to the working definition of bodily autonomy, this certainly refers to having control over or governing one's own body. It means that another person or entity cannot encroach on one's own personal agency in choosing to have the child or procure an abortion. As the pro-choicer will readily offer, the choice is not simply for the abortion, but for the female's choice. Yet, the idea of intentionality is key, in that one's rationality is permitted to choose the goal. Consider that Kant offered this idea of autonomy, as stemming from his view that the human will can direct an individual to align with moral laws that are discoverable by reason alone. Later, this autonomy will be tethered to personhood, which for Kant, applies to only rational autonomous agents that can exert their will in the form of a choice. Autonomy, which in truth should be understood as *respect for autonomy*, is derived from Kant's humanity principle, which holds that, by reason, ethically no person can be used as a means to an end. From that, then, this autonomy must exclude any external coercion or enticement if it is in conflict with the female's original intention. Perhaps to offer a comparison, in medical ethics this arises primarily as personal consent in terms of choosing or declining a course of treatment, and that includes the autonomous decision to not pursue treatment even if it is in conflict with the determination of the medical team. That is only mentioned because autonomy, though derived from rationality, must not be understood as "doing what one wants" with one's own body.

Two aspects of a qualifier must be addressed in terms of bodily autonomy. The first is the degree to which such autonomy can be rationally expressed, and the second is if there exists any ethical limit on that rational expression. If, by Kant's principle, bodily autonomy is primarily tethered to the human person's rational capability, then this rationality is not attached to every individual who is counted as a member of the human species. Some humans lack such capability. There are those with developmental disabilities where it might be reduced, those in an unconscious state where it is either temporarily or permanently gone, or adults with diminished rational capacities that, either dynamically or globally, have had their rational capabilities reduced or severed. Examples could include, but are not limited, to individuals in shock, those under the influence of legal medications or illegal drugs, those with dementia, or an individual who has experienced a brain injury. Now it is true that such desired expression of one's autonomy can be transferred to a proxy or substitute, so that such autonomy is still attached to the person in those examples by someone designated to judge on their behalf. A further qualifier would be that this rational agency is age-specific, as even though minors may indeed have rational capabilities, there remains an insufficient capacity recognized for direct expression.

The second aspect of the qualifier for bodily autonomy was already used as an example in the section explaining terms and the First Act of the Mind. It was offered that bodily autonomy is more exact a term than *free to do what one wants* with one's own body, since one cannot ethically self-harm and cite respect for bodily autonomy in defense. And then further that bodily autonomy is only a clear term if it is understood as *respect for bodily autonomy*, which is to represent the rational and intentional exercise of personal autonomy. For example, in rare cases of body integrity disorder (BID), where a body part, say a person's leg, is sensed to not be their leg, it has been reported that only amputation was thought to be a remedy. But it remains unethical to acquiesce to a person suffering from BID to ethically permit amputation, even if there is reported relief from those who by their own initiative have taken action. The point is that respect for bodily autonomy could not hold the same meaning as *bodily freedom,* which connotes no existing restraint toward a goal with the body, whether self-harming the body or seeking amputation. So then, bodily autonomy cannot be reduced to the exercise of personal freedom, which would affirm one is at liberty to execute one's own will, to do with one's own body as one wills.

In truth, it should not be controversial to state that neither sex has absolute bodily autonomy, even if there are extreme libertarians who would argue otherwise. For example, whether euthanasia is expressed as medical assistance in dying (MAiD) or the right to die, the appeals to autonomy framed under the notion of personal agency (realization of will) are not without regulation. Under personal agency, presently any access to legal euthanasia is considered ethical (by even the advocates) only if the person is terminally ill with minimum life expectancy, yet in all circumstances it is governed by strict criteria that extend beyond that. There remain ongoing public arguments to widen access for including physically chronic and mental illnesses, but presently there appears to be no rational campaign to hold that bodily autonomy applied to the "right to die" should be extended to physically healthy and psychologically competent people. In short, no longer willing one's own self to live is not an acceptable reason for euthanasia. So, though end-of-life issues are often structured in terms of a right, that right cannot be merely predicated as an assertion of one's will. If autonomy were absolute, then the right to autonomy would only be constrained by an evidentiary reduction of reason found present in the rational agent. In other words, if the person lacks sufficient rationality and therefore cannot be afforded bodily autonomy, then the *right to die* could not be summarily honored at their request.

Another application that challenges autonomy as absolute would concern the selling of nonvital organs while alive. There are those with libertarian persuasions that argue it should be legally permitted based on bodily autonomy, but the ethical consensus is that voluntarily selling nonvital organs while alive is contrary to the principle of body integrity. That is to claim ethically that the body, except for reasons of preserving one's own physical life, is to remain whole. There is further concern that other injustices would arise, such as the poor and powerless likely being the ones "voluntarily" selling their nonvital organs. In other words, it would appear to be voluntary but, in reality, would be nothing but an act of desperation by the "donor" to abate a socio-economic injustice.

What is singularly significant to this line of argumentation is that valuing bodily autonomy is something held by all, but the degree to which such autonomy can be rationally expressed remains the contention. The pro-lifer would be in ethical error to merely state that a female *does not have* an ethical argument concerning abortion that can be based on bodily autonomy, just as the pro-choicer would be in ethical error to merely state that a female *does have* an ethical argument concerning abortion based solely on bodily autonomy. The first argument attempts to dismiss the rationally based value of autonomy that governs the human person, whereas the second argument adopts irrational reasoning that bodily autonomy alone is sufficient to warrant ethical access to an abortion. It is not enough that bodily autonomy is predicated on the rational expression of the human person; also to be considered is the degree to which this rational expression can ethically be expressed before the tipping point determined by value is reached.

This then sets up the second aspect of the qualifier to determine if there exists any ethical limit on the part of the "donor" on that rational expression of bodily autonomy, regardless of degree. This is a different tipping point, specifically to determine if there exists any point where female bodily autonomy (again, in truth bodily autonomy for either sex) can have no ethical expression. This judgment should not be a controversial issue, but the ramifications of the judgment will cause certain dispute. The principle is that *one's own bodily autonomy ethically stops at the threshold of another person's bodily autonomy*. In other words, without very serious reasons and at the risk of ethical repercussions, one person cannot assert their own bodily autonomy that results in the reduction of another person's autonomy. Though the section that will contain the arguments on personhood lies ahead, at this juncture there arises tension that must determine what the unborn *is*. If the unborn is *not a person* (at any point in utero), then the female's bodily autonomy can be rationally exercised, unrestrained (prior to the point in utero where personhood is recognized). There is no reduction of the bodily autonomy of the unborn nonperson, for there is only the consideration of a single person at stake with claims to bodily autonomy—that of the female carrying the fetus. But if the unborn is accepted or determined to be a person (originating at whatever that point in utero may be), then the female's bodily autonomy cannot be rationally exercised. By this judgment, it would unethically override the bodily autonomy of the unborn person, for there is the consideration of two persons at stake (originating from the point in utero where personhood is recognized). Much needs to be discussed concerning personhood, but regardless of how that judgment is recognized or determined, the principle of one's own bodily autonomy ethically stopping at the threshold of another person's bodily autonomy stands as the ethical limit for any individual to rationally express their bodily autonomy. This is easily demonstrated to be ethically correct, for once the unborn's head has vacated the vaginal cavity of the female (legal personhood), the newborn is afforded bodily autonomy rights based on the recognized personhood.

Now it is ethically valid to argue that the idea of bodily autonomy is connected to personhood, but that does not disregard some value that can be ascribed to living nonpersons. That is to say that the expression of rationality with bodily autonomy may be binary as it relates to persons alone, but there can remain some value of the unborn nonperson. For example, if the unborn is not a person but is granted some degree of moral value, then the female's autonomy is proportionately weighed against that moral value of the unborn, which may or may not be ethically aborted dependent on the circumstances. But this is dependent on the nonpersonhood status of the unborn, and then the value the female person has determined to recognize or apply to the unborn nonperson. This is not simply theoretical, as a very practical scenario would arise with surrogacy. If the surrogate expresses bodily autonomy by carrying a fetus to be parented by someone other than herself, then it follows that for either altruism or some form of compensation, the unborn (even as a nonperson) retains value for the surrogate, and perhaps logically also for the intended parents. The arrangement by the intended parents may have stipulated that if any undesirable prenatal abnormality is detected in utero by imaging, the unborn is to be aborted. Legally, although the female perhaps could not be forced to abort the unborn nonperson, other factors such as immigration status and financial concerns will nonetheless weigh against the female's expression of upholding her bodily autonomy. In short, the female can be pressured to abort the unborn, and thus the value of the unborn nonperson will not be realized. The converse of this scenario is also applicable; the female might desire to terminate the unborn against the desire of the intended parents. Though with that, the same concerns of immigration status and financial obligations will weigh against the female's expression of bodily autonomy to terminate the pregnancy. Thus, despite the female's desire to express her bodily autonomy, outside factors may inhibit the expression.

This section on the value of bodily autonomy was not an attempt to provide a full treatise on the issue or to placate all objections, but to offer considerations as to how it is not the value itself but the application and relation to personhood that need to be addressed. The aim was to remove any facets of the application of bodily autonomy that can evidently cause unnecessary division. Such consideration is a distinct perspective, which by itself transcends any claim that bodily autonomy is the sole factor to retain under consideration. Perhaps that notion alone allows an opportunity for both the reduction of polarization and a readjustment in the approach for a more authentic and fruitful dialogue on the topic of abortion.

THE VALUE OF PRESERVING LIFE

The parallel argument to the valuing of bodily autonomy is the valuing of preserving life. Since a stand-alone chapter directly addresses the meaning of the term *life*, this section will be restricted to the aspect of *life* being a shared value. As with the idea of bodily autonomy, the first aspect of preserving life is not so much a matter of degree but of assessing the tipping point where the priority of one succumbs to the other. And again, to that point specifically, this notion of valuing is in contrast to holding to an ethical indifference. It stands contrary to both common sense and logic for any individual to remain ethically indifferent to the preservation of life, and from that point the opportunity arises to initiate a dialogue. Once more, here is that point stated in a series of syllogistic arguments. The pro-choicer would argue to the pro-lifer that—

P1 If you want to demonstrate that you value preserving life, you will support a female having access to abortion.

P2 If you support the preservation of life, then that demonstrates you value preserving life.

C1 Therefore, if you support the preservation of life, then you will support a female having access to abortion.

And in reply, the pro-lifer would respond in like manner to the pro-choicer that—

P3 I do want to demonstrate that I value preserving life, but I will not support a female having access to abortion.

P4 I support the preservation of life, demonstrating that I do value preserving life.

C2 Therefore, I support the preservation of life, but I will not support a female having access to abortion.

Notice that P2 and P4 appear as tautologies because each premise presents itself as a presupposition—namely, that X is done because of valuing X. It is still important as an affirming position. But it also presents a distinction, as the preservation of life in contrast to bodily autonomy results in consequences of no reparable remedy. The result is unrecoverable, and thus permanent. The unborn, regardless of recognized or assigned personhood, will be terminated; the fetus will die. This is not true, of course, in consideration of valuing bodily autonomy. With bodily autonomy, when it can and will be applied to the female, whether reduced or severed, there remains an opportunity for restoration as the result is reformable and thus not permanent. That is not to suggest that there are no serious conditions to consider with the diminishment of bodily autonomy, which span from physical to psychological needs and well-being; but in stark contrast, the choice of life is irrevocable.

First though, the working definition for *preserving life*, in this context, refers to the safeguarding of an innocent person's physical and mental integrity from violation by another. That term *person* is a necessary part of the definition, not to dismiss any value to a nonperson's life, but only to hold that the acknowledgement or assignment of personhood must be an initial consideration. The key term in that definition, which is *personhood*, suggests that unless one is a person, then the term *preserving life* will be weighed by other values. Where this becomes complicated, by issues of comparison, is that even with human lives recognized as persons there are proportional elements to safeguarding life, limits to control that safeguarding, and the issue of innocence concerning the life. So in the prohibitive sense, preserving life could be understood as not killing an innocent *living human person*, or not allowing an innocent *living human person* to be killed, without serious moral justification or proportionate reasons. It also should be kept in mind that here, too, there can be value to a life, even if that life is considered a nonperson.

To be clear, there are no exonerating circumstances that ethically permit one person to take the innocent life of another intentionally and summarily. This is true even when an innocent person is killed either intentionally or unintentionally, for the ethical calculus that differs between those becomes the degree of culpability. That is why murder and manslaughter are determined by the degree of culpability. But the varying degrees of murder address culpability and not the ethics of killing an innocent; otherwise, they still violate the safeguarding of a person's life as defined for the purposes here. But not all killing, even when intentional, is unethical if the person being killed is not deemed innocent. For example, the issue of killing another in an act of self-defense is not unethical, even if intentional, because it is understood as necessary for the preservation of one's own life. Further, some accept the intentional killing of a convicted criminal for capital crimes or the ethical killing of combatants during a justified war as the preservation of justice within a society. Mentioning these is not to judge or equate their ethical legitimacy relative to the abortion topic, but to make the simple point that any ethical justification for evaluating the preservation of life is directly connected to self-defense and the preservation of justice, which both sides would value and hold. Further, both of those concepts, self-defense and the preservation of justice, likely have import into the abortion dialogue.

With that last claim, the dialogue becomes ethically muddy as the variances of valuing the preservation of life are sometimes extended by each side comparatively into the abortion conversation. For example, if the unborn is interpreted as a threat to the well-being of the pregnant female, the idea of preserving life then weighs the value of the female's well-being over that of the intruding fetus. The argument then retains the value of preserving life, but the resulting death of the unborn can be framed as unintentional, even unfortunate, but still ethical by virtue of self-defense. In terms of the preservation of justice, an abortion will be argued by a particular stance without ethical implications in those cases where rape or social conditions have systemically fostered circumstances that limit viable options. By that logic, the unborn as the result of rape becomes an extension of the criminal act. Likewise, some articulation can be forwarded within particular societal conditions; the continued pregnancy becomes an extension of unjust forces that must be countered to alleviate such societal injustices. Here again, the argument retains the value of preserving life, but the resulting death of the unborn, though intentional, is weighed against parameters framing a female's bodily autonomy as it relates to proportional justice against an individual or society. So, even in an atmosphere that allows safe and rare abortions, such elements of prohibition and mitigating levels of guilt can allow the taking of an innocent unborn's life, while still supporting the value of preserving life. In terms of abortion, they simply have differing applications of how such a value is ethically applied.

The dilemma for both sides pertaining to the abortion issue arises, then, that the value of preserving life cannot be absolute. It follows logically that if valuing the preservation of life is not absolute in cases of a person's physical self-defense and the preservation of societal justice in terms of crime and perceived interests, then by extension it is not absolute in cases of rape or preserving personal justice in terms of inequity and other social injuries. In the same way that the pro-choice and pro-life "sides" can be argued as false absolutes that lack nuance, the value of preserving life can share that same evaluation. Though perhaps articulated differently, this is to some degree the practical public consensus because, in reality, those in the pro-choice camp accept in some instances conditions in which the life of the unborn should not be treated simply as an appendage solely to be controlled by the female's autonomy. In that case, the unborn nonperson retains value. And correspondingly, there are instances where those in the pro-life camp accept some conditions in which the life of the female should not be treated simply as an incubating means to deliver the unborn. In that case, the female's autonomy retains value. Think of all the varied reasons that give rational people a reason to pause and consider possible exceptions to defending an abortion in order to preserve the life of the unborn, or to oppose an abortion in order to not endanger the life of the pregnant female. In fact, the value of preserving life, if held as an absolute for either side, would be more ethically challenging or likely exacerbate the justice sought from each position.

The pro-choicer must determine those instances where mitigating circumstances hold that the life of the unborn must ethically be given primary consideration, even if it results in loss of autonomy of the female. The pro-lifer must determine those instances where mitigating circumstances hold that the life of the female must ethically be given primary consideration, even if it results in the death of the unborn. What impedes the abortion conversation is the perception that if either side concedes those conditions, they undermine their own side's position. Or another interpretation would be that those elements of nuance are downplayed or avoided altogether for fear of cooperating with or conceding to the opposing side's agenda. Accusations of hypocrisy also fester, even if the actual stance of not accepting the nuance is more akin to being inflexible rather than standing on one's ground of the recognized value.

These exceptions are often exposed in the difficult cases. It is usually then that the nuance of valuing the preservation of life becomes evident. And though the difficult cases may be rare, they are most suited for study in that they test the veracity of the theoretical points each side champions within their position. For this topic of the value of preserving life, without providing conclusive judgments to aid either position, two simple scenarios will serve as case studies to test the practicality of the base theory of each side in terms of the preservation of life. To first illustrate the limits of the pro-life view of preserving life, an analysis of an *ectopic pregnancy* fits that model. For the second case study, provided to illustrate the limits of the pro-choice view of preserving life, the analysis of an *abortion later in pregnancy* will serve the analysis. The incidence of each is less than 2 percent of all pregnancies.

An ectopic pregnancy, which occurs with 1 to 2 percent of all pregnancies,[1] takes place when a zygote (fertilized egg) attaches outside the uterus. The term *ectopic* comes from the Greek word meaning "out of place." With the vast majority of ectopic pregnancies, the blastocyst (implanted zygote) implants into the fallopian tube. There is no practical way for the fertilized egg to develop in the fallopian tube, and on most occasions this will resolve naturally. But it is not impossible for the unborn to gestate for many weeks, and though the unborn would perish due to lack of nutrition, by that stage it can rupture the fallopian tube. Left untreated, the woman will experience abdominal hemorrhaging, which at the very least can affect future pregnancies and present other complications, but the situation can also be catastrophic. In fact, ectopic pregnancies remain a significant cause of maternal deaths. The pro-choicer will claim the valued life of the female requires preservation and will disregard recognizing any moral value of the fertilized egg in the fallopian tube. The pro-lifer will claim the valued life of the fertilized egg must not be disregarded, but cannot ethically discount preserving the valued life of the female. For the pro-lifer, intuition will favor preserving the life of the female. Since this action does not preserve the life of the unborn, it may be reached by proportionally weighing the two lives involved and the practicality of the possible outcomes. It might be framed as mimicking the issue of self-defense.

The ethical dilemma arises as the female's life cannot be preserved without the termination of the fertilized egg. If the ectopic pregnancy is treated pharmaceutically to end the *pregnancy* (another term that requires a precise definition), the fertilized egg's tissue will be absorbed into the female's body. If the medical issue is treated surgically by removing the fertilized egg from the fallopian tube (salpingostomy), though the fertilized egg will die, the fallopian tube may be preserved. If the fallopian tube is removed with the fertilized egg remaining within the tube (salpingectomy), the fertilized egg will die, and future fertility will be compromised. If expectant care warrants medical intervention, the pro-lifer will have to determine how to judge the action as ethically acceptable knowing that in order to preserve the female's life, that judgment is in tandem with having moral certainty of not being able to preserve the life of the fertilized egg. There is much more that can be ethically applied to address this analysis, but here the point is to illustrate the tension

1. Lee and Barnhart, "What Is an Ectopic Pregnancy?," 434.

that arises for the pro-lifer when the judgment to save one life ends the life of another. On the surface, the resolution appears antithetical to the pro-life position. But an inability to articulate how to ethically resolve the dilemma explains why the persistence of the argument stubbornly remains a pro-choice demonstration of the inflexibility of the pro-life sloganized stance.

A bit of an aside is necessary here to define *pregnancy* and avoid another instance of equivocation. It does not change the ethical evaluation just presented, but clarity always helps in understanding as the definitions of pregnancy do vary. The American College of Obstetricans and Gynecologists (ACOG) defines the term *pregnancy* as beginning with the fertilized egg's implantation in the uterus.[2] Technically, by that definition, an ectopic implantation is not a pregnancy, and therefore the death of the fertilized egg is not an abortion. Some medical establishment definitions concur. That is an important distinction because if fertilization has occurred, the use of hormonal contraception, particularly so-called *emergency contraception*, can have the intended effect of the uterine wall becoming hostile to implantation of the embryo. If that is the case, the fertilized egg that is unable to implant may or may not be considered a pregnancy, dependent on one's definition. The argument then becomes that if there was never an implantation, then hormonal contraception cannot be referred to as an abortifacient. The definition of a pregnancy requiring implantation is what is referred to as an *established pregnancy*; the female is not pregnant until the fertilized egg has implanted into the uterus. This text's definition cited an abortion as the termination of a fertilized life. The scientific literature on ectopic pregnancies will cite a pregnancy as the attachment of the fertilized egg within the body of a female, not specifically the uterus. By those latter two definitions, an ectopic pregnancy technically results in abortion. This is a good example of why one must first define what they are referring to in order to avoid equivocation. And it should be stated clearly that dictionary definitions are not the solution, as they are descriptions and often include only the prevailing thought of a culture; they cannot function as an authority for any position and should be avoided as they are simply not definitive. The issue of equivocation, then, is what would constitute the termination of a pregnancy versus the termination of a fertilized life. It is important to be aware of these distinctions during the abortion conversation, although

2. Chung et al., "Obstetrician-Gynecologists' Beliefs," 132.e1.

as stated they do not alter the fundamental tension that arises in the case just presented.

Now to address the limits of the pro-choice view of valuing the preservation of life, an analysis of an abortion occurring *later in pregnancy* will be constructed. Notice the use of the term *later in pregnancy* rather than *late-term abortion*, as the latter is not a medical term. These abortions on average account for a little over 1 percent of all abortions and would occur under the conditions of twenty-one gestational weeks or later.[3] That gestational age (GA) is at the low end of fetal viability. There are multiple factors that require consideration, and the term *viability* itself is not standardized across regions. The reasons for abortions later in pregnancy can include financial and logistic barriers, the pregnant female's unawareness of her condition earlier in the pregnancy, or the discovery of undesired fetal abnormalities. The latter in particular can include newly found genetic anomalies, the determined likelihood of a nonviable fetal delivery, or organ development issues of the fetus detected during scans. A reason could also be possible health risks directly to the pregnant female. The pro-lifer will claim the innocent life of the unborn requires preservation, but under the conditions of expectant care, which holds to monitoring rather than immediate intervention.

But many who side overall with the pro-choicer will claim that although valuing the preserved life of the female must be paramount, one cannot ethically discount valuing the preserved life of the unborn at this stage *later in pregnancy*, which is at the onset of viability, or perhaps even postviability. The pro-choicer will have to ethically determine if anomalies such as Down syndrome or cleft palate constitute undesirable conditions for a pregnant female to exercise her bodily autonomy for an abortion. And if it is those conditions and not the preservation of the life of the female that form the calculus, then is any ethical consideration granted to the viable and near-born fetus? Even in cases of the baby not surviving long after birth, the ethic of terminating the unborn while still in utero would require an ethical judgment other than valuing the preservation of life. Like the previous scenario, there is much more that can be ethically applied to address this analysis, but here the point is to illustrate the tension that arises for the pro-choicer when the judgment to value the preservation of one life ends the life of another. This is particularly acute if the preservation of the female's life is not directly

3. Gomez et al., "Abortions Later in Pregnancy," para. 7.

health threatening or when, in the case of undesired health conditions of the unborn, an abortion *later in pregnancy* is chosen for lifestyle factors. Here again, an inability to articulate how to ethically resolve the dilemma explains why the persistence of the argument stubbornly remains a pro-life demonstration of the inflexibility of the pro-choice sloganized stance.

Two brief issues are necessary as asides to avoid yet further instances of equivocation. Though this may seem overly technical, the proper apprehension of terms is required in any rational dialogue in order to apply critical thinking. In the following scenario, as in the ectopic pregnancy case, the concern is to distinguish *intentional killing* from the *unintentional foreseen death* that will occur in certain cases where the female's physical life is in peril during pregnancy. For example, consider the case of a female who has been diagnosed with endometrial cancer while pregnant. The most common treatment for endometrial cancer is a hysterectomy, the removal of the female's uterus (womb). As with the fertilized egg within the fallopian tube, to remove the uterus will certainly terminate the prenatal life developing inside. But under the principle of non-maleficence, secular medicine has adopted the Principle of Double Effect (PDE), which itself was adopted from Thomas Aquinas's ethical stance on self-defense. Aquinas held that self-defense is not murder provided four conditions are met. The first is that what is being done as an act is good or at least neutral. The second is that only the good effect is intended even if the bad effect is foreseen. The third is that the bad effect did not cause the good effect, and finally the fourth is that there is due proportion between the two effects.[4] In the case of endometrial cancer, PDE can be applied in this way: first, treatment of the female's cancer is good; secondly, the curing of the cancer is the goal, and the cessation of the fetal life is foreseen, though not intended; thirdly, the cessation of the fetal life as the bad effect does not produce the cure for endometrial cancer, which is the good effect; and fourthly, the life of the unborn is not proportionally greater than the life of the female. By this analysis, to do no harm (non-maleficence), the value of preserving life is upheld and not in conflict with the foreseen, though undesired, outcome.

The second issue to be addressed to avoid equivocation is rarely defined in private and public debates on abortion: what exactly is meant by the term *life of the mother*? At first glance, death being the opposite of life, the value of the *preservation of life* is thought solely to mean the

4. See Aquinas, *Summa Theologica* II-II, q64, a7, 1465.

female will not die; therefore, the contrary of *life of the mother* is commonly held to mean the *death of the mother*. But that is not the technical meaning, and acknowledging this is important in the actual abortion debate. The term *life of the mother* is held to include other important factors that contribute not just to physical life but also to living, understood as thriving. In the 1973 U.S. Supreme Court case, *Doe v. Bolton* (the lesser-known case decided on the same day as *Roe v. Wade*)[5], the term *life of the mother* was broadened to include various other factors. It was held to mean physical life, but it also means a serious maternal injury from the pregnancy, the mental or physical defects of the born child, the psychological and emotional condition of the female, and/or her family dynamics, which includes the female's age.[6] The point is that these are not unimportant health factors to consider for the pregnant female. But if a pro-choicer is arguing the abortion is necessary for the life of the female, and the pro-lifer is explaining the female will not die or be physically harmed, they are not disagreeing over the threat of physical death. Each will continue arguing *past* the other solely because neither has cleared up the equivocal term of what *life* means in this context. As presented, the abortion conversation must engage to what extent both the pro-choice and the pro-life camps essentially support the value of preserving life. The point of this argument was not to seek common ground, but to resolve unnecessary division caused by the equivocation of language and unclear thought.

ETHICAL CONSISTENCY AND WHAT A THING IS

The values and beliefs one holds shape an ethical evaluation. One's values reflect the standard for ethical evaluations, and one's beliefs determine the ascent to that judgment. That was a clear reason to investigate the underlying values and beliefs of respecting bodily autonomy and the preservation of life. And as was argued prior, it remains unclear to what extent a culturally influenced evaluation affects one's values and beliefs, or vice versa. And along with that, it remains unclear whether or not something foundational for each argument remains unexpressed. But if one can set aside consideration for the aspects of values and beliefs that

5. See Roe v. Wade, 410 U.S. 113 (1973).
6. See Doe v. Bolton, 410 U.S. 179 (1973).

are articulated, there remains an even more foundational inquiry necessary for any ethical evaluation: until one knows what the thing *is* that is the object of those values and beliefs, no consistent ethical judgment is possible. Ethical judgments follow from values and beliefs, and from those judgments knowledge is deduced, thus forming rational principles that can be called scientific discovery. This is demonstrable knowledge that leads to understanding. For the Ancients, the study of *science* did not have the narrow connotation generally accepted presently, of holding to empirical pursuits. In Ancient Greece, the term for the study of knowledge was *epistêmê*, translated into Latin as *scientia*. That term can be accepted as *the state of knowing*. From that, the term *science* is derived, which in the broad sense and as used here would refer to any systematic way of knowing.

With that understanding in place, the branch of philosophy called *metaphysics* is the science that pursues basic realities such as consciousness, free will, universals (how things are unified), change, time, etc. Perhaps it is easier to say, in brief, metaphysics is the science of all fundamental reality. Aristotle, in his book *Metaphysics*, explains that there is something primary that everything else that is pursued as knowledge depends upon first and foremost. That first principle is found in the pursuit of *ontology*, which is the *study of being*. The term *being* here refers to what a thing *is*. It follows, then, that for philosophical thinking, one must grasp the first causes and principles of a thing (*being*) prior to any further investigation, particularly anything that falls under practical philosophy such as an ethical evaluation. Without initially considering this principle, ethical consistency is at risk, and one proceeds to argue *what to do with something* without first determining *what it is one is arguing about*. Here is that claim presented as a logical inference, known as a *modus tollens*. This is similar to the *modus ponens*, which claimed that when "If P, then Q" is true, then whenever P is true, so too will Q be true (P, therefore Q). The distinction with the *modus tollens* is that it infers if both the claim and implication ("If P, then Q") are true, then whenever Q is not true, so too will P not be true (not Q, therefore not P). What follows is that logical inference.

> If a person first determined as the primary principle what a thing *is* (P=*the being of what one is arguing about*), then they made an ethically consistent judgment (Q=*arguing what to do with that being*). A person *did not* make an ethically consistent judgment (Q=*arguing what to do with that being*); therefore,

> they *did not* first determine as the primary principle what a thing *is* (P=*the being of what one is arguing about*).

Once the object (*the being of what one is arguing about*) is claimed to be known, then every ethical evaluation involving that same being must not deviate from ethical evaluations applied in other scenarios. Granted, circumstances intervene, but even then, justification is required to maintain the ethical consistency that remains predicated on what the being *is*. The point here is that in order for one to maintain ethical consistency, the standard is determined by *the being of what one is arguing about* and not some value or belief tied to a dogmatic or ideological stance.

This first principle as the foundational axiom, in tandem with the necessity of ethical consistency, is quite simply explained by a thought experiment. There is nothing manipulative in its design, and by itself it changes no position on this topic of abortion. Here is the scenario. A bulldozer is brought in to demolish an old house. The contractor is responsible for the safety of all during the demolition. The contractor asks the crew on the ground if there is any living being in the house before they begin the demolition. If one of the crew responds, "Yes, there are live rats in the house," the demolition will proceed. If one of the crew responds, "Yes, there are live rabbits in the house," the demolition will likely proceed, though there may be an attempt to remove the rabbits or perhaps allow them to escape during the demolition. But if one of the crew responds, "Yes, there are live dogs in the house," the demolition would halt, and all reasonable attempts would be made to rescue the dogs. But finally if one of the crew responds, "Yes, there are live human children in the house," the demolition ceases, full stop, and will not proceed until the children's safety is assured.

In each variation of the thought experiment, the goal of demolishing the old house remained (Q). But what altered the ethical judgment (i.e., to proceed with or halt the demolition) was based on determining what the *being* (P) in the old house was. What the living thing *is* was the *being* that determined the ethical judgment of whether to proceed with or halt the demolition. So, the claim here is that ethics begins with being; or, restated, an ethical evaluation must first establish what a thing *is* (P), prior to any ethical judgment of what to do with or to that thing (Q). The tethering of ethical consistency to the *being* of a thing holds that if *being* determines the course of the ethical judgment, then in all instances concerning that same *being* (what it *is*), the same ethical judgment will be applied. What it *is*, determined as *being*, becomes the standard in the ethical evaluation. That is a logical, necessary inference.

Perhaps demonstrating this by way of a fallacy will be helpful. The reversal of a necessary inference is a logical fallacy known as *affirming the consequent*. One expression of an *affirming the consequent* fallacy would be a *converse error*. It can be expressed as "If P, then Q; Q, therefore P." Notice a correct *modus tollens* is "If P, then Q. Not Q, therefore not P." But the fallacy arises from the logical inference being severed when the statement affirms a necessary condition that does not logically follow. This is apparent once that formula is applied to a concrete example. Consider the following illustration of that claim.

> If a person takes a shower (P), then they will be wet (Q). A person *is wet* (Q); therefore the person must have *taken* a shower (P).

Although it is true that taking a shower will make a person wet, the fact that they are presently wet is not sufficient to logically infer that they did take a shower. They may simply have become wet from various other causes; it rained, they fell into a pool, etc. To demonstrate an *inverse error* using the original *modus ponens*, which argued for the primacy of ontology (what a thing *is*) prior to arguing what to do with that *being*, the fallacy could be expressed as follows.

> If a person first determined as the primary principle what a thing *is* (P=*the being of what one is arguing about*), then they made an ethically consistent judgment (Q=*arguing what to do with that being*). If a person *did not* first determine as the primary principle what a thing *is* (P=*the being of what one is arguing about*), then they *did not* make an ethically consistent judgment (Q=*arguing what to do with that being*).

This may appear to offer a sensible point in a very confusing manner, but it is important to show the logical inference as necessary, prior to stating the claim that is central to the abortion dialogue. That is, in the dialogue on abortion, any ethical analysis must first engage and judge the ontological question to identify what the unborn *is* (which includes assessing moral value), prior to claiming as a logical inference any evaluative judgment of whether it is ethical or unethical to abort. If one simply asked, "What is it that is being aborted?" more than likely the pro-choicer would respond, "It does not matter because the female's bodily autonomy is primary," and the pro-lifer would respond, "It matters because the unborn is a living human." Each, as will be demonstrated further along in this text, is insufficient to be put forth without the logical underpinning of *being* determined. The issue of what a thing *is* would be dismissed without the necessary background exposing why such inferential judgments are necessary, while otherwise circumventing them leads to fallacious reasoning and derails rational dialogue.

With those explanations of logical inferences in place, to deduce that what a thing *is* (being) is primary for any action (doing) to be ethically consistent, one may now apply the thought experiment of demolishing a house to the abortion dialogue. The judgment to demolish the house would be analogous to a judgment for having an abortion. The contractor would align with the people making the judgment for an abortion, who here are responsible to identify what *is* the living being in the uterus, or the ontological status of the unborn. The ontological status of the unborn (P=*the being of what one is arguing about*) must be determined prior to an ethical judgment about the abortion (Q=*arguing what to do with that being*), in the same way the crew would need to determine what living beings were in the house to be demolished. Like the lower-valued beings found alive in the house, if the unborn (P=*the being of what one is arguing about*) is not a person or is a person valued less than the pregnant female, or is a nonperson with some value that is less than that of the pregnant female, then one *may proceed* with an abortion (Q=*arguing what to do with that being*), in the same way the contractor may proceed with the demolition. But if the beings found alive in the house are human lives or valued beings, then similarly if the ontological status of the unborn (P=*the being of what one is arguing about*) is a person or is a nonperson with value less than the pregnant female but sufficient to preserve, then one *may not proceed* with an abortion (Q=*arguing what to do with that being*), in the same way the contractor may not proceed with the demolition. The point is simple: in the same way the contractor could not move forward with demolishing the house (Q) until it was cleared of valued living beings (P), so too with an abortion, until one determines the ontological status of the unborn (P), any action taken (Q) will logically result in an unethical act, or an act ethically inconsistent. That claim is not ideological or dogmatic, but if maintained it affords the means to avoid an ideological or dogmatic judgment and succeeds in first determining what it *is* prior to determining what to *do*.

In the section on the "Value of bodily autonomy," the principle of one's own bodily autonomy ethically stopping at the threshold of another *person*'s bodily autonomy was proposed as an axiom demonstrating the ethical limit for any individual to rationally express their own bodily autonomy. The key term *person* thus calls for the judgment of personhood as an ontological status. This does not reduce the value of bodily autonomy, but only logically claims (given the previous thought experiment and logical inferences) that bodily autonomy cannot be exercised prior to the judgment of what a thing *is*. That may seem like it defaults to the judgment of the pro-lifers, but not sufficiently so. In fact, applying this to the abortion debate does not solve the issue ethically, as one would still have to contend with the necessary (biological) relation of the unborn to the female, as well as with the notion of how to ethically resolve the value of one person (unborn) placing another person (pregnant female) in danger. But what this ethical axiom does recognize is the fact that until each agrees as to what the unborn *is*, the judgments when in dialogue will be about differing over the action (abortion) and likely fall prey to a *converse error* (autonomy over ontology). It can be expressed as "If I determine the unborn to be a nonperson of no or less moral value (P), then I judge the abortion as ethical (Q). I judge the abortion to be ethical (Q); therefore, I determined (actually did not consider) the unborn to be a nonperson of no or less moral value (P)." In this fallacious logical inference, the judgment of the abortion claimed to be ethical, regardless of any inquiry as to the ontological status of the unborn. The lack of consideration for the latter is the source of the fallacy and an indication that some necessary factor was not being critically examined, for reasons undetermined.

There are further considerations, relative to the thought experiment, as to yet apply to the dialogue on abortion. As with any analogy, all analogies limp. That is to mean they are useful for comparative purposes, but one-to-one parallels should not be assumed. If the unborn is living but *does not* have the same moral value of being as that of a natal child (a nonperson with moral value), then the pro-life position is not absolute in the same way that other nonperson living beings, in the thought experiment with similar ontological worth, *did not halt* the demolition. Likewise, if the unborn is a nonperson living being and *does* have the moral value of a natal child, then the pro-choice position is not absolute in the same way that the living child in the thought experiment *did halt* the demolition. The argument for the what (action) is arguing about procuring an abortion. The argument for *the being of what one is arguing about* (ontology), regardless of judging personhood or moral value, must precede *arguing what to do with that being*, which may or may not ethically halt an abortion. The *being* of the unborn in the pregnant female, just like the *being* within the thought experiment's house to be demolished, is not predicated on the mere fact that the unborn *being* is living. Just like the rat, rabbit, and dog, the unborn is biologically living. The reality of that will be explained in the following chapter. But in the thought experiment, the fact that the *being* was a living *human* (presumed *person*) changed the dynamics of ethically evaluating the action. Thus, the beginning of ethically evaluating whether or not to terminate the unborn in the conversation of abortion can only be based on the ethical judgment of what the unborn *is*. If what was explained was read closely, it should further demonstrate the defect in the pro-choice and pro-life sloganized positions. Rather than center the argument on the bodily autonomy of the female, or the biological life of the unborn, neither stance adequately addresses the personhood or moral value of the unborn, which has been demonstrated as primary for the dialogue on abortion.

The strength of this claim, holding that it is the only logical foundation for the abortion conversation, requires unfolding and development. But stated succinctly, the ethical judgment prior to autonomy can be reduced to *either some living humans are persons, or all living humans are persons*. That is it; there is no other way to logically begin the ethical evaluation of abortion, with hope of avoiding equivocation or fallacious inferences. And regardless of *what* is argued "for or against" in the abortion dialogue, one must first address the *is* as the primary ethical concern. The chapter titled "Personhood as Qualifiable?" will deal thoroughly with the concept of *personhood*, so it would be unconvincing to present a condensed summary in this section. Further, the chapter on "Human and Life as Quantifiable?" will deal directly with the terms *life* and *human*. It will be demonstrated they are neither as clearly understood as many assume, nor are they as vague as some propose them to be. In brief, the essential categories for the abortion conversation are not expressed by the terms *life* or *human*, and also not *autonomy*, but *personhood*. This redirects the conversation away from the polarizing pro-life and pro-choice positions and reorients it to a single goal: determining what constitutes the *being* to which any action is directed.

4

Human and Life as Quantifiable?

We would be in a nasty position indeed if empirical science were the only kind of science possible. —Edmund Husserl

One's convictions can be subjected to empirical tests. —Steven Pinker

Ever since intelligent beings began to be in contact, and consequently friction, they have felt the need to guard themselves against each other's encroachments. —Pierre Teilhard de Chardin

Facts are nurtured truths. They are more akin to a cut diamond than the raw stone. Facts, unlike speculation and opinions, are thought to not so easily bend and are thus used to support one's values or beliefs, rather than aligning one's values or beliefs with the facts. There is some truth in making these claims, of course; but facts are like artifacts discovered during an archeology dig—though held in the hand with certainty, they must be furbished, placed in context, and the veracity interrogated. Some facts presently known will not change. They are like the artifact held in the hand that is tangible and solid. Other facts must be refined as they are better understood relative to like things. They are like discovering whether the artifact is a functional tool or a ceremonial object. And in other instances, facts have even been found to be in error and thus a present fact is reformable. They are like discovering that the artifact has been improperly dated. That does not infer facts are unreliable, but it does mean they are reliable only to the degree presently understood and applied. In his book *The Half-Life of Facts*, Harvard mathematician Samual Arbesman made precisely that point: knowledge expressed as a fact has an expiration date (which, rightly stated, was the subtitle of the book). For example, that Pluto exists and orbits the Sun is a fact that will not change, at least not while humans are observing it. The fact that Pluto is a planet is no longer true, but only because of the uncertainty of Pluto's mass, which has been recalculated no fewer than four times.[1] It has therefore been reclassified as a dwarf planet. And finally, observation has led *most* planetary scientists to agree there is a liquid ocean beneath the icy crust of Pluto,[2] which may be entirely true as a fact or perhaps that "fact" may prove quite erroneous. So, some facts are known and will remain true, other facts will change as the things that form them are understood more clearly, and yet other facts are susceptible to adaption based on further discovery that may confirm or deny the premise they are based on.

All things considered, it might be argued that the appeal of facts, and the claim of knowing facts, unlike values and beliefs, offers something objective *outside* the fact holder. That is the strength of a fact. It can be appealed to independently of one's own values or beliefs. Facts, then, generally speaking, are thought to represent a *verifiable truth* independent of personal preferences and cognitive bias. Even if one holds to such claims, pertaining to the abortion dialogue, the facts of what constitutes the terms *human* and *life* may be more akin to the classification of Pluto as a planet or dwarf planet; but, ironically, even once the criteria for the classification of *human* and *life* are established, in truth, those facts alone will not be able to settle the ethical issues surrounding abortion. The reason is that neither of those facts is self-interpretive (what is the purposeful meaning?), the aspects of those facts can be used selectively (have the logical implications been left aside?), and too often those facts may be fallaciously used in an argument (do they support the conclusion?). More on each of those will be explained shortly. For now, the central point is to consider the perception of facts. If referring to something as a *fact* is colloquially thought to convey some irrefutable and definitive quality, which the fact cannot do, then one must accept that facts are not the secret weapon able to "win" the debate on abortion. In terms of

1. Arbesman, *Half-Life of Facts*, 149, 155.

2. Betz, "Underground Liquid Ocean," para. 4, emphasis mine.

human and *life*, facts concerning each, even once known, cannot settle an argument. Any facts used to form those two terms as known concepts are necessary and must be determined at the beginning of any dialogue. Beyond that, though, it is the way that facts are appealed to that requires attention.

On that point of appealing to facts, two truths need to be stated. The first, which offers no controversy, is that simply calling some claim a fact does not, by that mere assertion, make it a fact. The second is that, as with the terms *human* and *life*, what facts are known of each will aid in ethical judgments, but they alone cannot bear the role of determining the judgment concerning a stance. That certainly depends on the ethical system upon which one expresses beliefs, and the value of the being under ethical investigation. For if it is true that facts change, depending on the veracity of the fact, to the degree that one tethers an ethical judgment to those facts or the value of being, then it follows that the ethical judgment and the particular value ascribed to any being will itself have a half-life. In terms of the Pluto example, it must be determined if one's ethical judgment on abortion remains predicated on permanent facts, such as Pluto existing and orbiting the Sun, or whether there are likely corrections ahead, such as whether or not there is water beneath Pluto's icy crust. And finally, one must consider if the evaluation of the ontological status or moral value of the unborn is more akin to the categorizing fact that Pluto is now a dwarf planet, because the scientific community altered the criteria of what constitutes a planet. This is to ask if the criteria for *human* or *life* will remain static or change.

Covertly embedded in any claim of fact is an interesting question one must wrestle with: are all facts empirical? There is great philosophical debate around that point. But what is necessary here to understand is that whatever facts contribute to determining the concepts of *life* and *human*, perhaps within accepted and established parameters, both can be quantified and thus empirically founded. In contrast, whatever facts are used to form the notion of *personhood*, as the subsequent chapter will reveal, is not something that empirical science can ultimately establish. Such value-laden judgments remain outside of the domain of empirical science. Science builds and organizes knowledge of what is measurable. The distinction, as it will be argued between the quantifiable terms of *life* and *human* in contrast to the term *personhood*, is that the latter will require deductive reasoning while the former two terms remain reliant on inductive pursuits. Thus, as inductive reasoning pertains to what is measurable, what is measurable remains that which is quantifiable. It is the basis for how knowledge is acquired in the empirical sciences. Empirical science uses inductive reasoning as a counterpart to deductive reasoning. Nonetheless, deductive reasoning, which has been the line of reasoning used thus far in reshaping the dialogue on abortion, forms an argument by first proposing general premises that then lead to a specific conclusion. Recall that with deductive arguments, if the structure of the argument (syllogism) is such that the conclusion logically follows from the premises, the syllogism is said to be *valid*. But if the conclusion logically follows from true premises, then the syllogism is said to be not just *valid* but also *sound*. Though empirical science utilizes deductive reasoning when it proposes a general theory prior to proceeding to specific outcomes, the observed data is acquired by inductive reasoning. That process is typically understood as the *scientific method*. This method of inductive reasoning is formed by arguments that begin with what is specific, and then make general claims based on what is observed. For contrast, here is an example of a deductive syllogism.

P1 I accept that everything that is able to metabolize is biologically alive.

P2 A sperm is able to metabolize.

C Therefore, I accept that a sperm is biologically alive.

Notice how the general claim, "everything that is able to metabolize is biologically alive," logically leads to the specific claim, "a sperm is biologically alive"? In contrast to that argument, here is an example of an inductive syllogism, to illustrate how an inductive inference is claimed.

P1 It has been shown that mandatory imaging of the fetus changes a female's mind about following through with an abortion.

P2 States that require imaging of the fetus are imposing a restriction on abortion.

C Therefore, imposing a restriction on abortion is an attempt to change a female's mind about following through with an abortion.

Notice how the specific claim, "mandatory imaging of the fetus changes a female's mind about following through with an abortion," was proposed to lead to the general claim, "imposing a restriction on abortion is an attempt to change a female's mind"? In the inductive inference, as it is predictive, the claim that "mandatory imaging of the fetus changes a female's mind about following through with an abortion" is only strong or weak, but not true or false. The claim is not that it will always or never occur, but rather it is a prediction that the restriction will increase in occurrence. In other words, some females will likely choose to not have an abortion after being required to view the fetus by imaging, but not every instance of imaging will lead the female not to follow through with an abortion.

Now, even though the inductive claim is strong or weak, the correlation can be offered as a *fact* that is held to be true or false; that is to say, it is true that it can happen. Yet, even if empirical studies demonstrate the strength of correlating prenatal imaging to not following through with an abortion, it is possible that the effect of viewing an image of the fetus will wane over time, as the culture as a whole becomes more accustomed to it. At that time, it may no longer produce any significant effect of reducing the number of females who choose not to abort after seeing an image of their fetus. Then the *fact* that *imaging is a restriction* will no longer be true because the observed inference of it actually occurring has become too weak to establish the claim. With that in mind as an example, the point is that although empirical knowledge might appear to offer the highest sense of certainty, it is limited to only that which can be observed, and thus substantiated, but ultimately remains susceptible to reform as conditions change and further inquiry is undertaken.

With those basic concepts of quantifiable knowledge understood, this chapter will consider what can be empirically known concerning the terms *human* and *life*. Both are central terms for the proposed foundational premise that *either some living humans are persons, or all living humans are persons*. Perhaps, like what is or is not a planet, the criteria for what composes the categories of *human* and *life* must be accepted by consensus, but applying the accepted consensus of what is a *human being* or what is a *living being* will not prove to be elements for interpretation. This chapter will stand as a caution for employing facts to disarm another's stance that one finds disagreeable. Further, it will discuss those two quantifiable terms, determining what is factually known; it will clear up equivocations; and it will explain what must be adequately understood for a fruitful and respectful dialectical conversation on abortion to ensue.

TERMS, CONCEPTS, AND FACTS

It was briefly stated earlier that dictionary definitions typically address only how terms are used in society and, as they are descriptive, rarely express what is essential about the term. But defining one's own terms in a discussion, not formally or exhaustively, but by remaining clear in the meaning, avoids equivocation, ambiguity, lack of clarity, and the resulting unnecessary disharmony. For example, consider the following unfruitful exchange that illustrates the ambiguity of the term *baby*.

> *Pro-lifer:* The fetus is a baby, and an abortion kills babies. You wouldn't support killing a baby, so why do you support someone having an abortion?
>
> *Pro-choicer:* First, most dictionaries define a baby as an infant. The fetus is not an infant, so an abortion does not kill a baby but only a developing fetus. Abortions are fine.
>
> *Pro-lifer:* Then why do so many pregnant females speak of carrying their baby in the womb? If it wasn't a baby, they wouldn't call it a baby until after it was born.
>
> *Pro-choicer:* Calling a fetus a baby doesn't make it a baby.

And so on . . . and so on.

This line of questioning over the dictionary meaning of the term *baby* resolves nothing and merely causes mental irritation. Initially agreeing what the term *baby* means would be helpful (born human infant less than one year old?). But unless the exchange migrated to determine first what the unborn ontologically *is*, and how to determine from that if the unborn has moral value relative to the female's bodily autonomy, there remains little sense in continuing. So again, the dialectical goal here is not to seek common ground or to win the discussion but, by utilizing properly understood terms, to move as near to truth as possible by means of critical thinking. Recall that to properly form any argument, one must begin with the first act of the mind, which results in the simple apprehension of a term. To avoid equivocation and confusion, the terms must be clear (known), unambiguous (hold a single meaning), and exact (precise).

A central reason for such care in the choice of terms is that they are only the physical element in the process of communicating. Considering this, what is shared between two or more individuals in any discussion are terms expressed as words, whether they are written or spoken. But those words are the only thing that others can publicly share of one's internal thoughts, and the words are all that can publicly be received from another. No one can *read your mind;* they can only read or hear what was written or spoken. So from the word written or spoken, each person hears or reads the word and matches it with their understanding of a *concept* they hold in their mind. The concept, as the interpretation of the word, is private and exists only in the mind of the hearer or listener. The concept is how the individual understands the written or spoken word. But there is more, as each concept projects in the mind a particular *image*, which is the mental picture of what the word is thought to represent. This image, like the concept, is private to each individual. Here this process can easily be illustrated, returning to the equivocation of the term *baby* with *fetus*. One person had an image in their mind of an unborn baby (picturing a soon-to-be-cooing infant) and wants to share that image with someone else. They use their concept of a baby (innocent and vulnerable) to convey what they are imagining; and they hope to represent that concept with the word *baby*, which they use in speech or writing, when referring to the unborn in the female's womb. The other person or persons must interpret that by first reading or hearing the word *baby* and then connecting it to their own concept of a fetus (developing human life). This word-to-concept-to-image then forms a picture in their own mind of a fetus (lacking aesthetic proportions), which by their interpretation is nothing similar to a soon-to-be-cooing infant. This all entails mental images, which then develop into concepts, when then are physically transferred by spoken or written words. It is not difficult to see how issues of miscommunication arise in this process. If anyone has ever found themselves in a conversation where the two parties suddenly realized they were not talking about the same thing, this illustration should make sense. This section, and the insistence on beginning with good definitions, is offered to clarify the terms *human* and *life* in the hope of alleviating the obstacles of miscommunicating the word-concept-image process, as it pertains to the public abortion dialogue.

But yet another issue arises in the way these concepts connect to how one relays *facts*. The concern is that connecting clear and exact terms to facts thought to be irrefutable is not as straightforward as one might suspect. This concern, then, extends beyond the problem of conveying terms and adds to it the misunderstanding of what is a fact. So, perhaps it is a definition issue, but it extends beyond that consideration. For example, a fact must carry a truth that corresponds with something observable in the world, and the understanding of that fact-to-observation relationship can be altered with further insight. This is to mean that facts can be reformable. To illustrate that, it was once thought that the fetus *became living* when movement was felt by the pregnant female.[3] This was referred to colloquially as *quickening* (16 to 20 GA weeks), but that is now known to not be true and thus is no longer a fact due to observation. Recall that a fact, though true or false, may not be absolutely true or false (half-life?). It is best to imagine that a fact carries a truth like a canoe carries a person. A fact could *carry* the truth of what a thing *is*, or a fact could *carry* the truth relation of a thing to some concept such as the *fetus is a living being*. Facts, in this regard, are whatever can be proven by observation and experience. And like all empirical *facts*, they are held as true until reason and experience dictate otherwise. At the expense of appearing to reverse the meaning of the term *idea* as picturing something, perhaps in order to understand this point well, one needs to temporarily clear that meaning and consider an idea as a relational operation of the mind.

The empirical philosopher David Hume made a distinction between ideas and facts. To Hume, an *idea* as something known without any experience (*a priori*) and is only and always true or false. Then, by contrast, a *fact* is a contingent truth that is sensed by experience (*a posteriori*) where the effect of a cause is observed. This may appear confusing, because the pedestrian use of the term *fact* conflates Hume's use of fact with idea. Here is what Hume meant. An idea is like a faint image that occurs during reasoning, and is known with certainty, unlike a fact that requires experience and cannot always be known with certainty. To clarify that, an idea does not require experience, so no new experience can alter it; therefore, it is irreformable. One example that Hume could offer is the idea that "2+2≠5," such that two plus two is not five, and never will equal five. Another would be that "all bachelors are unmarried males." In philosophy, this is known as a tautology, as it is always logically true in that the term *bachelor*, which necessarily contains the concept of an *unmarried male*, can never be anything else. Therefore, the claim, as a self-evident truth, can be held with certainty. The drawback, if one may phrase it that way, is that even though *ideas* provide more certainty (they are always true or false), unlike *facts* based on experience (which is empirical), *ideas* offer less knowledge about the world.

3. Loseva and Gladyshev, "Beginning of Becoming Human," para. 2.

The point to be gleaned from this brief interlude of the relation of ideas to matters of fact, known as Hume's Fork, is that colloquially in public dialogue if both terms are considered facts, and facts are thought to establish the truth and validity of a position, then whether the claim is indeed a fact or idea will affect the premise of established truth or validity. When facts change, people become skeptical. But in fairness, some facts known by experience are set (the fetus is human), or perhaps are at least very unlikely to change (fetal cardiac activity is detected at five to six GA weeks). That means some facts are more reliable than other facts. For clarity, reliable *facts* can be understood as *established facts*. That is closer to the current popular understanding. Two examples of these *established facts* would be that the Earth is orbiting around the Sun and that the smallest particle in the universe is a quark. These types of facts, though sensed, are objective and independent of personal preferences, which is what the concept of a fact is hoped to offer.

Will the Earth one day no longer orbit the Sun? Perhaps, as some post-historic event—but that is irrelevant to any argument trying to claim it presently does not. Therefore, the argument "the Earth does not orbit the Sun" is factually in error. Likewise, since atoms were once thought to be the smallest particle in the universe, but now it is accepted that quarks are the smallest particles, it stands to reason that one day that too might be reformed. Yet, presently it remains an established fact and can be both held and claimed with confidence. Now, relative to the abortion dialogue, concerning the terms *human* and *life*, perhaps someday a post-human point will arrive that distinguishes the *post-human being* from a *present human being*. But that cannot dismiss what is presently understood to be a human being; as something cannot be *post-X* without knowing what *X* is presently. Likewise with the current understanding of the term *life*, perhaps someday new criteria will determine that something thought presently inert was, in fact, living. But that cannot dismiss what is presently understood to be a living being; as the new criteria will likely be an expansion of what is known presently of the criteria of life. The reality of this concern is that if one is seeking understanding on the relevance of facts, even if the fact can be verified to carry a truth, if the fact can change then so to with it the truth that is conveyed. But for the sake of an argument, even if it is accepted that a present fact can be verified and tethered to an irreformable truth, there remains one further concern: established facts are not self-interpreting. That is not to conflate fact with opinion but speaks to relevance or access to the actual state of affairs.

As an analogy, in a courtroom, the judge or jury is to be the trier(s) of facts. But those facts, once proven to be truthful, then must be weighed, and their relevance deliberated. If it remains true that facts, unlike values or beliefs, are thought to be *the truth* independent of personal preferences, then they cannot simply be the whole truth. Otherwise, lawyers and expert witnesses would not try to persuade judge or jury; the facts would simply be presented as self-evident and then, without subjective appraisal, be submitted to some calculating algorithm to provide a verdict. But, alas, that is not the case with facts in the courtroom—or with facts in the public dialogue on abortion.

This then is why, when pro-lifers refer to the unborn as *human*, it does not end the argument. The pro-choicers, who should both concede and accept that established fact, will determine its relevance to the values and beliefs they hold. The pro-choicers will attempt to address the fact of the fetus being human, by aligning a female's autonomy with their values and beliefs in terms of abortion. The same application can be demonstrated for the term *life*. In regard to each, it is crucial to understand that a fact, held to express a truth, is not an independent authority. All facts need to be placed into a digestible form that properly represents and is able to address the concerns of the issue. Facts, unlike Hume's self-evident ideas, must continue to be questioned and challenged in order to ferret out any fallacious interpretations or to determine relevance. This would include issues with the methods and the uncovering of any implicit biases. The upcoming sections are devoted to that specific task for each term (*human* and *life*); and then once the quantifiable terms of *human* and *life* are defined and understood, they will be contrasted with the definition and understanding of *personhood*.

HUMAN AND LIFE AS KINDS OF THINGS

Prior to directly addressing the definitions of *human* and *life*, it is important to know what kind of things *human* and *life* are. Everyone needs to organize concepts in order to make sense of them—that is, to claim that some things are like other things, and yet some things are dissimilar to other things. Therefore, to determine first what kind of thing one is claiming to know is a priority. Philosophically, this is another arena of metaphysics known as the study of universals. Universals are also known as the *nature* of a thing, or perhaps what such things have in common.

That term *nature* refers not to what is in the natural world, but to what (if anything) is innate and makes the thing what it *is*. For example, the term *writing instrument* supposes a handheld device that can be manipulated to mark a smooth surface. So, pens, markers, pencils, and crayons are alike by what makes them writing instruments, and yet different by what makes them specific, one from the other. The quality of difference is known as *individuation*, or what makes it distinct from other things with which it shares a nature. But the idea of a writing instrument did not fall from the sky, nor was it perhaps even discovered in nature; maybe an early human realized that a stone scratched on a cave wall makes a mark, and a conception was realized. So, some will argue that writing instruments have no nature *per se*, and others will argue that they do. But such considerations as to what type of universal categories there are (if any) is very useful for the knowledge of a thing and for communicating that knowledge with others. If one speaks of a writing instrument, the other person can share the internal concept attached to that term and form in their mind an image of a pen or crayon. This would also be true for things such as lithium or flying, in that once discovered, human society simply gave names to the element of lithium and the observation of flying. There are two ways of categorizing ideas (not Hume's ideas) in the world. One would be understood to have a nature, or essence, that makes it what it *is*. The other category is mind-dependent ideas that are useful but, for lack of a better term, can be considered social constructs. This distinction is known as either a natural or social kind.

Social kinds reflect human interests, and natural kinds reflect the structures found in the world. For example, the use of *money* and the idea of *race* are social kinds. Money developed as a standard for exchange, and it is given value based on the interests of peoples. The idea of race, which is formed from distinct phenotypes, perhaps determined by skin color or specific cultures within a region, developed as a cultural phenomenon and reflects human categorization. But in each of those ways presented, both *money* and *race* are mind dependent; without some intentional classification by the human mind, neither money nor race would exist except as subjective categories. In a way, that can mean they are not real things, which is to hold that there is no substance to them; any more than that is a topic for another time. One must be careful to not let that suggest that if money is not real, then there is no such thing as poverty, or that if race is not real, there is no such thing as racism. This may mean, though, that there is nothing essential about money or race, as the human community has changed the way they understand both over time, and the concepts of money and race will continue to adjust by cultural use and attitudes.

Concerning natural kinds, silver and polymers may have been named by humans, but they would exist as they are even if no human had ever lived. Silver will never be lead, even if someone insisted on calling them both by the same name. They differ essentially. The same is true for polymers that occur naturally, like silk and wool. Silk will never be sandstone, even if someone insisted on calling them both by the same name. They, too, differ essentially; but unlike social kinds, they are not mind dependent. These categories are not developed by human interests, but discovered. The application to the public abortion dialogue should be both evident and crucial. Are the ideas of *human* and *life* natural (discovered) or social (composed) categories? Unless the definition of each addresses the natural or social element of categorization, the use of the terms will lack clarity when applied to the argument of this text and cause unnecessary confusion.

There must be one last consideration before addressing these points of social and natural kinds in relation to the ideas of human and life. The reality is that social kinds do not lack a logic to their organization. So, something being constructed does not mean the relationship is arbitrary and can be changed for any reason. The category of *writing instrument* is mind dependent, but what ties items in this category together is their ability to be used in some form of written communication. A coffee mug is not excluded from being a writing instrument by mere consensus, but because it cannot perform the desired function of marking a smooth surface in a controlled way to communicate. There was a time when quills and a stylus were the known writing instruments, and ballpoint pens were not yet invented. But once introduced, ballpoint pens did fit the function and were added based on the constructed properties of what constitutes a writing instrument. Of course, some argue otherwise; there are those who embrace the theory of social kinds, who accordingly deny the existence of any nature to a thing, be it lithium or a writing instrument. There is a version of social kinds that is a new twist on what has traditionally been termed *nominalism*. This idea is typically attributed to William of Occam, an English philosopher and Franciscan friar of the thirteenth century. Nominalism (from the Latin *nominalis*, having to do with names), at least in one form, is a metaphysical idea that holds that there are no such things as universals (a nature to a thing), but rather things are categorized (named) by some common feature. So, lithium and polymers by this theory both exist; but, according to nominalists, neither possesses a nature that can be said to be essential.

Here is the application to the abortion dialogue. As one begins to define and understand what the terms *human* and *life* entail, are they social kinds like *writing instruments,* which are mind dependent and perhaps malleable? Or are *human* and *life* natural kinds discovered and in possession of an unchanging but knowable nature, like *lithium*?[4] People who ascribe to the latter would be essentialists, who hold that the attributes of a thing are necessary and the thing cannot be what it is without those attributes. (They are realists who accept universals.) But some argue that there is no such thing as essentialism, for the common usage may not align with actual properties. (These are nominalists who accept only general ideas.) So, for the purposes of the present point of the terms *human* and *life*, what properties of each need to be present for essentialism to hold or, contrarily, to adopt a social kind? The following analogy is not perfectly aligned, but it may aid in understanding this metaphysical issue. Ask what essential properties might be necessary for something to be understood as water. Is water the chemical formula H_2O, or is water more like the sensible properties (use of senses) that people experience that are included within the social kind of water? People look at the rain filling up a bird bath and would refer to it as water, but it likely contains dissolved gases, which means the water in that birdbath is more than the chemicals of hydrogen and oxygen. In fact, few people would look at the liquid in a bird bath and think of those two chemicals. This requires consideration, because for the topic at hand, it is important to be precise as to the meaning of *human* and *life*, and ask if it can be reduced down to sensible qualities. But one must also not get lost in the weeds of arguing about the chemical composition of a human or the finest thread of distinction between what is living and what is not living. To do so is a logical diversion strategy to overwhelm the opponent with technical information and then, thinking the opposing point defeated by not being able to respond accurately, to contend that the opponent's entire argument is unsound. It is, in short, uncharitable. The point of a dialectic is to aid the other person in understanding, which includes clarifying terms and precludes using terms to obfuscate the underlying point. The average person may not know all the chemicals present in the water of a bird bath; but if someone was told to rinse off their hands in water, the liquid

4. See Mason, "Metaphysics of Social Kinds."

in a bird bath is a choice—even if the essential nature of water remains more than what is immediately sensible. The fundamental point here is that the starting point must be what kind of thing either *human* or *life* is. Are things that are unknown about the terms *human* and *life* essential (like lithium), or like the water in the bird bath (sufficient to make a judgment), or like writing instruments (convenient categories)? It is not possible to proceed in a fruitful and constructive dialogue on the relation of those terms to the topic of abortion, without both understanding and properly conveying the meaning of the terms. And if human and life are judged to be social kinds, one is obliged to ask who decides (power or consensus?) and why are they placed into such a category (convenience or ulterior motives)? The following sections will explain that further. As this text proceeds with what *kind* of things the ideas of human and life are, it is equally crucial to ask what *can* be and *is* known, and finally what *cannot* be and is *not* known about the ideas of human and life. Then from those points, it is crucial to ask why the terms *human* and *life* cannot offer final judgments in the abortion conversation, but must yield to the nonquantifiable but central idea of *personhood* that ultimately must be determined to be either a natural or social kind.

ON THE DEFINITION OF HUMAN

The confusion and frustration that arises from equivocation has been addressed repeatedly. The solution offered was to both define one's terms well and endeavor to filter the meaning through context. The principle of charity in this regard avoids one immediately assuming an adversarial position and thus stifling the dialogue. The term *human* has various connotations, and the circumstances in which it is used are necessary to discern. Etymologically, the term *human* (*humanus*) has within it the root *man*, which in this instance is not sex-specific, even if such usage often presently leans toward referring exclusively to a male. During the early part of the second millennium, the sexes could be distinguished by the use of *wer* (male) and *wif* (female).[5] One can see derived from *wif* the term *wife* (married female), and from *wer* the term *werewolf* (male wolf-person). At that time, and remaining as a remnant, the term *man* (female and male) was connected to the term *human*, where both held the meaning of belonging to a race of peoples. Vestiges of that connection

5. See Riedinger, "Lexical Inequities in Marriage," para. 2.

are evident in the present vernacular use of the terms *manslaughter* (the killing of a human), *inhumane* (savageness to a human), and *mankind* (the human people). But yet the term *human* continues to be used in such a broad sense by colloquial statements such as "I'm only human," which is meant to convey a sense of one's limitations and frailty. So then, in the abortion dialogue, it is easy to detect that when one argues over whether or not the unborn is human, the appeal is an attempt to suggest the unborn does not yet fulfill some condition—perhaps not being part of the human community, or even not yet capable to fall prey to limitations and frailties.

The equivocation of such interpretations should suggest that the usage of *human* in those circumstances is much nearer to the use of the term *person*, though the adopted characteristics would be extremely minimal and remain vague descriptives. Objectively, the term *human* refers to a species—a modern connotation, as prior to the eighteenth century it is unlikely someone would have thought in such a fashion. Since ancient Greece, philosophers had provided classifications for animals and plants based on various attributes, such as the presence of vertebrae and blood. But not until general acceptance of botanist Carl Linnaeus's binomial pairing of genus and species did such categories begin to be readily adopted. The terms *human* and *person* likely would not have been thought of as distinct historically; but, regardless, it is the present state of things concerning the term *human* to be designated as a species, and so it respectfully solicits consideration. Yet even from this coupling of human and species, someone may reply that the term *species* is not easily definable, and that is true. This is known as the species problem.

The species problem recognizes that, as a concept, the terms *species* arises as a taxonomy to include, or exclude, like animals or plants in a particular category. Here one is speaking about a social kind, but certainly not an arbitrary one. Generally speaking, biologists accept a species as something that can interbreed. Yet, some animals from different species can interbreed. Other times a new species is discovered because what was thought to be a single species was determined to be distinct. Additionally, in some instances, two animals thought to be of different species were discovered to be a male and female of the same species. As to humans, the modern human as a species is identified as *Homo sapiens*. It is unclear which species came immediately before the *Homo sapiens*, as it might depend on the geographic location. The immediate predecessors are thought to be the *Neanderthals*, located in what is now known as Europe, or the *Homo bodoensis* in what is now known as Africa. And though it was long held as a fact that there was no interbreeding between these species, it is now commonly accepted that they did interbreed (the fact changed by observation). Both fossil evidence of the multiple species' coexistence and DNA analysis have strengthened that claim. In fact, a theory known as the leaky-replacement hypothesis makes a claim that the *Neanderthals* and the modern human were functionally similar. It has been postulated that some modern humans, depending on the region, may actually carry up to 4 percent of *Neanderthal* DNA.[6] What does all this mean for the issue of the unborn being classified as human? Nothing! Why then address it? Because on one side there are those who, in an attempt to affirm the right of the unborn, illogically think that making the case that the unborn *is a human* will ethically solve the issue. Likewise, there are those who, in an attempt to affirm a female's right to bodily autonomy, illogically think that making the case that the unborn is *not yet a human* will ethically solve the issue in favor of their stance. The term *human* is part of the foundational claim that *either all living humans are persons, or some living humans are persons.*

So, it behooves one to at least define the term *human*, but it also is imperative to place the claim in the proper condition of the argument (more than a fact is necessary). Recall that ethics begins with what a thing *is;* and although trying to make the argument that the unborn *is* a human may state a truism, it is not sufficient as it lacks the qualities of life and personhood. Even if the condition of life is assumed, the concept of personhood has not been addressed. Likewise, trying to make the argument that the unborn is not yet a human does not state what it presently is, only what it is not. If it can be assumed that the pro-lifer offers the unborn as a human, it stands as an insufficient claim. Likewise, if it can be assumed that the pro-choicer offers the unborn as unspecified, it stands as lacking any ontological basis for the claim. The former places too much emphasis on the unborn belonging to a species, whereas the latter argument leaves one with no identified thing upon which to make an ethical judgment. To the first case the ethical concern becomes, "It may be human, but *is* it a human *person*?" To the second case the ethical concern becomes, "If it is not human, what *is* being aborted?" Neither has asked the foundational concern addressing if the unborn human *is* a person.

6. Teague and McRae, "Ancient DNA and Neanderthals," para. 26.

As it stands presently, from the moment of fertilization the unborn belongs to the human species. Referring to it with an added adjective as a *developing human* does not alter any fact of the fertilized but yet unborn being remaining solely within the human species. The pro-lifer gains no ethical ground to insist that an abortion is unethical based on the humanness of the unborn. Likewise, the pro-choicer loses no ethical ground by conceding that the unborn belongs to the human species. To claim that science does not yet know everything about what constitutes the taxonomy of being a member of the human species cannot, and does not, alter what is known about the fertilized human being. To make that point simple, when a human person visits the zoo there is no confusion as to what is human and what is not human. In the public abortion dialogue, any discussion surrounding the unborn's humanness, or lack thereof, is a diversion tactic and an attempt to obfuscate the issue. If one insists that there is more to being human than merely belonging to the species *Homo sapiens*, then clarity and charity should compel them to define what constitutes this lived experience. And they must first demonstrate, by critical thinking and an appeal to reason, why that is a clearer definition than to claim that being a *human* is to belong to the species of *Homo sapiens*. Then they must also argue convincingly why some humans would be excluded from this category of species and why. This is true not just for the parameters applied to the being in utero but also for identifying the definition of *being* for end-of-life issues.

It will be found that if one intends to reduce the membership of what is human, separate from a species, it is better to make the argument that only *Homo sapiens* who share the lived experience X or characteristics Y are to be referred to as humans, as opposed to all beings who simply belong to the species. This material on the definition of human, and addressing the concept of there being a *species problem*, was introduced to illustrate that there are elements to an argument that, although true (it is not clear what a species is), are irrelevant in that there is no such thing as a neutral species (humans beget humans). What *is* known about the term *species* (i.e., that humans beget humans) is sufficient to address the abortion issue. To argue that there does exist a species problem does not logically mean there is a problem knowing the species of the unborn. And to be clear, this is true even at the single-cell stage. The rebuttal to an embryo not being part of the human species is simple: "There is no such thing as a neutral species." That means that there is not a generic species at the simple stages that can possibly morph into another species. If that as a present fact is potentially reformable, then that argument must be made convincingly. If not reformable, which is the claim here, then any argument over the humanity of the unborn must be set aside.

ON THE DEFINITION OF LIFE

The confusion surrounding the term *life* suffers from much of the same poorly aligned logic and equivocation as does the term *human*, but will take a little longer to dismantle and uncover the fallacious applications to the abortion conversation. One reason for offering a more thorough treatment concerning the term *life* is that the abortion debate has long been assumed to revolve around the question of *when life begins*. This section will demonstrate that notion must be set aside. It also immediately needs to be stated clearly from the beginning that even if it becomes verifiable that life is present from the onset, the arguments of each stance are not fundamentally altered. The pro-life position gains nothing with life beginning at fertilization. Even if granted, the argument will immediately turn toward either the primacy of female bodily autonomy, the lack of personhood of the unborn, or even the moral value of the unborn in relation to the pregnant female's autonomy. It then follows, given the lack of logical potency of the points, that the pro-choice position concedes nothing by agreeing that life begins at fertilization. Even so, the follow-up issues of bodily autonomy, personhood, and moral value of the unborn must still be ethically reconciled before a sound argument can be put forth.

Now, a modern colloquial expression claims there is no such thing as a bad question, implying that the only bad question is the one never asked. But in the context of the abortion conversation, it is genuinely a bad question to ask, "When does life begin?" Here are some typical replies. The skeptic may respond, "It is impossible to know when life begins," in an attempt to argue that since science has not settled the issue, as a non-fact, it cannot be part of the ethical judgment. Then perhaps the pro-lifer as a person appealing to facts might offer, "Science proves life begins at fertilization," as an attempt to settle the ethical judgment in favor of their stance. Or perhaps the pro-choicer will contend, "There is no scientific consensus as to when life begins," which implies that perhaps one day empirical science will settle the ethical judgment but at present it cannot be claimed as a fact substantiating any premise, so their stance remains correct.

The question itself is bad because life, as understood in relation to the fetus in the abortion dialogue, does not begin; it continues. It is true that the term *life* has varying criteria. But logic reveals as a truth (as does empirical science) that no living organism can come from something inorganic or inanimate. That statement does have an obvious *proviso*, for life obviously did once arise from something inorganic when *living matter*, whatever definition is used, came into existence from *nonliving matter*. But that describes not fertilization but *abiogenesis*, which is the clear term expressing the origin of life. To answer "As to whether an embryo is living, it is impossible to know when life begins," one need only to reply, "It is only impossible to know when there began the *abiogenesis* of life; but since that moment of *abiogenesis*, presently only life begets an embryo." In response to "Science proves life begins at fertilization," one need only to reply, "Science has not proven when life begins, but science has proven that life continues at fertilization." Finally, to correct the claim "There is no scientific consensus as to when life begins," one need only to reply, "Not only is consensus not necessary but, if it is thought to be necessary, there certainly is consensus that no living organic embryo can come from a nonliving inorganic matter." The point is that bad questions solicit bad responses, and judgments formed from bad responses only perpetuate unsound arguments.

Now it is true that the definition of life will require experts from various fields weighing in, and it is further true that presently some criteria are considered necessary (each that is required), while there is no consensus as to what list of criteria remains sufficient (all that are required). This may be akin to the species problem. However, this does not undermine the previous criticisms because regardless of the definition of life that one holds (sufficient criteria?), except for the origin of life, life in the context of the public abortion dialogue does not begin, but continues. Here is the argument expressed as a deductive syllogism.

P1 The living sperm and ovum that combine originate from a present living human organism.

P2 A living fertilized embryo is from the living sperm and ovum that combine.

C Therefore, a living fertilized embryo originates from a present living human organism.

The rebuttal would have to be that the sperm and ovum are not alive, and then to further claim that something that is not alive *becomes* alive by some process when it forms as an embryo. The term *dead* might be problematic here to refer to the sperm and ovum that are argued to not be alive, but it helps to clear up the issue. If the sperm and ovum are *dead* (not alive), then something not alive (choose any point from fertilization to birth) must logically come from something that is dead. This must hold as true that the male and female living organisms produced the living gametes, and then the living gametes, though themselves not organisms, produced a new living organism from a sperm and ovum that were argued as nonliving material. By this reckoning, it could then be argued that life *begins* at fertilization, rather than *continues* through to fertilization. Perhaps one might frame it as not simply living, but a *new life*, with unique DNA. In light of these points, it would be false to state either that life begins at fertilization or that one does not know when the life of the unborn does begin. The concern here, as with other issues, is that either the scientific fact that life is a continuous process is known and not admitted (deception), or one is uncertain and makes no attempt to rationally satisfy the logical judgment and form a conclusion in line with reason (ignorance), or they are equivocating and meaning by the term *life begins* that the new genetically distinct being is now a life (equivocating).

Regardless, there are some current definitions of life that are being offered by the disciplines of biology, chemistry, and philosophy of science. To offer the primary criteria under scrutiny, here is a sampling. The definition of life could necessarily include as one aspect the concept of reproduction, meaning that only something that is living can reproduce, such as by the process of cell division. So, by that criterion, a sperm and an ovum would be alive but neither is a living organism, while the embryo is a living organism. The definition of life could include the property of metabolism (chemical reaction/energy). On that criterion a sperm[7] and an ovum are living, as is an embryo. There is also the idea of this metabolism existing within the context of genetic information, so the transfer of DNA might be necessary for the definition of life. Both gametic material along with an embryo satisfy the transfer of DNA. Further, as crucial to the definition, life defined might require the notion of being self-contained and self-regulating—that is, capable of homeostasis

7. See Alberts, *Essential Cell Biology*, 453.

and reliant on energy. On that criterion a sperm and an ovum are part of the process, and the embryo is the product of both. Finally, perhaps the notion of adaptation and response to stimuli must be included in the definition of life.[8] It is far beyond the scope of this point to delve into the issue of sperm and ovum stimulation, though an embryo satisfies that criterion. With all that said, there yet could be other elements and notions, of course, or variations of those elements combined with notions for the definition of life.

The point is that there is a temptation to make the definition of life narrow or more lax if it fits the goal of a position. To illustrate that, here is a quick thought experiment. What would be the definition of life, if it was claimed that life had been found on another planet? What required criteria would be necessary regarding something found in fossil form, to say that there was once life? Or perhaps for consideration, if a living single-cell alien were found on another planet, would the scientific community declare, "Life discovered on another planet"? Because such a finding would be fantastical, likely minimum criteria would be accepted. So even the fact that there are varying definitions of life that create varying standards does not preclude what is known of the concept of life. The manipulation of definitions should always serve as a red flag for uncovering bias and dislodging ideologies; but, in reality, it remains that *life*, like the term *human*, has a certain mind-dependent character to it, and from that some criteria are known well and accepted. Further, despite the mind-dependent character of the term *life*, one would be mistaken to think that a certain level of construction implies the criteria are arbitrary. (Consider why Pluto is no longer a planet, yet it is known what constitutes a planet.) For example, there is an argument that viruses are not living systems because they do not have cells, cannot transfer DNA, do not self-reproduce, and so forth. So, the final word on whether a virus is alive depends on how life is defined, but the consensus that it cannot be classified as living is not arbitrarily applied or ideologically developed as a bias against viruses. That same indifference to the definition must be adopted in the abortion dialogue.

An embryo, though, is not just living, but a living organism. Further, the distinction between an embryo and a fetus would be one of maturation, and not an ontological question of its inclusion in the species of *Homo sapiens*. If one holds that the category of *life* depends on a

8. See Gómez-Márquez, "What Is Life?," para. 6.

consensus, whatever that consensus is in terms of living organisms, then one must also hold to life being a continuous process. To reiterate, the alternative makes this clear, as the embryo is not something that originates out of inorganic matter. Perhaps someday that *fact* (living matter only from living matter) as being contingent on present-day technology will change. But as interesting as that might be, it has no effect on the fundamental use of the term *life* for the present public dialogue on abortion. An embryo is a living being, and by virtue of the reality that it does not begin, it therefore cannot logically mark the origin of life. This is logic and critical thinking applied to the abortion dialogue. It is rigorous, even if not exhaustive. The power of logic and critical thinking is that one need not be an expert themselves, nor perhaps is it necessary that one is able to address the scientific consensus, to settle this definition of life in the context of abortion. An understanding of inferences and logical relations (that only life begets life) will suffice. Even if and when synthetic sperm and ovum are available for human reproduction, the basic claim stands that the sperm as the male reproductive gamete contains half the DNA of the living human—and, likewise, that an ovum as the female reproductive gamete contains the other half. If they each are not considered as *living*, then life cannot be a chain, but rather must logically have an abrupt beginning either at fertilization or at some point prior to birth. As this is not true, life does not *begin* at fertilization but instead *continues* at fertilization as a life with unique DNA from the sperm and ovum. Even if one prefers the term *new human life*, one cannot, because of the addition of the adjective *new*, either claim that life has begun or sidestep the inevitable ethical judgment questioning the issue of the embryo's personhood or moral value.

If there still seems to be some issue with the logic of either the sperm or ovum being living cells, and from that the inference that only life can beget life, consider two scenarios. Each of the following scenarios involves an equivocation. The first is a meme-like contention that has been fallaciously levied to argue that if either a sperm or ovum is living, then to purposefully not preserve it must be considered killing. If it is argued that killing a living embryo is unethical, then why does not that same judgment apply to the killing of sperm or ova? To satisfy this equivocation, if it is not obvious, the notion of killing (murder?) is exclusive to the intentional death of living, human persons. No one makes the argument that a sperm or ovum is a living human person, only that the gametic material are living. And though the sperm may survive outside of the human organism for up to five days (sperm in the vaginal cavity)[9] or the ovum one day (ovum released into the fallopian tube), the fact neither survives past those points cannot be considered killing. The argument remains valid that the living cells of the sperm must come from a living human male and the ovum from a living female, despite the inability of each to survive outside the intended environment or process. Something living has ceased to live, but it does not constitute killing.

Then with the second scenario, it is an attempt to equivocate the sperm and ovum as natural living substances with possible synthetic sperm and ovum as nonnatural and thus nonliving substances. This would contend that the latter would not constitute life, implying in this instance that life can and does come from nonlife. Someone asserting this issue of equivocation concerning artificial material might retort that abiogenesis can possibly occur with every instance of fertilization, if the gametic material is not natural but becomes both natural and living once an embryo. Consider this *future* argument. If every male of the human species were extinct and no viable sperm were available, the females could continue the species only for one more generation unless a fertile male is born, or if artificial sperm is possible. If every female of the human species were extinct and there were available no viable ova, the males could continue the species for only one more generation unless a fertile female is born, or if an artificial ovum (and a womb) is possible. Those two last statements, and the possibility of technology such as artificial sperm and ovum, will be very briefly addressed later in the chapter "The Arguments Ahead." But for now, the argument stands that if life comes from life, and living material from living material, can biological life be said to begin at fertilization if the gametic material was artificial? This is in fact simply an equivocation of the term *artificial*. The artificial sperm or ovum would be produced from living stem cells—either those of humans or perhaps mice. What is authentically meant by the term *artificial* is not that the sperm and ovum are not living, but that they were either stimulated or adapted into existence rather than originating from gametic material. Equivocations always have a ring of truth to them and typically require more effort to disentangle than to simply state. Most sense something is awry in a fallacious claim, but it takes a disciplined mind to clearly state the lack of clarity and to demonstrate how it affects the issue logically. That is the danger in their use, and they persist in public dialogue

9. Kölle, "Sperm-Oviduct Interactions," para. 4.

because many do not feel up to the task of proving the fallacious thought as an error, so the topic under scrutiny remains flooded with distracting assertions.

AN ARGUMENT TO CONSIDER

Although the terms *human* and *life* obviously relate to the abortion conversation, as secondary to the issue they remain necessary but not sufficient to reach an ethical judgment. As the foundational question remains to ask whether some living humans are persons or all living humans are persons, the terms *human* and *life* must be addressed only to clear away the confusion in popular debates. The principle of charity ethically requires one to demonstrate the weakness in the arguments of those who frame the ethics of abortion surrounding the understanding of these two terms.

The definition of what constitutes a species is admittedly problematic, and thus defining the term *human* must allow for both flexibility and the possibility of change. And one must recognize the reality that for the term *life,* neither biologists nor chemists nor philosophers of science are able to agree on what is essential, so it too must be allowed to evolve in its meaning and application. But the uncertain definition of "human" does not leave anyone confused over what the species is of the male or female gamete contributors, or the species of the fertilized offspring regardless of gestational age. And the lack of consensus over what essentially forms an understanding of "life" does not leave anyone confused over the reality that the fertilized embryo did not arise from nonorganic material. All the facts surrounding the exploration of those terms do not alter the logical reality that what is known about the unborn as being a human life is known by logical inference with certainty.

Neither the term *human* nor *life* is assigned to some unborn individuals but not to other unborn individuals. If one attempts to do so, they are logically and ethically bound to state what the unborn nonhuman or nonliving being is, if not living or not human. If the unborn individual is not human, then they must state what species the unborn individual is *or* that there is an indeterminate species that will become human at some point. And if the unborn individual is not alive, then they must state that the unborn individual is presently inorganic material that is capable at some point of becoming alive. To sum up this line of critical thinking, some things are not entirely known, such as the exact parameters of the terms *human* and *life*, but also some things are entirely known, such as "humans beget humans" and "life continues from life." These facts and conditions are both necessary and sufficient for the argument that the unborn, from the moment of fertilization, is a human life.

Each of the concepts behind those terms has been determined by empirical science. They have been found to be certain by direct observation and can be explained by reason. Because what has been stated about the concepts of *human* and *life* are facts, again that does not mean that either side of the abortion issue can claim victory in championing their position. The amount of ink, paper, and mental energy that has been misused and depleted to argue for or against those terms in hopes of putting the issue of abortion to a resolution is staggering. It is also, quite frankly, disappointing. But a dialectic demands to listen and reply, so listen and reply one should. That is why this text has explicated it as such. But a dialectic also demands clarifying the terms and reorienting the conversation to the substance of the argument. That is what this text intends. Both the pro-lifer and the pro-choicer may, at this point, find themselves reflecting on their positions in an attempt to find continuity with their preexisting positions. But further, each supposed "side" will be logically forced to assimilate their tenets, as presented in this section, into considerations of the next section on personhood. If the pro-lifer can demonstrate that all human lives are persons, then their point will be settled and abortion at any stage is unethical. If the pro-choicer can demonstrate that only some human lives are persons, then their point will be settled and abortion up until the point of personhood will be ethical. The argument may not be easy to make, but the parameters of the resolution are not complicated.

5

Personhood as Qualifiable?

I seem in just this little thing to be wiser, that what I do not know, I do not think I know either. —Plato

We are not smart enough to decide which pieces of knowledge are permissible and which are not. —Carl Sagan

Wonder rather than doubt is the root of all knowledge. —Abraham Joshua Heschel

THE TERMS *HUMAN* AND *LIFE* were presented as quantifiable, where something can be measured. When considering the idea of personhood, one enters another domain. In determining if a species is human, DNA can be tested. When one is determining life, cell division can be observed. But neither cell division nor DNA will settle if a living human is or is not a person. This endeavor traverses from the realm of empirical science into the domain of philosophy and theology. Personhood does not fall into consideration as strictly a social kind or a natural kind. But personhood must be determined by accepted capacities, or recognized values, or as a nature inherently attached to all living humans. Those are the choices. The first two form determiners or qualifiers for personhood, while the last one simply accepts personhood as the default recognition of a living human. Most in the public discussion surrounding abortion do not consider such a question; or, if they do, the legal assignment of personhood is accepted. Rarely is the idea of personhood and what it encompasses contemplated, yet it is an essential element to ethics and goods proper to individuals. Consider that when one speaks of the self in the first person as an *I* or refers to another in the second person as a *you*, it is usually done with little reflection as to what this *I* or this *you* actually is. That is perhaps ironic in one regard, and tragic in another, because a distinguishing achievement for the human species is (1) the cognizance of this self as separate from the world as an *I*, and (2) the capacity to recognize the value of a self existing in another as a *you*. This *I* is, without exaggeration, the source of one's own dignity, and the *you* identifies the other's moral value. Consider how casually people claim "I deserve justice" or "They must treat you with fairness," without full consideration of the *self* to whom they are directing the claim. It may not be explicitly expressed, but this *I* and *you* presuppose an autonomous moral agent whose inherent dignity is recognized simply by the fact they exist and thus are recognized as living human persons. Any claim to justice and fairness must be worked out according to the significance of the *I* and the *you* that are implicitly assumed to represent the self or the other as persons. Wars have been fought and civil rights have been championed to secure recognition for this very personhood of each *I* and the proper dignity afforded to those persons referred to as *you*. This section explores not just how one is to consider the meaning ascribed to this idea of personhood, but also how personhood itself may be understood. The three basic alternatives are to question (1) whether personhood is accepted as essential to all human lives; or if it is not, then (2) what capacities or (3) what values are sufficient to ascribe moral value.

THE PROBLEM OF PERSONHOOD

It is argued that this *problem of personhood* is central to the public dialogue on abortion; but, in truth, it is foundational for any ethical issue that affects the human community. Here for example are a few applications demonstrating that premise.

In ethics for medical professionals, such recognition is the basis for *personal* medical privacy (what information is being protected) and the value of *personal* patient consent (agreement to treatment). Regarding the former, the personal information is an extension of autonomy. Regarding the latter, the patient must be free from undue influence and afforded adequate information to make a decision. For end-of-life issues, the determination of personhood affects modes of proportionate care that allow each individual to determine their own *personal* treatment or, if so desired, to not proceed with intervention and accept life's finality.

This idea of personhood also has far-reaching implications for human interests of civil and social justice. The implementation of immigration policies requires *personal* protection and respect for basic needs and safety. Within any society, for the *personally* marginalized and destitute, justice requires persons to be afforded adequate monetary aid and opportunity. Another instance is that during times of armed intervention, civil crisis, or political upheaval, *personal* rights and liberties are sought to be gained or maintained. The list can easily be expanded, but the term *personal*—and why it is the impetus for such protection, aid, liberties, and such—cannot simply be glossed over. Anything that is argued to be *personal* is predicated first and foremost on what constitutes this living human person.

As another consideration, the role of personhood might not come directly to mind with the ethical treatment of nonhuman animals. The idea of the *humane treatment* of animals is an outreach advocacy determining to what extent even nonhumans deserve the proportionate extension and protection afforded to human persons. That is, the term *human* is purposefully used equivocally to extend the moral value of *human* to nonhuman animals. Perhaps this extension of animal rights would be comparable to the unborn nonperson, where one might argue that even if not a person, the fetus may have the same moral value as a nonhuman animal. So, this idea of personhood, or just the fact that it is a designation for ethical value, is much more radical than first thought, for on the recognition or designation of personhood hang rights and privileges. Yet, most individuals use the term *person* frequently without ever stopping to consider its meaning—until there is a recognized reduction in the dignity that one thinks should be afforded to a human being. Then the dignity of person is invoked as an attempt to criticize the unjust goal. Since, as was stated earlier, the meaning of the terms *human* and *person* are sometimes used interchangeably without conscious cause, an appeal to each surfaces without delay whenever the due consideration for either is ethically questioned.

If personhood is tethered to humanity, one way to easily demonstrate how ethical adversities follow the dismissal or reduction of personhood is by the way an individual or group's *humanity* is dismantled.

Often, when another individual or group's humanity is questioned or reduced, so too is their personhood and the result is genocide. A clear, tragic example is the 1916 Armenian genocide, during which the Ottomans raped and massacred more than a million Armenians. Another infamous case of genocide began in 1941 with Nazi efforts to exterminate Jews, Gypsies, and other racially mixed or "unfit" populations. In this attempt to purify the Aryan race, any groups that threatened that goal were thus deemed inferior, losing their *I* status, and were set apart for extermination. More recently, a Hutu politician in Rwanda referred to the minority Tutsi population as cockroaches who should return to Ethiopia, thus inciting the Rwandan genocide of 1994. No longer recognized as humans, the Tutsis as the other *you* were reduced to an *it*. Consider further the Rape of Nanjing, when in 1937 Japanese soldiers ravaged, raped, and killed well over two hundred thousand Chinese citizens. Finally, in one last example, the Sudanese government in 2003 set out to systematically eradicate the Darfur people in what is sometimes referred to as the first genocide of the twenty-first century. (Referring to it as the *first* should be unsettling in itself.) They "succeeded" in killing or starving an estimated two hundred thousand civilians. Those same atrocities resurfaced in 2023 where at least another two thousand human persons suffered ethnic violence.

There are unfortunately too many more historical instances, but what links them all together is that in order to justify the atrocities, regardless of any claimed motivation, the targeted individuals first had to be dehumanized. Once individuals or a population can be reduced to nonhumans whose moral value is less than that of humans, they are no longer granted the dignity of an *I* or a *you* but are reduced to an *it*. And from the lack of recognizing their humanity, any ethical standard proper to a human person vanishes and the atrocity, recognized by a legitimized intention, is thus nefariously justified.

The same sinister logic is used wherever and whenever an individual or group's humanity is accepted but their *personhood* is detached from that humanity. Rather than resulting in genocide, in this case the outcome is prejudice and/or subjugation by other humans, in whose estimation (according to their own determining values or necessary capacities) those *others* do not merit the status of personhood. These individuals are still considered *human*, but the lack of *personhood* becomes the means for the dominant groups, whose status remains that of persons, to justify the control or prejudice toward the others designated as *human nonpersons*.

The most widely recognized manifestation of human depersonalization is slavery. Human slavery has taken many forms, and history is replete with one group forcing other vulnerable population groups into slavery. Records of institutionalized slavery date back to 3500 BC in Mesopotamia.[1] For centuries in the medieval and modern eras, slavery was a structured reality in societies throughout Europe, Africa, and Asia; and from the seventeenth century, the transatlantic chattel slave trade developed institutionally. Opposition to one person or group of persons enslaving another person or group of persons has become *nearly* universally denounced only in very recent times. But even in the twenty-first century, regardless of disputed statistics that vary by definition, the number of forced-labor and sex-trafficked slaves may be in the tens of millions. Even if wildly inaccurate, such present multitudes might likely dwarf the enslaved populations of the previous, sad occurrences of slavery.

Yet, slavery is just the most notorious instance of not recognizing the personhood of humans. The multitude of other instances could include the improper treatment of prisoners and poor prison conditions, or the mistreatment of those who, perhaps because of economic injustices, diminished willpower, or poor choices, are culled into pornography, the sex trade, and prostitution. In domestic settings, there are unfortunate cases of one spouse subjugating another spouse or significant others. Whether resulting from that or independent facts, depersonalized children are being subjected to mental and physical abuse in unstable families or neighborhoods. Then, of course, even in developed countries, one can witness substandard employment conditions that are dangerous or intentionally demeaning. As with dehumanizing genocide cases, the listing of these depersonalizing cases can go on and on.

With all of these sad realities, the common thread is that whether dehumanized or depersonalized, the goal is to ease the conscience of the perpetrators, so that human persons as an *I* and *you* can be reduced to an *it*. Then, in the minds of the oppressors and suppressors, the *it* can legitimately become a means to their own goals. Stated plainly, no individual can be reduced to an instrument for the use, pleasure, or profit of recognized persons without first being recategorized as nonhumans or nonpersons themselves.

1. Reid, "History of the Slave Trade," para. 2.

Since the concept of *human* was covered in the previous chapter, it should require no ethical defense to claim that to be human has the minimal and sufficient criterion of belonging to the species of *Homo sapiens*. Even within the concept of personhood, little effort is required to identify the injustice of slavery, sex trafficking, improper treatment of prisoners, spousal abuse, intentional or culpable mental and physical abuse, and even the depersonalization caused by substandard housing and underemployment conditions. But within those conditions, or the myriad of others that can be disclosed, a proper understanding of what exactly makes a human being a person is often left unarticulated. This leads to the perpetuation of injustices, at worst, and to being ethically inconsistent, at best. Personhood, and the subsequent dignity, must not simply be accepted in the abstract. How one accepts personhood as a standard for the ethical evaluation of a living human becomes the standard upon which ethical evaluations will be judged. Recall the premise that ethics begins with *being*, what a thing *is*, and it is imperative that one determines what this living human *is*. Is every living human a person, or are only some living humans a person? If one does not first determine this source of dignity in the living human person, different standards will inevitably be applied to comparative evaluations, which logically and inevitably results in an injustice. One definition of an injustice is disclosed when two standards are applied to situations like this. That is to argue that the standard (what constitutes a person) must be determined prior to the ethical application and judgment, or comparable situations will yield divergent judgments and thus an injustice.

Here are the three possible variations of the standards of human persons. In justice, some concrete claim must be that either (1) all living human beings are persons, or (2) some identifiable and articulated criteria constitute personhood, or (3) agreed-upon values are extended to form personhood, so as to afford some living humans the dignity exclusively. Only one of those, or perhaps some combination of the latter two, can be the standard for personhood, and that standard must be maintained across ethical applications. This is simple logic applied to the notion of what constitutes a living human person, as the fundamental consideration in any ethical judgment.

So, what then would be used to form a judgment in the absence of one of those three concrete understandings of personhood? Each judgment will be rendered by either one's own expressed ideology (political party, culture, or worldview), unconscious bias (individual ignorance or disregard for differences), or settled belief (dogmatic stance or ingrained prejudice). This means that without conscious consideration of what makes a living human a person prior to the ethical judgment, the ethical application will simply conform to whatever form of individual or societal ideology, bias, or belief persists in the individual or group. Any position on personhood, if accepted by default, will result in an injustice or ethical inconsistency formed by one's ideologies, biases, or beliefs. This can be no substitute for critical thinking. The case of determining what *is* a person requires reflection and dialogue.

Any lack of reflection and dialogue, as the latter tests the veracity of our arguments, inevitably makes one's view of personhood self-contradictory in its application to ethical judgments. This may not be necessarily so, but premising one's view on ideologies, biases, or beliefs will likely result in affirming what aligns with each individual by those surrogate standards, at the expense of pursuing truth. Applied to the public abortion dialogue, for example, if one holds that an unborn at any particular stage is not a person by virtue of lacking consciousness, pain sensation, or the like, then it logically follows that an adult with the same conditions in an end-of-life scenario would also have diminished personhood. Therefore, if it is licit to abort the fetus determined to be a living human but a nonperson, then logical and ethical consistency must hold it is also licit to harvest vital organs from a living human in like condition who is determined to be a nonperson. Someone might add that at the end of life, one has memories, which the unborn does not. Of course, that is not necessarily true, as the individual at the end-of-life stage may not retain any memories or identity. Others might retort that the person at the end of their life has an invested moral value, in the sense that they *were* a living human person at one time. But even if that is true, would relationality be a factor for personhood? This is to question if an *I* is only a person with another *you*, or is a person an isolated *I* without consideration of any other *you*? Setting aside the beginning and end-of-life comparison, another question is if there can be any ontological distinction between a fetus at twenty-eight GA weeks and a forty-two-day-old infant in a minimal conscious state? Is the location (inside/outside) enough to change the moral value of the being, or is continued dependency based on the reality that human infants maturate slowly enough to link them? The point here is not to settle any of these situations ethically by making a judgment. The point is to merely recall that just as in the thought experiment involving the demolition of the old house, the only element that changed the response to the prospective demolition was an ethical judgment based on an evaluation of the *is* that was found in the house. As in the thought experiment, where the demolition of the house was the action, abortion is the action when applied to the topic at hand. The beings found in the house align with a determination of the being in the womb of the female. Is the fetus more akin to the living nonhumans found in the house with no moral value (developing tissue), or the living nonhumans found in the house with moral value (desired fetus, born but pre-maturation), or the living human person found in the house (maturated infants)? One cannot justly and consistently determine the *action* without first judging ethically the ontological status of the *is*.

Just because individuals do not consciously settle their views on personhood does not mean they are without an intuitive sense of personhood's centrality to ethics. But in the same way that studying critical thinking and logic elevates one's intuition about not just sensing but uncovering the specific error in another's argument, reflecting on the issue of personhood elevates one's ethical reactions beyond the reflexive counter, "It's just not right!" Without the ability to articulate why something is "just not right," one is left with a vague appraisal, and discouragement to engage ensues. Here is a concrete example.

If someone is asked to explain why they find sex trafficking ethically repugnant, pinning it to the reduction of dignity afforded by personhood is a better argument than simply adopting some personal or cultural aversion. It is much more convincing when worked out. So, rather than "it's just not right," one would do better to argue it is unethical because *a person is to be self-determining* and therefore cannot be a means to another's end; *a person is to be free from unlawful constraint* and therefore must not be held against their will; *a person is to be an autonomous agent* and therefore must be afforded respect and rational choices; and so on. With self-determination, freedom from unlawful constraint, and personal autonomy as established characteristics of personhood, sex trafficking can be demonstrated as unethical, predicated on the reduction of dignity afforded human persons. Then the affirmation "It's just not right!" can be vindicated by an *expressed standard* of the reduction of dignity based on what constitutes personhood, rather than a despondent verbal repudiation. And contrarily, then, if a person wants to ease their conscience for some level of participation in sex trafficking, they will have to demonstrate that the expressed standard does not apply and thus no dignity is warranted. For example, they would need to explain that self-determination, freedom from unlawful constraint, and personal autonomy are contingent on other factors or qualities not inherently tethered to the idea of personhood, or simply that the individuals being sex-trafficked are not persons. In other words, those individuals who are sex-trafficked, for reasons explicitly stated or implicitly held, must be shown to not be afforded any semblance of personhood. Sadly, when this occurs, it is simply not articulated by the perpetrators. Their action (sex trafficking) simply considers those trafficked as a living being in the house to be demolished, with no possession of personhood or moral value. They *feel* vindicated by either repressing any rational evaluation or thinking an individual (perhaps even a person) can be used as a means to an end. The tragic irony, and what history has demonstrated, is that whenever an injustice like this has occurred, any determination of what constitutes full personhood is retained by those groups or individuals who perpetrate the injustice. In other words, anyone who classifies other individuals as nonpersons always excludes themselves from that category of nonpersons. In reality, when personhood becomes an exclusive category, those forming the category begin with qualities they themselves possess. The nefarious practice of sex trafficking becomes acceptable to the perpetrators because those reduced to an *it* lack adequate advocacy, are marginalized by society, or do not resonate with the dominant ideology.

The point is that if what constitutes a person is not established prior to an ethical evaluation, then the goals of an individual or society will prevail at the expense of the person or group of persons. They will *feel* justified reducing the dignity of others, which itself has been untethered from being inherently tied to personhood. And even if there remains some understanding of the presence of personhood in an individual or group, but it is not adequately worked out due to either blatant disregard or lack of reflection, that category of personhood will simply be reduced in moral value whenever the goal is deemed worthy or necessary. One stalwart of the human psyche is to ease the conscience in the face of perpetrating ethical injustices. To remedy this, individuals and groups become quite skilled in rationalizing their actions and then working backwards, projecting the necessary values (or lack thereof) to those who are being used as a means to an end, so as to align their nefarious *action* with the deficient *is*.

MORAL VALUE AND PERCEPTION OF PERSONHOOD

The concept of moral value in this context does not create a weighted category necessarily *in between* what is thought proper to a living human nonperson and a living human person. Moral value simply ascribes a quality conferring worth to the nonperson or person. So, if there are privileges that adhere to a living human person, then some of those privileges are extended to the living human nonperson, for various stated and unstated reasons.

Returning to comparing the issues of abortion and end of life, it was presented that even if both the unconscious unborn near birth and the unconscious adult near death share the status of being a nonperson, intuitively a greater moral value will be attributed to the unconscious adult near death than the unconscious unborn near birth. An expanded rebuttal to equating the two could include the following. First, the now-dying adult nonperson seems to have accrued some level of moral value during all the years they *were* conscious. By contrast, the unconscious unborn nonperson does not have those vested years. Further, even if neither has conscious memories presently, one might argue that at least with the unconscious adult nonperson, other persons have conscious memories of them that are not restricted to some future point, as would be the case with the unconscious unborn nonperson. This is to argue, then, that any action or inaction ethically considered for the dying adult nonperson might retain a certain amount of respect for who they were. In other words, they are not treated as a mere potential harvesting opportunity, even if at present they are still living but no longer considered persons.

With that last point, the same theory of assigning moral value could be applied to some degree with the unconscious unborn nonperson. This might be particularly true—even more so—if the unconscious unborn nonperson is at a more developed gestational age. If one holds that the *not yet person* cannot be granted the full dignity due to a person, obviously it will not necessarily follow that the unborn is ethically comparable to a tumor or an appendix that may be removed without any ethical conflict. Perhaps the unborn in that scenario may be equated with something akin to the dying adult who might be considered a nonperson, who is granted a moral value greater than a being maintained for a potential organ harvest. In other words, one may argue that the unborn can have a moral value, even if they are not yet considered a person. Against that judgment of the unborn, someone would need to clarify the ontological difference (what it *is*) between, say, a twenty-four-week-old fetus and an hour-old infant. Unless the moral value is tethered to something more than mere sentiment, it becomes susceptible to oscillation or fluctuation driven by feelings. As to what might evolve as the recognition of the moral value, some standard should be articulated and held as a bulwark against fluctuating perceptions.

Many factors affect the *perception* of personhood. This section will briefly consider five. The first is the issue of aesthetics of the unborn and 3D imaging. The second is a consideration of moral value linked to the issue of physical dependency and infant maturation. A third is the critique of and possible solution to the case of monozygotic twins and ensoulment, which leads to the fourth that provides insight into philosophical notions of potentiality and actuality that aids in determining a nature from what can be sensed. Finally, there is a brief explanation of the idea of quickening as the anachronistic point of the beginning of life, which can be (and has been) construed as an argument that value is not easily connected to changing positions on personhood.

To the first point, it may prove interesting to explore the argument attributing moral value to nonpersons, where the rationale is aesthetically grounded. As the first premise, *what* an unborn being looks like affects the *is*. On this, Friedrich Schiller (d. 1805), who pressed back against Kant's distinction between aesthetics and ethics, offered that mere analytical thinking remains incapable of "pure reason in human beings" without an "interchange of matter with form."[2] To state it simply in context, if the appearance (matter) of the unborn invokes sympathies, a moral value (form) is ascribed from that. It might seem an odd point to make at first, but if one allows the argument to be presented and considers it in relation to the available imaging of the unborn, it is not without merit. Granted, the idea of aesthetics as a factor might vary quite a bit between individuals and cultures; but in reality, regardless of the variation, if it affects moral value, then the premise stands as true. The point is that many individuals who are affected by the aesthetic elements absorbed through media and culture may, from that, form an ethical stance. This means that often the way one perceives something or someone may be rooted in passive experiences that are not recognized as influential but remain influences nonetheless. As a prime example for this aesthetic

2. Schiller, *Aesthetic Education of Man*, 95.

consideration, though not implying an analogy, take into account the psychological factors of animations and advertising that can be projected onto the unborn or even nonhuman animals. (With nonhuman animals, one might call it the *anthropomorphic effect.*) Here is one of the premises. Though the human person has always had an imagination, the humanlike behavior portrayed in animation by talking bears, lions, snakes, and so on is culturally but passively embedded collectively into people's minds. This does not suggest that one thinks bears, lions, and snakes are human; but because they are portrayed with humanlike qualities and behaviors, the anthropomorphizing will affect human emotions and attitudes toward those animals when encountered as pets, at the zoo, or in other settings. This then forms and projects a moral value. Animated characters are able to evoke compassion and rouse indignation that not so much draws the human into their world, but stretches the reaction to the moral value of those animals *into* the human world. The point is that these images have formed the imagination of the masses to the extent that the actions and behaviors of animals encountered can be accepted as the similar exploits and manners of living human persons. This cinematic effect is not exclusive to pets and zoo animals, as movies have also portrayed infant humans who talk fluently, or even baby geniuses that interact with adults. Though obviously fantasy, the social interactions experienced in home viewing and cinema, along with the character's ability to form relationships and manipulate others, coupled with animated personalities, psychologically gives both the nonhuman animals and even the unborn (nonperson?) projected qualities that mimic those once exclusive to born human persons. In the time before film and animation, perhaps shared stories and even illustrated books may have had a similar effect. In terms of access and the ubiquity of present-day exposure to the effect of this experience, it pales by comparison. In that regard, without overplaying the point, it stands as worthy of consideration.

Illustrating this effect of projected sympathies is not an attempt to draw a strict parallel between unborn living humans and nonhuman animals or living human infants. Rather, it serves to offer a proposition: the anthropomorphism in the case of nonhuman animals and the personality projection to the unborn have influenced the emotional cues of adults envisioning each in reciprocal relation. If this claim appears yet to be a stretch, consider further the effect of the perception gained from enhanced diagnostic images of the unborn. To some extent, *seeing* a picture of the unborn can be a source of both exhilaration and stress, as it presents the reality of parenthood and all that it entails to the parents. But the ultrasound examinations are very interactive with the imagination and can easily provoke deep emotions as one witnesses the *real-time*, high-resolution 3D ultrasonographic images. They provide a *window to the womb* where the female can experience the otherwise invisible unborn with a grimacing face, yawning mouth, hand on head, cradled position of the body, and so on. Added to the culture at large, there are textbooks and a plethora of websites that offer illustrations of embryonic and fetal development. In past generations, this was exclusively a hidden process; but even nearer to the present, those images were line drawings, textbook illustrations, or perhaps sonogram images that lacked detail. This then brings up the other premise to the argument, that the more easily one can detect in those images any simulation or projected sense of a born infant who is accepted as a person, the greater the moral value ascribed to the unborn even when understood as a living human, but yet nonperson.

At the embryonic stage of the first couple weeks, there is no resemblance to what would pass for a culturally accepted understanding of the physical form of a human person. Perhaps nearing the end of the embryonic stage, when the limbs become more pronounced with bending elbows and distinct fingers, the image begins to appear more humanlike, and perhaps increases the unborn's moral value as they *appear* more like a person. But being less than two inches in length, with major body disproportions, there is little to provoke animating sympathy. It is not necessary to apply this notion to the entire gestational development of the unborn. It is enough to show the strength of this thesis by simply pointing out the connection between those in the pro-life camp who want to mandate ultrasounds prior to abortions and those in the pro-choice camp who oppose it. The advocacy and opposition precisely form because those in both camps are aware of this potential projection. The pro-lifer would be attempting to trigger an emotional connection between the female and the unborn to thwart her from proceeding with the abortion. The pro-choicer understands this and attempts to expose it as nothing more than a thinly veiled motive to impinge on the female's choice by personifying the fetus. For a female during pregnancy, ultrasounds are routine. Three-dimensional ultrasounds presently are not, but will likely become more common as their use shifts beyond purposefully detecting fetal anomalies. Experience has shown that as technology becomes more readily available (which is particularly likely to happen if, like this imaging, the technology is not invasive), so too will its use expand. What is novel typically becomes routine, and it is not a stretch to think that high-resolution images will be sought, if for nothing else than an opportunity for mementos and keepsake photos. But that aside, in regard to any abortion procedure, an ultrasound of any kind is not routinely necessary. The insistence to make them mandatory is in service to a goal. So any pushback to the mandated imaging becoming a tool for the goal of provoking sympathy is based entirely on the aesthetic import of the unborn and, from that, the projected moral value it likely will solicit. Here is that claim illustrated in a syllogistic argument.

P1 Exposure to the real-time aesthetics of the unborn affects the moral value ascribed to the unborn.

P2 The high-quality imaging of the fetus in the female's womb is exposure to the real-time aesthetics of the unborn.

C Therefore, the high-quality imaging of the fetus in the female's womb affects the moral value ascribed to the unborn.

This point should not be overstated to mean that because one sees the high-quality imaging of the fetus in the female's womb, they immediately attribute characteristics of personhood to the unborn. But neither should such a connection be dismissed, to mean that cultural influences and those high-resolution images do not enter the psyche and facilitate judgments of moral value ascribed to the unborn. The causal relation may be subtle, but that does not mean it is insignificant. Personality projection to the unborn has produced reciprocal emotional cues, becoming an element of both persuasion and evaluation of personhood in the public dialogue of abortion.

Now to further test this issue of moral value concerning the unborn, without attempting an exhaustive survey, consider those who do not accept personhood of the unborn but may or may not find value in preserving the unborn due to the dependent nature of the developing human life. Here is a way to work through that without getting into the details of what particular characteristics or values must be present to determine personhood. First, if it is both legally founded and accepted in the popular mind of many that personhood occurs at birth when the child has evacuated the vaginal opening, then the idea of personhood has some connection to dependence on the birthing female. That is a reasonable assumption for the grounding of such a policy and its likely consideration for personhood. Until that moment the fetus evacuates the vaginal cavity, some would argue that the moral value is determined solely by the female; but after the head evacuates the vaginal cavity with personhood accepted, the moral value is no longer in the sole domain of the birthing female. An attached umbilical cord is of course still present but not necessary for sustenance. Yet there are many pro-choicers, and likely all pro-lifers, who do not think the "inside-outside location" closes the case on the onset of personhood. They might further posit that the dependency argument is not satisfied, as the necessary dependency simply migrates from the birthing female to another person or persons. It is accepted as an irreformable fact that humans do not emancipate from the birthing female as quickly as other species. The now-born child requires constant care (parental care?) and will not persist while underdeveloped. This post-birth period of infant immaturity and dependence is known as *altriciality*. The logic would be, then, that if the child is not a person inside the womb because of the dependency on the pregnant female, then if once outside of the womb some dependence remains necessary, would not the issue of dependency simply transfer to another during that period of altriciality? The ethical question is whether or not the personhood designation, once solely in the domain of the birthing female, now transfers to the caregivers. An important relational-duty distinction to keep in mind, of course, is that even if one grants autonomy to the unborn, because there remains an existential dependence of the unborn to a caregiver, the pregnant female exclusively has a developmental alliance that remains distinct from post-birth caregivers. The point there is to ask if the form of care is significant enough to warrant the birthing female to retain a right to designate personhood to the unborn, which the caregivers of the birthed infant would not. One is a biological dependence (development), while the other is a physiological dependence (maturation). This matter of burden-shifting of post-birth care may not be a central issue presently. Nonetheless, the same burden designation will be necessary for preborn living humans, if artificial wombs become an option (whether for development of pre-viable unborn or, if and when possible, from fertilization), or to some degree within the pre-birth responsibilities of using a third party to carry out the developmental functions (surrogates). To that last point, the question remains whether surrogates have bodily rights if not specifically contracted as such, ethically probing if a bodily right can even be surrendered to another under a contract. A case for consideration would be if a receiving couple contracts a surrogate but detects an undesired anomaly during pregnancy screening; can their exclusion of any moral value of the unborn override the surrogate female? The point here is not to flesh out those similarities and differences between the "inside fetus" and the "outside infant." The various scenarios are presented to contend there can be a moral value argument (none, full, or any intermediate position) made on behalf of the unborn even in the absence of personhood status, if any premise rests on dependency to someone other than the pregnant female or contracting couple. Here is the foundational claim presented as a syllogistic argument.

P1 The attribution of moral value for a living human being is granted by the providers of development or maturation.

P2 Both the birthing female and post-birth caregivers attribute some moral value to the unborn or born living human being.

C Therefore, attribution of moral value for a living human being is granted by the providers of development or maturation.

The soundness of this argument rests with the veracity of P1, but it must be kept in mind that there is both a distinction and a necessity for the providers of development (including a surrogate or the caretaker[s] of an artificial womb) and for those responsible for maturation (guardians or caregivers). So, even if the unborn is not afforded personhood, the moral value argument arises by questioning if there is any point where the value of the unborn (viability? point of transfer to artificial womb?) can eclipse the bodily autonomy of the pregnant female. The next section on "Personhood defined" will offer the parameters necessary to address and respond to that concern with more substance.

Another consideration involves a theist/nontheist issue embedded in the public abortion dialogue, as to what value the possession of a soul constitutes. As will be affirmed, the argument should not center over whether or not a soul exists, as it is more useful for dialogue to explore (1) to what extent holding such a position (i.e., that a soul exists) determines the moral value and (2) whether personhood is ascribed or recognized. Various criteria and values can be attached to either functionality, dependence, or the immaterial soul. For the theist (or any individual who holds to an immaterial soul), that dogmatic claim may appear satisfying, but alas it is not sufficient. First, there is the reality that some people who hold to the concept of a soul that does not simply incarnate (etymologically, to come "into flesh," understood as a body/soul composite) with the born infant at birth will still support a female's option to terminate an unborn with a soul. But that situation is not found difficult to defend for many who oppose an elective abortion, as those "supporters" are thought discredited by their lack of dogmatic consistency. That concern is not central to the point being made presently, so any further comment will be set aside.

Nonetheless, a more substantial challenge can be put forth to any who espouse the soul's incarnation at fertilization as the argument opposing female bodily autonomy: how to properly account for ensoulment relative to the onset of personhood when the unborn are monozygotic twins. Though it will not be directly addressed, what follows could also be applied to fused embryos, where two embryos that fuse together as chimeras can be said to pose an equal case against ensoulment of the fertilized ovum. Referring to identical twins, consider that they form from a single fertilized egg (embryo) dividing into two fertilized eggs, who each share the same genetic material and thus the same sex. The concern, then, for ensoulment is this: if personhood (ensoulment) is present at the moment an ovum is fertilized, then when the embryo splits, how does the single soul (original embryo) become two souls (monozygotic twins)? Initially there is a single embryo with a single soul; then after the split there are two embryos with two souls. If the soul *is* the person, then does one embryonic person keep its soul and the other embryonic person receive a new soul? Or does the soul split? Or does this infer that the ensoulment argument is unsound (an untrue premise)? This offers not merely a thought experiment, but both an actual and frequent occurrence. Although such twinning occurs naturally with a few pregnancies per thousand, there has been an increase in occurrence due to more females conceiving at a later age and more females seeking reproductive assistance.

Now, a reply could include the adoption of Aristotle's view of what constitutes an individual person. One would find this rebuttal, offered as a solution, from the Roman Catholic Church, which employs Aristotelian metaphysics. The idea is that all persons are made of matter (the physical aspect of the body) and form (the spiritual concept of the soul). In other words, a person does not have a soul, but every person *is* a body and soul (a composite being). The body is the material aspect, and the soul is the immaterial aspect. It would follow then that if there were a fertilized embryo, the material of the embryo is composed of a soul that constitutes a single person. But then if the embryo splits, that second embryo, as the new material, would receive its soul at that time. It should not be understood as one person being split into two persons, but rather as a new (second) person forming as material originally shared, but now distinct and uniquely composed of a soul that can now be referred to as two persons. Here it is expressed as a syllogism.

P1 After a single embryo divides, monozygotic twins have unique cells (material).

P2 The soul (form) is attached to unique material after a single embryo divides.

C Therefore, the soul (form) is attached to unique material as monozygotic twins have unique cells (material).

Again, this is not to be understood as a split person argument; it is offered here to suggest that for personhood, wherever there is unique human living material, there also is a composed soul so as to hold to the understanding of a separate composite being. To briefly apply this to the case of embryo fusion, one person (material/form) would cease to be living. In essence, one living human person ceases to exist. One may speak of the death of the twin; but (as would also be the case when one twin is absorbed by the other, known as vanishing twin syndrome) without the possibility of intention or negligence, there is no culpability attached to the "death." So, the logic remains the same, except that rather than "there was one; now there are two," it would be ordered as "there were two, but now there is one." It should be clear how not addressing this argument leads to confusion and frustration when determining the moral value of the unborn.

Not all are convinced by this logic, but it does hold to an *internal consistency*. If the proponent of ensoulment affirms the body/soul as the onset of personhood, then that determines the moral value. If their assertion of moral value is questioned, it needs to be confronted by virtue of that claim. The term *internal consistency* is important for any argument within the abortion dialectic. This means that one should not argue outside of the terms and premises used to form the conclusion. The rebuttal to the ensoulment of twins should not be, "There is no God and therefore no soul." If the person making the point holds that an unborn (matter) has a soul (form), then one must argue why it is problematic on their terms, demonstrating a lack of internal consistency. And likewise, this is why an atheist's support for a female's right to choose an abortion cannot simply be rebutted by the pro-lifer arguing, "The unborn has a soul, and therefore it is a person." If the atheist does not use the soul as a premise in their argument, then claiming its absence as an error will not suffice to demonstrate the atheist is in error, because the theist's argument against them is not internally inconsistent.

Another instance of internal consistency that has bearing on the moral value of the unborn leads to discussion of the misunderstood term *potential* and its related counterpart, *actual.* Each affects the perception of personhood when speaking about the physical *changes* of the embryo as it develops into the fetus, which itself becomes an infant and will continue to *look different* through adolescence and adulthood, while still remaining the same being. Again, it does not settle the issue of the abortion dialogue, but correctly addressing the meaning of each term removes unnecessary strife. The misunderstood term is *potential,* which is intimately and always related to the idea of *actual.* The term *potential* arises during the abortion dialogue, when some claim that the zygote is a potential human or a potential life, or, as more commonly phrased, that the fetus is a potential person. The fallacy, and its relation to an apparent internal inconsistency, is when the term *potential* is equivocally used. The common usage or colloquial grasp of the term is that potential is held to mean *some possibility in the future.* As the case in point, an assumption of this potentiality is that the unborn can *possibly* at some future point be a human, or be living, or become a person. The last possibility is the topic of this section. But first (setting the equivocation aside for a moment), even if the colloquial use of the term *potential* is held in that way, the presenter of the argument is beholden to state what the unborn *is* presently, which will equate with its *actuality.* This returns to the issue of ontologically stating what a thing *is*, prior to the ethical judgment. Now, in addressing the equivocation, the term *potential* in a philosophical sense does not mean *in the future* or *any possibility*, as in the potentiality to be what one desires; instead, the term is used to speak of *change* (zygote-to-fetus-to-infant) by an *inherent power that is present within the being for a definitive act.* It is assumed, by this thinking, that change cannot come from nothing, but the realization (act) of some power (potential) that is restricted only by what is possessed within the nature of that being. And this power, unless something interrupts it as the being's potency, will become actual in accord with the nature of its being.

A proper understanding of these notions clarifies, and sometimes changes, the argument. To the first problem, one may make the valid argument that the unborn is a potential person, provided it is in the nature of the unborn living human to become a person. That is universally accepted by the pro-choicers and the pro-lifers. If there were no potentiality for a developing living human to become a person, then personhood would be outside its nature. To the point of the working thesis of this text (*either some living humans are persons, or all living humans are persons*), anyone asserting that some living humans are not persons would still need to offer what makes any living human a person (qualities, etc.) and then explain why the unborn is not a person. Further, along with that claim, they would also need to settle if the unborn, even as a nonperson, possesses any moral value.

But that aside, two things need to be addressed in terms of moral value to keep the conversation centered on well-understood and common language. The first crucial point is that if referring to the unborn as a potential person is by one's assessment still legitimate, even then the unborn cannot be referred to as a potential human or potential life. Otherwise, one would be beholden to explain how something not human changes to become human, or how something not living might change to become living. The qualities of human and life are determined quantitatively, and a nonhuman cannot become a human any more than a nonlife can become a life. That judgment was explained in the previous chapter. The second point stems from the first: even if one does not accept the concept of a soul, there remains *something* of what this living human is that would make it unlike other nonhuman living beings and, by virtue of that, be granted moral worth because of value X or quality Y. The question to ask is, does value X or quality Y, which may grant moral value to a nonhuman animal (higher primate or aesthetically formed attachment), have any semblance to the unborn, living human? If so, then the moral value of the unborn, even if less than a "born living human person," is not null, but exists as an ethical judgment along some spectrum to be determined and defended. To the second problem, in everyday speech, one must return to the term *potential,* which refers specifically to that inherent power that is the *only* future because of some capacity that the person has by nature of being a human. For example, considering human developmental stages, a fetus has the potential to be a toddler, and a toddler has the potential to be an adolescent, and so on.

In each of those instances, the inherent power of being a toddler is the *only future possible* for a fetus. So, a fetus has the potential to be a toddler, and when the toddler stage is reached, that is referred to as the toddler's actuality; potentiality leads to actuality. Of course, not every fetus survives. But then the death of the fetus is not another potentiality; it is simply the unrealized or, to be specific, the unactualized potentiality of a fetus to become a toddler. The same could be said for the quality of a human's ability to reason. The ability to reason is not actualized in a fetus any more than it is not actualized fully in a toddler. But it exists *potentially*, in both a fetus and a toddler, as a possibility to be actualized as the being changes. Unless something or someone intervenes, when the fetus or toddler reaches a certain stage, that potential rationality will become actualized, and the individual will be able to reason.

Why are potentiality and actuality important for the relevance of moral value in relation to the abortion topic? If moral value is pinned to what a thing is (the human nature of the unborn), which contains its potency, and the moral value is not simply predicated on any actualization identified by the stage of development (what the fetus "looks like" or some other criteria), then the moral value of the unborn is determined not by the actuality, but by the inherent potency. This would be an argument that moral value, not unlike the presence of a composing soul, is attached to the nature of a thing and not the developmental stage.

This might be easier to introduce by what is known as the acorn argument. It attempts to suggest how a nature remains stable as each potentiality (the inherent power, or what it will be) becomes actualized (changes into what it *is*). The important thing to keep in mind is that regardless of the stage of actuality or the remaining potentiality, according to the logic of the acorn argument, the nature of the being (oak) does not change; only the accidents (i.e., the nonessential qualities or properties of the being—here, what the oak looks like in actuality) can and will change. It can be illustrated as follows.

> When one has an acorn, the actuality is the acorn, and the potentiality is a sapling.
>
> As the acorn *changes* to a sapling, the actuality retains the potentiality of a tree.
>
> As the acorn *changes* to a tree, the potentiality has been actualized.
>
> Only the accidents *changed* as each potentiality was realized (acorn-sapling-tree).
>
> The nature of the acorn, sapling, and tree was always that of an oak.

Transferring this logic to the living human, it would follow as such.

> When one refers to a fetus, the actuality is the fetus, and the potentiality is a toddler.
>
> As the fetus *changes* to a toddler, the actuality retains the potentiality of an adolescent.
>
> As the toddler *changes* to an adolescent, the potentiality has been actualized.
>
> Only the accidents *changed* as each potentiality was realized (fetus-toddler-adolescent).
>
> The nature of the fetus, toddler, and adolescent was always that of a human.

And finally if the concept were to be illustrated in a syllogistic argument pertaining to the relative moral value of a fetus, toddler, and adolescent (FTA), it may be expressed as follows.

P1 The inherent capacity of the FTA (potentiality) is not limited by what can be sensed (accidents).

P2 The nature of a living human (fundamental qualities) is determined by the inherent capacity of the FTA (potentiality).

C1 Therefore, the nature of a living human (fundamental qualities) is not limited by what can be sensed (accidents).

***

P3 The inherent qualities form a being's nature (what it *is*), rather than a judgment based on the being's stage of development (what can be sensed).

P4 The moral value of the living human FTA is determined by its nature (the fundamental qualities) as the inherent qualities form a being's nature (what it *is*).

C2 Therefore, the moral value of the living human FTA is determined by its nature (the fundamental qualities), rather than a judgment based on the being's stage of development (what can be sensed).

In the public abortion dialogue, the "sides" of the analogy would be either (1) a fetus is potentially a toddler, so a fetus has moral value relative to the actuality of a toddler's moral value, or (2) a fetus is not a toddler, so the moral value of a fetus is determined by its own actuality and not relationally to the moral worth of a toddler, which remains only the fetus in potential. The pro-lifer might argue that the *actuality* of an acorn, because it is potentially an oak tree, should be granted the same care (moral value) as that of an oak tree, even though it is not presently an actual oak tree. The pro-choicer might argue that the *actuality* of an acorn, even if it is potentially an oak tree, should not be granted the same care (moral value) as that of an oak tree, because of the certitude that it is not presently an actual oak tree. It should be clear that this does not settle the issue, but it does offer clarity in addressing the stages of development and how moral value might be ascribed based on something inherent in the being, as opposed to what can be sensed.

The strength of the acorn argument is that it does not rely on the aesthetics or the functionality of the unborn to determine moral value, but relies instead on the nature of the unborn as a living human that situates value in a thing's potency. In the same way that an acorn and the tree that grows from it both possess the nature of an oak, the fetus and the toddler both possess the nature of a human being. Those who hold this argument worthwhile would say that its detractors are confusing a nature (what a being is) with development (what stage a being is in); they would also argue how moral value is attached to a nature and not a stage of development. The weakness of the acorn argument is that it does not properly consider the aesthetics or the functionality of the unborn to determine moral value, as it would logically demand that the moral value of an embryo (which even as a living human has only genetic potentiality) be considered equivalent to that of an adolescent (which is a living human with expressed genetic actuality). This stance may even agree with the nature of the unborn as a living human that situates worth in a thing's potency. However, a simple thought experiment does test the efficacy of placing value on the nature of a human rather than on the actualized stage. One must ask oneself, if forced to choose in saving humans from a structure fire, would the preference lean toward one living human adolescent or one thousand frozen embryos? Which would possess greater moral value: one living human with potential actualized, or one thousand living humans with potential unactualized? There are solutions to that, but it stands as a consideration.

To reiterate, it is important to point out that this does not pit the pro-choice stance against the pro-life stance, or vice versa; nor does it favor one over the other. Understanding this relation of "potency to act" only reframes the argument of moral value, and ultimately personhood, away from the present public categories of bodily autonomy and when life begins. Perhaps it can be said that, at the very least, it removes certain considerations as stumbling blocks to fruitful dialogue. To consider the nature of an existing thing (being), if one is to argue there is a stable nature to a thing (refer back to "Human and life as kinds of things," which discussed social or natural kinds), is to try to determine what is known as essential (the nature) for that being to be what it *is* (oak or human person). To describe what a thing looks like at different stages of development or to describe characteristics that are not essential is to list the accidents of the thing (acorn or fetus). To avoid equivocation, philosophically the term *accident* is not understood as a mishap or adversity, as in a traffic accident. Rather, accidents are those things that are not essential to the nature of a thing but yet remain how a thing is sensed and thus known. For example, if one accepts that there is a nature to a living human, then the color of one's hair, having four limbs, and being able to speak are all things that can change within the lifetime of a living human, and thus are accidents. But even without those accidents (observable features), the individual remains a living human being; they just look or function differently. To the abortion topic, then, it may be argued that value X or quality Y is lacking as an ability or feature with an unborn human being as compared to that of a toddler. But the fetus has different accidents, while sharing the same nature as (and having the inherent potentiality of) the toddler. Again, this does not close down the argument for pro-lifers or pro-choicers, but it does assist in centering the focus on personhood and even moral value, while offering a common language for productive and fruitful conversation.

Finally, prior to working through possible definitions of personhood, one last aspect here to be addressed is when judgments of moral value are confused by anachronistic views. First, the term *anachronistic* is a relational reference to the past but does not mean "old fashioned." An anachronism projects the present connotation of a term, attempting to apply it in the same way onto another historical time that may have understood the same term differently, if it existed at all in that period. It is a chronological inconsistency, or the equivocal comparison of a term across time periods. It is simple to grasp by analogy if you consider how odd it would be to watch a Victorian historical drama and notice one of the characters wearing sneakers. Because those sneakers do not belong to that period, they are *out of place* and historically inaccurate, resulting in an anachronism. This is relevant for the abortion topic in that sometimes the understanding of an action or term taken out of place historically is used to make a present argument appear inconsistent. If one is ignorant of the anachronism, the comparison appears true. When the anachronism is uncovered and understood as historically inaccurate, the argument fallaciously falls apart, much like claiming people wore sneakers in Victorian England. This dissolves the premise for the argument; further, it damages the credibility of the claimant.

In the public abortion dialogue, the following anachronistic argument is sometimes made but only causes confusion. There are claims that in the past, some in society and some major religious belief systems had no ethical issue with abortion until movement in the womb was felt (quickening). It follows from that premise that because they now do consider abortion unethical prior to quickening, they are at best being ethically inconsistent or, worse, unable to argue why their position has changed. It follows then that they can and should be called out for their change in position.

First, the term *quickening*, though no longer commonly used, was the way one referred to the sensation of feeling the unborn moving in the womb. It is derived from the Latin term for "quick," which is *vivus*, that itself literally translates as "alive." This quickening then was typically experienced at some point in the second trimester of gestation, anywhere between sixteen and twenty-two weeks of pregnancy. The importance of this sensation was that for even some stalwart pro-life stances, like that held by the Roman Catholic Church, this fetal movement indicated the *moment* the unborn *came to life*. So, the logic then was that prior to the unborn being alive (indicated by quickening), there technically could not have been an abortion if an abortion is understood as the termination of an unborn's life. The argument is meant to demonstrate that there are those presently holding the pro-life stance who have changed their position from an earlier period and thus are either hypocritical, ideological, or ignorant that their "side" once held a more reasonable and relaxed position on abortion. The response, regardless of one's position, is simply that it was the knowledge of when life begins that changed, not the position on abortion.

Once more, understanding this anachronistic argument does not settle the debate on personhood or the public abortion dialogue, for two reasons. First, demonstrating the hypocrisy of the other side does not prove one's own position. But, more importantly, if the comparison is anachronistic, then there is no veracity to the claim that the present stance is inconsistent, so in reality, the point is moot. It is being addressed here as it is simply one more diversion that does need to be cleared up to save the abortion conversation from needless frustration and antagonism.

For the sake of thoroughness, the unsoundness of this argument (its untrue premise) is easily demonstrated here. To be internally consistent, prior to modern times and presently with theists who accept a human soul, a body without a soul was not a living human person; for something to be alive, it must have a soul. This was and is true for plants, nonhuman animals, and human beings. So, the premodern understanding was that the unborn at some point was imbued with a soul, and only at that time did it *come to life*. When the unborn came to life, the unborn moved, and the female felt the movement. In the prescientific (empirical) world, this quickening was confirmation of the unborn animating in the womb. That term *animate* is crucial. It derives from the Latin term *anima,* which itself translates into English as "soul." To this day, the term *animate* holds that meaning of "coming to life." Consider cartoons, where still drawings come to life when shown rapidly in sequence. It is literally referred to as *anima*tion. But empirical evidence now holds that not only does life not *begin* at fertilization, but life *continues* through fertilization. And even if fertilization as the onset of a new life is contested, there is no empirical way to uphold that the unborn is inert (nonliving) until quickening. So, as is often the case with facts, the understanding that life begins at quickening was a fact that has been reformed, and thus is presently accepted as empirically false. Then, to expose the original argument, here is how it could be illustrated that even though it is valid (maintains proper logical form), it is unsound (based on an untrue premise) and thus must be rejected. To follow this, first recall that an abortion is the intentional termination of a prenatal living human. Secondly, realize that though the argument may seem correct upon first hearing, the equivocation based on the anachronistic use of *comes to life* derails the veracity of the conclusion.

P1 The same people who used to believe that the unborn *comes to life* when movement is felt in the womb (quickening) are those who historically held that abortion was ethically *acceptable* during the first two trimesters.

P2 Those who presently hold that an abortion is ethically *unacceptable* during the first two trimesters are the same people who used to believe that the unborn *comes to life* when movement is felt in the womb (quickening).

C Therefore, those who presently hold that an abortion is ethically *unacceptable* during the first two trimesters are those who historically held that abortion was ethically *acceptable* during the first two trimesters.

Perhaps it would be illustrative to simply use colloquial speech to hear how it sounds convincing.

> Some pro-lifers can be so hypocritical. They claim it's wrong to abort a fetus not only at or after twelve weeks, but at *any time* after conception. Didn't the famous theologian Thomas Aquinas specifically say that the soul doesn't even enter the fetus until near the end of the second trimester? But now they have changed their minds and try to argue that an embryo has a soul. It would be much easier to have a reasonable discussion if they simply returned to their previous position.

Now, are there more scholarly ways to address what is deemed ensoulment and generation as applied to premodern notions of embryology and fetal development? Certainly, there can be a deeper analysis, but it is not within the scope of this text. Further, that material is readily available as research for anyone interested in understanding it more authentically. An example is that one would likely find that Aquinas, like Aristotle, separated the soul into three powers, the vegetative (growth), animal (sensory), and intellective (rational). The embryo, even prior to quickening, was a living soul but not yet a living rational soul. Therefore, at least for Aquinas, it was still unethical to expel the unborn prior to quickening, but it differed by culpability (guilt or penalty), as that was not accepted as the termination of a rational human soul. The purpose at this juncture is not to parse out the details of those philosophical and theological claims, but to offer an insight into how an anachronistic notion creeps into a contemporary debate and causes confusion.

To reiterate the original point, and to be clear, if it was always unethical to intentionally terminate a human life in the womb, then it was not that position which changed, but an understanding as to when the unborn *comes to life*. So, it is anachronistic to claim that some have changed their stance on abortion when what has changed was the understanding of when life begins. Here is the argument to explain the reformed position in syllogistic form.

P1 Because empirical science corrected the anachronistic understanding of when the unborn is alive, it does not mean a judgment on the ethic of abortion has changed.

P2 People once held life begins at quickening until empirical science corrected the anachronistic understanding of when the unborn is alive.

C Therefore, because people once held life begins at quickening does not mean they changed their judgment on the ethic of abortion.

With that last claim addressed, two points remain necessary to make. The first is that a reader can grow weary of working through all these elements that arise in the argument about abortion. Something to always keep in mind concerning any ethical judgment is that *claims are much easier to make than to dismantle*. But such vigilance and perseverance are crucial to overcome ideological stances, or those accepted merely because of some political affiliation or worldview. Abortion is an important and enduring ethical issue, and to offer a mature contribution to the public dialogue, one must allow for and invest the time and discipline for the critical thinking required as preparation for a constructive conversation. The second point is that what was unveiled by empirical science has not made this issue easier to ethically work through. In fact, although science has made some aspects of the discussion clearer—such as an understanding of fetal development and what constitutes biological life—those insights have provided more elements now necessary to the public dialogue that must be comprehended to envelop into the discussion and ethical evaluation. Science, technology, and culture have changed the way individuals view and understand an unborn living human, and thus the ethics of abortion must contend with those progressions in a logical way, with applied critical thinking open to critique and reform.

ON THE DEFINITIONS OF PERSONHOOD

Although science has contributed to the comprehension of the terms *human* and *life*, empirical science has little insight to offer into personhood and none in terms of an ethical judgment. Science allows insights concerning the qualities of function or capacity, but it cannot determine the moral value those might evoke. Personhood is, quite simply, outside the domain of empirical science's competence (more on that shortly).

What does inform one's understanding here, if not empirical science? Helpful in answering that is some explanatory background on how an understanding of the living human person came to be realized. The term *person* itself has developed quite a bit historically. Initially, it was a term used in ancient Rome that play-actors assumed while wearing masks in their roles. Even presently, one can speak of actors assuming the *persona* of the character they portray. The fourth century saw a migration of persona as a role to the persona as an individual, when the Christian Church set out to explain the deity of Jesus the Christ while maintaining a monotheistic comprehension of God the Father. To metaphysically express how Jesus can be God even as the Father is God, while remaining monotheistic, the term *person* developed and was adopted to help explain that relationship. To this end, the church fathers employed the term *hypostasis*, a Greek word used to connote the individual *person*. In context, it was to represent the underlying reality of Christ, allowing for a separation of each *Person* of the Trinity, thus providing a distinction of persons while also permitting each to share the same *ousia* (essence). Thus, by this metaphysical appraisal, the separation of Persons preserved a monotheistic God and is referred to as the hypostatic union. The idea of that underlying reality, now offering a mechanism of expression, has come today to be understood as *personhood*. Yet, from that early period, this term *person* continued to develop and to be defined.

In the sixth century, Roman senator and philosopher Anicius Manlius Severinus Boethius (d. 524) offered the definition of the living human person as a *rational animal*. Definitions attempt to arrive at the essence of a thing, to express what it means to be that thing, and then to denote how that thing is known. It may appear ironic, but even the term *definition* requires defining—there are at least six definitions of it. But one way to understand a definition, and the means Boethius adopted, was to combine a universal genus (animal) with a specific difference (rationality). In his work *Against Eutyches and Nestorius*, Boethius proposed that a mortal person is an individual substance of a rational nature.[3] If one further connects this notion of a rational animal with Aristotle's concept of a soul (*anima*), one sees the rudimentary form of what is now understood as the individual person. For Aristotle and the church fathers, there was some dualistic or composite form of the living human person, which represents the "I" so often casually used without consideration. In irony, and to the public abortion topic at hand, contemporary persons rarely consider the depth and development of implications when declaring "I think" or "I choose." Not only is what this "I" constitutes simply taken for granted, but the terms *think* (which requires justifying one's beliefs as true) and *choose* (which requires intentionally forming ethical judgments) are assumed as some default position, given without reflection. An appreciation for how early thinkers devoted much time and thought to what today is understood as *person* should, at minimum, cause one to pause and appreciate the development of this idea of the living human person. Suffice it to say that later thinkers did and continued to wrestle with the significance of an individual human being referred to personally as this "I."

This composite view of personhood as a body and soul persisted through the sixteenth and seventeenth centuries until the Enlightenment pillars of reason and scientific investigation overtook any divinely grounded authority. During this time, philosopher John Locke (d. 1704), who coined the phrase "life, liberty, and property" as the three natural rights, proposed an understanding of personhood (or personality theory) based on psychological continuity. In simple terms, for Locke a *person* is a person based on continuity of memories. By his reckoning, this continuity of memories, as one's personal identity, can be understood as consciousness. Here one witnesses a move away from personhood understood by virtue of the soul as the necessary underlying substance that both theists and ancients accepted, to Locke's continuity, expressed as shared memories across one's lifespan.[4] For example, if a teenager (B) has memories from when they were a toddler (A), which persists when they are an older person (C), then the memories during the stages of life (A-B-C), by remaining the same, signal it is the same person at each stage of life by virtue of that continuity. Apparent issues surface with this "memory as personhood" concept, which later philosophers challenged;

3. Boethius, *Tractates*, 85.

4. See Locke, *Concerning Human Understanding*, 134.

a few will be mentioned. But it is at least worth consideration because when someone has lost their memory, perhaps from old age, injury, or disease, it is not uncommon to hear someone say about them, "They are not the same person anymore." Within that, one can hear the whispers of Locke's notion that has supplanted the underlying reality of the *hypostasis* that Aristotle and the church fathers adopted.

Issues with Locke's theory were brought up by more recent philosophers of the twentieth century. A condensed response would be to consider how past experiences shape the present individual, regardless of recollection. Consider that some things that may have happened in one's past—even though not remembered—still have significant influence for the person in the present. Perhaps a tragic event was suppressed, or an idiosyncratic quirk or habit is present while the origin is unknown. Some unrecognized compulsive behavior may have developed from an unremembered reason; contemporary philosopher Marya Schechtman, in her article "The Narrative Self,"[5] expresses this as unconscious memories, where the habit still exists even though the reason for its onset is unknown at present. The point is that something in the past initiated an aspect of the present person, but the *why* remains unknown. If this is so, how can conscious memories be *the person*, if those memories do not exist in continuity? The opposite, of course, is also true; people often have false memories. It is not uncommon for someone to swear that something specific happened or that some person said some specific thing but be entirely in error. They are not lying if they earnestly believe it and their intent is not to deceive; they simply do not recall correctly. So, whether the memory is forgotten or false, those past memories shape the identity of the present person. And further, often anxieties about the future, which are obviously not memories, can also affect what is held as the present person. These "future memories," as Bernard Williams (d. 2003) would assert in *Problems of the Self*,[6] are expectations of the present self that cannot be directly attributed to some continuity of memories, past to present. Such a demonstration of the *person* persisting, in spite of proper recollection, challenges Locke's theory of psychological continuity.

With no underlying immaterial substance, something else (memories, emotions, same body, etc.) must serve as the connection between the developmental stages of a person's life, to account for continuity of

5. See Schectman, "Narrative Self," 394–416.

6. See Williams, *Problems of the Self*, 46–63.

the same person. It is safe to assume that contemporary secular society dismisses the soul. For comparison, then, quickly reconsider Aristotle's view, which was based on a theory known as *hylomorphism* offered in his book *Physics* as a means to explain change. If you recall, Aristotle (d. 322 BC) proposed a natural science with the idea that persons are a composite of *matter* (the physical) and *form* (the spiritual). What underlies this, and accounts for continuity, is a stable *ousia* (the essence). That essence, or underlying substance, was the same theory to explain the unity of the three Persons of the Christian Trinity. Hylomorphism, then, held that the material cause (the body) was the potency, and the immaterial cause (the soul) was the act—so, once again, another application of both potency and act. Since this comprehension considers two contributing ideas of the living human person, it is a variety of dualism that shares some similarities with the Judeo-Christian view. With John Locke, who held onto the existence of an immaterial soul (and perhaps an immortal soul), it was conscious memories and not the individual soul that accounted for the human person, and thus one's identity. He demonstrated this with a thought experiment of a prince and a cobbler who swapped memories. Which one, after the switch, would one consider the real prince or the real cobbler? He contended it was the one who held the same conscious memories, regardless of which body those memories inhabited. This should serve as an observant point—that, as stated, in the absence of the soul as the form (act?) of the human person, it will either be the body (potency?) or perhaps the mind that must take the place of continuity through all the various stages of life and constitute what is referred to as the *person*.

This brief survey, as it continues, offers an important observation. It is crucial to keep in mind that individuals form their ideas dependent on the philosophical understandings of the age in which they exist. This is not obvious to all of those who hold the ideas, neither historically nor in the present. For example, to speak of what is important considering the human person, it may seem intuitive to claim, "It's what's inside that counts." But that is not an original observation. The ancient Greeks, the church fathers, and present holders of body/soul composite would find it problematic. Perhaps each would understand that one cannot be judged by appearance, but they would find it odd (and erroneous) to consider the person as something "inside" the body. That notion arose from one other interpretation of dualism that comes from the seventeenth century, as French philosopher René Descartes (d. 1650), a predecessor to Locke, tried to work out how one can know things with certainty. Descartes's concern was what to doubt, what to be certain of, and how one might distinguish between the two. The method he used was to whittle down all dubious claims to knowledge. The process he used coined the now-famous phrase, "I think, therefore I am" (*cogito ergo sum*),[7] which really should be understood as "I doubt, and I know it is I who is doubting." In other words, if there is anything Descartes could be certain about, it is that at least he himself is the one doing the doubting, and this he knows with certainty. He did not think the "outside" world was *not* really there, but he was looking for something foundational to be certain of before he accepted knowledge of the exterior world as being *really* there, and not derived as a misconception from his senses. How this bears on the Cartesian position on personhood is that an understanding of the person as "the self" (the "I") is not *in* the mind, but "the self" as the "I" . . . *is* the mind. Locke's view of personhood is an extension of the dualism offered with Descartes. The distinction is that though Locke was an empiricist (knowledge through the senses and thus experience), Descartes was a rationalist where reason alone can bring certainty.

Perhaps a polar opposite to this theory is that the material aspects of the body make each person who they are over time. But the notion of *the same body as the same person* has not held up so well in the course of history. That was in part why Locke proposed his psychological continuity theory, as a way to account for moral value and culpability via the string of memory. Perhaps consider that according to Locke's views, one can *own* themselves; and then as responsible persons with property rights ascribed to each person, they can be held accountable whether in the pursuit of happiness or individual liberty. One can sense the fermentation of civil law that Locke both adopted and offered. But, with that said, it is not some underlying substance or simply the organism called the human person that accounts for ontological continuity. Rather, it is a psychological identity that can grant present rights while holding the individual ethically responsible for past actions. Yet, returning to the counterproposal, the idea of any material aspect of a person or thing being the reason each remains the same person or thing over time was actually refuted in ancient times as implausible. Some philosophers questioned how something could remain the same over time simply because it is composed of the same material (human body?). One critic in particular

7. See Descartes, *Meditations*, 63–69.

was Heraclitus, a fifth-century BC pre-Socratic philosopher. Heraclitus is well known for the axiom arguing that *everything is change*. Others have attributed to him the famous expression that "no one ever steps in the same river twice." So, if everything changes, the body (the material) is not what constitutes the cohesion of personhood. Another challenge arose with Plutarch (b. AD 46), who addressed the unlikely claim of bodily "sameness as identity" with a paradox known as "The Ship of Theseus."[8] A paradox is a thought experiment intended to show how something seems to be true but ultimately is self-contradictory and therefore contrary to what one expects. To paraphrase Plutarch's proposal, consider a ship that, due to damage, wear, and rot over the years, has had every plank, board, sail, and nail replaced. If the ship at some future point has none of the original (same) materials that it had when it was first built, can it be said to be the *same* ship? The ship is not a perfect parallel to the human person. Yet, the point is that if the human body *is* the human person from birth, through adolescence to old age, then what accounts for the continued identity over time, considering the physical changes in organs, tissues, and cells from birth to old age? Much of Descartes's and Locke's views of personhood have persisted, but the material (body) understanding of the human person has not. A cultural acceptance of the latter in contemporary society has generated a separation of any understanding of the human person who is thought of as what is interior. This was, and is, a separation of the interior person from the exterior body. So, it is one thing to consider that an individual human person is not reduced to their body, but another thing to consider is that the body is not connected to the human person who is interior. That is another issue with implications for contemporary culture, but it is outside of the quest of this venture.

Another position on personhood is that of the eighteenth-century rationalist philosopher Immanuel Kant (d. 1804). One would be remiss not to introduce this concept. Kant, along with other Enlightenment thinkers, elevated reason as the authority over revealed truth and, from that, came to propose the human person as a *rational agent*. It was stated earlier that for the abortion discussion and medical ethics, here one finds the origins of bodily autonomy. This autonomy stemmed from his view that the human will can direct an individual to align with moral laws, which are discoverable by reason alone. His concept of personhood is

8. Audi, "Ship of Theseus," 842.

tethered to one's ability to rationally choose, which is why autonomy is crucial to Kant. This, then, likely confines the human being to a rational autonomous agent who can exert their will in the form of a choice. From that premise, this can exclude certain members of the human species who either never had or have lost that power of rational agency. Think in terms of those born with cognitive disorders who suffer from a severe loss of mental capacity, or even those who, because of an accident or disease later in life, lose their reasoning ability and perhaps their status as a rational agent. Some would argue that in those cases Kant's view would hold they never were, or are no longer, persons because of that lack of autonomy. Others would point out that those individuals who fall short of rational agency are not without moral worth and may be understood as *analogous persons*. An important consideration of Kant, to keep in mind with autonomy, is his expression of the categorical imperative known as the *human principle*.[9] It holds that by reason, ethically no person (notice the term *human* is referring to the term *person*) can be used as a means to an end. In other words, a person can only be used for their own good, and not for the good of another. That term *categorical imperative* is simple to understand when the term is broken down. The term *categorical* means always and everywhere, so think of categorically denying a false accusation. Then the term *imperative* means obligatory and mandatory. A *categorical imperative* then is something that must always be done without exception, and here Kant offers that no one can use another as a means to an end, ever, without exception. But some have argued that this categorical imperative does not apply to all human beings, only those deemed rational agents. So, to use it for the abortion conversation would require a specific argument, demonstrating how it can be convincingly applied.

Next worth considering are the ideas of twenty-first-century American cognitive philosopher Daniel Dennett (d. 2024), who proposed specific conditions for human beings to be considered persons. The terms *necessary* and *sufficient* introduced earlier are important here. Recall that what is necessary is something that must be included, but is not enough in itself for personhood. Likewise, then, sufficient would refer to the entirety of conditions needed to satisfy the full meaning of personhood. In truth, Dennett may not hold that any concept of personhood is somewhat coherent, as he did not think there was sufficient objectivity

9. See Kant, *Metaphysics of Morals*, §429, 36.

to form the notion.[10] Nonetheless, following at least Kant's view of a rational agent, Dennett holds as the first condition that a person must be a rational being. Another element is that everyone is conscious of something, as one cannot be said to be conscious if they are not conscious of something. That is not meant as a semantic jumble, but simply holds to the claim that to say one is conscious of nothing is to hold they are not conscious. This aspect he refers to as intentionality. This is tethered to the third point: that to be intentional also means that a person holds a position—what he calls a stance. Working off that third condition of a *stance*, he then states as the fourth element that a person must be capable of reciprocating that stance. The fifth condition may need more nuance than is possible in a short sentence, but the capacity for verbal communication is key for his version of personhood. This begs the question as to whether some living humans and other animals may be excluded because of that requirement. The capacity for communication is tied to a reciprocal attitude, and also insists a higher order of communication (thinking about thinking), so a squirrel chirping would not likely suffice. The sixth and final condition is consciousness itself, which by some is understood as self-consciousness. Now these are not to be understood as the entirety of what is sufficient for personhood. Humility compelled Dennett to realize these could not provide a comprehensive exposition of personhood. In other words, more criteria *may* be needed. For instance, you can think of the first three criteria pertaining to nonhuman animals, and the final three conditions may or may not include certain individual human beings who are deficient in one or more of those capacities. That being said, he admits to himself these are ideals and recognizes some instability in what is proposed.

At this point in offering definitions of personhood, a quick recap as to the varying positions is warranted for the distinct purpose of generally explaining their relation to the public abortion dialogue. Some of the thinkers addressed the abortion issue directly; with others, a position can be conferred from their stance on personhood. Though not merely speculative, in instances where no direct stance was addressed (this is rarely the case, which itself speaks to the perennial and persistent doggedness of the public issue of abortion), varying interpretations nonetheless can be pieced together. This brief survey is only intended to offer insight for reflection and makes no attempt to be either exhaustive or conclusive.

10. See Dennett, "Conditions of Personhood," 145–67.

So then, beginning with Aristotle, the principle of potentiality is important. To terminate a being with potentiality (the fetus) that will lead to an actuality (the infant) where terminating that actualized being is unethical, then it might follow that terminating the being while in the potential state (the fetus) is equally unethical. Others would argue that to simply equate a potentiality (the fetus) with an actuality (the infant) is a misapplication of an ethical judgment. Yet specifically in "Book VII" of Aristotle's *Politics*, he spoke directly that no deformed child (the infant) should live.[11] Perhaps this exposure, as infanticide, represents the unactualized potency that was present in the fetus. Further, Aristotle explicitly held that an abortion is permissible if it precedes the onset of the "sense and life of the unborn." To that point, one must not simply make the leap that he would support an abortion as presently defined. Recall that for Aristotle, life "began" at the point of *quickening*, so his view on abortion perhaps is in line with the historical view of fetal development, and one would need to argue from that to form a present stance.

Moving now to the views of Boethius, who as a martyred Roman Catholic held a stance aligned with the church fathers and the entire Catholic/Orthodox Church of the period, the uncontested position is that an abortion is unethical. It should be noted that outside of Christianity, the unborn was *a part* of the pregnant female. In contrast to that long-held pagan position, Tertullian (d. after AD 220) in his *Apologeticus* states that the unborn is "the fruit already in seed"[12]—and whether a life is destroyed either born or coming to birth, it is, by his account, murder and forbidden. Yet the same anachronism of when life begins (ensoulment at quickening) would again need to be addressed, as it altered the understanding of when life began. However, one clear distinction from the culture in which Christianity arose is that the early Christians adamantly opposed the exposure of infants. Ample historical record indicates that infanticide was widely practiced in the Greco-Roman world, as well as in regions of Asia and what is now known as the Americas. As an example of that historically accepted practice, the ancient Roman statesman Seneca the Younger (d. AD 65), expressed clearly in his *De Ira* (*On Anger*) that it is an act of reason to drown children born with a weakness or deformity.[13] It was precisely in response to such a practice that an early Christian document known as the *Didache* (The Lord's Teaching

11. Aristotle, *Politics*, Book VII, §16.10, 2119.

12. Tertullian, *Apologeticus*, 25.

13. Seneca, *De Ira*, §15.

Through the Twelve Apostles to the Nations) specifically stated that not only is abortion murder, but it is wrong "as well to kill the newborn."[14] This opposition to both abortion (from the onset of life/ensoulment) and infanticide (neonatal euthanasia) persists to modern time with Christian groups that boast an ancient heritage, notwithstanding those who reinterpret and, in varying ways, diverge from inherited Christian faith expressions to support a female's reproductive autonomy. As within secularism at large, one is required to investigate the arguments of the Christian expressions in continuity and consistency within the revealed tradition they claim. That is not in line with the project at hand and, if pursued, will likely require an appeal to dogmatic claims, which is the argument here that they have limited export into the public dialogue on abortion as fallacious arguments to authority.

Moving now into the Enlightenment period, recall Locke's view of psychological continuity. Though Locke was an empiricist (knowledge through experience), and from that a level of skepticism arose to the extent that facts do change, he did extend some level of certainty to the moral sphere. Locke held to a form of natural law (not simply some "law" found "out in nature") that is reflective of a higher will. In *An Essay Concerning Human Understanding,* though, Locke also pointed out that few adhere to an internal "veneration for these rules" that comprise such a natural law confirmed by experience. To mitigate this unruliness of the human mind and will, he supported *sanctions*, which for Locke was God's way of ensuring compliance. So, although not merely from a crass dogmatic stance, Locke nonetheless cited in his *Essay* that to procure an abortion is in opposition to the worship of God.[15] This notion of Locke is rarely discussed, as his medical ethics is an interesting, but often poorly studied aspect of his moral philosophy.

Next to consider is René Descartes, whose views of epistemology (how one comes to know) formed his philosophical anthropology (who is the human person). In *Meditations on First Philosophy*, the Cartesian view of the human person set out to doubt what cannot be known with certainty. That led him in the "Second Meditation" to view himself (personhood) as the *thinking thing*. By the "Sixth Meditation," he concluded that not only was he the thinking thing, but he was *only the thinking thing*, as the sensation he has *of* his own body (pains, hunger, etc.) do

14. *Didache*, §2, 16.

15. Locke, *Concerning Human Understanding*, §12, 19–20.

not come *from* his own body. He concluded that they must come from *within* the body, and he confirmed that God (Descartes was a Catholic) is no deceiver, so these ideas of himself that are sometimes erroneous (phantom pain?) cannot come directly from God or be mediated by some other creature. Now, specifically to abortion, Descartes understood that the generation (reproduction) of beings comes from the same kind (humans beget humans). And from this, his view of the person as the thinking subject would seem to exclude the prerational fetus. But yet, the *cogito* (the thinking thing) is not without a body. This remained true even if, as he put it, he is the pilot of the body, and he as the thinking thing must be conjoined to the body that senses. So, is the fetus, even if not yet rationally actualized, an embodied mind? In one of the many replies Descartes afforded his detractors, he entered into a debate with the contemporary Antoine Arnauld on the possibility of a *thinking fetus*. Much could be said, but let it suffice for the point at hand that Arnauld found Descartes's proposition of a thinking fetus absurd. And Descartes defended his own claim by speaking of the infant as capable of confused thoughts (that are not the sole domain of a being in utero) that did not persist into a conscious memory after birth.[16] That is, he argued that the fetus does think, even if what is thought cannot be recalled post birth.

Finally, to sum up the Enlightenment period, perhaps with Kant, like many moral philosophers, one can find various interpretations that support varying stances on abortion. First, Kant did not address the abortion issue directly. Since his rationally based ethics formed a duty premised on a categorical imperative (CI), that is the lynchpin in determining a stance. Recall that a categorical (always and everywhere) imperative (required action) has no exceptions. Further, as this CI maxim insists on both consistency and universality, the stance on abortion depends on how one builds the duty. Is there a duty that a female's bodily autonomy is paramount, or the unborn's right to existence? If the CI is expressed as the humanity principle (cannot use another person as a means to an end), then could the female be used as a means to the end of the unborn, or the unborn as a means to the end of the pregnant female? His views on agency that formed modern bodily autonomy, as was stated, are crucial to his moral philosophy, but this autonomy is never absolute. Such bodily autonomy cannot include harming other persons or intentionally harming oneself. Perhaps if there are competing universal claims—that

16. See Schmal, "Virtual Reflection," 730.

is, an equal CI duty to the female and unborn—then one must argue whether, why, and to what extent the pregnant female or unborn has a higher moral value than the other. The obvious tension is that one CI will inevitably restrict the other CI; and like the underlying premise for this text, since one's bodily autonomy halts at the threshold of another person, first the notion of personhood of the unborn must be settled, and then Kant's CI can be readdressed in light of that.

Though a time leap from the Enlightenment period, a short view of Dennett would be to understand his Darwinian underpinnings. Dennett subscribed to an unguided process of natural selection, which for him replaces the idea of a Creator God. This, for Dennett, led to the eponymous title of his *Darwin's Dangerous Idea*. Add to that notion his view of consciousness as a necessary criterion for the human person, and one would be hard-pressed to argue successfully that the unborn is conscious in the way he proposed. This consciousness for Dennett is not simply "dropped" into the mind. It is developed as one engages others and culture over time. If this consciousness *is* the self (personhood), then as he offered in *Consciousness Explained*, in the same way a spider spins a web without understanding what it is doing, so too an illusion of the personhood is spun, from which the self is created and consciousness is formed.[17]

In summation, a very important point must be gleaned. In the brief consideration of these thinkers, one should pause and consider that any position on abortion, whether implicitly or explicitly held, did not arise from some ideological or partisan position. They developed and adopted a position on personhood and, coupled with an intentional formation of an ethical system, a stance on abortion was determined. Whatever position on the abortion stance was formed or can form, it was, and must be, molded by an *intentional* ethical stance and became permeated by a *reflective* view of what constitutes the living human person. If any arguments for or against abortion would conceivably arise, they would not be defended as simply a "right to life" or the "right to autonomy," but an argument over how an ethical evaluation can and should be applied to an expressed view of the human person. With these thinkers' views and that aspect of ethical consistency now briefly addressed, the next consideration with the concept of personhood is to what extent the individual is an isolated being or whether personhood requires relationality.

17. Dennett, *Consciousness Explained*, 416.

PERSONHOOD AND RELATIONALITY

A hint of relationality surfaced as a compelling feature of the human person in Dennett's view of personhood, with its fourth condition of reciprocal stance. Those who held to ensoulment (the form) implicitly require relationality in their idea of personhood, though the body (the actuality) *perhaps* remains the individuating factor, with intentional emphasis on *perhaps*. The church fathers and subsequent Christians are an exception, given the inherent relationality of the Trinity; if it is accepted that the human person is created *imago Dei* (in God's image), then this hypostatic union of Three Persons is extended as the relational underpinning of each created person. Boethius would have held to that dogmatically, even if his definitional view did not cite relationality as a necessity. But through Kant, Locke, and the others who sought to refine his idea of continuity, any astute thinker would have noticed that the concept of personhood was very isolated. According to those views, one could be a person regardless of other persons existing. Asking what a person *is* was more like dissecting the pertinent factors and treating them like parts that formed an individual. By analogy, it is akin to asking what an ant is and then understanding the essence of an ant isolated from its colony. By doing so, one misses the fact that it might be only in relation that human persons form as dynamic and functional beings. This section will consider the notion of personhood beyond the isolated being as an individual. Thinkers who venture into the necessity of relationships for the living human to be regarded as a person will be considered as a necessary condition. In other words, the question of personhood will be reframed to ask if anyone can be a person in isolation from other persons.

In truth and as stated, to a certain degree any concept of a soul implies this relationality. Recall that the soul is not simply something held by modern-day theists who maintain a present-day expression of a creator Deity, but also by the ancient Greeks and Romans, along with those who hold to an immaterial nature of the human person. To reiterate, it was explained earlier that the soul is the form of the body. Then, further, the concept of one individual being as distinct from another is called *individuation*—that is, as the person is a composite of form and matter, the distinction is the matter. The form is the essence, and all beings that share the form are necessarily related by that essence they share in common. If all share the same form, although it is the body as the matter that would make each *person* a distinct individual, the form *is* the reality of relation for all.

With that in the background, just five expressions of the necessity of relationality for personhood will be put forward here. First will be the view of an African understanding of personhood known as Ubuntu, which was advocated for by former South African president and revolutionary Nelson Mandela. Second will be the relational view of Jewish philosopher Martin Buber. Third will be the twentieth-century philosopher Judith Jarvis Thomson, a secular Jew born of a Catholic mother and a socialist Jewish father. Her take on what one person owes to another would become a famous defense of abortion that accepts personhood, but nonetheless advocates for an abortion of the unborn person once a particular proviso is accepted. The fourth view is that of the Catholic philosopher Sir Roger Scruton, which leads rather naturally into a final but brief explanation and application of Natural Law.

Adding to those four brief treatises, the subsequent section will address the understanding and admission of the human person in terms of biological and mental functions. That treatment will examine to what degree the conditions of functionality and mental capacity are able to determine what constitutes personhood. This present section and those that follow will each present available determiners in one's necessary quest to define personhood.

In the wake of the South African apartheid (early 1990s), the communal philosophy of Ubuntu became popularized. The healing of racial segregation was determined to come not from seeking retribution but from the unity and healing resolution to be found in Ubuntu. This was particularly the case with both Nelson Mandela (d. 2013), who was imprisoned twenty-seven years for his opposition to apartheid, and Anglican Bishop Desmond Tutu (d. 2021), who championed it as both a source of personal dignity and a model of forgiveness. Ubuntu is a philosophy of personhood that is often translated to mean "I am because we are." Ubuntu certainly has long-standing indigenous roots, though its present expression does seem to have been given form in the mid-nineteenth century and to have evolved to a social ethic by the latter part of the twentieth century. To hold that the "I" comes to be *from* the "We" is not to suggest one's personhood does not have an individual expression, only that there is a necessary relation that constitutes personhood between the values of the individual and the wider community.[18] This is to claim that the well-being of the community is never distinct from individual needs. It does not carry the connotation of social status as widely understood in the West, but there is a hierarchy of personhood present nonetheless. Children will have less personhood than elders and must respect them for the sake of representing their family community well. The same would be expected of in-laws, and this personhood extends to ancestors no longer living, as well as to children not yet conceived. This view of togetherness has some unique concepts. One is that if there is an offense, be it theft or murder, the social stigma of the thief might be understood as a reduction in personhood, while a marriage between the families of the murderer and the victim would be an attempt to reconcile the social ties. This is not a concept that easily translates into Western notions of community, justice, or ethics. The common character of the philosophy might analogously have implications similar to what the term *form* has held for the West. There are various takes on Ubuntu; and as a philosophy, it does not fit neatly into the concept of interior personhood as held by Descartes or the communal understandings of the two philosophers who will follow. But if personhood is tied to humanity, then not to regard another as a person affects all humanity, in the same way that each individual's personhood is tethered to another. The implications are relevant and will be considered shortly.

Concerning the thoughts of Martin Buber (d. 1965), this twentieth-century Jewish existentialist philosopher offered a view on personhood that speaks of the experience and meaning that can and must be found in personal relationships. There is a relation between each individual (an "I") and other persons (a "Thou"), where either one sustains the other or one objectifies the other, reducing the "Thou" to an "It." The "I-Thou" relation speaks of an integrity found in each person. Think of the notion of personhood as *being whole*. This *wholeness* then is recognized in the other person, so that the "other as an I" is never reduced to an "objectified It" that is no longer bound to the "I." Buber does speak of memories, but unlike the continuity of Locke or emotional import with Williams, he holds them as healing aspects to ground one in the present and not something to be analyzed for continuity of personhood. It might help to understand this notion as treating the *other* on their own terms, and not by what experience they provide. Then perhaps in contrast to

18. Nwoye, "An Africentric Theory," 53.

Ubuntu, Buber does not stress any degree of personhood dependent on such relationships, as for him, personhood is present by virtue of a divine image. In fact, though not sharing the divine image in the same way, the "I-Thou" relation extends even to nonhumans and inanimate created things. The human soul is not simply the Platonic soul that unites each person with another person, but a soul that unites all *with* the Creator. Consider that to overstress what unifies all created things can lead to collectivism, in much the same way that to underappreciate it falls prey to individualism. To balance that, Buber's view holds for mutuality, and anything short of that mutuality is also short of being a fully human person. This is to be understood as a reciprocity of persons. It is important to note that someone is not a person because of the other but because of *the consideration* of the other. So, it may be argued that if a person who has lost their memory from injury or disease cannot reciprocate, their personhood is sustained by the *wholeness* of the one who initiates the relation.[19] Personhood is only damaged when the other is reduced to an object and, once thus reduced to an "It," is treated as less than a person.

Ethicist Judith Jarvis Thomson (d. 2020), a prominent thinker who appears in the public abortion dialogue, considers the issue of dependence of one person to another, specifically the dependence of an unborn person on a pregnant female person. Thomson worked out some responses to the popularly known "trolley problems" proposed by philosopher Philippa Foot. Those trolley problems were designed to press an ethical judgment between two highly undesirable outcomes. If one does nothing, allowing the trolley to stay on the original track, that inaction results in the death of multiple people tied to the trolley tracks. But if one pulls the lever to redirect the trolley to another track, then the one person tied to that alternate track is *chosen* to be killed. Each remains an ethical choice, one of either inaction or direct action. The ethical question is which choice makes a person responsible, and to what degree. That scenario, although interesting, does not directly relate to the present concern. But addressing the undesirable outcome of abortion, Thomson offered a thought experiment, creating a dilemma of her own to test if there is a necessary ethical relationship that creates a duty on the part of the pregnant female to the unborn child. Her scenario is nearly universally referenced in the ethics of abortion and thus should be understood sufficiently. A point that should be made clear is that Thomson did not

19. Buber, *I and Thou*, 62.

argue against the personhood of the unborn. Her argument for the ethical case of abortion concerned weighing the female's prerogative against the fetus's needs. Here is a paraphrase of her proposal, with the intended parallels embedded in the description.

> A man with the suitable blood type has been kidnapped by the Society of Music Lovers, in order to save the life of a famous violinist who, worthy of being saved, lies unconscious with a failing kidney. The violinist will die without having the now-kidnapped person lying next to them, circulating blood for nine months (paralleling, of course, the fetus's dependence on the circulatory system of the female for the duration of a pregnancy). Now, this scenario is claiming that the famous violinist (representing the fetus in the analogy) has a right to live as a person. But does the violinist's (fetus's) right to live sufficiently compel the kidnapped man (pregnant female) to offer his body as the means to recovery. Or, with its meaning simply stated, although the fetus has a right to life and subsequent birth, the fetus does not have the right to compel the female to sustain it for nine months, any more than the kidnapped man can be compelled to sustain the famous violinist for nine months.[20]

One can easily see the clever import of Thomson's argument. First, it disarms any contention that an abortion is unethical because of the personhood of the unborn. It perhaps is not even strictly the bodily autonomy argument many currently make, as Thomson does not claim that because a female has bodily autonomy, she must be permitted to exercise an unlimited expression. Her point is that it would be ethical to extend one's body for the purpose of a transfusion (famous violinist) or gestation (fetus), but it remains a prerogative; thus, such an ethical claim cannot be mandated. So, it does remain a choice for the pregnant female and in that way upholds autonomy, but it is not clear from the thought experiment if, and to what degree, that prerogative wanes as the pregnancy progresses. In other words, though nine months might be too great an ethical imposition, would one month warrant the same evaluation? It is likely on her account that the time frame does not alter the proposal. Nonetheless, Thomson's claim offers consideration and scrutiny. Like the trolley problem, there remains an ethical choice where either inaction or direct action results in an undesired outcome that remains tethered to personal responsibility.

20. Thomson, "Defense of Abortion," 48–49.

Moving on, although of course there are many other relational philosophies of the human person to consider, the last individual whose ideas are to be explored here is the British philosopher Sir Roger Scruton (d. 2020). He intentionally attempts to strike a balance between a human person understood as a biological animal, which humans are, and the notion of personhood where empirical science must withdraw its competency. Scruton's field was philosophical aesthetics—broadly speaking, the study of beauty. Most think beauty is subjective and accept the often-heard maxim, "Beauty is in the eye of the beholder." Yet, prior to the Enlightenment, most all philosophers understood beauty as something objective. For example, Aristotle referred to beauty as the splendor of truth; and in his book *Metaphysics*, he presents *beauty as an ordering of symmetry*.[21] (Think of the beauty of mathematics as an example.) According to Aristotle, if this beauty was connected to truth, and truth was held as objective, then there is an objective aspect to beauty. But even if one thinks beauty is governed by taste, as in the "eye of the beholder," not all tastes or eyes are equal in their discriminatory tasting or seeing. If that were not true, one would have to accept that there are no standards for beauty and that one painting, movie, or novel is as good as any other. But holding to a standard for beauty, Scruton offers an analogy to speak to the objectivity of personhood: consider an oil portrait, where the pigments and canvas are akin to the biological material of the face. Beyond simply viewing the pigments, the beholder absorbs the beauty of the image beyond the physical. In other words, one does not see just pigments and brushstrokes but rather the whole image, which presents itself as this beautiful portrait. Could this beauty be an insight into how personhood is distinct from the biological material each human is composed of? In his book *On Human Nature*, Scruton holds that personhood emerges from the biological material in the same way the portrait's face emerges from the pigments and brushstrokes.[22] And as with Aristotle, by this reckoning, each person is capable of conceiving themselves as an "I" with (but not reduced to) their own material body. The human person, for him, cannot be reduced to some arrangement of matter, but rather is an embodied moral agent *bound* to others, either with or without the consent of another. What emerges from this image of the relational person is consciousness, and each human being's personhood

21. Aristotle, *Metaphysics*, Book XIII.3, 1078b1, 1705.

22. Scruton, *On Human Nature*, where he holds personhood as an "emergent feature" (31) and "a way of becoming" (110).

then is irreducible, inasmuch as the parts are not the person, for even the whole is inadequately described when isolated from others who possess a relational consciousness. Yet, although this "I" must be understood in relation to others, it is not dependently so; even in physical isolation, the "I" persists as a person in relation, regardless of any lack of the physical presence of the other.

Though Scruton was not directly making a Natural Law argument, it should be briefly addressed because that theory explicitly extends the inherent notion of relationality to all human individuals. First, Natural Law is not to be conflated with the Law of Nature; the latter pertains to necessary physical properties that guide empirical inquiry. That perhaps is one understanding of Kant's view from his *Critique of Pure Reason*, or perhaps even the naturalism from Hume's *Treatise of Human Nature*, where an understanding of such laws is accepted for being processes of nature. As a matter of fact, to the point at hand, that is what caused Hume to situate ethical evaluations in passion and sentiment rather than the empirical natural world. Further, the Law of Nature is also not what is found in the natural world, so it would exclude extending the polygynous mating of animals (single male, multiple females) or cannibalistic behavior among like species, to evidence the lifting of ethical restrictions for human beings because they are deemed natural. This means that simply observing that something occurs in the natural world (i.e., other animals do it without ethical qualms) is not sufficient reason for it to become an ethical standard for living human persons (therefore, the human animal can ethically do it). Offering those contrasts is important to disentangle the term *natural* from those connotations *in nature* or *of nature*, so as to avoid equivocation by restricting the term *natural* to what constitutes the *nature of the human person*.

Here is Natural Law explained. In ancient Greece, the Stoics' worldview accepted that god as Logos was a deity of order, and thus all of the world—and all in it—has some ordered stamp of divine design. There were variations and challenges to this theory. The empiricist Hume would find the idea of God problematic because this God could not be sensed; and Kant, though critical of religion overall, did hold to a rational faith where justice must align with God's design, which at least can be practically derived. But in contrast to each, what developed within Christianity first took what was deemed worthy from the Stoic vision of Natural Law. Then, not limiting it to either human rationality or knowledge derived from the senses alone, they found evidenced in the design of the human person certain attributable moral propositions given by God that were both authoritative and universal. It is important to understand that the term *law* for Christians cannot be reduced to a legal prescription or binding custom. As inherited from the Jewish faith, law as a pattern of belief was how God revealed himself to persons and to the world. In fact, the Roman philosopher Cicero (d. 43 BC) in his *De Re Publica* is credited with claiming that any *true law* should be accepted as "right reason in agreement with nature."[23] The Christian heritage adopted that definition, adding that it remain in accord with the common good. This then aligned with a view of Natural Law explicitly stated in Paul's letter to the Romans, which holds there is a *discernible nature perceived* in the things that have been made.

As the theory developed, the Oxford-trained Franciscan John Duns Scotus (d. 1308), known as the Subtle Doctor due to his finely nuanced arguments, extracted from this *discernible* reality of the created order certain standards that can be rationally deduced. Thus, for him, that which is proper to Natural Law forms an ethical stance, provided it is derived from the first principle. This first principle for Scotus, as a self-evident truth, is that God should be loved and, by extension, so should all created beings. Thirteenth-century Dominican theologian Thomas Aquinas (d. 1274) offered an expanded understanding of Natural Law, grounded in Aristotelian philosophy. He proposed five *natural inclinations* of the human person. These five inherent dispositions are discerned and observed from the design of the human person; when coupled with rational knowledge, they provide an ethic guiding one's action or judgments. For instance, for Natural Law, if X *is proper* for an authentic human goal, then X *ought to be done*, and if X *is not proper* for an authentic human goal, then X *ought not to be done*. As an example to the present point of this section, one such inclination is *relationality*. (Related inclinations, although not covered here, would include to do good and avoid evil, to seek truth, to preserve one's own life, and to procreate and educate offspring.) This relationality is not to be understood as mere interconnectedness, but an inherent need of the *other*. If the human person is made in the image of God, and this God ontologically is three Persons in relation, then it logically follows that the human person cannot exist in isolation from this God or other persons due to the ontological nature of their own being. Consider the idea of language as a practical example. It has as its goal

23. Cicero, *De Re Publica*, 240.

to communicate with another. If language is innate, which many contemporary linguists accept, then biologically the human person is *built* (designed?) to communicate—an action or function that presupposes some relation with others. Natural Law understood in this way locates a self-evident truth within human nature—here, relationality—that can be rationally grasped and thus presented as a law that *should* be ethically pursued as it is demonstrably good for the community of persons.

How, then, might these thinkers and philosophical positions on personhood affect and apply as ethical propositions to the public dialogue on abortion? Beginning once again with an African view of Ubuntu, the reality of personhood forms a tension. One consideration accepts that the unborn has less relational standing than a born person. This does not discount the personhood status of the unborn, but it does weigh the unborn's integration as "relationally less" than the contribution of the more fully integrated pregnant female. Practically, one might argue that Ubuntu could easily side with Thomson's view of what the pregnant female "owes" to the unborn, in terms of sustenance and continual care. However, it is not clear if the responsibility to preserve the female's well-being, though perhaps never entirely absent, is more pronounced when there is a threat to the pregnant female's life or livelihood. Yet, as persons being determined by their value to the larger community, each individual cannot be understood simply as a pure utilitarian metric, as in judging one's dignity by how much, and to whom, they contribute. Another person, even of lower moral value, still remains a beneficiary of communal welfare. The conversion of "I am, because we are" would not remain valid to become "Because I am, you are not."

So then, even if the relational status *determines* personhood, this does not suggest a crass individualism. That would violate the moral possibility of the human dignity of all within the community, including the unborn, living, and deceased. It becomes difficult to understand this view of personhood on a gradient that, unlike Western versions of utility, remains connected to communal well-being. It also should not be thought that this philosophy simply aligns with the Western notion of autonomy, which has taken on a "personal rights" connotation in the popular mind. For example, even if the unborn has a reduction of personhood compared to the pregnant female, it could be that the pregnant female herself has a significantly reduced personhood, where the calculus is not simply decided by the assertion that it is "her body" and therefore "her choice" to continue or terminate the pregnancy. Taken to the logical conclusion, one may argue that the reduced personhood of the unborn extends to the newly born who suffers from a debilitating condition. To argue otherwise, one would need to determine to what extent infanticide can be an autonomous choice for the new mother over the dependent newborn child. In a similar way that there exists a recognized relationality between the spouses, the result (the unborn) of their consensual sexual encounter can be conceived as an extension of their spousal relationality. This concept of "extended relationality" would be akin to the relation of spouses to a born child with severely diminished mental and functional capacities. The disabled child is cared for, and granted moral status, based on a dignity prescribed by those who care for the individual. This is not a possessive relation (spouses own the offspring), but perhaps a form of proxy where, in line with Ubuntu communal philosophy, the disabled child is granted dignity in their stead. Perhaps consider the thoughts of African theologian Bénézet Bujo (d. 2023), who wrote in his *Foundations of an African Ethic: Beyond the Universal Claims of Western Morality* that a life force (*Okra*) of the unborn is embraced both by the visible *and* invisible community formed by Ubuntu.[24] It appears his claim is more ontological, yet invokes that born "moral agents are taken to have a stringent moral duty to ensure the safe arrival, all things being considered, of the unborn."[25] However, one serious caution must remain in any positive or negative critique: not unlike all metaphysical approaches, each must be contextualized within the "world" in which they were formed and do exist. Both the language employed and the subsequent understanding that seeks application need to maintain a certain ethnocentric humility. This aids one to understand that exporting one worldview to another is not without risk of misinterpretation and lack of nuance. Nonetheless, Ubuntu requires respectful consideration in the public dialogue on abortion and offers an admirable insight into the role of relationality.

Returning to the thoughts of Martin Buber, nothing conclusive will be offered here either, as philosophers have used his "I and Thou" concept of personhood in defense of both stances. But the considerations are whether or not the unborn is reduced to an "It" by the circumstances or desires of the pregnant female, or if it is rather the pregnant female being reduced to an "It" by the requirement to carry the fetus to term. Following Buber's understanding of God as the ultimate "Thou" that is present

24. Bujo, *Foundations of an African Ethic*, 88–89.

25. Molefe, *African Ethics of Personhood*, 77.

in each "I" will compel one to ethically work out the nuance of affirming life at any stage, including fetal life, without simply equating to the unborn what may be proper only to a born person. Yet, Buber's notion of the human person as an "I-Thou" relation at least offers a sensible and credible basis for determining how and to what degree the personhood of the unborn (if that is accepted) relates to, and perhaps governs, the ethical judgment of an abortion in consideration of the pregnant female's personhood and the dignity that entails.

From Judith Jarvis Thomson's conversion to Judaism, it may be assumed her position is similar to Buber's. Even though her thought experiment accepts implicitly the personhood of the unborn, that may have simply been a mechanism to logically address the abortion issue without being bogged down over the argument of personhood. Yet, from that thought experiment directly addressing abortion, something clearer as a response can be gleaned. If, in fairness to an application of her "famous violinist" scenario, any critique is limited to pregnancies that are either unexpected or nonconsensual, one may begin with the premise that the condition of the pregnancy does not change the personhood status of the fetus. This was to claim that even the innocent life of the fetus as a person does not compel the pregnant female, who is also a person, to allow use of her body for nine months of gestation. A critique would begin that in order to sustain this analogy, one must equate the relation of the famous violinist and the kidnapped man with the relation of the unborn fetus and the pregnant female. In light of that, this thought experiment may seem a stretch, as the relationship between a pregnant female and the unborn is not the alien relationship of the kidnapped man to the famous violinist. But, perhaps in cases of unexpected or undesired pregnancies, this scenario maintains sufficient import. In that case, Thomson's thought experiment makes a strong point. When the pregnancy is not consensual, she may argue that an abortion is permissible because the fetus does not have "permission" to use the female's body, even though as a person the fetus does have a right to life. This condition appears to equally extend to serious threats to the female's physical life. Now, it was not Thomson's intention to limit this argument to rape or unintended pregnancies, though that does appear to be a sensible application. So, with Thomson's scenario, one may circumvent the notion of fetal personhood derailing either stance; but the analogy must be consistently applied, and the conclusions logically accepted regardless of one's position, for any fruitful dialogue to ensue.

The last individual thinker examined earlier, Sir Roger Scruton, was a Roman Catholic whose views on the ethics of abortion aligned dogmatically with the Church. One might do well in beginning to consider his position in terms of a view to beauty. As beauty became subjective at the onset of the Enlightenment, so too by Scruton's account did the objectivity of truth wane. This worldview then produced a *false consensus* that resulted in an impoverished ethical view of the human person, whose value must then be granted rather than recognized. Thus, perhaps one can argue in his stead that this evolved subjectivity further calculated a "human right" to be an extension of the individual will, rather than one connected to an objective inclination. Then from that, the collective will of a populace ultimately becomes enshrined as a right reducible to an expression of the State. Further, whether one intends to uphold bodily autonomy or the life of the unborn, it follows that opposition to or support for abortion will be framed as the legal violation of a "human right," and not a right predicated on human nature. Further, it will not simply enter into the ethical arena from the legal sphere but will ethically be presupposed as a criminal offense. This is because in any ethical case, not being able to attach the objective judgment as an authentic good of the human person (as with beauty) can only be absorbed by society as a legal prescription. This then forms each "side" to determine what is ethical for the other "side," inasmuch as civil law, once championed, can compel others to abide by the legal finding and force legal adherence. Once the underpinning of this logical evolution of the "ethic-to-legal prescription" is forgotten, which usually happens in a generation, then those who inherit such an evaluation tend to only determine what is unethical by what is legally impermissible (e.g., it has been like such and such for forty years). The contrary then rationally follows, that because something is legally permissible, it is therefore held as ethical because the pendulum swung with the law in what is interpreted as a corrective measure. At that point, one is faced with a circular fallacy, where "if A, then B" is accepted as readily as "if B, then A." Once a law can no longer explicitly express the preferred ethical judgment in society, then those who hold to a differing ethical evaluation recognize the law as an unethical civil imposition. This is true whether it is to support a female's right to bodily autonomy or to support the life of the unborn. The critique (and the frustration) is that opposition to the State or anyone "telling others how to live" in society cannot seem to be disentangled from the fact every ethical judgment excludes the goals of those who are opposed to it on principle. Therefore, by logical implication, every position or stance excludes "the rights" of those who do not experience the judgment positively. The irony is that such frustration with a law not aligning with one's stance tends to default to a libertarian position. From that point, one returns to the "bad" argument thinking it is simply wrong to "tell others how to live," lamenting that their ethical position is not framed by civil law. Again, this is an extension of the objectivity Scruton would hold of the human person and, by extension, to the unborn. It is not one he has explicitly made. But it is based on an anthropology he accepts in view of beauty and the human person. And it is logically in line with his notion of the *calculus of rights forming duties*, which, unless tethered to a discernible and stable human nature, results in the tyrannical imposition of a subjective and *false consensus*. Finally, any opposing stance deemed in conflict with a perceived and likely unarticulated human right is expressed as unethical, where the ethical correction lies solely in the domain of civil sphere.

Prior to explicating this last segment of the relational considerations of personhood concerning Natural Law, notice that those previous thinkers or philosophical positions, although embedded in theological traditions (perhaps with the exception of Ubuntu, though there is an intertwined history), did not form their arguments dogmatically. Both Buber, who worked out the "I-Thou" relation, and Scruton, who connected beauty to objectivity, formed their theories rationally. Neither habituated their positions directly to Sacred Scriptures or theological traditions, in order to prove their understanding of relationality. The same may be said of the formation and subsequent use of Natural Law theory. This theory holds that the human person is imbued with rational knowledge and, from this ability to reason, can deduce from human nature certain universal and objectively binding ethical standards. It is a nondogmatic appeal to something outside of each individual. As a historical example, consider civil rights activist Martin Luther King Jr. (d. 1968), who pleaded a Natural Law argument in his "Letter from Birmingham Jail." When he was unjustly arrested for protesting, he argued that he did not break any law, but that the *supposed* anti-segregation law under which he was legally charged was in fact not a law at all; therefore, because he had not *really* broken a law, his charge and arrest were unjustifiable.[26] King, quoting the previously mentioned Thomas Aquinas, borrowed his argument that any civil law not embedded and in accord with Natural Law

26. King, in *Testament to Hope*, 293–94.

is, by virtue of that fact, not a law at all. In fact, King also quoted Buber's "I-Thou" principle, directly concerning the unjust segregation he was protesting, citing the false sense of superiority one senses by reducing another "Thou" to an "It."

This Natural Law tradition has an ancient history. The Stoics' version begins with the consideration of an observed purposeful order of the world, while the Christians developed it further by locating from this ordered design an inclination of the human person as created *imago Dei*. Natural Law does presuppose a worldview (metaphysical position) as the framework by which one recognizes the reality of such a design or order. But every metaphysical position requires a presupposition—a starting point without which one cannot build a worldview. One can argue that a theistic worldview (design) is necessary for this relational view of human personhood and thus Natural Law, but it cannot be argued that an atheistic worldview (no design) is a default position and therefore correct because it appears untainted by religious underpinnings. Every individual, either consciously or unconsciously, forms and adheres to a metaphysical position. Even those who deny having a metaphysical position do indeed have one. In fact, not being aware of one's metaphysical position likely means that one has a *poor* metaphysical position. Then everything that filters through that metaphysical position, which happens necessarily, is filtered through an *unknown* and possibly *poor* metaphysical stance. So, returning to Natural Law, it sets out to form an ethical implication that is universally binding on all. In terms of personhood, neither *the order* nor *inclinations* are tethered to any individual's value (worth) or function (ability). As inherent qualities of the human person, moral value is necessarily tethered to human nature, and cannot be severed from the fact that each individual simply belongs to the human species.

So, in that regard, what is inherent in a born person is also inherent in an unborn person, and thus abortion is a violation of Natural Law. That being said, the differing version as proposed by the seventeenth-century English philosopher Thomas Hobbes (d. 1679) might very well be in contrast to that claim, contending certain liberties must be curtailed for the sake of civil order. Thus, in his *Leviathan*, some such liberties must be surrendered to a sovereign. But it neither is clear nor settles to what extent the ideas of liberty and life are in conflict given his analysis, even if it might be easier to argue he elevated life over liberty. In short, it is unsettled as to how one might form the judgment on abortion, given his perspective. With the Thomistic version of Natural Law, it does draw again from the Epistle to the Romans that "they [all peoples] are without excuse"[27] and thus are bound to its precepts. But the primary precepts (natural inclinations) must be rationally engaged to form secondary precepts. And those secondary precepts are not, per se, absolute. Here is what is meant by that: the primary precept to *preserve one's own life* rationally leads to the secondary precept to *preserve another's life*. For example, if as a primary precept an individual (the "I") cannot harm themselves, then it forms a secondary precept that another individual (the other "I") cannot be harmed and thus their life too must be preserved. By the way, that is a Natural Law argument against murder. Notice it rationally "makes the case" against murder, without an appeal to the dogmatic commandment "Thou shall not kill." This secondary precept further extends to a third level, or what is referred to as a *remote precept*, where it remains rationally arrived at, but the application is more difficult for some to grasp. An example would be the Principle of Double Effect, and from it the determination to what degree and in what manner another's life might be preserved when there is a foreseen, but unintended and undesirable, consequence. Recall that PDE made a distinction, arguing that saving the life of a pregnant female with endometrial cancer by removing the uterus and fetus was not considered a direct abortion.

One final thought on Natural Law is worth making clear. The idea of freedom is typically understood in contemporary society as a *lack of restraint*. Under that notion, any form of law seems to be an imposition on one's freedom as one incurs restraint. But according to this ethical theory, if the choice is in line with one's design, then freedom becomes defined as *doing what one is designed to do*. An analogy to bodily health and human physiology offers an easy way to understand this. If a type of food is known to be in line with the body's physiology, then *eating* that healthy food is not an imposition or "external law," meaning one should eat it to maintain bodily wellness. Rather, it should be understood that *not eating* the healthy food will result in a lack of bodily wellness. So, even though an individual may balk at a physician's nutrition standards for bodily health, it is not seen as an arbitrary standard imposed on the individual. With Natural Law, then, in the same way that to "eat what is good for the body" is not an impediment to *doing what one is designed to do*, then to follow a discernible inclination of human nature is also *doing what one is designed to do*. Rather than signifying a lack of freedom,

27. Rom 2:15b, *Revised Standard Version, CE*.

bodily health and natural inclinations can each be understood and upheld to be expressions of freedom. To work against one's own ethical good founded on an objective inclination, as Martin Luther King Jr. explained, would not be in accord with Natural Law. Anything otherwise would be considered going against one's nature and thus a lack of freedom. The point is that according to Natural Law, any right to bodily autonomy or fetal life would have to argue to a sense of freedom in line with a discernible design that can ethically support an action, or inaction, by applying reason to human nature.

PERSONHOOD, CAPACITY, AND FUNCTIONALITY

The claim thus far is not that personhood is *never* considered in the public abortion dialogue, but only that it is *rarely* considered—and when it does become a factor, more often than not the stance precedes the determination. Stated colloquially, it could be framed as, "My position on abortion is X, so therefore my view on whether the unborn living human is a person is Y, because of X." Those who first make an ontological argument for the unborn and then use it as the determiner weighed against the female's bodily autonomy are in that *rare* category. But when personhood does enter the dialogue as a stand-alone factor, it tends in the popular mind to be derived from some value assigned to a capacity, or from the unborn living human's degree of functionality. This section will not be exhaustive, but from the variety of capacities and functions available for consideration, among those to be examined are *fetal heartbeat*, the detection of *brain activity*, fetal *pain sensation*, and the *birth event*, with a more extensive review offered on fetal and infant *consciousness*. For the sake of expediency, each of these considerations will be presented as the possible onset of personhood and therefore the threshold at which the ethical consideration of an abortion will become doubtful. The value of the female's bodily autonomy is not discounted but would necessarily be measured against the value of the unborn or infant if either is deemed a human person. The basic parameters will be offered for each consideration, with no attempt to settle them as an ethical judgment.

One central concern to evaluating the impact of each of these considerations, likely from both sides of the public abortion issue, is that if one capacity or function is conceded as the threshold of personhood, then such an admission would be a tactic for *incrementally* slipping closer to the oppositional stance. Often, because of that possibility alone, any rational consideration of changing one's mind is rejected, such that stubbornly holding a present position forms the defense tactic of maintaining the original stance. The result is that dialogue ceases and ideological or dogmatic stances become more entrenched. That predicament warrants consideration prior to evaluating the actual capacities and functions as potential, positional boundaries, for determiners of personhood and the subsequent ethical judgment.

The concern of incrementally slipping closer to the oppositional stance is known as the *slippery slope*. It is a commonly used term, but one not commonly understood well. The basic argument is that if one accepts some claim or judgment, then it will lead to the acceptance of the next claim or judgment in the logical chain. The overarching concern is that eventually this will conclude in an undesired stance or repugnant advocacy. To map it, if judgment A is accepted and thus conceded, then that might open the door to necessarily accepting judgment B. That only leaves one last "slip" to judgment C, which will alter one's advocacy for the pro-choice or pro-life stance. In the popular mind, it seems like a logical tug-of-war where the loss is repugnant, so to gain or impede the momentum becomes the ultimate strategy.

The *slippery slope* argument is so effective because it is both easy to understand and also sometimes true. It happens that the acceptance of one judgment can logically lead to the acceptance of another judgment. The importance of considering it here, in terms of capacities and functions, is that if one biological function or capacity of the developing fetus is accepted or rejected as a criterion for personhood, each side is concerned that then the next one will become the new battlefront. In short, the concern is that the goalposts will move in favor of the side who wins the point *for or against* the personhood of the fetus.

Sometimes when confronted with this approach, it is resisted by citing it as a logical fallacy. What is lesser known is that the slippery slope argument can be a fallacy, but it is not *always* a fallacy. So it is neither a good strategy nor constructive to the public abortion dialogue to consider all sequential logical connections a *slippery slope* fallacy. But it is equally important, if not more so, to know when it is a fallacy and thus how to counter it. It is a fallacy *only* if the underlying premises that connect A to B to C have changed; otherwise, the argument may be not only valid but also sound and thus should be logically adopted.

Here is an example of how a slippery slope argument should be accepted to a certain point, but rejected when it becomes a fallacy. At the cusp of the third millennium, smoking began to be banned in public restaurants on the premise that (A) authorities must safeguard health in public establishments. Some people argued that the authorities would eventually (B) ban smoking in public bars next. Advocates of the smoking ban tried to alleviate the concern of those who believed in "smoking rights" by claiming that if the bar does not serve food, there will be no concern for a sequential smoking ban. However, the premise was not simply that they served food but that "authorities must safeguard health in public establishments." Both the restaurants and the bars were public establishments, and the "smoking rights" advocates knew that. In this slippery slope scenario, discrediting step B (banning smoking in bars) was disingenuous on the part of the ban advocates, and resisting the next step was a legitimate concern for the smoking advocates. Since a restaurant is a public establishment, and public "authorities must safeguard health in public establishments by banning smoking," that premise (A) used in restaurants was logically applied to bars (B). Historically, this was borne out, as it was not long after public restaurants banned smoking that public bars followed suit. Yet, nothing up until this point constitutes a slippery slope fallacy. The same premise (authorities must safeguard health in public establishments) was applied to both restaurants and bars. Yet, further concerns among some smoking advocates arose. They felt that because of this "borne out" sequential result (from restaurants to bars), eventually the smoking ban would "slip" further and extend to individual homes. But to sustain that logical progression, the ban advocates would have to change the premise of "authorities must safeguard health in public establishments" to "authorities must safeguard health in private homes." As the premise changed, so did the fundamental conditions change for the argument, creating a slippery slope fallacy.

The point, as it relates to the topic of abortion, is a concern that any acceptance of an earlier (or later) functional criteria or capacity marker will cause the advocacy position for either the female's bodily autonomy or the life of the unborn to ebb or wane, to the degree those positions are accepted to be the onset of personhood for the unborn. But like the previous analogy, the underlying premise for each functional criteria or capacity marker should be the concern. It would remain to be seen to what degree any connecting premises can be sustained in the chain argument, but it is a lapse in critical thinking to simply argue in opposition to a true premise out of concern for how else that same premise might be applied. All involved in the conversation should concede to reasonable premises and logically accept valid and sound arguments, regardless of their present stance.

To keep the scenarios simple, so as to make the points relevant for illustrative purposes, recall it will be accepted that each of the criteria or functions addressed bears enough moral value, equivalent to personhood, in order to question the ethics of an abortion. That is to say, for the sake of argument, each will be considered the threshold, after which one *should* not abort the fetus.

The first idea to examine is the functional criteria of a *fetal heartbeat*. It has become popular for pro-lifers to argue that the detection of a fetal heartbeat is the threshold for an ethical abortion. The reason is not explicitly stated as to why a heartbeat qualifies a living human to be considered as a person, but that is the weight behind the claim. Now, there is a certain logic at play in ascribing the onset of a heartbeat as a marker for personhood, as the end of personhood (death of biological life) is thought in the popular mind to be determined by the cessation of a beating heart. The issue with this logic is that it may be a false equivalence. For example, nonlife follows the loss of a heartbeat, but nonlife is not what precedes the onset of a heartbeat. The latter is known as death, but there is no corresponding concept for the former, as the unborn prior to a heartbeat is biologically living. So, death is accepted as the end of personhood, but do the beginning stages of a vital organ warrant the same threshold for the onset of personhood? The conversation, being scientifically informed, has begun to speak of those early stages of this development not as a heartbeat, but rather as "cardiac activity." Technically, they are distinct. In consideration of those two terms, critical thinking reveals that the gestational age (GA) difference between cardiac activity (six weeks GA) and a fetal heartbeat (nine weeks GA)[28] is only three weeks. That is not significant; if the pro-choicer concedes to fetal heartbeat or the pro-lifer concedes to cardiac activity, there are negligible gains or losses for either stance. The question to ask is this: if the pro-choicer succeeds in arguing the onset of personhood is not determined by a fetal heartbeat at nine weeks, does that then concede that an abortion is unethical *after* nine weeks GA, once cardiac activity is present? The pro-choicer would not accept that judgment. Likewise, if the pro-lifer

28. See Omni, "How Soon?," para. 4. Using a standard stethoscope, the heartbeat is audible by 20–22 weeks.

succeeds in arguing the onset of personhood is determined by a fetal heartbeat at six weeks, does that then concede that an abortion is ethical *before* that six weeks GA? The pro-lifer would not accept that judgment. The centrality of the personhood argument as a determiner for moral value, which is the central theme of this section, is not affected by the nuance between those two terms. Discussing a distinction between cardiac activity and a fetal heartbeat is interesting, and differentiating the two is accurate, but it is not productive for setting the onset of personhood. The discussion is merely interested in incrementally gaining ground toward a concession if either side accepts the other's position. Interestingly, though, the pro-choicers' issue with this distinction (and the reason they prefer the term *cardiac activity*) is that when medical professionals allow the pregnant female to listen to the baby's "heartbeat" during imaging, they are rightly concerned that such phrasing psychologically *projects* certain sentiments to the unborn. So, perhaps this is a varied element of the aesthetic issue addressed earlier, where sentiment is brought into the dialogue as an emotional appeal.

Another major consideration to mark the onset of personhood is *fetal brain development*. A related concern is consciousness, but that will be addressed separately. Perhaps it is best to understand there are levels of consciousness, as there are phases of brain development. That may help keep the terms *brain function* and *consciousness* separate at this juncture. The brain is an organ—not in the same way that the liver or the skin is an organ, but each organ does have its distinct biological functions. Each person, as they deliberate on this issue, will have to judge to what extent they hold that the brain *is* the mind. A scientific materialist would hold that the "material" brain *is* the mind, where the processes of the mind are simply the result of the brain's interaction with the physical environment. In the same way, someone who accepts immaterial reality (spiritual?) would consider that the brain *is not* the mind, but rather that the brain is the material organ of the "immaterial" mind. This must be considered for clarity in the abortion conversation, where each is permitted to form their metaphysical view and be critiqued in accordance with their own internal consistencies or inconsistencies. Nonetheless, the important consideration here is the determination of "brain activity" and the presence of sufficient conditions, since that is what can and will be measured.

A further consideration is not simply the presence of brain activity, but the *level* of such brain activity that would be the benchmark to determine personhood. The reason is that even in the determination of human death, there is a distinction between higher brain functions and whole brain death. The term *higher brain* typically refers to cerebral abilities that provide memory and awareness. For those who hold that *the human person is the mind*, this is critical. If the mind is the brain and by that they mean "high brain," then by their account, the degree to which memory and awareness are necessary conditions for personhood would be the degree to which personhood could be present. In contrast, the term *whole brain* would then include the functions of the stem that regulate breathing and heart rate, among other basic bodily functions. Contemporary bioethics relies on the moral certainty of whole brain death prior to declaring one deceased, and thus it stands as a determiner for the loss of personhood, which legally precedes the possibility of vital organ donation.

On the surface, it may seem noncontroversial to argue that vital organs should only be harvested from a brain-dead deceased donor. But it is not that simple, or the dead donor rule (DDR) would not be necessary. In fact, some currently claim it should be re-examined, if not altogether abandoned. First, the idea of brain death (BD), introduced in the United States in 1968,[29] has persisted in its common form since 1981. The controversy centers around several questions: (1) what standard is used (inconsistent BD criteria by clinical state?); (2) whether the standard is a barrier to other goods (patient missing opportunity to donate vital organs?); (3) if there can be an agreed-upon standard (honest dispute over what constitutes BD?); and, if so, then (4) whether the agreed-upon standard is even followed uniformly by medical professionals (some using less rigorous BD criteria). In each of these considerations, moral certainty is required, but justice requires consistency and fair evaluation. But again, the term *justice* needs to be explicated. Is it *just* for a willing donor to slip into unconsciousness with the full expectation of having their vital organs donated, only for the family to experience that once extubated the patient persisted past the point of organ viability? The other side of the issue is that there remains a certain line between the moral certainty of irreversible cessation of brain activity, prior to vital organ removal. Otherwise, what was thought to be the ethical removal of vital organs then causes the death of the patient. If one is in error, even legally, then the donation is no longer *just* and can be classified as homicide.

29. See De Georgia, "History of Brain Death," 673.

One very real issue is that, in some cases, conscious brain activity has been discovered in the hypothalamus even after all other BD criteria have been met. Though rare, some individuals have regained consciousness and, without alluding to any out-of-body experience, have explained in great detail what they witnessed from their bed. Without expanding on any of this end-of-life concern, the purpose in introducing it is to call attention to the difficulty in determining the moment all brain activity ceases and thus when to ethically declare the person to be dead. The point is that those trying to determine the beginning of brain development will likely encounter the same uncertainties. Therefore, as empirical science continues to unravel what is known about brain development during the fetal stages, the findings may not provide any clearer moral judgment. For the public dialogue on abortion, there arises the concern of getting bogged down in each newly discovered scientific insight of fetal brain development. It can leave the impression that this issue is unable to be settled—or, if it can be settled, that it will be determined by empirical science. The term *functioning brain* is not clear; and though science will contribute greatly in this regard, science will not discover that the functioning brain *is* the person. The subsequent arguments will center around disagreements over the point at which the development of the brain becomes sufficient to possess the aspects of personhood that society then can claim to value. If one engages in the argument that personhood begins when electrical activity can first be detected, then that places the onset of personhood at eight weeks GA. If one rather argues that personhood does not begin until there is enough organization of the brain to warrant a claim it can function to do A or B, or possess the capacity to do C or D, then those particular functions and capacities must also be logically accepted as markers for the cessation of personhood (that is, the markers of death). That, simply stated, is the expectation of ethical consistency. Again, broader considerations first warrant scrutiny. Specifically for those in dialogue, it is critical to first consider if the brain *is* the mind, which would lead to some level of brain function determining personhood that includes some living humans and excludes others. The other option is that the brain *is not* the mind, in which case there then exist other identifiable notions to define what constitutes a living human as a person.

The next consideration, that of *pain sensation* of the unborn, arises as a sympathy concern for abortion advocates, as well as an emotional tool used by those opposed to a female's bodily autonomy. The fundamental question is at what point does the unborn human life experience pain? It is considered unethical, even by abortion advocates, to inflict pain on nonhuman animals. In fact, such an occurrence is referred to as *inhumane* (etymologically formed by *in*- as "non," thus "nonhuman"), so it should apply more so to an unborn human animal, regardless of the stage of fetal development. In short, it is uncomfortable to even consider that the unborn might experience pain during an abortion. With that sentiment in mind, those opposed to abortion present the experience of pain as a cruelty factor that requires consideration. The concern is whether or not the brain is sufficiently formed and the nervous system sufficiently developed for the unborn to experience the sense of pain. The key phrase to focus on is not simply *to sense pain*, but *to experience pain*. They are not the same thing, and that will require unpacking. First, there is no straightforward response to determine what is required anatomically to sufficiently form a judgment that the unborn has such a capacity. The question is how one would verify the sensing of pain? There are parts of the brain that specialize in interpreting chemical signals to detect physical threats, such as heat, pressure, or other various stimuli. This signal interpretation, known physiologically as *nociception*, is how the nervous system reacts to such triggers.[30] But to maintain that an abortion is unethical, premised on the procedure itself causing pain to the unborn, the argument cannot simply demonstrate a reaction to painful stimuli, but must address what unfolds as the experience of pain.

There is wide scientific consensus that the brain cortex is necessary for the sensing of pain, and also that the cortex does not sufficiently form until the third trimester—that is, on or near the point of viability. Yet, some research holds that pain receptors develop in the first trimester, so there perhaps are neural pathways present much earlier than current consensus concludes. The underlying purpose of this text is how to develop a logical strategy that addresses issues with competing claims. Here, it is seductive to think empirical knowledge and brain science will settle the public abortion issue, where each side awaits the latest research to use as ammunition in the debate. Those of the pro-choice stance can correctly explain the distinction between sensing and experiencing pain. Ultimately, it only removes the emotional burden of having to imagine that the fetus, while being dismembered during a dilation and curettage procedure (D&C), may sense pain but not hold an experience of pain.

30. See Armstrong and Herr, "Physiology, Nociception."

Even with other methods used in the first trimester, such as medication abortion, which purges the uterus, or a vacuum aspiration, which uses an anesthetic while a vacuum tube is inserted, the same distinction between sensing and experiencing is necessary to demonstrate. Extreme examples are rare, but they often provide the means to analyze an issue ethically. So as an ethical case study, and to play devil's advocate, even though the percentage of abortions after the twenty-fourth week are likely less than 1 percent of all procured abortions,[31] it is a fair question to ask if the *experiencing* of pain should be a consideration for abortions in at least those instances.

One cannot fear what one has not experienced, either personally or by explanation. That is why toddlers must be protected from the dangers of electrical outlets or an open flame on a stove. Once experienced or explained, then the pain from some external source is not simply sensed, but feared. This then creates a pain experience. As previously mentioned, the term *future memories* represented the philosopher Bernard Williams pushing back on Locke's view of personhood. Recall that for Locke the human person was determined by psychological continuity (memories); but Williams demonstrated through a thought experiment (apprehension of future torture) that an event not yet *sensed* could nonetheless cause development of anxiety and thus a painful yet present *experience*. The point is that it is one thing to *sense* a painful stimuli, and another thing for that painful stimuli to be *experienced* as pain. So, in the case of fetal pain and the experience of pain, is the experience simply the pain event, or the psychological fear of the pain event? The psychological fear includes the unpleasantness associated with anticipation of the pain event, so the ethical judgment may therefore not be the same for an unborn as for a conscious toddler or adult experiencing a pain event. But that aside, simply because a pain event may or may not produce psychological fear does not make the intentional cause of pain ethical. For example, would the use of anesthesia satisfy the ethical qualms for abortions later in pregnancy? That would certainly mitigate the sensing of pain; and since the unborn experiences no anticipation of the abortion, there could also be no argument for psychological apprehension. The reality is that such an argument would not satisfy most in the pro-life stance, and it would seem closer to a euthanasia argument for those holding to the pro-choice stance. One can see how this line of reasoning will not solve

31. KFF, "What the Data Show," para. 2.

the issue. And to the point of this section, it is clear that personhood is not convincingly predicated on either pain sensitivity or experience. The scientific evaluation of what is *sufficient* to declare that the unborn will sense or experience pain at point A should be part of the public dialogue, but it has limited import. Admittedly, the sensing and experiencing of pain for the unborn will likely remain a sympathy concern for abortion opponents and an emotional tool against those opposed to a female's bodily autonomy. Empirical science will offer insights as this concern develops. But if one judges that the unborn (dependent on the stage) *is a person*, then whether or not the unborn senses or experiences pain is an aggregating element to demonstrate an atrocity but would not alter the pro-life judgment that an abortion *is unethical*. Likewise, if one judges the unborn *is not a person* (dependent on the stage), then whether or not the unborn senses or experiences pain is a deliberating element for a more compassionate termination but would not alter the pro-choice judgment that an abortion *is ethical*.

Now, in consideration of the *birth event* being the onset of personhood, whether vaginal or cesarean, some aspects have already been addressed. Here they will briefly be restated, and then further factors will be considered. It is worth noting that viability also is a persistent marker, but it is distinct from the birth event. The ethical issue of personhood relative to viability will be directly addressed in the chapter "The Arguments Ahead" under the section "Future human wombs." So, here with birth as a marker, the strongest point to be made is if one speaks of the unborn's personhood in terms of independence or in terms of entering into society as a tangible and autonomous being. It is true that a born infant, as with adult living humans that have limited functions or capacities, is not entirely independent, as others are necessary for care and personal needs. But the point stands that any born living human is not physiologically dependent as is a fetus in utero. In fact, this is likely the major reason the birth event marks a legal definition of personhood, where rights can be ascribed and legal protections can apply. In the previous section "The value of bodily autonomy," it was stated that to be both correct and accurate, this legal personhood arrives only once the unborn's head has vacated the vaginal cavity of the female. At that point, even prior to the cutting of the umbilical cord (provided the infant is past the point of viability), the now-born infant is capable of surviving without sharing the circulatory system of the child-bearing female. But an advocate for the birth event as the marker of personhood will have to address any relationship between prenatal and postnatal dependence of care and sustenance from the female (or some surrogate) for continued post-birth maturation. In fact, Thomson's "famous violinist" thought experiment unwittingly probed that logic in the analogy. The ethical question is whether the same premise could be extended to post-birth care. In Thomson's analogy, the born individual is a person just as the fetus is a person. Thomson argued that the kidnapped man was under no ethical mandate to remain attached via blood lines to the famous violinist. Though the violinist was recognized as a person, the kidnapped man retained the prerogative to withdraw essential support. The point was that it logically follows that the pregnant female was under no ethical mandate to remain attached via "blood lines" to the fetus, who, regardless of the personhood recognition, could not override the female's prerogative to withdraw essential support. It appears that the premise is not simply a physiological dependency (physically tethered), but perhaps can extend to the interdependencies of caregiver and born child for all necessary postnatal care and sustenance. In short, can such postnatal care be an ethical mandate, if the prenatal care is not? The applied critical thinking would need to investigate whether the pregnant female's bodily autonomy in Thomson's scenario can ethically (and logically) extend to the bodily autonomy of the post-birth female or caregiver. The public dialogue does need to address this, in the determination of the birth event as a marker for the onset of personhood.

What makes the birth event marker of personhood both persistent and unique is that there are few who would consider the "minute-past-birth" living human to not be a person. The ethical question then to ask is if the "minute-past" post-born person is any less of a living human than the fetus a minute prior to birth; and further, if so, why and under what conditions? One of the dilemmas with those who hold the birth event as a marker is that there is no developmental distinction between a "minute-past" born person and a "minute-prior" unborn fetus (except for the difference of both location and physiological dependence, which was previously considered). For many, regardless of stance, the moral value of the child *during delivery* does not seem to be reduced because of any lack of separation from the female, and the moral value *after delivery* does not seem to increase merely because of separation from the female. If that is the case, then the separation from the female (birth event) would be a weak marker to suggest as the criteria for personhood. Yet, because it is so popularly held that living humans become persons at birth, sufficient reflection gives way to impulsive acceptance.

Two concepts have been confirmed. First, it was already stated that legal personhood begins at the birth event. It was also stated that one should be vigilant not to fall prey to allowing the legality (or illegality) of something to form the basis of an ethical judgment. Recall that when one generation enshrines in law, the subsequent generation that inherited the law deems those who adhere to it as following an ethical course. The converse is also true, that what is legally impermissible during the age one is born into will appear unethical by default during one's lifetime. A legalistic ethic, the idea that an ethic is determined by what is legally prescribed, can be an adherence to the whims of an age and thus not the development of an intentional ethical stance. It is the equivalent of comparing dead wood floating down the stream to an individual intentionally fighting the cultural current. But remaining within the context that a living human "becomes" a person at the birth event, it logically follows that to voluntarily terminate the life of a newborn is infanticide and thus unethical (and currently illegal). Then an inconsistency surfaces when, in some instances, the murder of a voluntarily pregnant female can be criminally tried as a double homicide. The inconsistency is that the prosecutor would not require the pregnant female's evaluation of the personhood of the unborn fetus, to warrant a charge of homicide for the fetus (which is the killing of a human person). That is, if the pregnant female terminated the life of her own fetus, it is not homicide; but if another terminated the life of her fetus, it could be classified as a homicide. One must reconcile the logical conundrum of advocating for the female's autonomy, which would support the choice of an intentional and legal termination of the unborn under usual circumstances, with the designation that the termination of the unborn during the homicide of the pregnant female is now a double homicide because it was the intentional killing of the female *and* the unborn, both designated as persons. That disparity between the ethical view and the legal precedents has not gone unnoticed. But despite it being a double standard, it still does not advance the issue of what constitutes personhood. It might be framed as follows: the pregnant female was murdered; the child, who was "wanted," was also a victim of the attack; and thus the moral value was extended from the female to the unborn who had a future expectation of personhood. But here is an ironic thought experiment: if the female and unborn were to survive the attack, and one week later the female had an elective abortion, what would have previously warranted the charge of attempted homicide is just one week later a choice in line with the female's expression of her autonomy. This is clearly an equivocation that has crept into the legal system.

There are two basic points to the brief criticism of the legal recognition of birth as the onset of personhood. First is to demonstrate the flaw of any legalistic reduction of ethics. Laws form precedents; but when acclimated to the current political will of the culture, if they prove unjust to a future society, reform is necessary. In justice, the law should reflect an ethical judgment; but in terms of personhood, the law must be predicated on an exterior standard. The other concern for the public dialogue is to disentangle an ontological grasp of personhood from a customary one, in which the birth event has long stood as seminal. The birth event can be observed. A recognized identity of the born person is legally certified by the day, month, and year. That is significant, for neither the moment of fertilization nor onset of ontological personhood is identified or recorded. The moment of birth is quite tangible, and the previously prenatal living human, now a born infant, can be recognized by others in society. A strong case can be made for the legal recognition of a born infant as a person, as many rights and privileges become attached to being a citizen of any jurisdiction. The public abortion dialogue must address that; but if it is to be held as the onset of personhood, one must demonstrate a convincing distinction that withholds personhood from the pre-delivery living human and the living human during delivery. Also needed is a clear distinction of how the post-birth dependency and sustenance differ significantly from the prenatal state to the necessary conditions of postnatal care, so that the latter level of dependency does not forfeit personhood where prenatally it did. These are but a few of the concerns that need to be addressed, if one is to hold that the birth event is the onset of personhood.

Finally then, one should consider the varietal parameters that may form the claim of *consciousness* being the onset of personhood. This treatment will be more substantial, as consciousness will be the criterion of the personhood argument, in the *some living humans are persons* framework. There is a lot to digest with the concept of consciousness, and more that could not be summarized or categorized. Understanding that alone should grant caution in the public dialogue. But pressing forward, there are three broad categories pertaining to consciousness, which include materialism, idealism, and dualism. Multiple layers and nuances exist within each of those main categories, and arguments abound as to the distinction of the thinkers who will be introduced. Many, if not most, thinkers do not fit neatly into one of those categories; in all honesty, as will be presented here, theists tend toward an outlier, integral approach. This treatise on consciousness is to serve only illustrative purposes. The main concern is to offer a sampling, so one may consider how an acceptable expression of consciousness may be the onset of personhood under the particular parameters by which each might make a judgment. It will not be exhaustive, and admittedly the risk of oversimplification remains. Importantly, no attempt will be made to present a definitive argument for why one expression or thinker may or may not be materialist, idealist, or dualist, though some tensions may be introduced. What must be kept in mind with each of these systems are the implications they hold. If consciousness is *the* factor constituting the onset for personhood, then one must first accept a metaphysical foundation, which then further requires a determination of what sufficient conditions are required for recognizing a conscious human being as a person. This is crucial to the public abortion dialogue. It is not an easy task, and there is no default position. If it is determined that a living human becomes a person *only* when consciousness is sufficiently present at point A, then *what* determines sufficiency, and at *what* time of gestation or maturation is point A? This is fundamentally the primary concern. Again, it will not end the argument—but in tandem with the female's bodily autonomy, both personhood and moral value can be discussed to determine the ethical evaluation of an abortion.

The first argument under consideration is the *materialist* view of consciousness. This holds that as there are physical laws governing the universe, it logically follows that *the mind is the brain*, operating under the same system and susceptible to the same physical laws. This places the idea of consciousness as a physical process, which, to be consistent, must discount any immaterial (spiritual?) source. Materialism offers that consciousness could be explained by neurobiological systems that stem from an evolutionary origin. It does explain the "mind and body" problem by pointing out that the mind is simply affected by, and reacts to, all physical causes present in and with the body. The critique is that materialism can account for the effects of and reactions to physical events, but not any source of unity of the natural physical world; therefore, it is more explanatory to the effect than it is proof that consciousness arises from the unconscious biological brain. Nonetheless, there are those who, though not properly within the materialist category, tweaked this into a form of naturalism. One such was the American psychologist John Dewey (d. 1952), who held rather than simply claiming because one has knowledge of the mental (consciousness), that if abstracted cannot be accounted for in the same way one may claim to have knowledge of the physical properties of the brain (organ).[32] Consciousness must retain an experiential character. Another was Dewey's contemporary, William James (d. 1910), who understood consciousness as cognizance of oneself that presents as alertness connected with awareness, along with attention and memory.[33] Both attention and memory concur with Locke's view of psychological continuity, while attention and memory may be rationally necessary. Both Dewey and James were Pragmatists, embracing a sort of middle path between the two inherited systems of knowledge, rationalism and empiricism. The philosophy of Pragmatism follows the basic understanding of its name: in terms of consciousness, the practical use of it (what one needs to accept) takes precedence, then theoretical speculation. James is credited with the term "stream of consciousness," in which consciousness is an intentionality that maintains the *ego* (the "I") to ensure survival of the human person. That is an example of a practical appreciation of consciousness. But more recently, in *Quantum Cosmology and the Nature of Consciousness* from Russian theoretical physicist Andrei Linde (b. 1948)—another outlier to the materialist perspective—consciousness is considered the function of matter, where it presents a description of the truly existing material world.[34] The strength of the materialistic view of consciousness is that most agree there is a physical aspect of the mental process in terms of demonstrating a result. The issue from critics would be its inability, by their account, to explain how the mind is composed of physical properties. If materialism is then carried to its logical end, one would end up in determinism (past events and biology produce all choices), which proponents of this theory understand and accept.

Next is the *idealism* view of consciousness, where *all reality is mental*, essentially. As mentioned earlier, all systems must be evaluated by their own internal consistency, which does not mean they escape critique; but rather, in the same way a theist must unconditionally accept that a deity exists, and a materialist must unconditionally accept that matter is

32. Dewey, "Psychology as Philosophic Method," 154, 161.

33. James, "Self," 131–37.

34. Linde, "Universe, Life, Consciousness," §9.

all that exists, so too an idealist must unconditionally accept that one's subjective experience is the primary and sole condition. Those are the metaphysical presuppositions for the applied rationales. The concept of idealism can be traced back to Plato in ancient Greece. Skipping ahead past various other advocates and into the eighteenth century, the Irish Bishop of Cloyne, George Berkeley (d. 1753), held that reality consists only of ideas of the mind. As to consciousness, in his *A Treatise on the Principles of Human Knowledge*, Berkeley explained in contrast to René Descartes's *cogito ergo sum* ("I think, therefore I am") that what is true is to rather posit *esse est percipi*[35] ("to be, is to be perceived"). This is to express that what one is conscious of, including the self, consists of bundles of ideas, to include the color, shape, scent, and more, but all remain mind dependent: no interior mind, no exterior reality. But he quickly pointed out that objects are not created and annihilated as any particular mind considers them, but that they exist dependent upon *all* minds. Then, presently, although a minority view, Dutch philosopher Bernardo Kastrup (b. 1974), in his *Brief Peeks Beyond,* continues to lay claim to the position that as the sleeping mind projects dreams, so too does the waking mind project reality[36]—the distinction being that the latter is perhaps a shared experience. Critics focus on his overall proposal, which they consider a strawman fallacy premised on his claim that any materialistic position would reduce mental states down to physical events. Others object that all idealists are in practicality "closet dualists" who propose something intrinsically dogmatic, and therefore the experience idealists propose as consciousness is unverifiable.

The third version of consciousness, known as *dualism*, holds that the mind and the brain *are not* the same things. So, unlike idealists who posit there are only mental states, or materialists who claim there are only physical states, dualists believe that both mental and physical states exist but neither can be subsumed into the other. Descartes was a dualist in that his methodical doubt revealed, by his reckoning, that he was the "thinking thing," for that alone gave him foundational certainty. But that same certainty eventually led him to accept the sensual, and thus physical reality. Aristotle also held to a dualism of the mind and body, as the soul (*psyche*) was the form of the body, which along with the body (matter) comprised what *is* the human person. And though Descartes held God as

35. Berkeley, *Principles of Human Knowledge*, 24.

36. Kastrup, *Brief Peeks Beyond*, 23–24.

the assurance against deception, and Aristotle held a place for the divine, contemporary theism would part company with either type of dualism. What is "real" cannot simply be a combination of the material body and the mind; although the soul (like Aristotle's form) can be affected by what the material body senses, the two are not extrinsically connected. For example, Christian dualism—specifically Roman Catholicism, which has historically engaged this philosophy of the mind conundrum—would reject the concept that the human person is composed of two parts. Rather, their metaphysics would hold that a human person is a composite, formed as a single substance. Therefore, by their account, the intellectual processes (knowing) are distinct from the material processes (sensing), but the former is affected by the latter. An inherited heresy (a Greek word meaning "to choose") of the early Christians was a philosophical movement known as Gnosticism, where the root is derived from the Greek word for knowledge, *gnosis*. Gnostics held that the body was but a shell, inferior to the "real" seat of personhood, the interior spiritual life. That type of dualism was rejected. Perhaps for theists, since they are a substantial part of the public abortion dialogue but are without category in this section, consciousness can be attributed to a hierarchical view of the Uncreated God over all created beings, where this God sustains those in the temporal sphere, who remain entirely contingent on the Uncreated God. Consider the Jewish grasp of the tripartite nature of the human person. The person is comprised of a body (*basar*) and a soul as the seat of vitality (*nephesh*), but is sustained and imbued with the breath of G-d (*ruah*). The strength of a dualistic approach in the popular sense is that there is something intuitive in claiming that thinking is radically distinct from what is physical. It is commonsensical to accept they are not of the same kind, though the connection between the body and mind would remain aloof (Descartes thought the pineal gland was the connection point). A practical weakness is that one can assume that this consciousness as "the person" is inside (modern Gnosticism), where a person will even speak of "having a body." Therefore, taken to its extreme, what is done to the body affects the person, but the body is not the person. This would incur ethical issues, where the "person" is disassociated from their body, affecting views on human sexuality and end-of-life issues and becoming a confusing determiner of the consciousness of the fetus with the abortion topic.

There are those who, in rejecting the materialist or the dualist position, fall into a category known as *panpsychism*. They would roughly represent an idealist position, though that is debatable. Nonetheless, they accept consciousness as *the hard problem*,[37] a term coined by philosopher David Chalmers (b. 1966) in the mid-1990s. Holding to consciousness in such a way will tend to land one's conclusion into accepting that consciousness is an illusion. To be clear, there are serious detractors to that claim; as with the other expressions of consciousness offered, here too there are varietal forms of panpsychism. Etymologically, that term is derived from the Greek, conjoining the prefix *pan-* ("everything") to the root *psyche* ("the soul" or, more specifically, "the mind"). This then holds that "all things" have the structure humans call a mind as some aspect of their fundamental existence. With panpsychism, some complexity or reality is woven through all things, but not reduced to the "mere" material of physical naturalism. It is what British philosopher Philip Goff (b. 1964) called the "third way," which was to be an alternative option to materialism and dualism. Goff posited that even the smallest of physical particles possesses what can be considered an *experience* in some fashion[38] (to be like that thing), and thus this experience can be spoken of as consciousness. This concept of consciousness would equate the mind with the brain and would offer a resolution of the mind and body problem as the collision of consciousness and physics. A forebearer to modern panpsychism, British philosopher Bertrand Russell (d. 1970), also attempted to bridge naturalism and dualism, proposing the term *quiddities* to integrate the two. Those quiddities are the properties that explain the observable physical causes, but remain integral to the explanation of consciousness. Although again there are varieties, Russell's theory is generally called monism, which is a term held to surmise the "neutral" elements of experience. In his *The Analysis of Mind*, published in 1921, Russell explained that such conscious experiences cannot be the essence of the mind.[39] Such conscious experiences are indeed distinct from the physical objects experienced, but there remains for him no "stuff" that can be said to comprise this consciousness. So overall with panpsychism, whatever gap exists in other explanatory systems does seem to wane by this account. But like its theoretical cousin of idealism, how one accounts for this theory cannot be accomplished with any empirical verification. If materialism gets the "cause" correct and dualism gets the "effect" correct,

37. See Chalmers, *Conscious Mind*, 4.

38. See Goff, "Top-down Combination Problems," in *Consciousness and Fundamental Reality*.

39. Russell, *Analysis of Mind*, 368–70.

then the question remains whether panpsychism really can bridge the gap, as its proponents claim.

What follows now is general information that both surrounds and encompasses the issue of consciousness as the seat of personhood, whether it stems from a materialist, idealist, dualist, or, for the lack of a better category, theistic point of view. Consciousness cannot be reduced to mere awareness. Discovering and recognizing that sufficient physiological mechanisms are in place during brain development cannot be, in themselves, evidence of the presence of consciousness. Such an inference, if intentionality is a determinant of consciousness, must logically support that one's experience and ability to hold to a desire are essential factors. The term *intention*, which draws etymologically from the Latin term *intendere*, holds the connotation of *attending to*, or directing one's attention toward an object. So, by that criterion, to be conscious of something is not simply to react to a stimulus of pain or pleasure but, as intentional beings, to *stand for* something. By this account, consciousness is more than just sensing the world and others; it is the *ability to experience* the world and others, along with *being intentional* in (i.e., directing one's attention toward) how it appears, and also being *attentive* from the "I" perspective. For example, there is a discipline within philosophy known as phenomenology. It is more of a method, a way of studying how objects *appear* to one's consciousness, rather than an explanatory process of understanding what an object is or how an object occurs. Perhaps think in contrast to rationalism, where one progresses to knowledge of an object from rational reflection, or empiricism, where the experience is the means to knowledge of the object from what can be sensed. In phenomenology, the German philosopher Edmund Husserl (d. 1938), who is often considered the founder of this method, presented the idea of intentionality to mean holding one's thoughts and experiences as deliberately directed toward an object. It perhaps is better understood if one accepts that an object is not brought *into* one's consciousness, but one is conscious *of* the object. Intentionality then, is the mind's direction *to* that object. The concept of intentionality offers this attentiveness of consciousness, which in fact Husserl gleaned from his professor, Franz Brentano (d. 1917), an ex-Roman Catholic priest. Brentano offered the notion that when an object is sensed, as it is presented to the mind there is an immanence, whereby the sensed object is acknowledged, desired, etc., and forms as a mental act of the mind.

At the risk of oversimplification, as this twentieth-century movement is diverse, what follows is the representation of a phenomenological experience of a person facing the exterior of a building (the object). They are able to sense the exterior walls, windows, landscaping, noises, and movement of people, all of which are in view from their perspective. But that is not the entirety of the experience of the building that is presented to their consciousness. The building has other physical aspects, which are simultaneously known, though not immediately sensed. The other sides of the building, though not immediately in sight, are known to exist. The building also has interior walls, doors, staircases, furniture, people, etc. And beyond the physical elements, one may have had past experiences in that building. This person may recollect walking up the stairs and may know where certain rooms are located. They might recall meetings they had with colleagues or friends within this building. Perhaps seeing the building brings back an unpleasant encounter or reminds them of a certain period in their life. Maybe the building has unique architecture, or it could even have historical significance where a famous narrative enters the experience. All of that *appears* to the consciousness simultaneously and goes beyond accounting for just the physical aspects of the building (empiricism) or what can be reasonably known of the building (rationalism); as an intentional experience of the building, it also accounts for a mental act presented to the consciousness (phenomenalism). This depth of consciousness is obviously more complex than simply recognizing oneself distinct from others (I am not the Thou), or sensing one's awareness of the self through pain or pleasure (I am tired, or my knee hurts). It also offers depth to the Thou one encounters, and the comprehension of them as persons.

One explanation of how such an experience translates into a sense of consciousness, and then how consciousness then may be understood as "what it is like to be that thing," was proposed by the twentieth-century philosopher Thomas Nagel (b. 1937). In his book *Mortal Questions*, Nagel (a panpsychist) offered the notion that since organisms have consciousness, and organisms are comprised of matter, then the matter itself must have some properties that appear as mental phenomena. He called this ubiquitous consciousness a "mental chemistry."[40] But the limits of this experience of another are that what is available to one individual (the *subjective* experience of another "I") is based on the perspective not

40. Nagel, *Mortal Questions*, 182.

available "outside" of the thing itself (the *objective* experience of oneself). He proposed a thought experiment, in an essay titled "What is it like to be a bat?" That essay, and the question it proposes, might appear somewhat absurd; indeed, philosophy is often chided for contemplating silly notions. But philosophy tackles the simple questions often thought understood, yet likely not—and unfortunately, that which is thought to be understood is typically left uninvestigated. Such thought experiments, like asking what it is like to be a bat, may help demonstrate (regardless of agreement with the position) if his concept of consciousness is really understood prior to dismissing it. So, for Nagel, if someone *pretends* to be a bat, they do not fly, echolocate, eat insects, and so on. They will remain human beings, flapping their arms, perhaps wearing a cape, hanging upside down, and running around erratically trying to mimic a flying bat. In other words, the *objective* experience of the bat is unique to the bat, and the human person has only their *subjective* appearance of what being a bat might be like. They always will remain a human being. Trying to function like a bat does not make someone a bat; but Nagel's point is that "what it is like to be that thing" is consciousness.[41] The hard problem of consciousness, which is Nagel's position, is that unlike biological functions where the eye, as the organ of the body, is the cause of vision, there cannot be a parallel where the brain, as the organ of the mind, can be said to be the cause of knowing. There always seems to be some gap between what is "in the world" and one's conscious experience "of that world." It should be clear that consciousness understood as such is much more than mere awareness. The question for the present topic is at what point would such sufficiency for consciousness arise, and how would it be verified for personhood?

A competing version of this "presented to consciousness" philosophy would be that of German phenomenologist Max Scheler (d. 1928), who perhaps might offer his own philosophical system to bridge consciousness to the idea of personhood. Each person has a conscious experience, but rather than frame it as a subjective experience of the other, Scheler offers the idea that each one's own objective sense of self is always an "experience in relation" to the other, which then provides objectivity of persons in communion. He described this concept of always experiencing a phenomenon with another as being a *member of a totality*. This totality is not to be understood as groupthink, but rather as, for example,

41. Nagel, "What Is It Like?," 437–38.

the intuitive awareness of the shared empathy between two or more persons grieving the loss of a child or parent. This conceivably closes the gap between what is "in the world" and one's conscious experience "of that world," in the sense that each is "of that world" together and thus a member of totality or the "coexperienced unity of experiencing."[42] It is then not an adopting of another's identity (what is it like to be a bat), but an "I" that is intimately involved with another "We" (or to use Buber's framework, no "I" without the "Thou"), as a collective identity. In a sense, the solidarity between the consciousness of each forms a totality that allows for individuality as persons without the possibility of isolation as persons. For Scheler, this is the love of the other that exceeds any rational foundation, where one does not merely appear as the experience but phenomenologically participates with another "I" as an act. Consciousness for Scheler, then, is a relation of one to another *and* to the world. One may glean distinct views of this expression of consciousness for personhood and its relation to the public abortion dialogue.

To address the topic of abortion directly, with the consideration of consciousness as a marker of personhood, two fundamental demands present themselves as questions to be engaged. First, what criteria of sufficiency are required for consciousness to be the onset for recognized or assigned personhood? And secondly, at what age then does this sufficient condition of consciousness arise? The answers are in the form of proposed arguments linked to age-related milestones, and those will be briefly addressed, working backwards from preteen to birth. The first to consider is the developmental *age of reason* derived from a sufficient level of consciousness. For the human person, there is wide consensus that the *age of reason* is set between seven and thirteen years of age. That explains the emancipatory stage markers of the Christian Confirmation rite (at least in the Western expression), or the Jewish bar and bat mitzvah ceremonies. This could not reasonably be argued as the onset of personhood, as earlier conditions for consciousness are obviously identifiable. So, perhaps this could be left as the onset of a rationally expressible consciousness. Then to speak of consciousness as the *moral self* where values and stances are sufficiently developed to incur culpability, those conditions may not appear until three to four years of age. From that point, there surfaces an elementary sense of right or wrong, perhaps better stated as a fairness forming the ethical awareness where judgments can

42. Salice and Schmid, *Phenomenological Approach to Social Reality*, 59.

be appreciated as personal considerations. This of course is provisional, as toddlers are not thought responsible for "getting into things" and are safeguarded from being "exposed to things" reserved for those at or beyond the age of reason. Rules without the underlying explanation of the perceived dangers or exposure are, for this age range, often the prescriptive means to preventing harm and forming conventional behavior for those persons prior to the onset of culpability. But nonetheless, they are accepted as being conscious, even if not fully conscious of the relation of judgments to actions. In his book *Phenomenal Consciousness*, cognitive scientist Peter Carruthers (b. 1952) claims this to be the age bracket at which consciousness *finally* emerges. For example, three-year-olds can focus not simply on the color red but how the color red *seems* and *appears* to them as a subject.[43] This level of consciousness—the criterion of intuiting how something both *seems* and *appears*—is certainly sufficient to determine the presence of consciousness, but remains farther than the point that most would convincingly argue to be the onset of a minimum level of consciousness as determined sufficient. And because it is determined as sufficient, they are considered persons with full autonomy, even if it is partially demonstrated through caregivers.

The remaining treatment of consciousness, which is to follow, can only be a consideration of some of the determinants. Each determinant, and its import into consciousness and thus personhood, is ultimately based on one's explicitly or implicitly held metaphysical view. From that, depending on the varietal form of consciousness one adopts, those metaphysical presuppositions will form what logically constitutes the onset of consciousness and, if consciousness is held as a marker, the onset of personhood. Recall that the following argument is only valid and sound (proper form and true premises) if one accepts that consciousness *is* the marker for personhood. So, now working forward from the fetal stages to the conditions sufficient for the moral self (two to four years of age), the first consideration is what is physiologically necessary for consciousness to be present. Consciousness includes the ability to sense pain, touch, etc.; and, as stated, those are present perhaps in the first trimester or certainly by the third trimester. Even the recognition of voice, which occurs in the first trimester of fetal development, would be an insufficient criterion for consciousness. Consciousness cannot simply be the computational act of the mind, like a calculator capable of transforming some

43. See Carruthers, *Phenomenal Consciousness*, 81.

input into a result. With consciousness, in the analytical sense, there seems to be necessary some interpretation of that input's meaning. A calculator processes input; it does not interpret any meaning of the result. If the mind were like the calculator, then perhaps one could equate the mind's processing to the use of digital software to interpret phrases from one language to another. Although each translated word independently is technically accurate, in context either the syntax is off or the translation as a phrase simply does not express the idea with the same meaning of the original language. Consciousness must exceed that. Perhaps as a response to this concern, American philosopher John Searle (b. 1932) argued in *The Rediscovery of the Mind* that any biological naturalism[44] holding to a conscious experience can be linked to some empirical observations, which means that consciousness is verifiable. He holds that perceptions, whether they are a reaction to pain or Scheler's intentional love, are brought into consciousness. Somehow, by his metric, these biological and of course materialistic particles "underneath" offer for the subjective "I" an experience of consciousness that provides unity to body and mind. Notice how consciousness in these categories is represented by biological criteria. That speaks to the material aspect of the human person; but for those who hold to a form that actualizes the potentiality, these are merely the observable qualities of consciousness that may not even be necessary evidence for its onset.

Now moving in the other developmental direction, rather than consideration of the period from preteen to toddler, here is an evaluation of consciousness from the fetal period to the six-month milestone. As the fetus develops and is nearer the birth event, neurobiologists explain that the thalamocortical connections (those connecting nerve fibers responsible for motor and sensory function) are not yet fully established until the fetus is well into the third trimester. It will be accepted here as occurring at or equal to 26 weeks GA (prenatal ≥26 GA). The fetus's ability to hear precedes this time frame, though it is not until this stage that the capacity for memory begins to appear. Blood oxygen levels, to the extent that they factor into the criteria for consciousness, are quite reduced for the fetus, as compared to the post-utero infant. After the birth event, the infant is capable of eye contact, responds to audible sounds, and will react to stimuli. Researchers from the neonatal research unit at Astrid Lindgren Children's Hospital in Stockholm, in a review titled "The

44. Searle, *Rediscovery of the Mind*, 93.

Emergence of Human Consciousness," quantitatively considered the level of consciousness of a preterm newborn (*ex utero* at less than 26 weeks GA) to be at what they deemed a minimum level.[45] Without making any value comparisons, this minimum level of consciousness at that "born" preterm stage would be analogous, by their interpretation, to that of a rat or mouse. If one holds to their conclusion, then one would need to deem a rat or mouse conscious in order to attribute consciousness to the preterm, now-born infant. But that is not a valuative comparison, and it is forming a consensus. If there is a reciprocal connectivity between an internal state (where the mind is disengaged from a task) and an external state (where the mind is engaging something in the environment), then this prenatal state of ≥26 GA can be conceived as the onset of sufficient consciousness.

Once into the post-viable fetal stage, the level of consciousness seems to differ little as development progresses into the post-utero range. Some neuroscientists theorize that as consciousness is connected to working memory, the capacity is in place during that developmental stage. More recent research has shown certainty that by three months of age, the mental function of attention is evident. The term *attention* can be thought of as "top down," which refers to the ability of "attending to" or "sustaining the focus" by intentionally selecting and rejecting objects of interest. This top-down attention, when observed in adults, connects brain activity with the sensory detection of objects entering the field of vision and stimulating the prefrontal cortex. It may or may not be valid to assume infants "attend" in the same way as adults; but in the absence of recognizable communication for preverbal infants, some standard for consciousness must be utilized. The methodological issues (how to study and measure) of determining infant consciousness is not without hazards. But the ethical implications reach far beyond the public abortion issue, as many adults enter similar states of unconsciousness, as do children who, in minimal conscious states from injury or disease, do not forfeit their personhood. Or *do* they forfeit their personhood, if personhood is pinned to the confirmation of a living human existing in a conscious state? Perhaps, at least, if consciousness can be measured by neural activity, infants of a certain age may be said to possess consciousness, since neural activity is noticeable as a pattern in infants as early as five months of age (although the activity is slower than that of

45. Lagercrantz and Changeux, "Emergence of Human Consciousness," 259.

adults). But—and this is the crucial point—if it is *not* measurable before that time, then from that lack of certitude it would logically follow that there is no scientific reason to think a newborn less than five months old possesses consciousness to be understood with the necessary criteria of a working memory, attention, and intentionality. That is to say, if they at that stage do not sufficiently respond to social stimuli, it would move the age level to a later age, where the increased required criteria for consciousness includes necessarily the ability to be self-reflective. By that evaluation, the onset of personhood would be nearer to fifteen months of age, post-uterine.

This is important for the rational consideration of consciousness as the marker for the onset of personhood. If the working definition of an abortion is "the intentional termination of a fetal human life," and that termination is premised as ethical because the fetal life is not yet a person, then when personhood is determined by the onset of consciousness at five months of age, would (or could) that logically lead to the ethical termination of a four-month-old living human? The premise remains the same, so this cannot be a slippery slope fallacy. The premise is an abortion being ethical because of the nonperson status. If the living human fetal life is a nonperson, then the living human four-month-old—also not a person—lacks the same necessary quality. The term *fetal life* is in the working definition of an abortion, but only because the legal sense of personhood is used. Once the legal sense is dismissed and an ontological or a reformed legal sense is used (consciousness), an abortion is simply redefined to be "the intentional termination of a nonperson human life." That does not differ essentially from the original definition.

Could this simply be the reintroduction of "exposing" undesired infants, which was an accepted Greco-Roman practice, opposed by early Christians as a fetal abortion is now? Before that is summarily rejected as hyperbole, a contemporary ethicist from Princeton University named Peter Singer (b. 1946) has advocated for the ethical termination of an infant's life based on that very criterion of consciousness. For example, the ethical status of a three-month-old infant, by his judgment, cannot be equated with the ethical status of an older child or adult, particularly if the infant has a severe or life-threatening condition.[46] So, the law and ethical sentiments that presently preclude one from killing a toddler would not ethically apply to an infant with diminished functions in its first

46. See Singer, *Rethinking Life and Death*, 215; pertaining to an anencephalic infant, 39; pertaining to an infant born terminally ill, 111.

months of post-uterine life. Singer does not think this decision should be left to the whim of the parents but should be made with physician consultation. If the criterion for personhood (consciousness) has not sufficiently changed from the fetal stage to the birth event, then infanticide is in actuality a post-birth abortion. If "post-birth abortion" carries offensive connotations, then this termination can be understood as active or passive "neonatal euthanasia." To make this point salient, the present use of neonatal *slow codes,* the practice of only symbolically responding with lifesaving care for those deemed unable/unlikely to survive long or perhaps for those with unacceptable abnormalities and severe health conditions, will likely be the bridge to this practice. This warrants further expansion in the later section "Potential humans and future offspring"; but to the topic at hand, slow coding can be understood as managing what was not achieved in utero, whether due to restrictions that did not permit an abortion or a variety of other reasons. Nonetheless, when advocates of post-uterine euthanasia are criticized, they may argue that the opposition is not ethically formed but rather is an emotional aversion remnant of a culture imbued with lingering dogmatic traditions. They could rightly claim this, as any "repugnance" will evaporate when society acclimates to a previously repulsive idea. Then too will the subsequent moral outrage wane, and the generations that follow will inherit it as customary. One can sense the transition of abortion from being "safe, legal, and rare" to a "reproductive right," while logically anticipating "slow coding" as being equally acceptable, provided the underlying premises for a prenatal abortion equally apply to the infant.

It is worth lingering on this point momentarily. Historically, though many practices or forms of conduct now ethically acceptable were once legally prohibited and fomented social outrage, the most evident and obvious example is abortion itself. Ethically, an abortion was nearly universally condemned in the West for many centuries. There were always advocates—but now, according to popular polls, access to safe abortions is favored by a majority. In fact, the migration of abortion from being ethically offensive, as evidenced by in-place civil laws and societal stigma, to now being held as "basic healthcare" for females represents no little shift in public attitude. It is further remarkable that this acceptance occurred within a half century. Could it not logically be held, then, that when consciousness is better understood, and if it becomes clear that consciousness is not present in an infant until five months of age, "infant euthanasia" will gain wider cultural acceptance, at least for those with severe health conditions? Although it is not popularly known, countries such as the Netherlands and Belgium have already decriminalized infant euthanasia.[47] They simply moved the standard for adult euthanasia to infants and applied it as a premise to legally permit neonatal euthanasia. It is possible that within a century, just as abortion has evolved from being held as ethically offensive to now being viewed as basic healthcare, neonatal euthanasia (slow coding) would evolve from being an ethically offensive practice for some to being framed as primary health-related comfort care for infants. Even if that never gains popular support, perhaps an infant post-birth abortion will at least be evaluated in line with comfort care for borderline viable fetuses.

A comparison of third-trimester abortions and neonatal euthanasia is stronger, as prenatally a fetus of that gestational stage shares like-levels of consciousness (and of most criteria, save physical attachment) with a newborn or one-month-old infant. Common to both scenarios, society can assume care. Admittedly, this is presently a minority view, but Singer is not the sole outlier. The American philosopher Michael Tooley (b. 1941) stated explicitly that one must determine the cutoff point at which it becomes morally relevant to not end the life of a human being.[48] Any individual, by his account, must form principles and not simply have the judgment stem from some mere discomfort level. Another American social philosopher, Jeffrey Reiman (b. 1942), offers the argument that the killing of infants is deemed by the populace as unethical, not because of any intrinsic value in the infant but because parents and other adults value infants predicated on a moral intuition.[49] This could be a nod back to the ethical inference of the psychological projection that adults place on infants and the unborn, or it could simply point to the idea that the infant's value is determined by the caregiver's desire. But in any case, the point remains that if one disagrees with this reasoning, one must refute their logic, which is more ethically consistent than arguments for personhood from the markers of cardiac activity, pain sensation, brain development, or the birth event. These thinkers that would support "infant euthanasia" do not do so from a dogmatic or ideological stance, but from first determining the sufficiency of consciousness as "the line" for judging the personhood of a living human, and then applying that criterion indifferently as a standard.

47. See Verhagen and Lantos, "Dutch Model," para. 1–8, table 1.

48. Tooley, *Abortion and Infanticide*, 14, 69, 170, 190; on infanticide, 330, 332. 357.

49. See Reiman, "Abortion, Infanticide," 181–200.

In conclusion, admittedly the average public view on consciousness is not developed; in fact, it is likely not considered. In the scheme of determining personhood, the idea of consciousness is not something tangible. That is why the public and media engage in determining markers such as the monitoring of a heartbeat, or considering fetal reaction to pain, or making the birth event as legal personhood the substitute for any ontological consideration, and thus the basis for an ethical evaluation on abortion. Philosophy of mind, the discipline that studies consciousness, seems ethereal compared to neuroscience that can address the empirical structure thought to permit the presence of consciousness. Yet, the fact that something is measurable does not ensure that what is measured is sufficient, relevant, or even applicable. What can be measured are the underlying structures thought necessary, and it may be satisfying to link those assumed structures with how consciousness *appears* to the viewer; but causal implications are fraught with uncertainty. Perhaps the relation of those underlying biological materials to consciousness is equivalent to Scruton's analogy of the pigments' and brushstrokes' relation to how the portrait *appears* to the viewer. The pigments and brushstrokes are the measurable idea of the artist and are necessary for the portrait to appear, but the form existed prior to the portrait with the artist.

The premise of this text stands, as *either every living human is a person, or some living humans are persons.* If only living humans are persons, then what constitutes a person for those "some" must be determined prior to declaring an abortion ethical at point X because of criterion Y. If the converse is true, that all living humans are persons, then the value ascribed to living human persons against respect for female bodily autonomy must be determined prior to declaring an abortion unethical. That would result in one of two further judgments. First, if and when that determined value of the unborn person *does* outweigh female autonomy, at that point an abortion is unethical (advocacy for the unborn). Secondly, if and when the determined value of the unborn person *does not* outweigh female autonomy, at that point an abortion is ethical (advocacy for female bodily autonomy). In tandem with the rigor of critical thinking, all in the public dialogue must concede to the equivalent meaning of terms and be committed to express their judgments by true premises. Then further, each must summon the ability and willingness to form a valid and sound argument. Only within those parameters, even given the reality of strong emotions and sincere disagreement, will the public dialogue on abortion be respectfully and fruitfully engaged.

6

The Death of Pro-life and Abolition of Pro-choice

IF ONE BEGINS AN inquiry or proceeds to intentionally form judgments based on a faulty premise, even the finest mind will end its journey in a convincing error. The public abortion dialogue, to the extent one can claim there is an authentic dialogue, has been riddled with misconceptions stemming from flawed starting points. That there are "sides" in the public abortion conversation is understandable and even sensible, given what each side holds as the sobering consequences capitulated to when each objective fails. Let it be accepted that each binary side produces a binary effect, as ultimately either a female's bodily autonomy is denied or the life of an unborn human is terminated. This chapter will attempt to form the proposal that rather than arguing an abortion is ethical because it supports the bodily autonomy of a female, it is clearer to argue that the unborn human life regardless of personhood possesses less moral value than the female's autonomy. Likewise, rather than arguing that an abortion is unethical because it ends the life of a living unborn human, it is clearer to argue that an unborn human life is a person with sufficient moral value. To that end, it is imperative for the ethical evaluation of an abortion to be premised on whether *some living humans are persons* or *all living humans are persons*. Then by addressing the premise of personhood, one can either *assign* moral value (traditionally the pro-choice stance) or *recognize* moral value (traditionally the pro-life stance). Furthermore, from that moral value predicated on personhood, an assessment logically follows that either a person *can ethically* end the life of another person (for necessarily proportionate reasons or lack of moral value) or that a person *cannot ethically* end the life of another person (PDE notwithstanding, as there is an equality of moral value). Admittedly, sides persist given the resultant ends of each; but, as will be argued, the single premise positioned as the major term in the major premise requires engagement, while not falling prey to the minor premises of bodily autonomy and fetal human life, which are inherently incompatible with a resolution. To reiterate and clarify, the first condition is that it rationally follows that such dialogue forms over arguing about either determiners for personhood (pro-choice?) or recognition of personhood (pro-life?). And secondly, this resolution must then weigh the value of those judgments against both the authentic goods of safeguarding female bodily autonomy and preserving fetal life as secondary premises. The inverse of the major and minor premises, in conjunction with two dissonant proposed premises, is offered for consideration as it presents the barricade to dialogue.

It would be helpful to consider the premises of one's argument according to the arrangement of a syllogism, determined by the positions of the major and minor premises. This was initially proposed in the "Discerning positions on value and belief" in chapter 3. Here the point is reintroduced as primarily illustrative, rather than a definitive response to the issue. The argument of this text is that unless the issue of personhood is first resolved, human dignity remains undetermined. Repositioning the major and minor terms of the present expression of the argument allows for both the essential ideas of bodily autonomy and biological life to remain in the public dialogue on abortion, but presents both as secondary (minor) premises which preserves the shared goal to uphold human dignity. Here are the two *present* public arguments based on the primacies of bodily autonomy or biological life expressed syllogistically.

Pro-choice	*Pro-life*
Human dignity requires *bodily autonomy*.	Human dignity requires *biological life*.
Being pro-choice upholds human dignity.	Being pro-life upholds human dignity.
Being pro-choice requires *bodily autonomy*.	Being pro-life requires *biological life*.

Both arguments, with each premise reformed to accept personhood as the major term, while retaining either bodily autonomy or biological life as the minor term, would be expressed syllogistically by the following.

Dignity Due Persons	*Dignity Due Persons*
Human dignity is tethered to *personhood.*	Human dignity is tethered to *personhood.*
Bodily autonomy preserves human dignity.	Biological life preserves human dignity.
Bodily autonomy is tethered to *personhood.*	Biological life is tethered to *personhood.*

These are not the sum of the arguments proposed for the public dialogue on abortion, but they are the first criteria necessary for reorienting and ultimately forming formidable advocacy arguments for either *some living humans are persons* or *all living humans are persons.*

These ostensible premises must first be dislodged from the town square, news, social media, and political discourse. That goal requires both the death of the pro-life stance and the abolition of the pro-choice stance signifying the arguments of either side. Further, it is not clear that any sloganized stance on personhood should be replace them, though perhaps *dignity due persons* might be a candidate, as it would logically include discussion of the personhood of the unborn fetal life and bodily autonomy as essential elements that then can warrant moral value. Though the sloganized premises of pro-choice and pro-life are binary sides and logically do produce binary effects, this does not necessarily imply they are *false* binaries. There remains a logic to resisting the effects that each judgment renders unethical and that those of each side thus render unacceptable. For example, regardless of how nuanced the position on abortion is for the general public, news media, politicians, and the like, when the premises of being pro-choice or pro-life are pressed to their logical conclusions, there inevitably arises a tipping point where each individual's judgments will favor the goal of one of those two camps. The advocate for the female's bodily autonomy will consider the value of the unborn's life but will stand firm by ultimately not capitulating the female's choice of accessing an abortion until some threshold of assigned moral value has been reached or exceeded. Likewise, the advocate for the life of the unborn will consider the value of the female's bodily autonomy but will stand firm by ultimately not capitulating the life of the unborn to an abortion at a threshold that does not align with the recognized moral value of the female's bodily autonomy and the life of the fetus. The pro-choicer will frame the preservation of bodily autonomy as a basic right, thus upholding human dignity. The pro-lifer will frame the preservation of the unborn as a basic right to life, thus upholding human dignity. From the 1970s to the present, these positions have organically arisen, and the public abortion debate has tacitly sanctioned the two sides as default adversarial positions. Each position carries attached values that, when adopted, press those in each stance to champion either "choice" or "life" as a perceived inviolable right for human dignity.

As the sides of the abortion issue continue to publicly ebb and flow with the tide of media interests, election cycles, and court rulings, the pedestrian experience confirms that any dialogue seeks to ferret out an ethical evaluation by the ultimate effects (autonomy or life) appropriate to the stance one holds. This means that when any emphasis is detected that one's position favors either of those two stances, the nuance evaporates as each individual is folded into the position that ultimately adopts an advocacy for female bodily autonomy or fetal life. This present treatise is intended to reorient the public dialogue so that even nuanced positions return one to the foundational question of personhood. Then, with such a common premise in place, this text offers the foundations for critical analysis in making judgments on acknowledged standards of personhood to which moral value can then be ascribed or recognized. The judgment of what sufficiently constitutes a living human *person* need not be shared for productive dialogue, but a recognition of the necessary elements that premise this personhood and moral value will develop during the form of engagement. Once committed to this single premise (rightly assigned major terms), each "side" can rationally argue whether their criteria or recognition warrants consideration and how it may be comparatively valued morally against other competing goods. This then is the role of dialectic, which reveals the resilience of one's argument to an interlocutor's logical scrutiny. Determining sides from the competing goods of female bodily autonomy and fetal life (minor premises) will only perpetuate the stalemate. The foundational reorientation to the common premise of personhood and moral value will likely retain sides, but any exchange on that single standard facilitates dialogue by necessity. Recall that an injustice can be framed as two standards applied to a single judgment. The goal here is to frame judgments achieved from a single standard. If the intended judgment is to be whether or not an abortion is ethical, then the standard cannot be about the primacy of either the female's bodily autonomy or the primacy of fetal life, where the gains are governed by the principle of zero sum. These standing binaries of pro-choice and pro-life, held as two distinct standards upholding human dignity, remain why each side persistently argues *past* the other. But once it is conceded that either some living humans are persons or all living humans are persons, then determining moral value from a single standard can be applied critically to the proportionate goods of female bodily autonomy and fetal life.

Furthermore, with each inherited sloganized position, even though the pro-choice and pro-life stances are not false binaries, both as binaries remain susceptible to logical critiques that undermine their acceptability. There are multiple approaches of dismantling each side's logic, but that task is reserved for other books. The present undertaking is to reorient the premises and offer a primer for the public dialogue on abortion. That remains unique and occupies a narrow niche. But to the point of each stance maintaining an ostensible premise, consider once more the assumption of fetal life and bodily autonomy as the major terms. They each attempt to affirm that either biological life or female bodily autonomy is sufficient in itself to sustain moral value convincingly to negate the value of the other. First, with the pro-life stance, although the fetal life is necessarily attached to human dignity, if one is to assert that an abortion is unethical because it terminates an unborn human life, one must first substantiate that *all* living humans are persons with moral value greater than or equivalent to that of the female's bodily autonomy. Turning then to the pro-choice stance, although the female's bodily autonomy is necessarily attached to human dignity, if one is to assert that an abortion is ethical because it upholds the unconditional expression of bodily autonomy, one must first substantiate that *some* living humans are persons, and that even if the conscious fetus or infant (for example) were allowed within that subset of "some," they lack sufficient moral value. Each is a presumptive claim and, as the premise, results in an unsound argument.

Two more problematic situations arise that, while not unresolvable, rest on the assigning of moral value to fetal life over bodily autonomy, or correspondingly to bodily autonomy over fetal life. Neither fetal life nor bodily autonomy is an absolute value. There are conditions in which the value of each cedes to the other. This is true regardless of a moral comparison of the fetal life to the female both as persons, or of the female person's bodily autonomy to the living fetus as a person. Each pairing demonstrates an instance where the value of one yields to the value of the other. First, regarding the moral value of the fetal life, consider an instance of ectopic pregnancy (explained previously), where the value of the human life of the embryo implanted outside of the uterus is equal to that of the female, yet will yield to the female's moral value as a human life. One may rightly argue that PDE applies to this scenario, as it would in cases involving uterine cancer treatment that would result in the death of the living human fetus. Other circumstances and medical conditions might press the limits of PDE. Without attempting to build the circumstances into case study scenarios, a few are presented here: depending on the GA, placental abruptions with concerns of hemorrhagic shock; or a female's water breaking prior to viability, which presents a situation, among others, where sepsis can become fatal with moral certainty, meaning not empirically verifiable but judged with high confidence. Secondly, regarding the moral value of a female's bodily autonomy, there are instances in which it yields to the moral value of the life of the fetus. As explained earlier, since Kant attached autonomy to rationality, autonomy is better understood as "respect for bodily autonomy." From that, then, it is an axiological maxim in bioethics that one's autonomy (which applies to either sex) ethically stops at the threshold of another person. No person can harm themselves or another (save perhaps in serious scenarios involving self-preservation); no person may sell a kidney, self-harm, or seek amputation, arguing their action is ethically permissible by virtue of their bodily autonomy.

That does not diminish the "respect for autonomy." The key term *person* is what upholds autonomy and yet preserves this autonomy from the encroachment of oneself or another to bodily integrity. It follows, then, that the claims of biological life and bodily autonomy, though tethered to human dignity, cannot be absolute. This means that even biological life and bodily autonomy rightly understood cannot settle the issue of how to determine moral value dependent on the ontological status of the living human pregnant female or the living human unborn. In estimation of the limits of the bodily autonomy of the female and the biological life of the fetus, it is more favorable to public dialogue to reposition the major and minor terms of the present expression of the public abortion argument to the shared goal of upholding human dignity.

SOME LIVING HUMANS ARE PERSONS OR ALL LIVING HUMANS ARE PERSONS

This section is the precursor to the advocacy arguments for either some living humans are persons or all living humans are persons. What follows is a brief explanation and evaluation of the possible markers for determining personhood. For the sake of convenience, the "*some* living humans are persons" stance will simply be referred to by the term *some*. Correspondingly, the "*all* living humans are persons" stance will hereby be referred to simply by the term *all*. A brief comment may appear for the *all* stance if it is relevant to include. But otherwise, since the *all* premise presupposes that a marker cannot exist for personhood essentially, as the unborn being is a living human, that self-evident conclusion need not be reiterated for why each marker fails as a sufficient condition.

Beginning with the marker of *cardiac activity* (along with fetal heartbeat), two critiques surfaced in a previous treatment of this text. The first was that as a marker, with present empirical knowledge, the distinction between cardiac activity and fetal heartbeat is only three gestational weeks. So, even if either side capitulated to the other, the movement of the marker would offer little to no significance, which would not permit endorsement or adoption of the contrary position. The other issue is to question whether cardiac activity can even properly serve as a marker. Though the lack of cardiac activity can be the determiner for the cessation of life, in terms of embryonic or fetal maturation, it does not mark the inception of biological life, as the embryo is alive prior to cardiac activity. That is to say that death follows the cessation of cardiac activity, but death does not precede the onset of cardiac activity. That remains a weakness perhaps for both stances, although the *all* stance may utilize the audible cardiac activity to contrive a psychological projection of personhood for the unborn, while the *some* stance may demonstrate that such a tactic is simply intended to sway public sympathies.

The second marker for determining personhood, *pain sensation,* is difficult to apply, as there remains serious disagreement as to the physiological conditions necessary for the unborn to sense pain. Some experts claim those necessary conditions for pain sensation are present in the first trimester, while others conclude they cannot be sufficiently formed until the third trimester. If one of those two judgments proves correct, it would simply extend or limit the time frame where the *some* side would have to accept denying female bodily autonomy after the point the fetus can sense pain, or the *all* side would have to accept the ethical termination of the unborn until that same point of pregnancy—because without pain there then is no person. The more concerning issue is that even if the onset of those conditions for pain sensation can be identified with moral certainty, the argument will migrate from being capable of sensing pain to determining if the unborn can experience pain. As a weakness for the *some* side, that will breach once more the sympathy concern, for it may not alter the judgment of either stance. The fetus could simply be anesthetized and thus no pain experienced, even if that becomes uncomfortable for some to consider. The second difficulty is that many nonhuman animals sense pain, and that indisputable fact does not impute personhood to those nonhuman animals based on that premise. However, that same point forms the strength for the *all* side, in that even inflicting pain on living nonpersons (dogs, cats, primates) is held as inhumane and thus unsettling. And just as was the case with being able to audibly hear the unborn's cardiac activity, if it can be determined that the unborn does sense or experience pain and consequently must first be anesthetized, the stirring of emotions from that notion both privately and publicly will likely surface as a point of contention.

Like the marker of pain sensation, the third consideration of *brain activity* as a marker of personhood is tied to physiological cues that are not easily pinned down with certainty. In the same way ethicists argue over what constitutes brain death, it is unlikely the argument will be easily settled as to what constitutes the onset of "brain birth" or the functioning whole brain. This marker evaluation suffers from the same false comparison that arose with fetal heartbeat and cardiac activity. Even if one can with moral certainty argue the "beginning" of sufficient brain activity to warrant the birth of the brain, it does not logically follow that the fetus was brain dead prior to that point; and then one will venture into the degree of brain formation necessary for sufficiency, which may include both a third-trimester fetus and the month-old infant in the same category by degree.

In short, for the markers *cardiac activity*, *brain development*, and the onset of *pain sensation or experience*, each is insufficient either substantially as an indicator or by the inability to confirm its actual subsistence. Therefore, they possibly may exist as necessary markers for personhood, but certainly fall short of qualifying as sufficient markers.

Reflecting on fetal *viability* as the sufficient criterion for personhood, it will be considered here in tandem with the *birth event*. The rationale is that although preterm viability does not presume survival outside the womb, viability is possible past twenty-two gestational weeks and is more than likely after twenty-eight weeks. So, even though many factors contribute to a preterm infant's health outcomes, any convincing ontological distinction between the fetus that is viable in utero or delivered post-utero is rather remote, if not nonexistent. Legal personhood of the fetus's head vacating the vaginal cavity, though it presently aligns with the birth event, is insufficient as a marker, for no other reason than as a recognition this personhood can be modified by social and political factors. That is not to suggest that a determination of ontological personhood cannot fall prey to those same factors, but one might more readily assume that legal determinations fall prey to ideology more easily than the development of personhood even as a social kind. Whether or not that is true, as it stands, any legal determination is founded on the placement of the fetus as unborn. By contrast, the ontological designation must make a distinction of both *what* the fetus "is" along with a determined moral value, as opposed to *where* the fetus "is" with the moral value assigned by legislation or the courts. So, in short, determining what a fetus or infant "is" simply by the "where" of the fetus or infant will not hold up to logical scrutiny. Previous discussions on consciousness and infant euthanasia spoke to that claim. As to abortions later in pregnancy, as mentioned, they are rare. When they do occur outside of a misjudged gestational age or logistical issue, the reason is often the discovery of a previous false negative prognosis or a newly confirmed fetal anomaly. That is not always true, of course, as ample anecdotal evidence speaks to the contrary—some abortions later in pregnancy are elective, falling under the wide definition of life determined by *Doe v. Bolton*. It is an aside, but to that point, reporting on abortions varies by state and country, and any requirement to provide a reason is often only available by testimonial. Nonetheless, each of those judgments will have to engage an ethic predicated on assigned values or desired functionalities of the fetus. But each must settle the *some* or *all* dichotomy prior to determining either the value or function deemed acceptable for the unborn, future offspring. An exception arises in the event that there is an identifiable and certain danger to the *physical life* of the mother, so much narrower than the definition of life with *Doe v. Bolton*, and likely more in line with the popular apprehension of the term "life of the mother." At that juncture, the remedy is less contentions by even the *all* side, who could ethically appeal to PDE and accept the "bad effect" of the unborn's death, which is proportionate to the "good effect" of preserving the physical life of the female. Finally, without revisiting the comparison of in utero and post-utero dependence, if the fetus viable in utero is born vaginally or by cesarean, the *some* side would be required to explain convincingly the ontological distinction predicated on that change in location. That is, they would be logically beholden to explicate how the "where" of the fetus is the sole indicator of the "is" of the fetus, without resorting to a legal determination of personhood. The necessary physiological care of the unborn by another or society is a factor; but, as was addressed, maintenance of the unborn's needs does not change substantially from the viability state to any point soon after the birth event and, more importantly, by itself does not determine the ontological status of the fetus or infant. This is evidenced by laws often more strictly regulating third-trimester abortions or the public's hesitancy of support, based on the assumption that society (or at least another besides the birth mother) can assume care. In conclusion, both viability and the birth event each present as substantially insufficient for personhood markers. They both solicit serious consideration, and should remain part of the public dialogue on abortion. If for nothing else, illustrating those markers' lack of sufficiency and inability to withstand logical scrutiny clears the way for the marker of consciousness, which is the stronger for consideration.

The final consideration for the marker of the onset of personhood then is *consciousness*. This treatment will require more nuance than the previous considerations. And it will be a modest sampling of the judgments that can be rendered from each metaphysical expression of consciousness that follows. Nonetheless, a basic understanding of each is necessary, as consciousness will be presented in the following section as the onset of and primary consideration for personhood in accord with those who assert the *some* stance, or *some living humans are persons* position. This claim of primacy for considering human consciousness solicits two necessary concerns. The first is that depending on one's metaphysical foundation, consciousness may require a minimum of physiological conditions to be present. That is particularly true for those who hold to materialism. The second is that those conditions themselves must be predicated on a philosophical assumption of what exactly constitutes consciousness. Rephrased, one must first intentionally claim a metaphysical position and then, through the lens of that metaphysical position, form a definition of consciousness. That does not make consciousness relative, or distilled down to what one "thinks," but it does presuppose that a viewpoint on reality must develop prior to determining the "is" of consciousness. Perhaps the only exception is if one's reality is projected by consciousness (solipsism). That is not meant to appear as a word jumble, but places the elements of critical thinking in their logical propositional order; counsel, reflect, judge, and adopt. The claim that one must first determine one's metaphysical view is the alternative to founding a position based on ideology, political partisanship, and naïve dogmatism.

So, too, the onset of consciousness, along with the sufficient conditions to argue its presence (if one holds there is an onset at all), requires no less than that level of consideration to first determine if one is a materialist, idealist, dualist, theist, or panpsychist. What follows will provide the pertinent criteria to consider—e.g., for consciousness, one would consider if there is something measurable, or if the sufficiency can only be rationally argued, or even if a position is to be accepted dogmatically. Unlike cardiac activity or a fetal heartbeat, consciousness is not so easily sensed and empirically verified. With brain activity or pain sensation, even the concern for pain experience and the presence of neurological conditions can be intuited from observed reactions and reportable sensations. Such intuited inferences are not absent with how consciousness may be observed; but as there are those who argue that consciousness can or cannot be equated with a reaction to a stimulus, or that it does or does not require some level of intentionality, the conclusion will depend on one's metaphysical view. This may remain true for both preterm viability and the birth event living humans, even as the former is measurable by health outcomes post-birth, where the birth event itself, though remaining an insufficient marker for personhood, is obviously tangible. So, if consciousness is to be the marker for personhood, there is no present consensus (nor will there be one) as to the "what" of consciousness. And when one does adequately argue the "what" to form a definition of consciousness, does that imply that the living human becomes a person *only* when consciousness is sufficiently present? Further, to be ethically consistent, whatever conditions are determined to grant personhood to a fetus (≥26 GA) or post-utero living human (≤5 months), those conditions must be applied consistently through the human's life to include minimal states or loss of consciousness due to injury or health conditions. Here is that argument in syllogistic form. Note that in the following syllogism, the Greek term for consciousness, which is *syneidēsis*, will be used to denote the range of the onset of consciousness as representing "≥26 GA to ≤5 months postnatal."

P1 To fulfill the accepted criterion for a living human to be a person, the condition of *syneidēsis* must be evidently present.

P2 An unborn or infant is not a person, unless they fulfill the accepted criterion for a living human to be a person.

C Therefore, an unborn or infant is not a person, unless the condition of *syneidēsis* is evidently present.

That is to hold that even a living human at the prenatal stage (≥26 GA) or postnatal stage (≤5 months) would no longer be a person if they ceased to be conscious, provided those conditions for consciousness are no longer sensed or measurable as evidently present. The criterion of *syneidēsis* is sufficient. What criteria are necessary for *syneidēsis*? That cannot be settled here, and accepted empirical findings may indeed have a half-life. But the logical relation remains that for a living unborn human (prenatal ≥26 GA) to be a person (evidence of consciousness), the same criterion must be accepted for a living born human (postnatal ≤5 months) to be a person (evidence of consciousness). In brief, personhood is determined by the evidence of *syneidēsis*. Of the multiple considerations as to the "what" of *syneidēsis*, the following synopses of various metaphysical views will be offered. Special attention is given to considerations for the public abortion dialogue, relative to adopting measurable consciousness as a sufficient marker for the onset of personhood.

The first to be reappraised for consideration is that of the *materialist* viewpoint. The main point of the materialist grasp of consciousness was that there is no distinction between the mind and the brain. It would logically follow, then, that until there is ample brain development, prior to the sufficient presence of such determined criteria, there can be no condition for consciousness and thus no recognition of personhood. This may prove to offer consciousness as early as the third prenatal trimester. As stated, the strength of the materialistic view is that a result can be verified, as the brain which *is* the mind proves capable of intentionally doing A or B by observation. One weakness remains in how to explain the mind as composed of physical properties. The caveat, though, in following an understanding of the concept of a "stream of consciousness" from James, or some semblance of maintaining the "I" as the *ego* necessary for survival of the person (psychologically?), one would be hard-pressed to ensure sufficient conditions for personhood prenatally until very near the birth event, as the development may not be present for the onset of complex brain functions. In fact, such sufficient conditions may not be present even early in infancy. If one takes an approach to consciousness explained by necessary neurobiological systems, research has linked brain imaging of conscious adults to like-states of consciousness in infancy. With infants (≤5 months), one may witness an integration of sensory capabilities. If that is accepted as evidence for a rudimentary form of consciousness, then some degree of that sensory integration is likely to be found prenatally (≥26 GA). Understandably, this consciousness is tethered to sufficient brain development, so although it is predictive and is not presently falsifiable (that which cannot be falsified is often considered to be outside of an empirical pursuit), it nonetheless remains a relevant theory with ethical implications for at least those rare later-in-term abortions. There are further implications in that consciousness may be determined by degree—that is, a fetus is less conscious than an infant, an infant is less conscious than a toddler, etc.—which would imply that with consciousness as the marker by degree, moral value would follow by degree. This, perhaps with a nod back to the concept of a "stream of consciousness," will also entail exploring to what degree the consciousness can be present if determined not as continuous, but incremental. That incrementality would be a necessary consideration in order to justify an ethical evaluation of personhood based on this criterion of awareness.

Unlike the mind as the material brain, with *idealism* all reality is mental perception where the condition for consciousness is one's own subjective experience. It can be summarized by Berkeley's formulation *esse est percipi* ("to be, is to be perceived"). Kastrup remains a modern proponent who holds consciousness to be the waking mind that projects reality, although his view remains an outlier in the philosophy of mind discipline. This idealism is the counterpart to the materialist position as a metaphysical view for explaining consciousness. Whereas a materialist approach pushed backed on the dogmatic (revealed?) underpinnings of the medieval period, idealism can be touted as a secular approach that both denies reductive physicalism and religious dogmatism. It offers the sense of a worldly mysticism that fills the gap materialism left void and forms as a resistance to the perceived imposition of orthodoxy. The brain remains necessary for consciousness with idealism; but strictly speaking, one's body need not be fully formed for consciousness to exist, as the embryonic, fetal, and infant stages would all possess consciousness prior as beings with a mental substance. The presence of consciousness may be continuous, but recollection would not be a necessary condition. During later, postnatal developmental years, consciousness may be tied to thoughts and memories, and thus memories are recalled; but during infancy (or perhaps prenatally), consciousness remains too mysterious to suggest that the mind of the infant or fetus is having intentional thoughts and resultant memories. One may claim that each memory from those prerational years would be swept away as lost memories in the same manner that most adults cannot recall conscious experiences from the first few years of age. With idealism, that lack of recollection is not evidence for any lack of consciousness. To the abortion dialogue, it is not clear then how early consciousness could be determined to exist sufficiently for the onset of personhood. There is a subjectivity to the idealism concept of consciousness that can be claimed as both a strength and weakness. The unrecollected experiences, or even the possibility of such experiences at the early stages of maturation (personhood?), is simply unverifiable. The reduction of mental states that still constitutes consciousness for proponents of idealism must then be accepted as the reduction of physical events. The appeal is that consciousness through the lens of idealism is fundamental to human existence and thus would prove a formidable marker as the onset of personhood that, depending on how it is framed, need not be tethered to any developmental stage.

Perhaps related to idealism is the notion of consciousness known as *panpsychism*. Although it does contain some link to idealism, there are those who consider panpsychists to be "closet dualists," so the distinction is dependent on how one expresses the notion. Nonetheless, as Goff pointed out, panpsychism posits consciousness to exist even in the smallest physical particles.[1] Would that logically infer that all matter is conscious? The short response is yes. But it would take much more to ferret out how the consciousness of a tomato compares to that of a rational primate. So perhaps the fuller response would begin with "Not all matter is conscious," and the reason for that response is that it depends on how one holds that a tomato can have a sentient experience in the same manner as a rational primate. It may be argued that each simply has a distinct form of consciousness.

To the abortion dialogue explicitly, even if one holds that the matter comprising an embryo is conscious, the likely inference would be that this level of consciousness still does not warrant any moral valuing of the fetus over that of a female's autonomy. In truth, Chalmers, among others, espouses an integration theory of consciousness. This theory attempts

1. See Goff, "Are Electrons Conscious?," para. 9.

to unify a sense of consciousness in the same way that the experience of reading is not mechanically interpreted as holding a book, looking at ink, thinking about sentence structures and syntax, etc. Chalmers and others then apply that type of unity to consciousness itself, which may prove distinct from the measurable mechanics of determining it. But this integration theory is not without its serious detractors, who claim that any method purporting to be scientific cannot be described by claims that fall short of what is measurable and thus empirically verifiable. For some, the unborn would possess consciousness to some degree, while for others panpsychism is simply pseudoscience wrapped up in scientific garb. With all things considered, the theory of panpsychism is that consciousness pervades all of the universe, known or unknown, so anything that exists, known or unknown, must share such a rudimentary conscious experience. This may prove counterintuitive to personal experiences of the world, but it also offers an integrative approach connecting all existence, as the name of the theory implies. That is attractive for some but obviously will not settle the ethical value issue tethered to the public abortion dialogue.

The alternative that tends to be the antithetical rival to materialism (physicalism) is the *dualism* concept of consciousness. Dualism admits as a premise that the mind and the brain are not identical. But it also accepts the material aspect necessary for consciousness without the reductive element. Recall the *hylomorphism* of Aristotle, where the soul is the form of the body (the essence) that, along with the body as the material element, comprises the "what" of the human person. This means every human person is a composite. The human person is not inside the body. Aristotle held that an abortion is permissible prior to the fetus being formed; but one must recall that with hylomorphism, the soul is the formal cause that the body receives in potency. Therefore, "formed" here cannot simply be held equivocally as development. On that point there remains a question for the *some* stance holders. Given Aristotle's claim that the soul's presence gives animation to the body (quickening), which was adopted by a now-outdated physiology, one would have to reconcile that antiquated view of ensoulment with present views on embryology and fetal development. Further, this would necessarily include consideration for Aristotle's *teleology*, where birth is the goal-oriented purpose of the sexual act and the female's reproductive system. The question is whether an abortion would frustrate that goal and for that reason be dismissed as disordered (not ordered to its proper end). Still, Aristotle's nuanced position can offer consolation for the *some* stance. One must keep in mind that Aristotle had concerns for population growth and supported the custom of exposure, which manifested either as passive euthanasia, in which infant children were left to succumb to the elements, or as abandoning of the newborn in a communal area in the hope that others would assume responsibility. This, in the ancient world, was practiced to manage fetal anomalies (which was encouraged by law) or, as stated, to regulate community growth. Overall, if one takes this dualism approach to its logical end, with the strength being that there is something intuitive by claiming that "thinking" is radically distinct from what is "physical," it also can be reduced to the consciousness being "the person" existing inside as a modern Cartesian expression of Gnosticism.

To the abortion dialogue explicitly, this view does require an acceptance of an immaterial aspect of the human person, who, as a composite, is a single substance of form and matter. This acceptance need not be dogmatic as with a revealed religion; but like the other positions on consciousness, it requires at least the explicit application of hylomorphism where the moral value of the unborn or infant is weighed against the value of bodily autonomy. An exception would be the Christian dualistic view, which leans to the dogmatic stance, rationally expressed. This holds that every living human being, as an ensouled composite, has moral value attached to the composite being and not to the presence of consciousness. By such a metric, any termination of the unborn would likely be limited to those instances where PDE would ethically permit an exception. Further, from the dogmatic stance it would be inconceivable how such an application could apply to any post-utero, living human, as was the case with ancient infant exposure.

This chapter began with the claim that if one's argument begins with a faulty premise, then no logical path to a sound argument or true conclusion is possible. Further, it is logical that there are binary sides in the present abortion debate, which themselves produce binary effects: ultimately, either a female's bodily autonomy is abolished or the life of an unborn human ends in death. But the binary sides—of female bodily autonomy and the life of the unborn—that ultimately result in those effects cannot themselves be foundational premises. Not only are they in tension; they are oppositional in that one logically impinges on the other. It was asserted that the ethical evaluation of an abortion must be premised on *whether all or some living humans are persons*, and the public dialogue needs to reorient to that single foundational premise. It was also admitted that sides will persist, but they would rationally form from determiners of the recognition or acceptance of personhood, which is a single, arguable premise. Finally, then, once a judgment on personhood is reached, it must be weighed against either safeguarding female bodily autonomy or preserving fetal life. Both premises of the original binaries remain, as autonomy and life are authentic goods that require consideration; but they are secondary to the ontological claim of the unborn. This task is no small one; it is a virtual reorientation of the default grounds that have been argued for half a century in the public square, on news programs, social media outlets, and embattled partisan platforms. The goal of focusing on personhood requires the death of pro-life and the abolition of pro-choice as sloganized stances. In their stead, what follows are two sections, each offering a defendable advocacy argument for either the premise *some living humans are persons* or the claim *all living humans are persons*.

A DEFENDABLE ADVOCACY ARGUMENT THAT SOME LIVING HUMANS ARE PERSONS

What follows are not arguments devised to satisfy all nuances of an advocacy position. Neither is each ensuing argument formed as a definitive response, but rather they are concretely designed to serve as templates for consideration in terms of their logical consistency and resistance to reform. Both advocacy arguments present how to "walk through" an argument that, as both valid and sound, may be tweaked within certain parameters to fit various fundamental definitions. That is to say, one may mold each argument in accord to a particular expression of *consciousness*, in the case of "some living humans are persons," or *fertilization* for the advocacy of "all living humans are persons." The premised terms, *consciousness* and *fertilization*, will then be considered against the value of female bodily autonomy and fetal life. It is important to note that each argument offered is intended to be a strong argument, meaning that they are resistant, not impervious, to being criticized through logical scrutiny and critical thinking. That is simply the humble acknowledgment that there is no single argument that is unsusceptible to being logically dismantled. Further, they are not the *only* strong arguments that may be made; but in light of what has been presented and within the principle of charity (not immediately asserting an adversarial position and thus stifling dialogue), they are offered as the most robust argument relative to each advocacy position. A warning is in order, though: a logically valid and sound argument may be resistant to being logically dismissed, but it does not ensure that the conclusion is either compelling or emotionally satisfying. And the truth of each premise that follows, in both this and the subsequent section, will not be reargued. That foundational treatment occurred elsewhere in the previous sections and chapters. But even if the premises are accepted as stated, along with appreciating the form of the arguments, it is realized that the rationally derived conclusion can never be the initial way to "win over" and convince the public masses. People must first agree to listen reflectively, engage respectfully, and, while being charitable, remain within the confines of rational discourse. That in itself may seem rather idealistic—and perhaps unrealistic. But that is another underlying theme throughout this text: assuming that the participants adhere to agreed-upon rules of logic, the more objective an argument's premises, the greater the hope of the public dialogue on abortion commencing both respectfully and fruitfully. That, quite frankly, was the reason for inclusion of "The elements of an argument" in the first chapter. To remain "logical" is not to discount the role of rhetoric, or even emotion, and certainly not passion. It is only to affirm that each of those, in the absence of the rules of logic and the discipline of critical thinking, will devolve into one "side" tyrannizing the other. When there can be neither appeal to rational discourse nor agreed-upon terms of public engagement, browbeating, shaming, or duplicity is the only avenue to forward one's advocacy position. That may very well describe the present state of things. But it was offered early on in this treatise that courage as a moral freedom is a welcomed virtue; it would then follow that such courage stands as a prerequisite for the notion of hope. Both courage and hope may be uncommon in the current public dialogue on abortion, but neither is exceptional as a personal trait. Therefore, for those in the public square—in news outlets, social media, and even the political sphere, as they are composed of single individuals or are simply groups formed as individuals writ large—the virtues of courage and hope remain possible and realistic.

To present a defensible argument advocating for bodily autonomy, which permits an abortion as an ethical judgment based on bodily autonomy, it is strongest (steel man) to argue that some living humans are persons. It has been argued previously that anyone's autonomy stops at the threshold of another person. If all living humans were persons, there would need to be an additional argument for why one person can summarily terminate the life of another for proportionate reasons, in order to substantiate a claim that an abortion is ethical. That is possible. But, to argue the *some* stance well, the necessity of consciousness for personhood offers the clearest and most defendable criteria. Specifically, the materialist and dualist expressions are both publicly defendable and palatable. As it has been presented, consciousness is not merely recognizing oneself as distinct from the world but would likely include (again, depending on the expression) the capacity for memory and some indication of self-reflection in experience. Those parameters for consciousness present a strong marker for personhood because, unlike heartbeat detection or pain reflex, consciousness seems to contain something substantial beyond physical functions, also a criterion that may be argued universally and thus valued. Regardless of one's definition of consciousness, here is the form of the argument.

P1 The possession of consciousness is the capacity for memory and some indication of self-reflection in experience.

P2 The marker of personhood is the possession of consciousness.

C Therefore, the marker of personhood is the capacity for memory and some indication of self-reflection in experience.

This assertion that a living human deemed conscious has value does not imply that prior to consciousness the unborn or infant has no moral value, only that the moral value is less than that of living humans who are accepted as persons and, by that designation, granted due dignity. The next premise to consider is that unborn nonpersons who lack consciousness are not granted unreserved expectancy to the preservation of life; therefore, the life of the unborn nonperson, when weighed against the female's bodily autonomy, results in an abortion as the ethical judgment. Here is that argument as a *modus ponens*, expressed here to favor the *some living humans are persons* stance. The argument would be as follows:

> If one affirms a female has the final decision of what to do with her own body (P = bodily autonomy), then the choice whether to carry a fetus to term is ultimately up to the female (Q = support for choice). A person affirms the female has (P) bodily autonomy; therefore, the person supports (Q) choice.

Once consciousness (marker for personhood) becomes the premise for determining the affirmation of the female's bodily autonomy, then based on the criteria of the capacity for memory and some indication of self-reflection in experience, the argument aligned with the value of a female's bodily autonomy can be syllogistically expressed as follows.

P1 Living humans without consciousness are valued less than a female person's expression of bodily autonomy.

P2 Those living humans who lack the capacity for memory and some indication of self-reflection in experience are living humans without consciousness.

C Therefore, those living humans who lack the capacity for memory and some indication of self-reflection in experience are valued less than that of a female person's expression of bodily autonomy.

This is not to claim that society assigns no value to the living human nonperson at the fetal or perhaps even infant stage because of the lack of consciousness; but, lacking the recognition of personhood, the value for such living human nonpersons is not greater than, or even equivalent to, the value of a living human person who is afforded bodily autonomy.

This argument is to affirm that the value of a *person* is preserved in dignity by the ability to preserve and express bodily autonomy. The acceptance of the value recognized for *nonpersons*, as those who are lacking consciousness, can be considered but cannot be imposed as an imperative. If it were to be imposed, that would undermine the autonomy of the female person and thus their dignity. Therefore, even if a value can exist for the preservation of nonpersons (the value of the fetus is not zero), it cannot rise to the level of an imperative and be ethically imposed. This then holds that the value attached to the dignity of the female person expressed by bodily autonomy trumps any value assigned to the fetal nonperson lacking consciousness. Restated, whenever such criteria for consciousness *is not evidently present*, the preservation of the unborn nonperson cannot primarily determine the ethical judgment of an abortion. This would logically apply to the living human nonperson in utero, during the first two trimesters. Also, depending on the expression of consciousness that one applies as the standard for personhood, that lack of primacy can and should logically extend to the unborn living human in the third trimester (as the fetus is still physiologically dependent), or even to the first few months of infancy (the infant is still in physiological need of continual sustenance and care). Here is that argument expressed syllogistically.

P1 If consciousness is not evidently present until five months of age, the primacy privilege of the infant is not equivalent to or greater than the expressed autonomy of the persons providing the continued sustenance.

P2 The value of living humans as nonpersons who are physiologically dependent on the female or surrogate for continued sustenance aligns with the onset of consciousness as not evidently present until five months of age.

C Therefore, the value of living humans as nonpersons who are physiologically dependent on the female or surrogate for continued sustenance, as the primacy privilege of the infant is not equivalent to or greater than the expressed autonomy of the persons providing the continued sustenance.

An immediate reaction to this argument would be that even after five months of age, when sufficient consciousness *is* evidently present, the five-month-old infant displays no substantial distinction from the born, preconscious infant in terms of physiological dependence on the female or surrogate for continued sustenance. But notice the change in the premise—and thus a slippery slope fallacy has formed by that assertion. The distinction at that point is that the onset of sufficient consciousness is evident, and thus the infant is *now a person* with a primacy privilege that *is* equivalent to the expressed autonomy of the female or surrogate. Admittedly, the argument that the primacy privilege of a preconscious but sustenance-dependent infant warrants less autonomy than the caregiver is emotionally distressing to accept. But that reality is due neither to the lack of logical validity and soundness of the argument nor to the inherent ethical consistency. The dismissal of the argument, if such an argument surfaced, would be predicated on a guttural reaction to the thought of psychologically accepting a post-birth abortion or infant euthanasia.

That can help explain why the argument of an abortion during the first two trimesters is more emotionally digestible and appears in line with present public sentiment. There arises something instinctual in providing sustenance for a viable fetus or infant. The image one holds in their mind of a fetus at that stage is much like an infant; and between the psychological projection of infant-like qualities to the fetus and its chronologic proximity to birth, the moral value of the fetus approaches that of an infant, which popular opinion assumes is a person because it is no longer inside the female's body. It has an effect if one considers that public support for a procured abortion begins to wane by the third trimester, in that female bodily autonomy tends to equalize with the public's ascribed value to the near-term fetus and born infant.

Another factor to consider, related to viability and sustenance, is the general acceptance that society can assume some responsibility for care. The emotive value placed on a near-term developed fetus's proximity to birth, in tandem with the notion of legal personhood assigned at the birth event where a "separate life" permits society to intervene, has ingrained public value. Here is that claim made syllogistically.

P1 An ingrained instinctual necessity to provide sustenance for a viable fetus or born infant diminishes public support for an abortion in the third trimester.

P2 The value emotionally ascribed to the fetus by the proximity to birth or the infant after the birth event itself ingrains an instinctual necessity to provide sustenance for a viable fetus or born infant.

C The value emotionally ascribed to the fetus by the proximity to birth or the infant after the birth event itself diminishes public support for an abortion in the third trimester.

This emotional value ascribed to the third-trimester fetus on behalf of the born infant is felt even more intensely toward the born infant. In the absence of evident and sufficient consciousness, the lack of primacy could and logically should extend to *the unborn* living human. That may be palatable to many. But, once again, to be logically and ethically consistent, if those same substantial conditions of insufficient consciousness and necessary sustenance remain even in the first five months of infancy, the premise remains that *the infant* as a nonperson is not assigned a moral value equal to the primacy of the autonomy of the female or caregiver. This is to claim that once the fetus is either viable or born, since the distinction is not based on a value ascribed to recognizing ontological personhood as the onset of consciousness but primarily to society being capable of assuming care, then any claim of early infant euthanasia is just an extension of the logic ethically to support a third-trimester abortion, which clearly also presents the conditions of society intervening. Obviously, this is publicly unsettling. But again, regardless of it being an emotionally charged judgment, it remains a valid and sound argument. Further, as the present proponents of infant euthanasia argue convincingly, their position is at the very least ethically consistent. They hold the "line" for personhood based on sufficient consciousness, understood as the capacity for memory and some indication of self-reflection in experience. That is more ethically consistent than those who simply draw the line at viability or birth. Both of those markers for the onset of personhood are predicated on either a "likely survivable birth" or an "outside of the body" argument that offers no substantial ontological distinction, but rather surfaces as an emotive attempt to satisfy what is otherwise an unsettling ethical judgment.

It is understood this is unlikely to be considered an effective argument, as it will not placate the masses. And it certainly is not intended to provide a reasoned judgment that can be accepted by both sides, as it is neither a compromise nor a concession. But it must be taken into account that a future society will likely habituate to this ethical judgment; as the pedestrian climate over subsequent generations simply becomes more comfortable with their inherited premises, those premises may possibly take hold in culture and become the new social justice expectations in future generations.

Consider again how, historically, the societal acceptance of abortion has changed drastically over the last half of the twentieth century. Procured abortions have always occurred; but, relatively speaking, popular moral evaluations and civil laws only recently offered abortion public support and legal protection. That attests to stringent opposition, at least aligned with public opinion, up until very recent times. Ethical evaluations and liberty-based reproductive rights from then have developed exponentially. End-of-life care for infants is ethically acceptable by all stances, and infant euthanasia has proceeded from that as ethically acceptable in a growing minority of countries. Even though third-trimester abortions are rare, it is not inconceivable that post-birth abortions can follow from the inferences of the same logic, if based on sufficient consciousness as the marker for personhood rather than a vacillating emotional designation. Perhaps they will gain wider acceptability, provided they are regulated with the same societal and legal intensity of third-trimester, pre-birth abortions. They may, to some degree, find parallel acceptance with the increased liberty and rising societal endorsement of MAiD for adolescents and adults, as the criteria now extends beyond terminal illnesses to include chronic health conditions,[2] which include mental illness, even for minors. In short, what may presently appear intuitively repugnant can possibly parallel the evolutionary acceptance of procured abortions and emerge as clear ethical thinking within the next half century.

If the terms *human* and *life*, used to refer to the unborn, are themselves sufficient categories to settle the abortion issue, which is a fundamental aspect of this argument, then it is not because a being is a living human that they are afforded autonomy; rather, that autonomy is attached only to the designation of personhood. But the term *autonomy* also remains ambiguous and unable to settle the issue. For even as autonomy ceases at the threshold of another person, if personhood is predicated on sufficient consciousness, and if prior to the third trimester there is no consciousness, then there is no personhood to curb female autonomy. It then logically implies that if the onset of sufficient consciousness is determined to not surface until five months post-utero (keep in mind there is no valid or sound argument that the birth event is the onset of consciousness), then an infant at that stage may have an ascribed value like the viable fetus but is not a person, and thus the autonomy of the female or caregiver remains primary. For an abortion advocate, which is certainly not derogatory if no "person" is being terminated, the argued-for conclusion of personhood is that sufficient consciousness, indicated by the capacity for memory and some indication of self-reflection in experience, is simply the least refutable marker for personhood and thus sets the ethical line.

Given that infant euthanasia seems to imply infanticide, and any support for infanticide might be perceived as a way to poison the overall position of *some living humans are persons*, further comments are warranted so one does not think the *some* position implies no ethical restrictions. Because a third-trimester nonperson (fetus physiologically attached to the pregnant female) or a nonperson infant (infant physiologically dependent on the pregnant female or surrogate caregiver) is a living human not designated as a person, it does not logically imply a lack of inherent moral value. For some, that lesser value in the nonperson infant, although present, is not sufficient to impede infanticide under certain conditions where low life satisfaction is foreseen or undesired anomalies are present. That is the proposal, in a nutshell, offered by some

2. See Fruhstorfer, et al. "Patient Experiences."

ethicists and philosophers in support of post-birth abortions. But the ethical slide down the slope to infanticide is not necessarily affirmed. That is, in response to the concern that this criterion of consciousness, when absent, must then lead to infanticide, the short answer is that it is not necessarily so. But the *some living humans are persons* proponent who accepts consciousness as the marker for personhood would have to refute such a judgment by articulating the moral worth of the born infant on grounds other than personhood. That is quite possible, as one option is the *potentiality of personhood*, which can especially be enhanced by the *nearness to personhood*, in the same way that nearness to birth offers moral value to the viable fetus. The determination of moral value is not binary but exists on a spectrum that is then proportionally considered. It may be accepted that at a certain point, even though the nonperson infant is less than the value of a being with personhood, enough moral value is present to warrant the reconsideration of what weight is assigned to the dignity of the female's bodily autonomy. For example, here is a thought experiment to explain such comparative valuing. With mass casualties, the medical principle of *triage* is exercised to identify those for whom intervention and treatment are deemed proportionate to the goal of recovery, who will receive treatment prior to others for whom treatment will not be as effective or for whom intervention would come at the disproportionate expense of those with greater expectancy of recovery. Giving this care and attention to those deemed *more treatable* is not done by summarily discounting those *less treatable*—that is to say, the less treatable are not without value. But given the circumstances and limited resources, their triage allocation is weighed against those who are prioritized not by some inherent or assigned value to their personhood, but by predictable outcome. Applied to the public abortion dialogue and the concern for infanticide, in the same way other goods such as the physical, psychological, and familial well-being are fundamental concerns of the caregiver and society, the infant nonperson will be valued against those goods in the same way a third-trimester fetus is valued. That is to claim that the third-trimester fetus, although a nonperson, has value that is closer to that of a lower triage determination. Again, this is being ethically consistent, as otherwise any advocate for a third-trimester termination would have to make an ontological distinction of greater value for the newborn infant, which cannot simply be predicated on society's ability to assume care and responsibility. It was explained that this is not a sound argument, so both the viable fetus and infant, according to the criterion of consciousness, lack personhood and thus share a value that is not substantially distinct. An advocate who accepts the termination of a viable unborn in utero should be prepared to extend that evaluation to the nonperson infant. It is a slippery slope for certain, but not a slippery slope fallacy, as each evaluation remains the logical extension of the same premise.

One might notice that the sufficiency of consciousness, with no consensus as to how early it appears, tends to parallel the emancipation for a living human's need for psychological sustenance and care. Specifically, in infants five to six months of age, most accept a sufficient level of consciousness to warrant and recognize personhood. And further, as the level of necessary sustenance and care wanes, the primacy of the female's bodily autonomy also diminishes. At the point of fetal viability, the bodily autonomy argument begins to weaken to the point that it is not so readily accepted as primary, or at least not primary enough to warrant an abortion for reasons other than the preservation of the female's physical life or fetus survivability. Prior to viability, there is presently no relative chance of survival, so it follows that at that point and earlier the female's autonomy would remain primary, and it is intuitively accepted as such. But at and after viability up until the birth event, given no other mitigating circumstances, the moral value of the living human unborn nonperson would be significant enough to warrant the consideration of an ethical judgment of delivery and subsequent care—and would not unreservedly be subject to the female's choice. On the surface, if this is true, it would appear to weaken the concern for infant euthanasia or post-birth abortions. But the premises do not change; only the "location" of the living human nonperson does. That is to suggest that unless a valid and sound argument is put forth for why a third-trimester fetus is susceptible to an abortion predicated on female bodily autonomy, where the fetus is ontologically distinct from an infant, then that argument's deficiencies will make post-birth abortions equally valid and sound.

There is obviously more that must be logically worked out in the upcoming years, as determining the ontological status of the viable fetus and infants with low expected health satisfaction will likely become an increasingly larger part of the public abortion dialogue. Any necessary response to this concern will only intensify over time, along the lines of two specific points. First is that technology will continue to lower the gestational age of viability. As the viability of gestational age decreases, any moral worth of the near-birth fetus will continue to extend to that earlier point. An advocate for *some living humans are persons* will have to logically accept that scientific advancements will change the premise of viability being substantially distinct from earlier gestational points of development, because there will be an increasingly ethical encroachment on the weight assigned to bodily autonomy and thus the cutoff point for an abortion in utero. Specifically, the intervention of society to assume care and responsibility will continue to occur earlier. The second point is that if moral worth is tethered to *what is valued*, improved imaging resolution along with intrauterine surgical interventions will increase the perception of that value. As screening resolutions become higher and three-dimensional images continue to be more realistic, those experiences will likely affect society's assignment of the ethical value to an increasingly lower gestational age, which will likely parallel the increasingly earlier point of viability.

Here is the terminal claim. If consciousness, as the capacity for memory with some indication of self-reflection in experience, becomes the onset of personhood, then the present "gray area"—from viability to the onset of sufficient consciousness at five months of age—will result in two distinct challenges. The first is that if the moral value of the fetus follows the lower viability age in an inverse relation, then those who hesitate to support the primacy of autonomy in the third trimester due to projection and nearness to birth will experience more restriction for an ethical abortion as viability dips lower than twenty-two gestational weeks. The second is that in the same scenario, those who support the primacy of autonomy in the third trimester may resist accepting any more restriction paralleling the lower gestational age of viability. In tandem they will have more difficulty arguing against the charge of accepting infant euthanasia. The reasoning is that in the absence of psychological projection or an emotive standing, there is no substantial ontological distinction on the low side between a viable fetus with a shared *syneidēsis* (more specifically a prenatal ≥26 GA fetus), and the "cutoff" for sufficiency of consciousness of a nonperson infant at postnatal ≤5 months or age on the high side. Here is a defendable advocacy argument that some living humans are persons, expressed in a series of syllogistic arguments, where the final syllogism's premises are drawn from inferences of the previous two syllogisms' conclusions.

P1 *Syneidēsis* is sufficiently present when there is measurable evidence of a thalamocortical structure capable of reciprocal internal and external states.

P2 The marker of personhood is when *syneidēsis* is sufficiently present.

C1 Therefore, the marker of personhood is when there is measurable evidence of a thalamocortical structure capable of reciprocal internal and external states.

***

P3 Those who lack measurable evidence of a thalamocortical structure capable of reciprocal internal and external states are deemed living human nonpersons.

P4 If a fetus ≥26 GA or infant ≤5 months lacks sufficient *syneidēsis* and thus lacks personhood, they lack a measurable thalamocortical structure capable of reciprocal internal and external states.

C2 Therefore, if a fetus ≥26 GA or infant ≤5 months lacks the capacity for memory and indication of self-reflection in experience, they are deemed living human nonpersons.

***

P5 The moral value for living humans that is tethered to *syneidēsis* is less than the moral value of the female's bodily autonomy or that to compel caregiving by another.

P6 If a fetus ≥26 GA or infant ≤5 months lacks the capacity for memory and indication of self-reflection in experience, they lack the moral value for living humans that is tethered to *syneidēsis*.

C3 Therefore, to terminate a fetus ≥26 GA or infant ≤5 months, the fetus or infant must have a moral value less than the female's bodily autonomy or that to compel a caregiver.

Those are the proposed steps to advocate for the *some living humans are persons* premise. One must argue for the definition of consciousness, which may not align with *syneidēsis* as "lacking the capacity for memory and some indication of self-reflection in experience," but the form of the argument remains.

In conclusion, here is the argument advocating for *some living humans are persons* in sentence form as a distillation of what has thus far been proposed. The marker for personhood, as *syneidēsis*, is the capacity for memory and some indication of self-reflection in experience. If living, human nonpersons (prenatal ≥26 GA to postnatal ≤5 months) lack this sufficiency of consciousness, they would therefore not be granted unreserved expectancy to the preservation of life. If they do have sufficiency of consciousness, then the moral value is not without consideration, but the human life of the fetus (prenatal ≥26 GA) must be weighed against the female's bodily autonomy, and that of the newborn (postnatal ≤5 months) against the caregiver's autonomy. This moral evaluation can result in an abortion as an ethical judgment, as the value of the female's bodily autonomy or that of the caregiver is greater than that of the unborn or newborn nonperson, or unborn or newborn person with insufficient moral value. This value of a pregnant female, as a *person*, is preserved in dignity by the ability to safeguard and express bodily autonomy. That is what is at stake. This implies, then, that whatever value is assigned to or recognized for the unborn or born living human as *persons* or *nonpersons* cannot be imposed as an imperative, as that would undermine the autonomy and thus the dignity of the female person or caregiver. This means that whenever such criteria for consciousness *are not evidently present*, it is the bodily autonomy of the female and not the preservation of the unborn or born nonperson (or those with insufficient moral value) that can primarily determine the ethical judgment of an abortion. It is then also true that the value of born living humans as nonpersons, as those who are physiologically dependent on the female or surrogate for continued sustenance after birth, is not equivalent to or greater than the expressed autonomy of the persons providing the continued sustenance. Once more, this asserts that autonomy stops at the threshold of another person, which by this scenario is present at about five months of age. This can be emotionally unsettling, as the premises logically support infant euthanasia. But in the same way that public support in the United States for an abortion begins to wane after the first trimester and more so in the third trimester[3] (28 weeks GA) because of the value emotionally ascribed by proximity to birth or the birth event

3. Crary and Fingerhut, "Most Say Restrict Abortion," para. 3.

itself, if those same substantial conditions of insufficient consciousness and necessary sustenance remain even in the first five months of infancy, the premise remains that the moral value of the infant as a nonperson has less primacy than that of a caregiver or of the female's bodily autonomy. Therefore, conditions surrounding infant euthanasia are not unlike the conditions of the abortion of a viable fetus post 28 weeks GA. As to it being unsettling, it is not inconceivable that a future society will habituate to this ethical judgment, in the same way that past public contempt for the death of a prenatal life has evolved in fifty years to the point of the present generation now accepting an abortion as basic healthcare. As the pedestrian climate over subsequent generations simply becomes more comfortable with the premise that *some living humans are persons*, and only persons are afforded primacy in the ethical judgment of an abortion, then ethical consistency and logical scrutiny will demonstrate that there is no *person* until sufficient consciousness is evident, so the abortion or termination of a living human nonperson is an ethical judgment.

A DEFENDABLE ADVOCACY ARGUMENT THAT ALL LIVING HUMANS ARE PERSONS

The advocacy argument put forth here in defense of *all living humans are persons* will assume the same conditions as the previous explication. To reiterate, this presentation is not designed to satisfy all nuances of this advocacy position and assumes no pretense as a definitive response. But, in like manner, it is proposed as a template for consideration, open to the possibility of refinement. An obvious distinction, though worth stating explicitly, is that unlike the previous argument, here one's expression of *consciousness* is no longer the premise for personhood. In fact, it is the very presupposition that because there *is no marker* for personhood, all living humans must be persons by virtue of simply being both alive and of the humankind. The two strongest claims for this *all* position are first that it circumvents the necessity to judge what criteria constitute personhood and, from that, the responsibility to determine which living humans are designated as persons. For the *some* stance holders, the "necessity to judge" must remain ethically and logically consistent, in that the criteria that apply to fetuses or infants must also apply to children and adults. In short, if a criterion is chosen, it must be universally applied to all living humans. That initial complication is no small concern to dispense with for the *all* stance holders, as not excluding any living humans from being persons also ethically circumvents the justice issue brought on with the related second claim. The second claim is that if only some living humans are persons, then the *some* camp must satisfy the ethical question as to exactly *who* determines what the criteria *are* to confer personhood on some living humans.

One should hover on that last point briefly, as it inevitably presents as one group of living humans determining the personhood status of other living humans. To grasp that thoroughly, here is an example by analogy. One can consider the justice issues that arise with determining normativity and disability with living human persons. It is clearer, though, to speak of impairment rather than disability, as impairment relates to reduction in function while disability connotes the consequences of that impairment, such as needing ramps, audio signals, and such. The point is that the disability from an impairment can be offered some compensation, and therefore the impairment can be mitigated, perhaps to the degree of not even qualifying as a disability. But to the point at hand, for this issue of impairment as a parallel to precisely who determines the criteria for personhood, two subpoints warrant notice. First, when one considers condition X an impairment, initially it must be argued why precisely it is deemed nonnormative. For example, some in the deaf community consider deafness not a disability but a culture—and, further, one which should be recognized and preserved. Secondly, regardless of an individual's sense of compassion, it is noteworthy to recognize that it is not uncommon for professional healthcare workers to deem life satisfaction of impaired persons as being lower than the actual impaired person would evaluate their own life satisfaction. In other words, the impaired person does not view their own condition nearly as limiting to their happiness as others might. This situation is referred to as *ableism*, where social prejudices form attitudes implicitly, and it results in discriminatory assumptions. These are two strong claims for this *all* position, and they each preserve any determination of personhood from the personal judgment predicated on what is deemed comfortable in terms of a function or a value. Any determination that excludes *some* from this category of persons also extends to excluding both natural rights and the fundamental dignity of those held to be nonpersons. Those who hold to the *all* stance are inoculated from excluding others who are deemed impaired or inferior, lack utility, or present as burdens to society. And by virtue of forming no exclusivity to this group deemed persons, no justice issue formed by power or transient values can be levied against them as singling out the vulnerable or disenfranchised, for individual, cultural, or even eugenic goals.

As to respect of the female's bodily autonomy, this *all living humans are persons* position does not summarily dismiss autonomy, but its value is weighed against the personhood of the unborn. In the same way one's personal rights stop where another person's rights begin, so too does the bodily autonomy of one person stop at the threshold of another person, whose bodily autonomy must be equally respected. However, as with the previous treatment of the *some* advocacy, to state that there is no living human who is not a person does not *ipso facto* resolve the issue of moral value or how to proceed when the goods of human life and bodily autonomy are in conflict or tension. With this *all* position, to circumvent the injustices that arise over determining *what* constitutes and *who* determines the personhood of another living human, to state that "all living humans are persons" from the moment of fertilization offers the clearest and most defendable point as the onset of personhood. To place the basic argument then in syllogistic form, it may be expressed as follows.

P1 There are no assignable criteria for personhood if every living human is a person.

P2 The onset of personhood is fertilization as there are no assignable criteria for personhood.

C Therefore, the onset of personhood is fertilization if every living human is a person.

Rather than with the *some* camp where the markers for personhood appear at various gestational stages or align with certain expressions of functionality, there is no need for this position to adjudicate each one separately. This is an affirmative stance, and a negative need not be proven. Still, the errors relating to each criterion that the *some* camp may levy against the "personhood at fertilization" position could be, and should be, globally addressed. Otherwise, one will fall prey to the Bulverism fallacy, which is to state something *is* in error without explaining *how* it is in error. In other words, this position is only credible to hold if each confronting argument is rejected collectively with the others; and in order to logically reject them, they must conjointly be demonstrated neither necessary nor sufficient. To state it plainly, as an argument, each criterion is required to be demonstrated unsound, fallacious, lacking logical form, or ethically inconsistent in unison with all others. If one criterion for personhood is determined as true, then the *all living humans are persons* premise falls by that single point. Similarly, if *all living humans are persons* is true, then all the criteria for personhood fall collectively. The point is that the single premise of concern over both *what* and *who* is determining personhood should equally apply to each possible marker offered by the *some* camp. So, an argument that fails to adequately address one does *ipso facto* demonstrate the *all* premise offered here as to be in error. But conversely, the argument here that adequately satisfies one of the *some* camp contains the framework that can be equally applied to all of the *some living humans are persons* advocacy in tandem.

An aesthetic point that fosters sympathy requires mention. The advocacy argument for the *some* stance places the marker for personhood at sufficient consciousness, which logically brought the personhood of not only viable fetuses but also of infants into the nonperson designation. For the society at large, even if the argument is rationally constructed, that is neither popular nor easily digestible. But here too with the *all* advocacy argument, the logical conclusion can provoke a similar knee-jerk reaction: just as it might appear both unsettling and dubious to assign a nonperson status to born infants, it would appear counterintuitive and equally dubious to argue that a 0.7-millimeter zygote, or even a six-week-old fetus merely 1.25 inches long that aesthetically resembles a tadpole, both *is* and *can* be argued as a living human person. But with the ethical judgments of either a zygote, fetus, or infant, the aesthetic factor must be set aside as the critical criterion for an abortion judgment. The determination of *what* a person is should not be resolved by what the person does or does not look like. Whether a zygote, fetus, or infant, each is a living human from a biological perspective. One may—and should—argue from either perspective as to what the recognition or assignment of moral worth is for the zygote, fetus, or infant; but once personhood is necessarily connected to any of the three, the ethical evaluation and moral value then exist between persons (female and fetus, or caregiver and infant) and thus respect for the autonomy of each must logically become a consideration. Where there is personhood, there is inherent moral worth; and as the moral worth is tethered to personhood, the ethical determination must be applicable to any age of a living human as a person. This position has logical implications. To reiterate such a point, the moral evaluation of a zygote based on personhood must be ethically consistent with a living human person at other stages of life. In the absence of such ethical consistency, any evaluation would necessarily reduce the moral value of personhood down to the evaluation of some persons over other persons. That is the primary discord revealed here with the *some living humans are persons* advocacy stance. If the personhood of some living humans is reduced for commensurate reasons, it will result logically in a judgment of subjugation and thus present itself to be ethically hazardous and subject to political and power manipulation.

In this advocacy argument of the *all* stance, if the personhood of the unborn is recognized, a primary and legitimate concern surfaces that the *life* of the pregnant female will become a secondary consideration to the *life* of the unborn. This stands as a sincere contention and should be addressed preemptively, demonstrating that support for female bodily autonomy will not fall prey to exaggeration of the unborn's moral value as superior to the female's life. The contention enters the public abortion dialogue in the form of a concern that imputes there would be no ethical intervention permissible for serious threats to the pregnant female's *life*. Because abortion is regulated by the State, which is warranted by virtue of the State's role of promoting and preserving public health through policy and legislation, abortion is often understood as a civil and legal justice issue. The *some* stance frames the State's involvement in terms of allowing access to an abortion, which is viewed as basic public healthcare, while the *all* camp envisions the law's necessity to impose a moral imperative in much the same way that the State weighs in on other threats to the physical life of persons. But while legislation and court rulings are an essential component of the public dialogue on abortion, the legal definition of *life* is not defined essentially, but rather broadly and equivocally. In terms of the ethical evaluation of the concerns of both stances, the State's definition conflates *biological life* with *what affects one's life*. For instance, as was explained in the chapter "Reorienting the Discussion," within the section "The value of preserving life," the pedestrian definition (the public's intuitive grasp) of what constitutes a "threat to the life of the pregnant female" is a potential for serious health risks that make the female's death certain, or that will likely result in an irreparable and serious health condition. But *Doe v. Bolton* (1973) set a legal and public precedent that widened the interpretation of "life of the female" to include any mental issues of the female, physical defects of the fetus along with ensuing care, the psychological and emotional condition of the female including her family dynamics, and, finally, the female's age during pregnancy. Both the *all* and the *some* camp may readily agree that those are mitigating factors, but they are elements of *what affects one's life* and are not identical with death, or the end of *biological life*. The term *life*, untethered from the qualifier *biological*, is quite relative and subject to political and policy persuasion. If one applies the *what affects one's life* rubric to born persons with established and recognized consciousness, then it becomes apparent that moral value attached to personhood cannot be so easily set aside. This is to mean that if a child or adult causes burdens due to physical defects, or instigates pressing psychological pressures on the caregivers, or contributes negatively to familial dynamics of the female, one may rightly state that those elements affect the life of the female and family but are not physically life-threatening issues. Logical and ethical consistency would require the same application of value across the spectrum of biological life, from fetal life through childhood and then adulthood. Ultimately, the term *life* requires defining in the public dialogue and subsequent acceptance of an essential meaning.

But that equivocation cannot skirt the issue that remains, under the assumption of the *all living humans are persons* stance: the authentic concern that, if the female were confidently in predictable physical harm, the life or well-being of the female is jeopardized without unfettered access to an abortion. The *all* stance can respond in varied ways, but one response to that concern could include an application of triage (priority of urgency) or even what is termed emergent care (observe and judge). Yet, a more thorough and less nuanced response exists, assuming that two biological lives (pregnant female and fetus) are in mortal danger, perhaps with an ectopic or some other form of high-risk pregnancy. PDE affords an ethical resolution; within specific conditions, the *all* stance could ethically permit the death of the unborn, in order to preserve the physical life of the pregnant female for proportionate reasons. An expected rebuttal, as an initial reaction from the *some* camp, might be based on the autonomy of the pregnant female superseding the unrecognized personhood of the unborn, suggesting that such proportionality, which the *all* stance is affirming, is not even a necessary consideration. But in any logical dialogue, it is the veracity of the premise that is to be confronted, and not an attempt to abruptly dismiss the nuanced ethical resolution. It is worth explaining this further, as it arises in the public dialogue on abortion. If the *some* side were claiming that the *all* side is disproportionately concerned with the fetus and not the pregnant female, and then the *all* side attempts to demonstrate rationally that they are considering both the fetus and the pregnant female proportionally, the response of the *some* camp should not be that "there is no proportionality to consider" because the female's autonomy is tantamount. That is a type of logical filibustering, more formally known as the *argumentum ad lapidem* fallacy (the appeal to stone), which is the repeating of an assertion that favors dismissing the other side's premise, rather than rationally engaging it to demonstrate it as unsound. If the concern of the *some* camp is that the *all* stance holders favor the life of the fetus over the life of the pregnant female, then the *all* camp's attempt to demonstrate that as not true must stand or fall on the merit of the argument put forth.

Next, to engage the premise of applying PDE, notice that the term "death of the unborn" was used rather than "termination of the unborn," which describes a procured abortion. This is to maintain both ethical consistency and proportionality, as aligned with PDE where the "death of the unborn" is anticipated as the foreseen bad effect but is ethically accepted to preserve the physical life of the female, which is the desired and proportional good effect. So, even if the death of the unborn is foreseen, because it is not desired or purposefully intended, it is situated as a viable and ethical option. Stated positively, the death of the fetus would be unnecessary if it was morally certain the pregnant female would neither suffer death nor incur serious ill health effects. Granted, several circumstances would need to be specifically addressed that extend beyond the present point; but provided the intervention does not involve the direct intention of ending the life of the unborn, the pregnant female's life and health may be ethically preserved in line with the *all* camp's stance on moral value and personhood of the fetus. And to address the concern and restate the premise, provided the moral value of the unborn living human person is not greater than that of the pregnant female—which it is not by an *all* stance under the rubric of PDE—the death of the unborn is ethically warranted in order to preserve the life of the pregnant female person. This argument as a *modus ponens* would be as follows.

> If one affirms that a pregnant female and the unborn share equal moral value (P = shared value), then when the pregnancy is biologically life threatening to the female, to foresee but not intend the death of the fetus is the choice of the female (Q = support for choice). A person affirms that a pregnant female and the unborn share equal moral value (P); therefore, when the pregnancy is biologically life threatening to the female, to foresee but not intend the death of the fetus is the choice of the female (Q).

An important distinction with this application of PDE is that proportionality is a key factor. The moral value of the pregnant female is equal to the unborn. That means that as autonomy remains a consideration, and since autonomy is attached to personhood, the autonomy of the pregnant female *and* the unborn must both be ethically considered. In that calculation, then, as a parallel to Aquinas's application of PDE used with the case of self-defense, one may frame the danger of the pregnancy to the physical life of the pregnant female such that under certain conditions the female is ethically justified to preserve her own physical life, even if doing so results in the death of the unborn. Both lives *are* proportionate.

P1 The female's autonomy remains a consideration, even when doing so results in the death of the unborn.

P2 Under certain conditions the female is ethically justified to preserve her own physical life, as the female's autonomy remains a consideration.

C Therefore, under certain conditions the female is ethically justified to preserve her own physical life, even when doing so results in the death of the unborn.

But in contrast to that, if one broadens the term *life* to hold the legal meaning of *what affects one's life*, then the key factor of proportionality is no longer ethically satisfied. The ethical calculation of PDE then would not find the death of the unborn to be proportionate to any concern for the care, conditions, and dynamics that have a lower moral value than the biological life of the unborn living human person. Thus, the death of the unborn, according to PDE, would in those circumstances fail the test of proportionality and be judged ethically illicit.

In those circumstances just presented, where the death of the unborn would not be framed as *an abortion* but as the *preservation of the life of the pregnant female*, this is not a semantic ruse. It is rather the proper identification of an ethical judgment, demonstrating concern for Aristotle's first act of the mind where the clarity of the terms is required to avoid equivocation. Rather than an ectopic pregnancy, perhaps a case study of a "severe placental abruption" could offer insight into the distinction between *lifesaving care* of the female, where the fetus will certainly perish, and a *procured abortion,* which would include the intentional termination of the life of the fetus. A placental abruption occurs when the placenta (the temporary organ during pregnancy that provides necessary sustenance for the fetus) detaches from the uterine wall. This detachment may be either partial or complete. Symptoms experienced include abdominal pain and vaginal bleeding. The blood loss necessitates transfusions; and if the abruption is severe, delivery of the fetus will be induced to preserve the pregnant female's physical life. Relative to that inducement, if the fetus's gestational viability is not compatible with survival outside of the womb, it is foreseen but not desired that the nonviable newborn will not survive. There are those who fallaciously call this a *lifesaving abortion* scenario, but in fact it is the *lifesaving care of the female*. Those two terms are not the same, and to refer to this scenario as a lifesaving abortion both equivocates the term *abortion* and distracts the dialogue from constructive and logical engagement. Here is that argument as a syllogism.

P1 Treatment for a placental abruption that ends in the unintended death of the fetus is not a procured abortion but the *lifesaving care of the female*.

P2 Delivering a fetus incompatible with life while preserving the physical life of the pregnant female is treatment for a placental abruption that ends in the unintended death of the fetus.

C Therefore, delivering a fetus incompatible with life while preserving the physical life of the pregnant female is not a procured abortion but the *lifesaving care of the female*.

At this point in the argument, two basic assumptions protagonistic to the *all living humans are persons* proposition have been identified and addressed. The first was the issue addressing any lack of proportionality, in response to the *all* camp's rebuttal that a lack of concern for the bodily autonomy of the female would result in her physical death. The second was the clarification of the term *abortion*, which, when conflated with *lifesaving care of the female*, distracts from resolving the point of the previous contention.

The survivability of the fetus, even for those holding the *some living humans are persons* stance, which predicates personhood on the substantiated presence of consciousness, will experience a specific tension as innovative technologies continually press on the public's emotional viewpoint as survivability inches closer to fertilization. To be clear, this is not to suggest the *some* stance holders will accept the personhood of the unborn or infant without sufficient consciousness as the marker, but that the veracity of the bodily autonomy argument will be affected because of lifesaving technology. The point is that the gestational viability age will decrease in inverse proportion to the perceived increase of moral value of the unborn. Here is that argument summarized as a syllogism.

P1 The gestational viability age decreases in inverse proportion to the increase of moral value of the unborn, because of lifesaving technology.

P2 The veracity of bodily autonomy as the main criterion in the public abortion dialogue will decrease as the gestational viability age decreases.

C Therefore, the veracity of bodily autonomy as the main criterion in the public abortion dialogue will decrease in inverse proportion to the increase of moral value of the unborn, because of lifesaving technology.

This will be covered in more depth in the upcoming section "Future human wombs." But for now, the idea of embryos developing into fetuses in an external womb is neither a present possibility nor a likely one for distinct reasons. Still, it would be ethically hazardous to discount *any* future possibility. Discarding prospective technological advances has, more often than not, proven to be naïve. So, for the sake of argument, if embryos can someday be incubated in artificial wombs, the body of the female would theoretically no longer be a consideration in the ethical evaluation of an abortion. The argument of this text, the centrality of personhood, will be the only relevant criteria in tandem with moral value. But, since part of the present argument for bodily autonomy, which necessarily includes dependent care, was extended to caregivers in the *some living humans are persons* argument, the consideration of artificial wombs may very well force that issue of dependency beyond the birthing female to be engaged. The distinction is that with an artificial womb, the familial responsibility for the "decanted fetus," as fictionally depicted in Huxley's *Brave New World*, may be perceived outside of any single individual's or even the nuclear family's care. It would be more akin to the fetus as a ward of the State or the responsibility of an assigned caretaker. Rather than a legal burden on the female, as it is with pregnancy, both the female and male's contribution to the maturation of the fetus would be limited to the donation of gametic material. In reality, there are too many variables to work out ethically in order to satisfy every misgiving, but nonetheless in a general sense there are specific scenarios that evidently align with the above syllogism; thus, it remains a sound consideration. Perhaps it would apply more readily to assigning moral value to cryopreserved embryos, which are presently considered property. As there remains a dependency of the cryopreserved embryos on caretakers in the present, any custody of the external womb would share a similar relation. But as dependency does not determine personhood status for the *all* stance holders, the location of the fetus-as-person does not alter the ethical determination that would not distinguish between the illicitness of an abortion and the illicitness of not providing sufficient care and dignity to the decanting fetus. Yet, as was argued, implicit in this future conjecture is that as the bodily autonomy argument erodes, the concept of personhood will present itself as the central factor in the public abortion dialogue, if for no other reason than as a matter of utility. In this treatise, the centrality of personhood is argued as essential. If bodily autonomy is removed from the calculation, then personhood is the point of contention by default, and the arguments put forth here will only become more relevant as technology advances.

It has been stressed that an important consideration is ethical and logical consistency. The moral value associated with personhood, and the subsequent necessity of care, must necessarily follow the recognition of personhood at all stages of life. If consciousness as the sufficient criterion for personhood may exclude viable fetuses and infants, then it equally applies to children and adults in minimally conscious states, or perhaps even to those with severe brain injuries. That consideration may not be thought central to the public abortion dialogue, but it remains the logical inference from the stance of the *some* camp who would hold consciousness as the marker for personhood. Of course, this would apply to any chosen marker. However, if the birth event is thought resilient in this case, one must recall any retreat to the birth event simply is the attempt to bypass an ontological designation and rely rather on legal findings of personhood, which are equated with citizenship.

So, then, for the *all* stance holders to form a necessary response to this position, two points arise for consideration. First, since medical technology has expanded the success rate of diagnosed prenatal conditions that now are survivable, this has permitted parameters of life for some infants who are successfully carried to term and delivered, but whose health condition does not rise far above the level of mere existence. In other words, in the same way that technology has created end-of-life ethical dilemmas by extending physical life with few quality gains by means of medical intervention, scientific technology will continue to create more ethical dilemmas by preserving natal life from conditions previously not survivable. But not unlike the minimal conscious state of a child or adult who lingers prior to biological death, the newly born infant may also linger prior to biological death. If euthanasia is acceptable for the child or adult in what is considered a low-quality life state that warrants consideration, then the same ethical metric must logically apply to the born infant in a similar condition of health.

The second point is sadly ironic to the first, that regardless of future "miracle treatments," physical death remains the impenetrable border. That is, regardless of continued advancements in care and treatment, medical interventions will also continue to be limited in terms of care and treatment. Setting aside any concern for infant euthanasia, this implies the question as to what constitutes disproportionate care, meaning that any intervention resulting in physiological futility (no chance of life) to qualitative futility (low value of life) will need to be addressed for persons at the beginning of post-birth life. In other words, as is presently the case, end-of-life care will become an option for some at the very beginning of one's post-birth life, but the parameters for post-birth euthanasia will at the very least parallel the culture's position on child and adult euthanasia. The criteria for what constitutes a chosen "happy death" are broadening, not narrowing, so there is no sensible reason to assume that the criteria for determining what qualifies one for euthanasia will become anything but more culturally indulgent. Further, though it may be unsettling to make care and treatment decisions based on resource allocation and futility evaluations, both staff and facilities as resources are never unlimited, and their use must align with concerns for not merely the justice of the newborn patient but also for the community that each newborn patient enters into. This is not to equate the conditions of considering infanticide to those of maintaining a life with only brain-stem functions, but they are the logical ethical dilemmas that will arise and must be addressed. In each of those situations, the designation of personhood cannot, according to the *all* stance holders, be reduced down to some metric of utility or societal burden. The issues of proportionality and futility are legitimate, but they apply much more distinctly to nonpersons than they do to living human persons. These issues may appear peripheral at first glance, but they hearken back to maintaining ethical and logical consistency. If the moral value associated with personhood and care does indeed flow from the recognition of personhood at all stages of life, then these issues are necessary elements of the abortion dialogue and must be engaged.

So, then, as with the previous "consciousness as personhood" presentation, now here for the *all living humans are persons* stance are two arguments presented in syllogistic form, again with each of their conclusions becoming premises in a third syllogistic argument, thus providing the terminal claim of this *all* personhood position.

P1 There are no living human nonpersons, if every living human is a person.

P2 There is no marker for personhood, if there are no living human nonpersons.

C1 Therefore, there is no marker for personhood, as every living human is a person.

***

P3 If all living humans are persons, personhood is not assigned but logically tethered to all human life.

P4 That all living humans have moral value is logically consistent with the claim all living humans are persons.

C2 Therefore, all living humans have moral value, as personhood is not assigned but logically tethered to all human life.

***

P5 No one can classify another living human as a nonperson, if every living human is a person.

P6 All living humans have moral value as personhood is not assigned but logically tethered to all human life, so no one can classify another living human as a nonperson.

C3 Therefore, all living humans have moral value, as personhood is not assigned but logically tethered to all human life, if every living human is a person.

Those are the proposed steps to advocate for the *all living humans are persons* premise. One may make arguments about moral value, particularly in the case of two competing goods, but it must be predicated on dignity and even rights connected to personhood. In presenting arguments, as laid out here in syllogistic form, it must be made clear that those are illustrations of the wider argument—i.e., the argument without all the gaps filled in. Someone may assume that the syllogism is the whole of the argument for either position. That would be neither accurate nor fair to the argument. Each is the compression of the argument in propositional form. Perhaps by analogy one might consider the syllogism a formula. Just because the formula does not convince one of something does not mean the full expression of what the formula represents is inconclusive. It is correct to expect that besides the form of the argument, each premise must be true for the conclusion to also hold true. But one should keep in mind that just because the syllogistic argument by itself may not appear convincing, that does not mean that the conclusion is false and thus that the argument is unsound.

In conclusion, here is the argument advocating for *all living humans are persons* in sentence form as a distillation of what has thus far been proposed. The clearest defendable position is that all living humans are persons from the moment of fertilization. Otherwise, with the *some* stance, some person or group must logically determine which living humans are designated as persons. That has never ended well historically. And further, those of the *some* stance must necessarily resolve which criteria constitute some living humans as persons, and why. What is known as certain is that those with power and influence will never place themselves, or what criteria they possess, to align with those who are designated nonpersons. Rights and dignity are tied to personhood. The implication is that if all living humans are persons, and bodily autonomy is tethered to personhood, then in the same way one's personal rights stop where another person's rights begin, so too does the bodily autonomy of one person stop at the threshold of another person whose bodily autonomy must also be respected. This means, and logically implies, that fetuses and even zygotes in the early gestational stages are persons. They are not "full" persons, as personhood does not permit a degree without the same justice issues of *why* and *who decides*. But then, if every living human is a person, the onset of personhood must logically be fertilization. It is worth recalling that a logically valid and sound argument may be resilient to being logically dismissed, but people do not always accept, or even easily conform to, a rational, syllogistic argument.

In the actual public dialogue, it was discussed how confusion arises when the term *biological life* is confused with the term *what affects one's life*. The circumstances for this equivocation arise with the ill-founded assumption that because all living humans are persons, the *all* stance holders would support the life of the fetus over the life of the pregnant female if the pregnant female's biological life were in physical harm. But in consideration of triage, emergent care, and PDE, the element of proportionality respects the autonomy of both persons (pregnant female and fetus); and therefore, under certain conditions, the female is ethically justified to preserve her own physical life, even when doing so results in the death of the unborn. That required the correct understanding of a distinction between the term *procured abortion*, as contrasted with the term *preservation of the life of the pregnant female*. It was explained that if a fetus were to be delivered incompatible with life while preserving the physical life of the pregnant female, what occurred was not a procured abortion but the *lifesaving care of the female*. But as technology inches closer to allowing the survivability of what is presently an unviable fetus, the public's viewpoint on personhood will be affected by emotive, if not rational, standards. This will in turn affect the veracity of bodily autonomy as the main criterion in the public abortion dialogue. The centrality of bodily autonomy, even for the *some* stance holders, will inevitably decrease in inverse proportion to the increase of moral value of the unborn because of the ongoing lifesaving technology. As the bodily autonomy argument erodes, the single focus of personhood will become more apparent.

While this public dialogue on abortion ensues, those in the *all* camp continue to argue that certain functions or values, such as fetal heartbeat, pain sensitivity, or consciousness, will each distract from a more central, clearer advocacy argument. Understandably, in all important topics that manifest as "sides," each side will utilize certain incremental points to "gain ground." Though it seems important rhetorically, they fail for the very reason that their ends of autonomy and life as determiners for the public abortion dialogue are false goals. As parts of an argument, the *some* camp would hold that whether as values or capacities, any criteria used to determine whether a living human is not a person will inevitably have to argue it on factors subjectively held and likely culturally formed. Those factors will not remain consistent over subsequent historical periods, as values and factors always change. The historical records are replete with conditions for personhood that, though fully accepted as rational at the time, are presently found to be aberrations of justice. It would be hubris to think that the present time period has become the pinnacle of moral evaluation. All born persons who suffer from minimal consciousness, loss of bodily functions, inability to communicate or reciprocate, with little to no memory retention, and so on, would otherwise pose a serious ethical dilemma if not accepted as persons. In terms of determining their personhood status, they logically must be recognized as living human persons until natural death, even if comfort care is justly determined proportionately. In summation, what was presented will likely require refinement and nuance in particular applications. But it does offer substantial grounding and insight and is intended to enable dialectical discussion.

Finally, the first section of the previous chapter was titled "The problem of personhood." Then within the text speaking about personhood, the term *problem* was clearly distinguished from the term *mystery*. On the surface, calling personhood a problem and then claiming it to be a mystery may appear as a contradiction or equivocation. But if the term *mystery* had been used in the heading, it would not have been understood the way mystery is to be defined. With that said, to use *problem* in its everyday connotation, as in the issue of abortion, connotes that the concept of personhood is a problem. But this section explored how one is to consider the meaning ascribed to the idea of personhood, how it may be understood and accepted as essential to all human lives. Personhood is not solvable. It is a mystery in the truest sense. And as anyone who can read this page must be a living human person, each individual person exploring personhood is embedded in the concept of personhood themselves. That is, only persons can read about persons, which means that persons cannot "step away" from personhood to examine it, as one would a problem. In the same analogous way, this text is presented to one's consciousness, and the person reading is embedded in the experience of reading. So, even for the *some* stance holders, only those with sufficient consciousness can examine human consciousness. Thus, whether one holds that only those with sufficient consciousness are persons or all living humans are persons, the idea of personhood must be much greater than simply part of the conversation. In fact, it must be the central and primary factor. But the idea of personhood can never fully escape the realm of mystery, with mystery properly understood. Personhood is fundamentally different than the terms *human* and *living*. Both of those are quantifiable terms. They may not be known perfectly, and the parameters may be argued and adjusted, but what is known presently about being human and alive remains sufficient for the abortion dialogue. Nonetheless, unlike the qualifiable term *person*, empirical science cannot assist anyone in this endeavor; there is nothing about personhood that can be measured and weighed. The disciplines of philosophy and theology must be brought to bear on the concept of personhood. Personhood is solely in their domain. It matters not which of those pursuits is used, provided the foundations of the argument remain rational and the means for thinking critically adhere to the rigor of logic.

7

The Arguments Ahead

It is said that the present is pregnant with the future. —Voltaire

The future depends on what you do today. —Mahatma Gandhi

He who marries the spirit of the times will soon find himself a widower.
—G. K. Chesterton

This chapter confronts what lies a generation ahead for the public abortion dialogue. With no attempt at impotent predictions, the goal is simply to outline the logical trajectory of technological advances, aligned with current cultural trends of how innovations tend toward liberal use in the future. Just as many of the elements of the present abortion conversation would be alien to the minds of those a half-century past, it is also true that what lies ahead will be equally foreign to the minds of those in this present generation. Perhaps that is not true for all, but it will feasibly be so for many. A theme will be developed here asserting that what is first thought innovative and exhilarating and is probably accepted with uncertainty will become customary over time and thus expected. As subsequent generations inherit an innovation, for them what is customary will shed the exhilaration and uncertainty. Becoming accustomed to its use, they will accept it as an expectation.

This is the legacy of technological innovations cycling through the culture over time. It is not limited to the innovations providing comfort and convenience, though central heating and air conditioning would certainly stand as an example. It is also not limited to the timeline of civil freedoms and attached privileges, though the rights of underrepresented groups certainly have benefited from the hard-won privileges of the prior marginalized. But specifically with the public abortion dialogue, though cultural projections may be difficult to forecast convincingly, there are identifiable signs that if things continue along a similar path, the trajectory will lead to predictable ends. That is, what lies ahead is not entirely unforeseeable, as the present recognizable signs point the way. A *sign* can be defined as a thing that represents something other than itself to a knowing power—in the same way that a downward-pointing triangle traffic sign does not embody the notion "to yield" the right of way but represents that notion to the human person who has the power to know its representational meaning. Likewise, in culture, the possible application of technological advances can form signs. Just as the present signs are not arbitrarily formed, neither are future manifestations of their inevitable outcomes. All such signs are the result of judgments that have been explicitly or implicitly adopted, either as inherited customary practices or present innovations that were approved without critical concern for how human persons will become instrumentalized by the logical applications of such technology.

This stresses the necessity of critical thinking and reflective consideration. It must be applied to not simply how technology may improve human flourishing and wellness in the present, but how and when further applications and developments, not immediately intended, will create ethical concerns often under one's radar. The following two sections of this chapter consider how technological advances will impact the public abortion dialogue in terms of future human offspring and future human wombs. If this seems to strike a dystopian tone, consider that both of those are ethically acceptable goals of the present technology, and the concern arises from foreseeable possibilities. Both are forming as present innovative technological advances: genetic screening and editing are intended to eradicate anomalies or diseases, while artificial wombs are hoped to increase premature infant survivability. The present good of these technological advances can licitly be embraced, although not without trepidation for future application or goals—goals that will not seem too much of a stretch as the development advances. All technology is to serve the good of the human person, which implies an understanding of both what a person *is* and what is *good* for the human person. If these technological innovations are for persons, and they are to serve persons, then the present judgments (obviously made by persons) must also ethically consider the impact on future persons and thus the collective society. In short, what is accepted in the present must run the gauntlet of critical, ethical analysis, both in terms of what is presently intended and what may be a probable future application.

When asked to consider such present and future concerns, it is common for someone to offer their assessment in the form of "Well, I think . . . " It is worth pausing on that phrase, because someone who utters the words "I think" offers a profound claim and does not fully appreciate the depth of the expressed meaning. This was already addressed, but it is worth revisiting. First, they recognize themselves as an *I*, grasping the notion of a self, a person. Secondly, they claim *to think*, but with little consideration for what such a pursuit entails. There is no default way of thinking; thinking must be intentional. Further, the issue is not whether or not one claims to be thinking, but *how* one is thinking. In like manner, there is no default view of personhood; the idea of personhood must be intentionally formed. Further, the very individual who claims to be thinking thinks as a person, which situates the ideas of personhood and rational thinking as both necessary and primary considerations. There is a third element to this chain of claims. When the "I" who is "thinking" forms an ethical judgment—in particular, weighing a present technological application in terms of how it may be used or abused in the future—there is no default way to determine an ethical judgment; ethical judgments must too be intentionally formed. Once the *I*, *thinking*, and *ethical judgments* are conjoined, they form the conclusion that *there is no default way to think through ethical evaluations predicated on personhood.*

By neglecting a view of determining personhood, two issues arise. The first issue is that one will not likely be consistent in their judgments between the varying applications of personhood. That was addressed as a concern in the last advocacy argument, where what is determined as an ethical course of action for the unborn or infant must apply equally to adults and all living human persons. The second issue is that when a view of personhood is adopted, the only certainty will be that it is inclusive. Anyone who determines what constitutes personhood will include themselves within the parameters of the value or capacity used as determiners. Once again, either all living humans are persons (all are included by all), or some living humans are persons (some are included by some). Plainly stated, no living human considers themselves a nonperson.

Regarding the method of judgment, the same is true for which ethic is used in any evaluation. As there is no default ethic, without one intentionally chosen, two more issues arise. The first issue is the same inconsistency of judgments between the varying ethic employed. But rather than an inconsistency with what constitutes a living human person, the variance will be between one adhering to rules, following their own intention, or trying to do what is thought best for the majority of living humans. Clearly, each of those systems will result in different judgments. The second issue involves an irony, which seems to contradict the previous claim: that is, without preconsideration, a default ethic does tend to emerge. But that default ethic will always be predicated on one's own preferences, which favor one's advantage. It need not be a crass egoism, but it will be formed in view of what is considered an advantage for the present, almost to the dismissal of future applications that may prove contradictory to the good of the human person and society at large.

In either case, without rationally working out one's view on personhood or determining an ethical system intentionally, the *default* of both will grant the preferences and advantages to those who have both the means and power to assert their own personhood and ethic as the standard. Thus, in the absence of an intentionally chosen ethic, what preserves or gains power will always become the rationalization. In fact, that was Nietzsche's point with his master/slave morality, where the master with the power determines what is "right" while the slaves determine the "good' as aligning with that "right." This, for Nietzsche, is not crass brutalism, but the means to form a practical ethic. Yet, in the reality of individual experience, anyone without means or power, unless advocated for by a majority group, will fall prey to the judgments of those who do have the means and power to assert their self-serving goals. In the absence of an objective view of personhood, ethical system, or rational form of reasoning, all that is left is power derived ideologically. Ideology is not rationally derived but rather is contrived and compelled, as there is no logical basis to which one can appeal. Calling out this tragic predicament resonates with the public, specifically because many become frustrated over not being able to rationally engage others. Most encounter not being able to enter into conversation over how relational justice or individual responsibility bears on the very significance of being a living human person. And all are quite cognizant that the ethic utilized in politics and government seems to continually favor those who will benefit from the judgment. This is the penalty of subjectivity or, at the very least, the penalty resulting from the lack of ability to engage in fruitful dialectical conversation. This reality is the *sign of the times*, a harbinger brought about by deficient reasoning and inattentive acceptance of either inherited cultural customs or the dismissal of foreseeable consequences.

One must not overstate this though. There is a Latin maxim, *abusus non tollit usum*, which translates as "abuse does not preclude use." Applied here, it means that there is much good in the present technological advances, and simply because they *can be* abused in the future does not mean that they cannot be used for the good of the human person in the present, or even that they *will be* abused in the future. That should be remembered. Yet another Latin maxim is *memores acti prudentes futuri*, which holds that "being mindful of those things being done also requires being aware of the things to come." In other words, the present bears responsibility for what is passed on to the future. That reality is a *sign for the times*, which, when inherited, also reflectively inherits ethical precautions and vigilance.

SIGN FOR THE TIMES

The two advocacy arguments on personhood in the last section of the previous chapter are not intended to resolve the overall argument this book is proposing. Instead, each was an attempt to reveal the point that the pro-life and pro-choice "sides" are woefully inadequate to address the complexities of the abortion dialogue or even the fundamental argument, which is that neither autonomy nor life are terminal goods. Both "sides" serve the dignity due to persons; but, untethered from the personhood that this dignity is predicated on, each needs to be discarded so that the dialogue may proceed. The lead-in to this chapter was to make the point that in moving forward in the conversation on abortion, one cannot think critically without adequately evaluating influences of the present ethos on their judgments. In other words, everyone needs to read the *sign of the times* and, once interpreted, enter the dialogue as a *sign for the times*.

The distinction between *sign of the times* and *sign for the times* is the difference between succumbing to a sign and intentionally engaging a sign. It is not merely a matter of directional influence, although it *is* that; it also pertains to the degree to which such an influence is allowed a stable home in one's own thoughts and judgments. The idea is to disentangle what is culturally inherited from what constitutes an intentional judgment, or to identify to what degree one's own ethical decisions are made distinct from the cultural milieu in which one lives and functions. It might be made clearer with an analogy. For someone who regularly swims in the ocean but has never seen clear blue ocean waters, they may be aware the water they are familiar with is cloudy, but that cloudiness is accepted as normal. As the present condition is their only experience of ocean waters, the swimmer not only accepts the cloudy water but, over time, loses their awareness of the water being cloudy. The ethos of any culture or time period is often like that. Everyone is born into a particular culture in a particular time. Only through personal reflection and cultural detachment can someone become aware of how other cultures and times are, or were, different from the "waters they swim in" presently.

This section will consider how the ethos of the time is often unwittingly absorbed as the *sign of the times* and how, with intentionality and reflection, it can become the *sign for the times*. There is an often-used maxim among artists that states, "One is only as original as the obscurity of their sources." The meaning is plain; people think of something as profound or creative if they consider it to be an original insight. If they later stumble upon the idea somewhere else, they realize what was first experienced was not original; then the notion of originality and creativity evaporates, as they realize what was accepted merely aligned with their uncritical experience. There are elements of the public abortion dialogue that seem "right" and originally derived by one stance or another. But once it is revealed how those elements are confined to the present time frame and culture, they are revealed as predicated on uncritically accepted notions that are embedded in the present waters; and as those notions wane in future generations, so too does their effect of persuasion.

Those points, along with some aspects of this section, may seem peripheral to the public abortion topic. But it is crucial to understand not simply that each time period will inevitably influence people of that generation in a particular way, but also that the present societal ethos always seems right to those whom that "truth" benefits, as though it organically surfaces to the supporting stance holder. In this way, what is uncritically accepted *seems* self-evident but derails any progress in the public abortion dialogue. This section will confront the idea that embedded cultural views are to be accepted uncritically and will underscore the point that without intellectual and ethical vigilance, what appears intentionally sought is more likely than not unwittingly accepted. People easily succumb and fall for the *sign of the times*. In addition to that basic point, three other influences will be introduced briefly: nominalism, postmodernism, and the notion of free will. They will be poised not as culprits but as considerations. The section will then conclude, proposing that only an arrogant thinker will assume their present generation's ethos or ethical view is the pinnacle of truth that future generations will hold in esteem. Those subsequent generations will subtract and add to what was inherited, just as every prior generation has done. Each generation thinks to subtract glossed-over errors and to add insights thought novel. But as the overarching premise remains that *either some living humans are persons, or all living humans are persons*, then one would need to make the argument that either personhood is discovered by a stable nature (it does not change) or it is determined by certain criteria and values (it changes because of X). Such determinations, provided they are not wedded to the age, require reflection, dialogue, and critical thinking. Those aspiring to become a *sign for the times* will resist submitting uncritically to societal influences, tethered to particular times.

Now applied to the cultural ethos, there is a phenomenon where present thinkers will readily consider their own view originally derived. But when confronted with intentional thinking and reflection, their position is soon discovered to be tethered to the present societal ethos, which they will part ways with once what is "new" finds popular acceptance. When the present idea is uncovered as unoriginal and merely part of the present ethos (which does not mean it is unethical), only then will it be discovered as stealthily influential. Here is a thought experiment, akin to "guess your age" carnival barkers ferreting out clues to determine an estimate of the patron's age. Consider speculating about the historical age that a person lived in by being given only their accepted social justice positions on marriage, their views of personal honor, and the acceptable source of ethical authority. Of the three scenarios that follow, each *aligns* with either the nineteenth, the twentieth, or the twenty-first century, in the context of the Western tradition. It should appear obvious which scenario aligns with which century.

> In this century, the couple *may choose* marriage but will likely require approval of the female's family. As a bride, the female will be in her mid to late teens. The couple probably grew up in close proximity to each other. Marriage is expected to be between one male and one female, for life. The father will give

away his daughter as a matter of authority. Marriage may be entered into because of love, though arranged marriages are not uncommon. The wife is expected to remain subordinate to her husband and would not be employed outside the home. If the female becomes pregnant before marriage, they are expected to marry quickly so that her chastity is not questioned. The wedding venue will likely be a church. The main reason for divorce is betrayal, but civil law will favor the husband. Personal honor is reputational and aligns with a cultural code. Honor is somewhat hierarchical and attached to privilege. As to the primary source of ethical authority, it would likely align with one's religious affiliation, or perhaps even the values of one's country.

In this century, marriage is typically chosen by the couple themselves, who are likely to be in their late teens or early twenties. The couple may have grown up together, met while traveling, or met when the family relocated due to employment. They chose each other because of romantic love, and the family is informed afterwards of the engagement. It is expected to be between one male and one female, for life. The father will give away his daughter as a matter of custom. The expectation is that the wife is equal in status to her husband but will maintain the home and children if she is employed. The wedding venue will likely be a church, in the hometown of the husband or wife. If the female becomes pregnant before marriage, the male is expected to "do the right thing" and marry the female. Divorce is regrettably accepted, with irreconcilable differences cited as the major personal reason. There is somewhat of a negative connotation for being a divorcee, so a second marriage is a fact sometimes kept private. Personal honor is attached to following one's conscience and upholding individual character, with a minor emphasis on not disparaging the family name. As to the primary source of ethical authority, it would likely align with one's religious affiliation, but rational explanations are more convincing.

In this century, marriage is always chosen by the couple themselves, who are likely in their late twenties or mid-thirties. The couple may have grown up together but, more likely than not, met in college or at their place of employment. They chose each other because of romantic love and may even have met through a matchmaker service. The couple likely cohabitated for a few years prior to the engagement. The family is informed afterwards of the wedding date, and announcements are sent to friends and extended family. Marriage is expected to be between two people, either of the opposite or same sex. Marriage

> is a consensual relation, and the initial intention is that this union is durable. The father may give away his daughter if the marriage is heterosexual; but, overcoming what was patriarchal, both spouses share household duties and the rearing of children regardless of orientation. Typically, both spouses are career oriented, a fact that probably extended the dating period and delayed the marriage. The wedding venue will likely be a civil ceremony, a destination spot, a rustic barn, or even the seaside. If the female becomes pregnant before marriage, it is not uncommon for male and female to raise the child together unmarried or even for the female to raise her child as a single mother, since marriage is not the social norm. Divorce is common and carries little social stigma, and being unsatisfied in the relationship is cited as the major personal reason. Previous marriages are no hindrance to future relationships. Personal honor is attached to being true to oneself and not allowing others to control one's path in life. As to the primary source of ethical authority, it would likely align with the notions of being tolerant of others and favoring liberty when possible; but without rational explanations, it remains individual preferences.

The reader will observe that each scenario's characterization of marriage, honor, and ethical authority mapped rather obviously to a specific century. That was the point. As stated, these are generalizations, and of course there are exceptions, as there were many individuals who, as *signs for the times*, became determined to change what was unjustly prohibited. But from the viewpoint of the vast majority who lived during those times, the scenarios were simply the "waters they swim in." Many of the forward thinkers, in retrospect, can currently be said to have been on the right side of history, though it was not known by them at the time; and one can find miscalculations in just as many "predictions" that did not turn out as ethically favorable. Even of the many changes that proved to be beneficial to individuals or society, some of the changes produced effects not immediately foreseen; yet the subsequent centuries inherited them as the base expectations, with or without their secondary, adverse effects. The point is that regardless of how original each individual thought themselves (or did not think themselves), none have arrived at their views independent of their embedded culture and age. And none will know otherwise unless some distance between them and their own culture and age is intentionally sought. The twenty-first-century observer will sense the nineteenth-century resident as being compliant and conforming with that century's ethos. But the twenty-first-century individual, if not self-critical, may unwittingly think their own ethical views and ethos equally originally formed, an improvement the next century will welcome. But with the passage of time, a twenty-second- or twenty-third-century historical observer evaluating a twenty-first-century resident will likely sense the same historical compliance and find some good, some bad, and even some unforeseen consequences that were not properly anticipated. They will conclude, save some outliers, that the average person conformed to the present ethical views and ethos in much the same way as previous generations. By knowing what the typical person thought in terms of marriage, honor, and ethical evaluations, they will be able to generalize, not unlike the carnival barker, the age in which the individual lived. It is sobering, and humbling, to acknowledge such a phenomenon.

Why does this matter for the public abortion dialogue? It matters because few consider how their ethical views on abortion and personhood have been shaped by the present "waters they swim in." And those who are a *sign for the times* can only be so by reflection and critical thinking, not by simply reacting from the position of one's allegiance to a belief, ideology, or socio-political affiliation, which typically mirrors the present cultural ethos. To separate oneself from the present ethos is a difficult and time-consuming effort, but to not do so is rationally passive and intellectually lazy. Here is a dichotomy to consider. If the current ethical trends on abortion are resisted and limits are sought, one is thought conservative and pro-life. If the current ethical trends on abortion are embraced and expansion is sought, one is thought progressive and pro-choice. Both are reactions, perhaps not without reasons, but each is conforming in their own way. It is often said that a conservative allows truth to get out in front, while the progressive ventures beyond the truth. It is not that the conservative "conserves truth" any more than the progressive is "anticipating truth." The reality is neither is aligned with truth, but each is more interested in preserving an expression of "truth" that coordinates with their ideology. Framed another way, as Chesterton remarked in the 1924 *London News*, the progressive and so-called advanced person is reckless rushing into ruin, while the conservative and so-called retrospect person tends to admire and feel at ease in the ruin.[1] This is about making mistakes and correcting mistakes, and too often is but a reaction to some current dilemma. Without critical thinking and

1. Chesterton, *Illustrated London News*, 164.

reflection, more often than not, one simply accepts by default the dictates of present ideologies, beliefs, or political affiliations, which results in neither the conservative nor the progressive thinking for themselves but merely thinking differently than the brand they oppose. One thinks by deficiency, and the other by excess. And not being sufficiently self-reflective, the confidence of each is only heightened by thinking their particular position has been arrived at by original, critical thinking, where they are either preserving or anticipating what will be the right side of history. This is so for all in the public abortion dialogue who, with unchallenged or reactionary thinking—that is, without a sincere public dialectical exchange—will either uncritically align with the present ethos or react indiscriminately against the present ethos. Both, as stubborn harbingers of ideology, leave the culture the worse for it, as fallacies and partial truths remain camouflaged under the guise of originality, if not even cloaked under compassion.

This is such an important concept to supplant the present state of things that it warrants being framed by another illustration, that of political philosophy. What follows may appear obvious, but the obvious is often that which eludes the brightest, who engage others with committed minds. Each period's ethos consequently develops a view on reason and authority, which subsequently forms implicit views of personhood. And not unlike present persons reacting to the preceding ethos, each cultural shift historically is a reaction to the thoughts and behaviors that preceded it. That is to claim that each period was, and is, shaped by the political and natural conditions of its time. Here is a brief survey of that reality.

Beginning with the twelfth to fifteenth centuries, known as the late Middle Ages, the cultural ethos emphasized authority and truth flowing from a Deity, through kings and clergy, to the people. It was the *Age of Belief*. The vast majority of people in the West were peasants who lived under the land ownership of a lord. Even among the upper class, the standard of living was beneath twenty-first-century lower middle-class standards. Cities were still under aristocratic rule, and one finds modern statehood began to emerge. This period witnessed the debate over what is known as *universals*. A universal is the nature of a thing, also called a *form*, which, as heralded by Plato and Aristotle, constitutes a philosophical system known as *realism*. But in contrast to that arose the idea of *nominalism,* which was popularly attributed to the Franciscan friar William of Occam. Nominalists hold that there is no such thing as a universal, and that things could be grouped together—perhaps think of it as a classification or taxonomy. This is not well understood by the public mind, but is critical in a determination and ethos of personhood. The reason is that if a person has a nature, then an ethic or action can be connected to that nature. What is good for the person is something objectively and identifiably good as it aligns with the nature of the human person. Think in terms of finding some unfamiliar and peculiar gadget at a thrift shop. If its use is unknown, someone usually begins to fiddle with it in an attempt to guess why it was designed a certain way. The design, or nature, is thought to be connected to its use or function. The debate during this period was whether that can be said of the human person. In the Age of Belief, this went beyond the physical structures of human males and females, extending to the essence of things like beauty, goodness, and truth. But to ask if one can know any truth, even beyond the patriarchal and dogmatic underpinnings of knowledge, it was accepted that there was indeed certainty of truth, even if it could only be known imperfectly. This was not the Dark Ages, coined by Francesco Petrarca (d. 1374), as the popular Black Legend perpetrated by the Renaissance thinkers and anti-Catholic stances made it out to seem.[2] Indeed, this period was in fact the birth of the university system, which itself was a growth of belief-centered monastic schools. The point is that one must try to grasp how these factors implicitly formed the cultural views of personhood of that time. One might summarize that persons received their nature from the Judeo-Christian God, where traits or inclinations can be gleaned from the design, and the good of the human person then is aligning those sought-after goods with the design of the human person. Even the nominalists, who accepted divine authority and would have dismissed such human nature, would have sought the good of the human person via the revealed truth they received divinely.

By the seventeenth century, there was a cultural explosion of ideas and development—the Enlightenment. It was formed in reaction to the previous ethos and was to exalt reason and empirical judgment over belief and dogma as the foundation for authority and truth. During this *Age of Reason,* the important distinction between Church and State took shape. And along with René Descartes's philosophy offering a "turn to the self," the empirical approaches of John Locke and Francis Bacon offered horizons for human happiness that stunned the imagination. With these and other thinkers, the science of God was eclipsed by the science

2. See Petrina, "All Petrarch's Fault," 152–53.

of man; here science is not meant only as *empirical science* but is understood by its etymology of *scientia* as the *ordered pursuit of knowledge*. Too, the rallying cry for the modern democracy arose championing life, liberty, and property. That phrase morphed into "life, liberty, and the pursuit of happiness" as adopted into the U.S. Declaration of Independence. During this time, economics developed as a discipline, seeking ways to explain and understand the principles of wealth distribution. The groundwork for the Industrial Revolution began to form. Truth and certainty were now to be pursued through empiricism, where knowledge originates from experience as inductive reasoning, alongside rationalism, where knowledge originates independently from experience as deductive reasoning. For the empiricists, the human person's mind came to be understood as a blank slate ready to receive experiences as knowledge; this persisted through Freud to very recent times. The rationalists questioned such certainty from sensory experience; to them, the nature of the human person was best displayed by their use of reason. In fact, they held that the senses could be distractions to certainty, as what is seen, heard, or otherwise sensed is often misleading. But it is important to note that during this period, the human person has become secular. Without the aid of an authority greater than the human person, the psychological self was formed, and for many the personhood became equated with the mind or psychological continuity. The world was interpreted through a lens of both the possibility of understanding and confidence in one's own judgment; and in the same way that the human person was set to conquer nature, the seeds were planted for using the same method to perhaps conquer human nature and constrain evil impulses.

By the onset of the nineteenth century, disillusionment with the promises of the Enlightenment began to swell, and another reaction to the previous system formed. Recognizing the limits of reason and empiricism coincided with the beginnings of the Industrial Revolution. Both the human mind and economic creativity have expanded exponentially. This was the *Romantic period*. On the heels of revolutionary wars and of philosopher David Hume's arguments for skepticism arising from empirical thought and rationalism's narrow capability, society began to side with the imagination as a source of truth. The movement migrated from the exploration of the mind to the exploration of sentiment. Great names in literature are remembered from this period, such as Victor Hugo, Jane Austen, Ralph Waldo Emerson, and Mary Shelley, the author of *Frankenstein* (subtitled *The Modern Prometheus*, taken from the mythical god who molded mankind from clay). Mary Shelley is noteworthy on two points. First, her mother was Mary Wollstonecraft who, as both a philosopher and author herself, is now labeled as a first-wave feminism founder. Secondly, although Shelley's *Frankenstein* is primarily thought of as belonging to the horror genre, it was a Romantic exploration of two ideas: (1) it addresses the limits and dangers of knowledge, and (2) it explores the crisis of being isolated from others who share one's own nature. The monster (though some argue that the monster's creator, Victor Frankenstein, is the actual monster) revolted, wreaking havoc. But Shelley has this created monster lament, "If any being felt emotions of benevolence towards me, I should return them an (sic) hundred and an hundred fold; for that one creature's sake, I would make peace with the whole kind."[3] In other words, if another being would feel emotions of goodness toward the Creature, then as a hideous creature he would make peace with all of mankind on account of that alone. Shelley would not have written such a sentiment had her experiences formed in another era. The words she places on the monster's tongue are not dogmatic or empirical, but imaginative. She too was influenced by the ethos of her period, as the term *romantic* came to be accepted as pertaining to the poetic and to things marvelous. The human person and the subsequent idea of personhood as formed in this environment elevated the imagination and came to know the conscience as the center of human authority. This was tethered to conscience being dictated according to norms of the time. An astute reader of Jane Austen's *Pride and Prejudice* will recognize how the author tried to capture those notions.

Into the twentieth and present centuries, now on the heels of the Industrial Revolution, the notion of personhood continues to be molded. As briefly mentioned earlier, marriage, if pursued, could only loosely be defined as one's consensual personal expression. The average forms of transportation and communication have become expedient and instantaneous. These progressions and conveniences have affective powers that inevitably influence one's view of the human person. As inherited, nature can be manipulated. But then, so too can human nature flex to present expedient and instantaneous desires, and the technological advances demonstrated that ability. And then there are the underlying philosophical views of individuals in the early 1900s that were as commonplace for them as divine guidance was for those living a couple centuries earlier.

3. Shelley, *Frankenstein*, 196.

The Enlightenment continues to be critiqued for not delivering on the hopes and expectations it appeared to promise. Mass production may have made things faster and less expensive, but those bonuses do not always seem to have translated into living a more fulfilling life. With the "assembly line" attitude for production, Karl Marx (d. 1883) unveiled the alienation of workers from the products they produced. For example, a cabinet is no longer crafted from beginning to end by a skilled laborer, as now an unskilled employee might have no more participation in the process than the sanding of the rough-cut door rails. Marx thought the proletariats, those who did not have ownership of the tools of production (capital), would cease tolerating such conditions and revolt. But they never seemed to rise up as Marx predicted. There were reasons offered as to why, but an Italian Marxist philosopher named Antonio Gramsci (d. 1937) proposed an idea. He held that it was not simply economic division that repressed people, but what he referred to as *hegemonic power*. In this line of thinking, the dominant ideologies embedded in culture were to blame, seemingly pacifying proletariats and repelling their awareness of their pitiful condition. Those ideologies, according to Gramsci, included religion, schools, mass media, and the nuclear family structure. The idea was that if people's thinking is formed by structures in culture,[4] then those structures must be disrupted to break the chain of power and control their hold over the mass public. This is referred to as *Critical Theory*, which begins to situate and understand the human person not with a nature, but as a being ever situated "against" power structures.[5] The remedy is to implore an ethos of emancipation. So, in short, the human person is always freeing themselves from some aspect of oppression, even if the goal is not clear. Basically, in the absence of a nature, the human person is constituted by this indeterminate angst.

In tandem with this, although distinct, is the onset of a philosophical movement known as *postmodernism*, which arose in the last quarter of the twentieth century. It is not easily defined because it is an approach more than a system; but, at the risk of generalizing, two concepts can be attributed to its ethos and how that may influence the public abortion

4. See Gramsci, *Prison Notebooks*, 353, where he posits that "the active man [is he] who modifies the environment, understanding by the environment the *ensemble* of relations which each takes part in, [where] one's own individuality is the *ensemble* of relations." Emphasis in the original.

5. What Gramsci would phrase as the "great masses, previously passive, [who] entered into movement," 228–29.

debate. It is in line with nominalism, which holds that there are no natures to a thing. So, postmodernism denies *a thing* possesses anything that can be essential to that thing, particularly human nature. And where there is no nature (essence or form), one is within the realm of a social kind rather than a natural kind. That distinction was discussed earlier. It is not accurate to state that if something is mind dependent and thus lacking an essence (social kind), it is therefore *constructed* without intent or rationale, though of course from societal interests. But it is safe to assume that without an essential nature, the "definition" is changeable, which means it can be altered by ideology and custom. When something is accepted by one culture or time period, and then is redefined, it necessarily affects one's understanding of that thing or idea. For example, if the term *procured abortion* or *living human person* is not "one thing" in particular, then disagreement immediately arises as each party talks past the other. (Recall that the only way to overcome equivocation is to be clear with one's terms.)

As for the other general concept of postmodernism, there is a disregard for any foundational approach for how one can come to knowledge. This is not to claim that there is no truth to be known—but only to say that with anti-foundationalism, in the absence of any underlying worldview (metaphysics) that can be inherited, no truth can be accepted or "passed on" with certainty. So, historical notions of truth propositions (what was known and ordinarily passed on) must be reinterpreted through the lens of the present, as the previous claims are always suspect. This goes beyond the normal skepticism, which would want to independently affirm what was received, in that it rather summarily discounts what was held by past ages. For the human person, this would mean that certainty can never really be achieved as to what constitutes personhood. Perhaps at the risk of oversimplification, it might be easier to understand this approach as suggesting that knowledge is constructed within the society and that both culture and ideology play a part in determining that construction. Because nonstatic norms logically change, knowledge will always be conditioned by experience and thus will also change, both within an age, and from one age to another. To the point of the nature of a human person, how does one come to a judgment as to *what* constitutes a human person, *when* a living human becomes a person, or if there is *even such a thing* as a stable human nature? It may be safe to assume with postmodernism that personhood is not predicated on an essential nature, but is only tempered as "true" by the social parameters of the present.

Regarding then the last element of this section, the notion of free will or free agency should be briefly considered prior to addressing the topics of future human offspring and future human wombs. Why is this crucial? Culpability, or being responsible for an action, is always connected to being able to choose otherwise, when compared to an established ethical position. For the public abortion dialogue, if a person does not have free will, then regardless of judging to override a female's bodily autonomy or to terminate the life of an unborn, each person is merely submitting to a determined position, with no possibility to choose otherwise. This is the logical result of a materialist (everything is made of matter and subject to the laws of physics) or nontheist metaphysical position. Such a position cannot be dismissed on that basis, any more than a religious or dogmatic stance could be dismissed simply because it is a religious stance. And to be clear, atheism is not neutral simply because it is not founded on a revealed belief. Both hold presuppositions—that either something came from nothing (nontheist), or something came from something (theist). To be clear, then, according to a nontheistic worldview, the destiny of all people is not predetermined, but it is determined by the materialistic nature of the human person and the influence of one's environment. As a materialist stance, atheism cannot accept any immaterial notion understood as *spiritual*. This means that in regard to free will, there is no explanatory way to account for such freedom in terms of behavior or judgment. That would require one to arrive at judgments by purely biological means, even if not immediately identifiable, implying that one is beholden to their biology, both innate and from environmental effects. Determinism does not claim that a person is incapable of making a left turn while walking or that they can prefer no ice cream flavor other than butter pecan by necessity; but it does suggest that there are forces either from some genetic predisposition or the environment that are simply unknown, but that nonetheless have preceded what appears to be a free choice.

In applying this to the public abortion dialogue, some background may help with the understanding of the free will issue from a materialist stance. The twentieth-century American physiologist Benjamin Libet (d. 2007), studying free will, demonstrated that the electrical activity of the brain precedes even the conscious decision to lift a finger, claiming that the *brain activity* necessary to raise the finger is present even before *the desire* to raise the finger.[6] What if all ethical action, which would be as physical as raising one's finger, came only *after* the necessary electrical brain activity and *prior* to consciously choosing it? If that is so, it demonstrates actions and ethical choices are not freely chosen—and that suggests that those who argue against or for a particular position are arguing *for* a stance they did not choose and *against* a person whose stance was also predetermined. That is a conundrum. If one accepts this materialist application to free will, consider how often those who fail to properly articulate their position are said to be ideologues, following the crowd, or not "thinking for themselves." Could any of those be a valid assumption? It is often a criticism of theists that the "parishioners in the pew" cannot articulate their personal beliefs well, which supposedly demonstrates their blind allegiance. But it is equally true that the average atheist "on the street" would not be able to adequately articulate the logical consequence of their personal nonbelief to the absence of free will, which would equally demonstrate the same blind allegiance to secular, atheistic tenets. But atheists who are philosophers know the free will paradox of its relation to ethical judgments well. American philosopher Sam Harris (b. 1967), who is also a neuroscientist and an avowed atheist, plainly calls free will an illusion. Daniel Dennett (d. 2024), who was mentioned earlier for his views on consciousness, also understands that atheism is incompatible with the notion of free will. He holds to the view of compatibilism, popularized by the philosopher Harry Frankfurt (d. 2023), which proposed that if one voluntarily succumbs to the predetermined choice, then that individual can still be held ethically responsible, even though the choice itself remains unalterable and thus determined. For example, a person "chooses" to fabricate a story (lie) in order to stay home from work, but even if they did not "choose" to stay home, the car battery was dead, and no assistance was available. The result was determined by past actions and present circumstances, meaning that whether that person intended to stay home or go to work, they would stay home that day. But the difference in this scenario, and why it is claimed that the person who "chooses" to lie can still be culpable (guilty), is that their internal choice (they lied in order to stay home) aligned with the determined result (it was inevitable they would stay home). Compatibilism is an attempt to maintain that there is no free will, but *sometimes* people can still be held responsible for their actions if the restraint is not external (in

6. Libet, "Do We Have Free Will?," 48.

the example, they chose to lie). Without free will, there is no choice, and without choice, there can be no ethical responsibility. As the late atheist and British journalist Christopher Hitchens (d. 2011) jokingly quipped in logical fashion, "Yes, I have free will. I have no choice,"[7] which is to offer the paradox that if it appears that one has free will, the judgment only appears to be freely chosen.

If this take on free will seems an odd claim, here is a thought experiment to help. Consider there is a perfect mind (not a god), who knew every existing genetic influence of each person, and every environmental effect, along with a perfect grasp of all the laws of physics. If nothing existed outside of the material world governed by these factors, would not every personal judgment or action be known perfectly and thus accurately predicted by this perfect mind? From a materialist standpoint, the response is yes. Here is an easier analogy to digest. Think of a person shooting billiards. There is nothing random about the force of the cue stick using the cue ball and cushioned sides to impact another ball, causing momentum that, with the precise angle of the bank, will retain enough velocity with the proper trajectory to sink the target ball into the chosen pocket. But for the pedestrian viewer, there appears to be sorcery behind those "trick shots" that seem to defy prediction. But it is the inability to predict, given the improper application of physics and geometry, that makes the shot appear magical. It is not random, not a trick, certainly not magical. Even someone aimlessly breaking a rack is entirely dependent on the laws of physics, from the perspective of limited ability to calculate the velocity of the cue ball, how tight the rack is, the friction of the table felt, the cushion of the bumpers, and so on. The successful shots and eventual resting position of the other balls appear impossible to forecast. Again, the end result *appears* random, but random is just an observational term for being unable to predict the outcome. If a perfect mind were able to accurately predict the final position of the cue ball and the other fifteen balls after the break, then in a real sense the event would be predeterminable and the illusion of randomness would be just that—an illusion.

If one would now export this example into the real world with value and ethical judgments, then some celestial "perfect mind" who knows all the physical laws and environmental circumstances would, with the ability to accurately predict outcomes, determine from known physical

7. WGBH Forum Network, "Great God Debate," 0:21:34.

laws and individual biology every judgment and result. All of the random elements that enter the public abortion dialogue, and all the judgments that pro-lifers level against pro-choicers and vice versa, while not preordained are predetermined; and holding those positions would be evidenced by factors unknown but knowable. The individual who supports a female's right to bodily autonomy or defends the life of the fetus as absolute really could not be said to choose to do so. Regardless of any nuance, the semblance of a choice only appears freely arrived at from the flawed perspective of a human who remains unaware of the influencing elements. Think how often someone is accused of uncritically accepting a position, when the "perfect mind," being aware of all the relevant circumstances that prodded and edged the individual to hold that position, would be able to demonstrate that it is the only possible position for that individual to hold. So, if an individual is a materialist, such that the human person does not have free will, the public abortion dialogue would fall to either power or ideology, as the judgments would have to be accepted as predetermined. It is an interesting factor to consider, and rarely if ever does this notion of free will relative to the public abortion dialogue enter the fray. It remains elusive from any review or reflection because, in all honesty, there is no resolution save that of compatibilism, which quite frankly is often criticized for conflating internal and external forces on personal judgments. Perhaps there are ways around this conundrum—but from a materialist standpoint, would not even those "ways around" be part of any predetermined circumstance? This is not simply interesting to ponder; it changes the tone and trajectory of the dialogue. By this reckoning, individual judgments on abortion are nothing more than the target ball in a game of billiards; the biology is the force of the cue stick, with the past physical laws representing the velocity, while present environmental conditions align with the momentum and side banks. Perhaps the paralyzing effect of such a realization of individual judgments being little more than the target ball sunk in the pocket is why the determinist concedes that accepting the illusion of free will is better than accepting determined consequences of ethical judgments that appear freely chosen.

The point of offering this brief historical survey is to argue that, for individuals and for society collectively, there are unconsidered factors *in the waters that all swim in* that affect an understanding of personhood. Ethical judgments on abortion predicated on one's understanding of personhood are not made outside of those waters. If a person "choosing an abortion" or a person "choosing the life of the fetus" is merely the product of biological forces and environmental experiences, then the argument on the ethics of abortion is naught. There is no reason to linger on this point, but determinism does not allow personal culpability, precisely because the action is not predicated on a free choice. This is an aspect of the public abortion discussion that rarely surfaces, perhaps because if it is true, there is no way to proceed ethically. Nonetheless, one's comprehension of the human person (personhood) either allows for free will or not, unless one does not have free will, of course. If this is the waters one swims in, it is not to claim people today or in past eras simply yielded to groupthink. And yet, upon critical thinking and self-reflection, their ethical stance may be unveiled as more customary to the time period than it is an original judgment reached by critical consideration. That begs the basic question: will the present ethos that forms and steers these seemingly intuitive views on personhood and abortion endure long? Though the following two sections will address that notion, it is right and just to consider the ethical and social justice parameters of the public abortion issue, as well as how popularly accepted ideas are affected and formed. There have been many well-deserved advancements historically on various issues of social justice. But for proper perspective, if it is true that every person *swims in the cloudy waters* of their own time—perhaps rephrased as one's ethical views are the fruit of the present ethos—then any hope for ethical truth and clarity is not a fruit best picked unripe. So, to what extent can ethical evaluations be used as standards from outside the present era and ethos? For the sake of illustrating this point in the political landscape, if conservatives in their effort to "conserve" a particular idea allow the fuller ethical truth to pass them by, that does not logically hold that what is being conserved in the present is ethically true and not in need of reform. Likewise, if progressives in their effort to champion "progress" exceed the reach of present ethical truth, that does not logically hold that what is in the present is not ethically true and requiring no such reform. An ethical error is an ethical error, whether it be conserving what requires reform, or progressing beyond what is necessary to conserve. Both excess and deficiency fall short of ethical truth. Only *in the future* will an evaluation be clearer when the perspective is wider, the influence of the present ethos is no longer present, and its often subtle influence is more easily detectible. For example, there are many past historical instances where present confidence was paired with now known ethical errors and atrocities. That should give everyone pause, as it makes sense that some confidences in the present that are now paired with assumed ethical truths will in the future be unveiled as ethical errors and atrocities. In short, the "right side of history" is only verifiable when the present is indeed history. It is quite easy to succumb to the arrogant thinking that the present period is superior to what came prior, or even that the present era is the pinnacle of ethical expression that will cause future generations to marvel at how well the ethical truth was reached so clearly. A magical moral time machine is not an option for those in the present to judge those of centuries past, any more than it is an option to project present ethical evaluations as being upheld in the future. On that premise, future generations will look at the present period with the same chagrin and eye-batting superiority that many in the "enlightened" present period use to ethically judge those in the "ignorant" past.

On the issue of personhood, all should allow reflection and humility to temper the tone of such absolute certainty. Humility is not self-degradation, but an honest self-assessment. When entering into conversation on the topic of abortion, consider the principle of charity as expressed in the 1899 poem "The True Gentleman," by John Walter Wayland. One line reads, in the context of correcting another out of necessity, that a charitable person is one "who is himself humbled if necessity compels him to humble another."[8] It speaks to seeking the good of the other in truth (is either of those objective?) and to not thinking of the other as a conquest whose lack of critical thinking skills or insufficient knowledge on a particular subject is a setup to exploit, thus gratifying one's own ego. And in the case that one's own logic does turn out to not be as superior as presumed, this expressed humility will shorten the distance that the overconfident will have to fall once found to be in ethical error. All should strive for truth expressed well but be ready and willing to accept correction. These are the characteristics of a mature intellect and properly formed will. The point being stressed here is that the concept of personhood and the way each person seeks certainty as to how one may ethically forecast the effect of technological advances is not formed in a vacuum. And further, how that concept of personhood affects the public abortion dialogue must be critically formed within that "closed" environment. Left unreflective, each person becomes susceptible to the cultural current. And just like a river where only dead things float with the current, in culture only the living things who "think objectively" by

8. Wayland, "Gentleman," para. 1.

recognizing the influence of *the waters one swims in* are capable of resisting the cultural stream. Merely following the *sign of the times* is to submit to the uncritical influence of society; one's mind is present to the issue, only in the present. Becoming a *sign for the times* neither discounts the water's influence nor succumbs to the current uncritically—rather, to the best of one's ability, the individual's mind becomes present to the abortion issue, discerning clearly how the abortion issue presents itself to society.

POTENTIAL HUMANS AND FUTURE OFFSPRING

The technological advances in fertility treatment, over the last half-century, have offered those in society opportunities that until very recently were only the stuff of science fiction. That statement contains two terms, often thought to be generally understood, that must not be glossed over and therefore require clarity. The first is *technology*, and the second is *society*. To most, the term *technology* is limited to the category of electronics or labor-saving devices. Technology, of course, includes things from both of those categories, but it is much broader. The term is derived from the Greek word *technê*, which refers to the practical application of knowledge. To understand this by contrast, consider Aristotle's three distinct types of knowledge. One is a theoretical knowledge (*epistêmê*), which is what the average person means when they claim to know or understand something. This would include what are held to be necessary truths, which can be scientifically engaged, provided one keeps in mind the broader meaning of science. Then there is a practical wisdom (*phronêsis*), which would include the art of living. This type of knowing is not necessary for other pursuits, as it is intended to be a good in its own right and attainable by experience. But *technê* is concerned with the practical application of knowledge. It is sometimes understood as a craft or, as a modern connotation might express it, a developed art. Unlike *phronêsis* or *epistêmê*, the idea of *technê* has a specific goal and use. So, as to a working definition of *technology*, it is best understood as anything in nature that is manipulated for the practical purpose of humans and their community. That last term, *human community*, also requires clarity as it is much broader than simply living among other people. Think of such a community in terms of what one means by referring to a society (*societas*). The term *societas* expresses cooperation between people as an intentional order, an association of human persons collaborating in their endeavors for the betterment of each, and thus all. This brief explication is necessary, because to otherwise assert that both *technology* and *society* always occur together can be reduced to a one-dimensional view, and can be thought too obvious to investigate the relation. As this section and the next present the influence of *future human offspring* and *future human wombs* to the public abortion dialogue, it is crucial to grasp society both as that which gives birth to technology and as the prism that refracts technology. Thus, technological advances are not formed in a vacuum; they simultaneously condition the perceived needs and desires and form as practical reactions to the perceived needs and desires that exist in the very society in which they arise.

Now with the understanding that the manipulation of nature is inseparable from the community from which those needs arise, the opening section of this chapter should not only enforce that claim, but appear evident why it was first necessary to introduce. If this still seems too obvious, recall that philosophy often unearths the unseen value from the otherwise obvious. To be clear, what is critical but often left unstated are two important concepts. The first is that *technology is not self-directing.* It requires goals in the form of wants and needs that the manipulation of nature for human society aims to fulfill. And because technology is tethered to society in terms of cooperation, those goals will *never be isolated from the very effects they produce.* Society is formed of peoples. The forces that ethically form individuals within society do not always have the same effect on society as a whole, at least not in the same way. Here is what is meant by that claim. The civil rights advocate Martin Luther King Jr. studied philosophy at Boston University, and speaks in one of his essays of engaging the thought of Reinhold Niebuhr (d. 1971), who himself was a twentieth-century ethicist and political commentator. Niebuhr proposed an idea known as the *dualistic ethic.*[9] This ethic addressed the dichotomy between moral individuals (the ethically formed individuals) and immoral society (the phenomenon of individuals in the group not expressing their own individual ethic). King shared how what is nurtured as good in the individual often disappears when the "good person" acts as the member of a group. To phrase it in terms of Martin Buber's *I and Thou* philosophy, the relationality in the group tends to decrease the

9. Niebuhr, *Moral Man*, 270–71.

force of the "I" as the number of "Thous" increases; and as more group members no longer recognize the other as an "I," the "I" becomes objectified and formed collectively as an "It." The danger, then, as society collectively becomes objectified, is the pitting of the "I" against the "It" that C. S. Lewis warned of in his 1943 *Abolition of Man*. Lewis explained in *Abolition* that technology is the precise means of reducing others to an "It." He claimed that as society wields power over nature, there inevitably emerges a situation of power by some people over other people, where the manipulation of nature (technology) is merely the tool to control society.[10] Virtue theory may govern individuals; but, in a pluralistic society, individual virtue caves to the ethos of seeking a means to an end. This public ethic often forms as a concession to that inevitable reality.

More often than not, the "public ethic" has been utilitarian, which holds that the goal is the greatest happiness for the greatest number of people. Such an ethic has a certain appeal, as it weighs the "goods" and the "bads" and then by that metric determines the means to the ethical goal. On the surface, it appears sensible in its consideration for the majority. But one of the recognized flaws of a utilitarian ethic is that only the current "goods" and "bads" can be considered; and as the unforeseen effects evolve, the novel has by then become customary and has thus embedded itself in the very society from which it has sprung. Anyone who has experienced horrific, or simply undesirable, outcomes from what otherwise seemed like a good, sensible idea at the time can easily understand this predicament. For example, in terms of fertility treatments, advances such as prenatal screenings, preimplantation diagnosis, and the genetic manipulation of embryos have become applications of technology with the end goal of increased fertility. But it is not always clear that what *seems* good in the present will ultimately *seem* good as the technology continues to advance. How it plays out in the future is something quite frankly experienced as championing the successes while the undesired effects will be formed as an ethical imposition, not chosen, yet endured. Historical occurrences of this already bear witness to uncertain outcomes for future human offspring from technological advances that seemed advantageous at the time but now are questionable. This is not a Pandora's box scenario, although that is possible, but the influence of the effects can be both subtle and even rationalized as worth the utilitarian calculation.

10. Lewis, *Abolition of Man*, 59.

First, the term *potential human* does not hold the same meaning as *future offspring*. As intended here, the latter refers to an embryo or fetus, which regardless of any designation of personhood is already a living human, while the former refers to gametic material prior to fertilization and thus denotes a future human. This is an important distinction that this section will make use of for comparative purposes, in its relation to technology and society. To clarify, think of *potential* in this context as having the power to become something—here, the human sperm and the human ovum possess the potentiality to become a living human embryo and thus a fetus. With a future offspring, the potential has already become actual; the living human embryo will be an offspring in the future, provided nothing adverse occurs. For example, for a young couple planning to start a family or for an individual considering having a child through gametic donation, the result will be a potential living human. Then, whether in vitro fertilization (IVF) is used to develop an embryo or a female has conceived and is carrying the fetus, the offspring is already a living human.

This section's focus is the application of technology within society relative to the potential human and future offspring, so it is about what *type* of potential human or future offspring the present-day living human persons are envisioning. Consider this practical point: to a degree, both potential living humans and future offspring can be selected using technology. If that sounds eerily inauspicious or ominous, it should. It is not so much that one person's "good" is another person's "bad," but that the means to achieve such a good may, when logically applied, turn out bad regardless of any good intention. Here is what is meant practically by that notion. Technology has addressed infertility, which society rightly considers a tragedy of the human experience. In many positive ways, this has allowed females to experience a pregnancy who otherwise would have remained infertile. But it also has allowed intervention to "weed out" genetic abnormalities and disorders discovered during screening and testing. On the surface, that is good. In the same way that one would not wish an abnormality or disorder upon an existing infant or toddler, why would not the ability to stave that off, prior to implantation, also be good? One would be hard-pressed to find any issue with some of those applied advancements when they address conditions that are undesirable. But the term of what is *desirable* is the issue at hand. Those seeking fertility treatments, along with their providers, do have control over *which* ovum and sperm become fertilized embryos as *potential living humans*. Then even once fertilized (thus either in vitro or in utero), there remains the further selection of the embryos, selecting out the *future offspring* considered undesirable prior to implantation. The argument is simple and should not be contentious: selection is available; selections will be made according to what is desirable or undesirable; what is desirable or undesirable is influenced by the cultural ethos and available technological advances; current technologies applied in society are presented to a future society, which in tandem impacts that future society's technological applications and conditions; and thus particular desirable or undesirable traits evolve within that ethos. Regardless of which "side" of the abortion issue one is on, if it helps referring to the positions yet as sides, selection even for reasons of benevolence logically results in one generation choosing the quality and capacity of potential and future offspring for the subsequent generation. Therefore, the living human persons of the present society, by their selections of what is deemed desirable and undesirable, determine the persons of the future society. That is simple logic to follow.

Next, consider that French philosopher and sociologist Jacques Ellul (d. 1994), in his 1954 work *The Technological Society*, speaks of the necessary subordination of technology to the respect for human ends, which is often set aside unwittingly. Ellul warns of the exploitation and suppression of the human person and, in its place, an indiscriminate and autonomous development of technology at the expense of the human person.[11] The issue, then, is *what*, or better yet, *who*, determines what is desirable or undesirable, in the present and subsequently for the future. And if, as claimed, what is deemed desirable or undesirable is formed by the current cultural ethos, by Ellul's concern, technology becomes a goal in itself and thus forms the ethos. As the ethos changes, with and by technological gains, then so does what is determined desirable or undesirable change, which becomes susceptible to the use of technology and how it is to be applied acceptably. The inheriting generation has no say in that determination but, numbed by customary use, falls prey without critical reflection to an involuntary consent under the guise of progress.

To systematically address the issue, it may be helpful to juxtapose it against the major theme of this text, that *either some living humans are persons, or all living humans are persons*. If only some living humans are persons, which can be framed as the *abortion advocate position*, then female autonomy governs the ethical judgment of an abortion prior to the

11. Ellul, *Technological Society*, 10.

onset of moral worth at viability and personhood at consciousness. As an ethic is dependent on *being* or what a thing *is*, in terms of any fertility treatment relative to abortion there are three distinct phases. Each phase is categorized by evident levels of *being* and thus will have corresponding ethical evaluations relative to abortion and bodily autonomy. They are (1) the sperm and ovum selection, (2) the postfertilization/preimplantation embryo screening and testing, and (3) the postimplantation blood testing or imaging diagnosis. The point here is that the primacy of female autonomy can logically be applied to the first phase of (1) sperm and ovum selection, or the second phase of (2) postfertilization/preimplantation embryo screening and testing. In either case, the *being* is at a stage prior to implantation, and as gametic material or nonimplanted embryos, the term *abortion* is not applicable. The case of (2) postfertilization/preimplantation would still be the termination of a living human, but not premised on a bodily autonomy argument. Regarding the ethical judgment in the first phase of (1) screening and genetic testing, the *being* would be described as living material that is not yet human. This analysis may appear pedantic, but such distinctions aid in clarity and retain the rigor of logic and critical thinking, permitting dialogue based on the ordinary understanding of terms. The ethical evaluation then is that if there is biological life (gametic material) but no human being, there cannot be a person, and if there is no person, then it cannot be an abortion. Keep in mind that abortion advocates would not likely extend a significant level of moral worth to this category, as there is a stark distinction between the termination of biological life *from* a human, and the termination of human biological life. That point may seem obvious, but it is necessary to affirm, as in the public sphere there has surfaced the conflation of an embryo and gametic material. There have been invalid pro-life rebuttals cynically asking who is responsible for the "killing" of the sperm that occurs with its expiration after ejaculation, if not intended and "used" to fertilize the female. Then, as to an ethical judgment on the second phase of (2) postfertilization/preimplantation embryo screening and testing, from the *some living humans are persons* position, the *being* would be described as a *living human* that is not yet a person. In other words, the embryo is *of* the human species; and since life does not *begin* but continues, the embryo is presently a human life although a nonperson. So, the issue of storage or discarding of nonimplanted embryos poses no ethical consideration for this position. Finally, the same judgment would apply to the (3) fetal stage pre-viability where the fetus acquires moral worth prior to consciousness, at which point the living human has yet to *reach* personhood status. In each preceding stage or scenario, for the abortion advocate, female bodily autonomy is the governing factor for the ethical judgment, and that is weighed against a determination of *being* expressed as (1) gametic material, living, nonhuman, nonperson; (2) embryo, living human, nonperson; and (3) pre-viable fetus, living human, moral value but nonperson.

To continue systematically addressing the issue for the other "side," one must consider the *abortion opponent position*, which holds that all living humans are persons. The abortion opponent will respect female autonomy but will recognize that such autonomy cannot trump the personhood of another after personhood is ethically established. So with the analysis remaining based on what a thing *is* (the *being*), personhood is accepted as necessarily tethered to all living humans. That is the ethical line. With the first phase of (1) screening and genetic testing of the *being* as *living material* that is not yet human, the ethical judgment would not differ in kind from that of the abortion advocate. There might be moral worth ascribed by both the advocate and the opponent, as the gametic material is living matter unique to humans—in fact, to a particular human—but not qualifying as a person. In fact, in instances of divorce or the death of one (or both) of the persons who contributed the gametic material, the cryogenically stored sperm or ovum would be considered property of the estate. It is noteworthy that property is always ascribed value, a consideration given more attention shortly. But then, with the second phase of (2) postfertilization/preimplantation embryo screening and testing, the *being* logically accepted as a *living human* would, by virtue of the premise that all living humans are persons, be in total contrast to the ethical judgment of the advocate. At this stage, neither female autonomy nor undesirable screening or testing would ethically alter the judgment of the now-living human person. Even arguments by the advocate that lean toward aesthetic or functional criteria would not reduce the personhood status for the opponent. And then, of course, concerning the third phase of (3) a fetus at either viability or consciousness, the *being* would unequivocally be judged as a person.

These systematic judgments presented as scenarios are not intended to be representative of all possible judgments on abortion relative to *being*, but only an application of what would be considered the strongest case for an advocate or opponent position on abortion, in view of personhood as the determiner for an ethical judgment. Here is the argument in syllogistic form for why this principle was chosen.

P1 All nonpersons can have their life discretionarily ended by another person.

P2 No *being* recognized as a person is a nonperson.

C Therefore, no *being* recognized as a person can have their life discretionarily ended by another person.

The strength in this claim of *personhood as the threshold for an abortion* is that it forces the individual (the present person) who is making the judgment to first determine what *being* constitutes a human living person and then compels a consistent ethical application. But as it was also argued that a nonperson *being* may possess moral worth and thus cannot have their life arbitrarily ended by a person, that suggests something else along with personhood forms a value as a determinant for an ethical evaluation. The previous syllogism would require altering to express that point in argument form. Here is that revision to include the valuing of moral worth.

P1 All who seek an ethical judgment would agree that no being of moral worth, even if a nonperson, can have their human life arbitrarily ended by a person.

P2 The abortion advocate and opponent are those who seek an ethical judgment.

C Therefore, the abortion advocate and opponent would agree that no being of moral worth, even if a nonperson, can have their human life arbitrarily ended by a person.

Again, this is not a simplification of the abortion argument in order to favor one side over another. Rather, it is the reduction of the ethical fulcrum to its logical end, that any ethical consideration of personhood is tethered to an evaluation of being. The thrust of this entire treatise is to narrow the conversation logically into the only arena that can accommodate fruitful exchange, as the idea of *personhood*, unlike *human* and *life*, cannot be empirically determined and so must be dialectically considered in a consistent ethical manner.

Now, an opportunity should be taken to briefly address the terms *opponent* and *advocate* relative to abortion, as in the pedestrian mind they can be easily dismissed as representing a false binary. The objection to those terms is that they do not exemplify *what one is for*, and so then each is but a canard used unfairly as an identifier to debase the other. However, this is another instance of either the use of a fallacious diversion tactic, or ignorance of the logical outcome of *opposing* or *advocating for* abortion. To state the issue, the pro-lifer may try to argue that they are not against female autonomy, but only supporting the life of the unborn. The pro-choicer may try to argue that they are not advocating for abortion, but only supporting female autonomy. Yet, logically, each ultimately becomes an opponent for either autonomy or abortion respectively, by virtue of the position each advocates for. It is true that some positions held do not result in zero-sum evaluations; but in this instance, the advocacy of one position logically results in the opposition to the other. Consider this: if a pro-lifer claims to support the life of the unborn and not oppose female autonomy, by virtue of what they support, in some instances they become a de facto opponent of female autonomy, if that autonomy would be exercised by choosing an abortion that ends the life of the unborn. Since one of the logical expressions of female autonomy results in the termination of the life of the unborn, claiming to support female autonomy while being opposed to abortion would be contrary to the pro-life stance. Such a position can only be semantically, but not practically, held. Not verbalizing one of the logical consequences of the position (the denial of female autonomy if it results in an abortion) may make the claim more publicly digestible, but it does not make the claim more benevolent, and it certainly cannot be practically held. It follows that if a pro-choicer claims to support the female's autonomy and not oppose abortion per se, by virtue of what they support, in some instances they become a de facto proponent of abortion, if that female autonomy would be exercised by choosing an abortion that ends the life of the unborn. Here, too, since an abortion is one of the logical expressions of female autonomy, claiming to support female autonomy and not being a proponent of abortion would be contrary to the pro-choice stance. As with the other position, this could only be semantically, but not practically, held as a position. Not verbalizing one of the logical consequences of the position (the acceptance of an abortion if it is necessary to uphold the female's autonomy) may make the claim more publicly digestible, but it also does not make the claim more benevolent, and likewise cannot be practically held. To state anything otherwise is either ignorant or fallacious.

There is another way to understand clearly that one cannot advocate for what is considered positive while denying advocacy of one of the logical results that is deemed negative. This can be shown by the use of the variant of a fallacy known as *reductio ad absurdum*, where one reduces the argument to its absurd conclusion by demonstrating the premise is false as applied in other instances and thus is unsound regardless. For illustration, one may take the premise of what is being asserted, substitute another term, and demonstrate how the claim is absurd by contrast. In this case, the fallacy can be illustrated by swapping out the term *abortion* and inserting the term *slavery*. One thing to know first is that this is not a false equivalency or false analogy. The term *abortion* here is not to be tainted by association with the unethical practice of slavery. They are not presented as interchangeable unethical ideas; they are presented for illustration, where the technique is to demonstrate that if the advocacy claim is absurd as applied to slavery, it is equally absurd when applied to abortion. So, the substitution of terms in such an instance is not an attempt at comparison. Here then is the rephrasing of the logical comparison, substituting the term *slavery* for *abortion*, where the terms for the abortion and bodily autonomy arguments are retained in parentheses, so the fallacious logic can be unmasked. If a pro-lifer claims, "I am not opposed to a female's bodily autonomy, but only support the life of the unborn," it is akin to arguing, "I am not opposed to a person's right to own slaves (female autonomy), only to slavery (abortion)." One may logically retort, "It is not possible to oppose slavery (abortion), while claiming to support a person's choice to own slaves (female autonomy), because the opposition to slavery (pro-life) is by de facto the logical opposition to owning slaves (female autonomy)." Then to counter the pro-choicer, if they claim, "I am not a proponent of abortion, only a female's bodily autonomy," it is akin to arguing, "I am not a proponent of slavery (abortion), only a person's right to own slaves (female autonomy)." One may here logically retort, "It is not possible to support a person's choice to own slaves (female autonomy), while claiming to oppose slavery (abortion), because supporting the right to own slaves (pro-choice) is by de facto the logical support of slavery (abortion)." From each perspective, the action of what is being advocated for cannot logically be separated from opposing the object (logical end) of that action. In summation, the whole argument that one can be for female autonomy without implicitly supporting an abortion, or that one can be for the life of the unborn without implicitly denying female autonomy, is a diversion. Each logically results, or at least is possible because of, the support or opposition to the other. To hold a view otherwise can only occur because either the fallacious logic of the claim has not been thoroughly considered or the individual is ignorant of the logical implication of what they claim to advocate for or oppose. If this explanation appears verbose, as is the case with most fallacious claims, more effort is required to identify, explain, and thus refute fallacious thinking than is required for the claimant to simply illogically assert it. Both the uncritical thinker and the ideologue are content with the semblance of a fuzzy affirmation, if what "sounds good and sensible" furthers their position.

This discussion is an attempt to address the reality within the public abortion dialogue: the choice of *selection* is not merely between the goods of female autonomy and fetal life but, by extension to issues of reproduction, logically applies to the selection of sperm or ovum, which embryo to implant, which fetus to reduce, along with which pregnancy to terminate. Therefore, female autonomy relative to reproduction will by extension support three types of selection. First will be the consideration of determining which embryos are genetically *fit* and what sperm may be excluded prior to fertilization based on predictable undesired factors. Secondly, there will be the ethical evaluation concerning the selection of fertilized embryos prior to implantation. And finally, during an established pregnancy, this section will address the ethics of the multifetal reductions that become the abortive selection of three or more fetuses when multiple embryos implant, but would also include the abortion of a single fetus. With either of these considerations, there logically remains the ethical choice of some *selection*. To the first, the *selection* is based on desired or undesired traits formed by preferences. With multifetal reductions, the *selection* may be pragmatic (not safe to carry multiple fetuses), but even then, the *selection* is not done randomly. It will consider which traits, if knowable and present, are desired and preferred that will logically form the society of future offspring. With those parameters explained, this section will address two considerations. The first is to consider if there is a logical relationship between the identification of what is or is not a desired and preferred trait, and then its relation to that of indirect or unintentional eugenics. The other consideration will be if there is any logical relationship between the undesirable traits and preferences in those three types of selections, with prejudice toward present people in society who exhibit those same or like undesirable traits and preferences. The broad point for each consideration will test one's present understanding or dismissal of personhood as it relates to abortion and autonomy, which must account for any technological advances in society in terms of influencing the idea of personhood for subsequent generations.

It may seem discordant for the conversation to speak of abortion, autonomy, and selection as having some connection to the depravity of eugenics. But to do so is neither a defense of the pro-life stance (it is safe to assume many pro-lifers are advocates of IVF and the unavoidable choices), nor a formal accusation of those who hold the pro-choice position. The primary point here is that when the choice is connected to desired outcomes, and those desired outcomes are further connected to the selection of future human offspring, it is logically impossible for eugenics not to be addressed. Eugenics is the principle of improving the future human population by controlled breeding. The goal is one of *fitness*, although that fitness is not self-defining but relative to the values of the present cultural ethos. The term *eugenics* was first coined by the cousin of Charles Darwin, Francis Galton (d. 1911). In his 1883 book *Inquiries into Human Fertility and Development*, Galton formed the term *eugenics* from two Greek words understood etymologically to mean "good birth." The logic of eugenics is simple: if one desires to improve the intellectual acumen of future and potential human beings, and if intellect and social rank are due to genetic factors, then those genetic factors, being desirable, are the ones to be preserved and encouraged by reproduction.[12] The reverse of this is also true, of course: the inferior stock must not be permitted or encouraged to reproduce. For these reasons, with the added angst of world overpopulation and the projected food shortages, the eugenics movement became an infamous hallmark of the early twentieth-century Progressive Era. It is historically understood now, regardless of one's political persuasion, that the Planned Parenthood founder and birth control advocate Margaret Sanger (d. 1966) spoke plainly about the failure of the *melting pot* mentality. While Sanger was editor of *The Birth Control Review*, her publication explicitly stated that the only way to save the race from deterioration was to have the families of better stock procreate and those of lesser stock contracept.[13] Those who were specifically targeted and thus deemed *unfit* at the time were Italians, Black people, and Jews. Further, it is historically known that the leaders of Germany in

12. Galton, *Human Faculty and Its Development*, 2, 57.

13. Sanger, "Birth Control Review," 7.

the 1930s praised the United States for this "eugenic science," evidence of which can be found displayed on a plaque in the United States Holocaust Memorial Museum. Located in Washington, DC, the museum houses an exhibit titled "Deadly Medicine: Creating the Master Race."[14] The reality of this sinister project sank in—and its subsequent repudiation came—only after the discovered horrors of the Holocaust, at which point such genetic engineering was condemned and discarded in the United States. And though eugenics is often accused of being a "junk science," if improving genetic quality through breeding were only a junk science, then animal breeders would never retain stud animals and breed purity could not "scientifically" be controlled. It was, and is, in fact, a *correct science*, albeit a correct science used for the nefarious goals of human selection. That is not to dismiss those aspects of the project that were in fact junk science, as the biological classifications of race, cranial capacity (anthropometry), and the linking of behavior to intelligence had no empirical standing. But accounting for the ethnocentric and racist claims that underpinned eugenics, the legitimate empirical applications that included controlled breeding are not just possible but are fully capable of reaching that *fitness* goal. And it should be known that this control of breeding through forced sterilization was not simply an isolated tragedy limited to a few decades. It continued well into the second half of the twentieth century. Even into the 1960s, the majority of states in the United States had eugenic laws that permitted sterilization without consent for those deemed feebleminded or diseased. The category of feeblemindedness included nearly any mental disorder or criminal deviancy, and those individuals considered diseased encompassed any condition from epilepsy to alcoholism and even masturbation, which was thought to be an obstacle to mental treatment.

It is not an exaggeration that the goal of eugenics in determining *fitness* was, and is, to depersonalize those with undesired traits. One may easily argue that with the Holocaust, the goal was to dehumanize, which is an enhanced indignity, but that does not detract from the point. The question, then, of contemporary society's selection criteria for gametic material, embryos, and pregnancy screening is to what degree selecting out nondesirables can be *implicit eugenics*. Put succinctly, will genetic selection from testing and medical imaging diagnosis lead to a new expression of prejudice through *implicit eugenics* that, while not explicitly

14. See Bachrach, "Deadly Medicine," para. 2.

targeting race or ethnicity, nonetheless reduces certain populations to less than persons? The ethical concern is not to ask if prenatal genetic testing can screen for serious medical issues, as it can and does, and within those parameters there is wide ethical agreement. The ethical concern may not even be whether conditions such as cystic fibrosis should be avoided, if and when possible, but rather if it is equally undesirable to select Down syndrome, deafness, assumed cognitive abilities, or developmental impairments as undesirable conditions for *potential humans* or *future offspring*. There may be no overt governmental or other authoritative pressure to consider such conditions as *unfit* for selection of the gametic material or embryo, but there has arisen apprehension connected to anticipated increased parental care (the psychological strain of responsibility) and perceived or actual societal medical burdens (is it ethical that society bear the burden for individual imprudent judgment?). The evolution of this *implicit eugenics* is that what begins as an *autonomous choice* may very well form as a societal pressure and thus be perceived as one's individual duty as a justice to society at large. Over time, societal pressure can implicitly evolve into a public mandate required by the present perception of social justice. Consider a couple bringing an embryo or fetus to birth, with an otherwise preventable impairment or health condition. While the individual parent or family predicates their choice on weighing personal burdens, such as if they are able to both mentally and physically support the *chosen* impaired human offspring, the choice will consider to what degree the *chosen* impaired human offspring may become an unjust burden to the future society and the present healthcare system. And if the choice for selection during pregnancy is without restriction even up until fetal viability, then would conditions such as congenital hydrocephalus (buildup of fluid on the brain), for example, with its associated life expectancy ranging from toddlerhood to early adulthood and its likely corresponding effects of learning disabilities and epilepsy, by default be something selected *out* as not desirable? Or even for treatable issues such as a cleft palate *discovered in utero*, which will require post-birth treatment and follow-up surgeries, will those factors meet the threshold of selection as *unfit* future offspring because of the subsequent care and burden that may otherwise be avoided? And though the sex (male and female) of the unborn is not an impairment, given that there is the ability to sex-select one's offspring by preimplantation screening or fetal reduction, would the undesired sex of the potential offspring or fetus be susceptible to parental desires and societal expectations?

To the issue of personhood status of those in the present society who exhibit those undesirable traits, as stated, there arises the question of whether such a relationship can logically be inferred between what constitutes an undesirable trait (in the potential or future human offspring) and prejudicial views (or treatment) of those presently in society with such undesirable traits. The initial reaction would be that the cases are distinct, and there is no correlation between a trait being undesirable and a person possessing that trait. But consider, for example, people with cystic fibrosis, who *themselves* would likely accept a cure, if possible. There may be little resistance to not perpetuating the disease, which means it would follow as unlikely they would sense disregard for their own personhood by others not desiring the condition they possess. But would the same dynamic apply for people with Down syndrome or for people who are deaf? It is not entirely unheard of for individuals to identify with these conditions. Would concern be more pronounced with conditions or disorders that develop character and form community more centrally, such as the Down syndrome community or the deaf community? For example, those in the deaf community may have a strong reaction to genetic testing that devalues their existence by *selecting out* those embryos and fetuses who would be deaf upon live birth. In fact, it is a matter of *ableism* (the favoring of able-bodied persons), from their perspective. Then with embryos or the unborn who are screened or tested for Down syndrome, will they be *selected out* on par with those identified with sickle cell anemia as the marker for an "unhealthy baby'? There is some evidence of this occurring; in Iceland over three-quarters of all pregnant females choose to test for such a condition, and the termination rate for those prenatally screened for Down syndrome is near 100 percent.[15] So to the argument of voluntary screening evolving into a public social justice obligation, if a couple in Iceland is determined to bring a Down syndrome child to birth, will that be prudentially questioned by the present human population as both perpetuating an undesired condition and burdening societal resources? Would that then have no logical inference as to the personhood of "born people" with Down syndrome?

To be clear, the concern arises as to whether or not a present human person with Down syndrome or an individual who is deaf would endure pressure to not have a potential human or future offspring with Down syndrome or deafness. In terms of justice, they may feel compelled to

15. See Government of Iceland, "Facts," para. 6, which states that two to three children per year are born with Down syndrome.

utilize IVF where gametic selection could control either condition existing in a potential human; or they may feel pressure to not implant an embryo or to seek an abortion if the condition is discovered postfertilization or in utero, in the case of a future offspring. The concern is that if those exhibited traits are undesirable for either potential humans or future offspring, is it possible to disconnect that depersonalizing based on undesired conditions from present human individuals who possess the same undesirable traits? It may not be a one-to-one causal link that simply implies that because one does not desire Condition X in a potential human or future offspring, that then those who presently have Condition X are themselves thought of as less than a person. But the concern remains valid, and it may be an issue of cognitive dissonance to assert otherwise. The primary ethical issue is in judging what is *less than perfect*, as determined by selecting traits and conditions for potential humans and future offspring that cannot be judged outside the cultural ethos of society (the waters one swims in). What is "less than perfect" has changed since the Progressive Era of the early twentieth century, and it will change again in the future era of the late twenty-first century. And even if present individuals with those "unfit" traits such as Down syndrome or deafness understand and agree to ethically support limiting each as sufficient conditions for selection of potential humans or future offspring, the calculus does not change. If those with Condition X are perfectly fine reducing the continuation of potential persons and future offspring with the Condition X they exhibit, the logic that one set of human people in the present is determining the "fitness" of human offspring for the future remains an ethical concern to be addressed.

The reality of the risk of depersonalizing is associated with the ability to select. When a choice is possible, then the choice must logically and evidently be binary. What is undesirable may not be held by a full majority, but ultimately either someone will select or not select what is undesirable in each individual instance. Then logically, if one must choose to select or not select, for those who do select, some desirable trait predicated on a perceived and knowable future fitness will inevitably be necessary as a value to determine moral worth. Logically, the concern is that any human person or societal group is ethically culpable when determining a "fitness standard" formed by a present desire, while determining potential humans or future offspring. Technology and society, as argued, are intrinsically linked. If the "fitness standard" that is applied to any potential human or future offspring is neither influenced by the current ethos nor applicable to any individuals in the present population who share such criteria, then one would have to argue they do not have that same "fitness standard," which would logically devalue the moral worth of present humans who already possess the undesired trait. The soundness of such an argument would be questionable (the premise would not be true), and the sincere application would be difficult to find convincing. Further, the next logical projection of this "selecting" is that if the present choice of embryonic or prenatal selections is predicated on female autonomy, then that present autonomy either permits or prevents a potential human from being fertilized (gametic material), or a *future offspring* from being implanted (embryo) or brought to term (fetus). The potential humans and future offspring will have been "selected out" by values that are ethically imposed by the present, and those *swimming in the waters of the present* will have to be honest in recognizing that their cultural ethos will ethically impose what is deemed as *fit* for future populations. If the standard of fitness was worked out in one generation (presented as novel to society), then that influence will be inherited as customary (received as ordinary to society). These conditions require stringent application of critical thinking and considerations that will leave a utilitarian ethic to ethically weigh the presently evident goods and bads as well as the foreseeable circumstances.

Here is a thought experiment that illustrates (1) how an opportunity for a choice will inevitably compel a selection and (2) how, because one selects what is personally judged to be a desirable condition, that action psychologically frames the judgment in terms of aligning individual or societal preferences with the available choices. The point is that any *selecting* logically creates a hierarchy of criteria to determine fitness that are judged by those selected preferences. That is straightforward. It is a neutral claim, free from bias or impartiality. There are those who screen for embryo viability to discover genetic defects that will likely result in failed implantations or miscarriages. That is more functionally based rather than preference selection, so for the sake of this illustration it can be set aside. In terms of preference selections, the selection of *fitness* in those cases is process related. In this thought experiment, from multiple embryos, once each is tested and screened, one, two, or more will be considered for implantation. Any *fit* embryos that are viable but not implanted will likely be cryogenically preserved (frozen), donated for research, or possibly made available for adoption. The *unfit* embryos will be neither donated, nor preserved, nor implanted. They will be discarded or used for research. For those that are not to be discarded due to unviability, prior to implantation, the sex (male/female) of the offspring can be selected with nearly 100 percent accuracy.[16] This may be done for family balancing concerns, or as a personal preference for the sex of the future human offspring. For example, the couple wants a daughter as they already have two sons, and the extended family is also predominantly male. So, in this thought experiment, the available selection of viable embryos is between one female and three males. The persons making the judgment desire to select the female living human embryo, but the female embryo has been diagnosed with genetic deafness, and the couple themselves are not hearing impaired. Though the diagnosis of deafness is accurate, whether or not the future human offspring would be deaf is not 100 percent certain. The couple must factor their selection based on *their* desirability for a *potentially* deaf, future female offspring. Will they consider deafness as an unfit trait or base their selection solely on the desired sex, as at this point they cannot remain value-neutral? Would their selection be influenced at all by family and societal approval? For instance, would they be able to argue why it was ethical that they *selected* a potential offspring, with a foreseeable impairment, to those who would judge this as fostering the impairment of deafness on a future child? Would they rebuff the concerns society might have that a deaf child was purposefully chosen, given that such a *selection* could have easily been avoided? Would it be considered a prudent judgment that intentionally places a burden on a future offspring and society at large? If so, are any of these attitudes relative to values or judgments of present living persons who are deaf? That requires reflection and will be a determining factor. Now, to tweak this scenario, what if the parents were both members of the deaf community themselves and purposefully selected the embryo because of the genetic deafness diagnosis? Another tweak would be if they, though members of the hearing community, see deafness as value-neutral. In that scenario, would selecting an embryo with a deafness diagnosis as *unfit* be seen as ableism and thus as prejudice toward those presently living in the deaf community? Would those in the deaf community see any *selecting out* as ableism and prejudicial? The point is that it is difficult, if not impossible, to make the argument that what is *selected* as *unfit* for future human offspring has no bearing on one's present view toward living human persons who possess that same characteristic deemed *unfit*. The act of selecting

16. Nucleus, "PGT-A Testing," para. 9.

logically creates a hierarchy of fitness determined by the preferences selected, which both are influenced by society and, in turn, influence future societal views.

To flesh out the connection between a preference and decision predicament, one more tweak is necessary that logically leads to societal prejudicial views of present human persons. This is merely the same previous thought experiment concerning a future offspring, now applied to *potential humans*. The distinction is that with the latter, fertilization has not yet occurred, so this concerns the selection of gametic material. In this scenario, the couple who wants to begin IVF belongs to the hearing community. Both have been genetically tested and now know they each have one copy of the gene mutation that causes deafness, meaning that it is likely their potential human offspring will be deaf. The couple decides they will seek sperm donation from a donor who does not possess the mutation for deafness, and then proceed with IVF using the female's ovum. The sperm selection will include consideration of various physical traits, taking into account anything from height to eye color. Other desirable criteria would include the sperm donor's education level, personal and family medical history, race and ethnicity, and so on. Here is the concern. If the sperm is healthy and does not contain the genetic marker for deafness, would they choose the sperm from a donor whose highest education level was a high school diploma, if equally *fit* sperm from another donor was available who had earned a graduate degree? If it were even between two donors with graduate degrees, would they choose the donor with a State School degree over an Ivy League degree? If they selected the Ivy League graduate, would that selection be made in the moral confidence that it is not because they deem that male sperm donor as somewhat better than the State School graduate? It would be fair to hold that if they claim otherwise, their selection betrays them, and reveals at least a modest prejudice that the more elite degree offers a greater *fitness*. This could be done for every criterion.

The logic is simple in that because one does have a choice and, in fact, one is compelled to choose something, then the choice would be based on more desirable preferences, which then forms a hierarchy in terms of *fitness*. It is difficult to perceive that a person may seek donated gametes without concern or interest in donor fitness. Though there may be important reasons for the anonymity of the donor, it does not follow that there would be a cavalier disinterest in donor fitness, as the application process and collected information attest to its importance. It then follows that whatever criteria are deemed of higher quality would be the factors in determining what is more desirable; and as one would be expected to choose what is deemed of a higher quality, the desires would form the preferences for selection of the sperm or ovum to be used for the potential human offspring, or selection of an embryo in the case of the future human offspring. Here is this claim stated in a series of syllogisms to argue that what is desirable and preferable is the basis for selection. This first syllogism presents the foundational claim—obvious for most—that when an individual is given a selection, that individual will choose in line with their desires and preferences.

P1 When a selection is available, a person will choose what is both desirable and preferable.

P2 In the case of embryo or sperm selection, a selection is available.

C1 Therefore, in the case of embryo or sperm selection, a person will choose what is both desirable and preferable.

As those selections result in a chosen ovum, sperm, or embryo and thus are either potential humans or future offspring, then those that are selected for the future are based on desires and preferences influenced by and with the present ethos and culture. Here is the argument.

P1 What is desirable and preferable is formed by and with both cultural and societal values in the present.

P2 Both potential humans and future offspring are selected by what is desirable and preferable.

C2 Therefore, both potential humans and future offspring are selected both by and with cultural and societal values in the present.

This argument demonstrates a twofold ethical issue. First, the worth of both a potential human and future offspring is determined by how their qualities will match individual present desires and preferences. And secondly, those qualities determined by preferences of individuals are inherited from a previous cultural ethos and are formed within the present set of adopted cultural and societal values, which itself has developed an underlying ethical ethos.

From that, a third argument logically forms. This argument holds that the preferences of the culture and society in the present become a basis for what is deemed *fit* for each offspring, and this in turn becomes that which is ethically inherited by the future society. That is, selecting more *fit* human offspring in the present logically is ordered to creating more *fit* human offspring in the future. One time period's ethos of fitness is inherited by a subsequent time period. Here is that claim illustrated as a syllogism.

P1 Selecting preferences for potential humans and future offspring in the present will create a more *fit* future society.

P2 What is deemed *fit* in the present society influences the selection of preferences for potential humans and future offspring in the present.

C3 Therefore, what is deemed *fit* in the present society will create a more *fit* future society.

This thought experiment serves only to demonstrate that present desirable conditions psychologically compel one to frame their selection. And thus, any present concept of *fitness* maintains a positive eugenic goal, even if subtly implicit based on the selection of the expression of known criteria. A likely rebuff is understandable: the selection of potential humans and future offspring, claimed to implicitly result in unintentional eugenics, is based on the beneficence of eradicating diseases and disorders that otherwise were not controllable in the past. But again, the concern is exactly which disease or disorder is *selected* and thus targeted for eradication. Is it cystic fibrosis, Down syndrome, deafness, and so on? Further, the available *selections* presented for consideration are not limited to those criteria. For those who would continue to claim that eugenics is merely a junk science or that what is presented here does not qualify as implicit eugenics, they would need to explain how the selections of sperm and ovum for potential humans, or the embryo selections and/or multifetal reductions of future offspring, do not share the goal of a "good birth" that the eugenics movement of the early twentieth century also sought. And further, they would need to argue that this is not done in order to improve genetic qualities through breeding of human offspring, by weeding out what is presently deemed *unfit*. It is intellectually honest to admit such selections are intentional, and then to recognize that eugenics is *technology* applied with science, as an aid to providing the "good birth" of a potential human or future offspring, for the benefit of *society*.

The ethical question, which must be pressed, is what preferences constitute a *good birth*. Yet, it must be kept in mind that the goal of eugenics is argued not to improve just one single individual but collectively to foster a more *fit* society overall. To that point, the argument of the second syllogism addressed that individual selections of potential humans and future offspring are influenced by implicit societal goals. So, if one can accept that culture has an effect on individual perception and complacency (that was Marx's and Gramsci's point concerning hegemonic power), and individuals rather than a governmental entity are making the selections in these individual scenarios, then the personal *selection* must account for an outside influence, with an implicit cultural goal to form a more *fit* society by influencing perceptions and anticipating complacency toward *fitness*. One "swims in the waters" of their own time and ethos. If the goal is to improve one's own potential human or future offspring through gamete or embryo selection, and there is some societal consensus that shapes those preferences for each person, then logically the individual *fit* potential human or future offspring selected will collectively contribute to a more *fit* future human society by means of the concurrent technology. There exists a concrete and verifiable case that explicates this trend from individual preferences, predicated on societal norms, utilizing technology for individual goals to align with implicit societal goals. It can be framed as a question. For those living in Iceland, would it be reasonable to expect there is some cultural influence that compels one to resist implantation or bringing an unborn to term if the potential human or future offspring were diagnosed with Down syndrome? With no explicit authority mandating to *not* implant an embryo or to abort a fetus with Down syndrome, the culture of Iceland has reached the same result that an explicit and enforceable mandate would achieve. The societal ethos has embraced an implicit eugenics, evidenced by *literally* only one or two live births per year of offspring with Down syndrome, in a country with thousands of annual live births. Without questioning the benevolent intention, one would be hard-pressed to argue there was not a cultural and societal expectation from which an ethos developed that infants with Down syndrome have been implicitly determined to be neither desirable nor preferable for human offspring.

Two risks concerning this claim require a brief explanation, to solidify this point that personhood is the critical factor in the ethical evaluation of autonomous choices manifesting in selecting *fitness*. The first point is to further respond to someone who argues that a preference for one's own future human offspring has no connection to any prejudice based on those preferences existing in present human persons. The second point is offered in response to someone who argues that the selection of preferences is not unduly influenced by society but rests primarily on autonomous choices, indifferent to the cultural ethos. The second point has already been addressed and stands or falls on the veracity of the first point, so it need not be directly confronted.

To the issue of aligning preferences for potential humans or future offspring with present prejudices toward those exhibiting the same expression, one must be keen not to overstate this connection. But the converse is also true: one must not summarily dismiss it due to its uncomfortable reality. For instance, it is an overstatement to suggest that because a couple does not want a child who is deaf, that they have an overt prejudice toward persons who are deaf. But it is reasonable to suggest that they do recognize the impairment of deafness as something *unfit* and would not select to have a deaf offspring, if possible. They might hold the same position for someone with Down syndrome or even ADHD, the latter of which has floating and oscillating conditions for a diagnosis, which imports an equally floating and oscillating ethical evaluation.

Now, to directly demonstrate the connection between *preference* and *prejudice*, one method would be to investigate cases of buyer's remorse. The term *buyer's remorse* is being used as a convenience for familiarity with the idea of what it means when expectations do not match outcomes. It is not framed in this manner to reduce the human offspring to a product, although at some point depersonalizing a potential human or future offspring may elicit that designation. When testing gametic material or embryos (although testing accuracy differs by condition), there remains the possibility of false-positive diagnoses, in which results presented as true are actually false, or false-negative diagnoses, in which results presented as false are actually true. If an embryo is "selected out" and is not implanted, but in reality it was both viable and fit, a living future human was unjustly not brought to term. Or if a fetus were not aborted because the type of screening or circumstances missed an undesired criterion, the *unfitness* that otherwise would have been selected out is now a live birth with the undesired criterion present in the offspring. In the first instance, it presents as an issue of nonrealization (the fit embryo was not brought to a live birth), though the inaccurate false-positive testing results will likely never be known. But what happens in the false-negative case, where the live birth results in the presence of an undesired *fitness* that was specifically screened to be *selected out*? In that scenario, even though one is informed that the fetus is *fit* and healthy, at birth the infant in fact presents with the undesired condition; what was judged *unfit* is now present in the live offspring. How would the female or couple react to this unexpected condition? The *prejudice test*, which is a clearer term here than *buyer's remorse*, is to ask if that scenario will be met with a level of indignation or disappointment, equal to the preferences that would have been *selected out* if they had known assuredly of the *unfit* diagnosis. The accuracy may be near 100 percent for Down syndrome, not as great for genetic deafness, and even less so for ADHD. If those conditions were accepted as not desirable (*unfit*) but became evident either later in pregnancy or post-birth, would the parents express disappointment or perhaps outrage, thus presenting evidence of present prejudice? If so—again, the relation is not to be overstated—the *prejudice test* exhibits a causal link between what is deemed *unfit* in the selection process and the same conditions existent in persons of the present society.

One other method to consider in demonstrating the connection between preference and prejudice is more emotive in tone. Even so, an affective argument is not an invalid way to discern prejudice, in terms of the criteria for testing and screening. Here is the question to ask: how would one explain their selection of undesirable preferences to an adult who possesses those very same *unfit* criteria? For example, if later in pregnancy or post-birth a diagnosis revealed that the fetus or child had Down syndrome or was deaf, how would one explain their autonomous *selective* choice for *unfitness* to an adult who has Down syndrome or a person who is deaf? With the awkwardness aside, one would have to articulate that they accept the individual person they are speaking with as a full person but would prefer that their own offspring not have Down syndrome or be deaf. One can, of course, substitute this preference test for any condition that the female or couple did not desire as a condition for their own offspring. Now, perhaps a person with Down syndrome or one who is deaf would understand and possibly even accept the premise that the criterion for Down syndrome or deafness is an acceptable selection of being *unfit* for future human offspring. Perhaps they are conciliatory, or perhaps without any reduction in their own personal dignity they hold that the condition is admittedly not desirable. But once again, even if true, that does not alter the premise that people *in the present* are selecting potential humans and future offspring based on criteria for preferences that have formed in society and technology. It may very well be that those who possess an unfit condition, formed with and by society, have themselves come to accept Condition X as unfit. The following syllogism is what requires satisfaction (some form of *being* addressed adequately) in terms of expressing that one's own preferences for a particular condition in a potential human or future offspring that would be selected as *unfit* does not causally infer that a present human person with that condition is characterized as *unfit*.

P1 As present humans will judge Condition X as unfit, there is no prejudice toward present humans with Condition X.

P2 Condition X is undesirable or unfit for potential humans or future offspring as present humans will judge Condition X as unfit.

C Therefore, Condition X is undesirable or unfit for potential humans or future offspring, as there is no prejudice toward present humans with Condition X.

To maintain the argument's conclusion (C) that deafness is considered undesirable or unfit criteria for offspring but does not infer prejudice toward human persons who are deaf, one must first either demonstrate as true P1 (although deafness is a lack of fitness, those who are deaf are not *unfit*), or P2 (although deafness is *unfit* for potential humans or future offspring, it does not mean that deafness is *unfit* in birthed persons). Arguing P1 only considers deafness in the abstract and in practicality is self-contradictory, meaning it would have to hold that deafness is *unfit* in one instance but not another. And as to arguing P2, it will eventually be self-contradictory also, because if deafness is only accepted as *fit* in adults, then the potential human or future person for whom it is *presently unfit* will somehow eventually be *fit* after the live birth.

None of this argument, as presented, is to assert that most rational people who have access to such testing and screenings are seeking to create *perfect offspring*. The concern of present persons forming preferences that manifest as desires, and which further result in choosing *potential humans* or *future offspring*, is not about designer children. Yet, present persons will desire what is currently deemed *normal offspring*, which can be accepted by the societal ethos as relatively free from conditions that would be seen as undesirable and thus *unfit* by present standards. That is a reasonable claim, and one that needs to be part of the public dialogue on abortion. Again, it seems intuitively good to want *what is best* for an offspring, in the same way that parents express they want *what is best* for the future opportunities of their children. In fact, it will be in consideration of future opportunities, by which the selection of *fitness* is determined. Is it not a societal bias that the concern for selecting *fitness* criteria is to ensure that those with Down syndrome or persons who are deaf have the very opportunities that are connected to perceived happiness? One might pause on that statement, and find it reasonable. But one would also need to consider how societal happiness is linked to utilitarian goals, and how what is perceived as *fit* constitutes a societal metric in determining the chance of *success*. So, if the strawman of a utopian ideal (creating designer children) can be set aside, the goal of selection, when available, implicitly seeks a perceived ideal, made against some standard that has arisen in the present ethos. There is no logical rebuttal to that claim. The question is what is that standard, how is it determined, and what influences the criteria that form that standard. It can be expressed as Condition X is preferable, so X must be the standard that the *selection* of Some X is determined against. This standard of X is not *one thing*, but it is included in those things collectively that are desired, preferred, and deemed as *fit* in society, which then are achievable by the means of technology.

There is a further question that bears on the ethical evaluation of *selections* based on *fit* criteria. If it was first asked *what* are those standards that comprise Condition X, then the logical follow-up concern is *who* is establishing those standards as Condition X? Those within the communities of present persons who are seen as less than X (less than preferred, and therefore not desired as potential humans or future offspring) are quite aware that their conditions will be *selected out*. Among those groups whom this would apply to, and who have been vocal about this very concern, are persons whose conditions include Down syndrome and those who are part of the deaf community. That is why those two conditions in particular have been utilized in the previous considerations. But without being exhaustive, one may add people with dwarfism, individuals with developmental disabilities, those with family histories of mental health issues, individuals with low education or modest IQ levels, and those with identifiable congenital or prevalent serious health issues, to name just a few. It is specifically among those conditions that the society-held forces of desires and preferences are working toward an implicit positive eugenics. Members of those communities understand that their status and dignity are predicated on societal perceptions; they realize their relation to the concept of *normal* and perhaps even a judgment of being *healthy* is questioned by the able-bodied population. They realize desires, preferences, and functionality comprise the standard of X, by which the term *unfit*, though not explicitly used, is nonetheless intuitively applied by the practice of *selecting out* potential humans and future offspring.

If someone from those marginalized communities—a dwarf or an individual who is deaf, for instance—seeks IVF therapy with the goal of having an offspring that shares their specific condition, it would pose an ethical challenge for many, if not most, able-bodied persons. Though it is not clear this is anything but a rare occurrence, if one continues with it as a thought experiment, it does test the limits of individual preferences of offspring influenced by societal expectations. So, it is a safe supposition that any human persons who belong to these communities also view their societal *abnormality* not as such, but rather as a positive marker for their own personal and cultural identity. That is to claim that there is pride in belonging to the deaf or dwarf community. The *abnormality*, though recognized as some impairment, is not thought of as a defect, and for all intents and purposes is acceptable and thus may be preferred for their own offspring. A nefarious colloquial term has been coined, pejoratively phrased as *deformer babies*, which refers to the desire of groups such as the deaf and dwarf community to have *future offspring* that are *like them*. This term is obviously intended to cynically parallel the concept of *designer babies*, where rather than trying to create a *more fit* offspring, their preference is not simply to allow but to prefer what is considered by the *fit* as a *less fit* offspring. As an aside, notice that the term *impairment* and not *disabled* was used in this illustration. The term *impairment* refers to the loss of function, and a *disability* is the degree to which that impairment restricts that loss of function within society. Any accommodations *do not remove the impairment, but do mitigate the associated disability.* This is mentioned to address two facts. The first is that what constitutes an impairment has a subjective quality, which is evidenced by the horizontal spread (the category broadens to consider an increasing amount of functional restrictions as impairments classified as disabilities). The second fact is that it is well-documented that able-bodied individuals view the life satisfaction of those with impairments as lower than those with the impairment view their own life satisfaction. This is to claim that the perception of an intolerable condition from a *fit* perspective does not align as intolerable from the individual with the so-called *unfit* condition. So, returning to the ethical question of whether it is licit to "allow" a female or couple to bring deformer babies to a live birth, would it not logically follow that those existing people with the same loss of function or conditions such as Down syndrome, dwarfism, deafness, ADHD, etc., should not only be denied future offspring themselves, but in lieu of their own lack of function or condition, be considered as *less fit* in society? The point is simple: there exists a two-way influence, in that any pushback that such *unfit* conditions should not be encouraged forms as an implicit societal force that deems those who exist within the categories of those reduced functions and conditions as being unfit themselves. In the same way that the early twentieth-century categories of what is deemed *unfit* have changed but have nonetheless influenced their present and subsequent generation, so too will the present-day categorization of those who are *unfit* influence both the present and subsequent generation.

If there is any substance to this argument, then the direct connection between the selection of potential humans or future offspring being conditioned by present cultural and societal forces is a social justice concern, impinging on the public abortion dialogue. Therefore, the cultural and societal forces of the present ethos impose an implicit form of eugenics that seeks to set expectations as the conditions for the ethos of the future culture and society. To reiterate for the sake of clarity, the concern is not for the *ideal offspring*, but that some capacity or value develops as the standard by which the selection is comparatively determined. These selections are neither made in a vacuum nor free from explicit or implicit influence. Historically, to repeat the truism, the powerful have never included themselves as those deemed *unfit*. The eugenic atrocities of the early twentieth century stand as testimony to that. That is not an isolated manifestation of prejudice relegated to that single historical period, as history is replete with such marginalization of the *unfit*. To not safeguard against such concerns would do nothing more than habitually perpetuate hubris. Technology, and its advances within and for society, are noteworthy. But the possibilities they offer have made ethical issues appear in the present, where such possibilities were only dreamt of as fanciful thought experiments in the very near past. Here is a quickly sketched example of how technology is ethically confronting the present and also how the present ethos will impact the future. Consider the possibilities of the gene-editing tool CRISPR (the genetic scissors). This technology was reportedly used to *fix* receptor gene CCR5, thought responsible for the transmission of human immunodeficiency virus (HIV), which, when not properly treated, results in acquired immunodeficiency syndrome (AIDS). This disease devastated minority communities in the 1980s, particularly same-sex males, and continues to harbor a stigma in China. To counter the onset of HIV and the resulting prejudice, a Chinese scientist named He Jiankui (b. 1984) in 2018 altered embryos during the IVF process to cut out the responsible gene.[17] On the surface this appears benevolent, as HIV is deemed undesirable. Jiankui reported success, which resulted in the birth of twins Lulu and Nana, both of whom are thought to no longer carry that receptor gene. This news from China was *leaked*, as this type of genetic manipulation is presently unethical by both international and China's scientific community standards. Again, the goal was laudable, to render the offspring no longer susceptible to the AIDS-causing virus, and thus eradicating the condition and attached stigma. The scientist responsible, Jiankui, was sentenced to three years and jailed for illegal medical practices. To apply this technology illegally, Jiankui reportedly forged ethical review documents and duped the physicians into implanting the embryos without knowledge of his genetic manipulation. But since Jiankui's release in 2022, he continues to research gene therapy.[18] Currently, the twins born from his experiment are alive and remain healthy . . . and continue to be studied. In reality, given the geopolitical aspects of the research and lack of access to the data, it is not clear and perhaps unverifiable that this project was a success. But that aside, the benevolence is questionable, because these targeted genes like CCR5 are responsible for more than a single function. That brings up yet another ethical conundrum of how presently formed, benign intentions, as they are developed in a current ethos, affect future communities by utilitarian goals where some unknown but perhaps foreseeable factors escape present consideration. What are referred to as off-target mutations of gene-editing *will* produce both unknown and presently undesired side effects. For example, a deficiency in the CCR5 gene that is intended to reduce HIV infection also increases the risk of clinical manifestations of the West Nile virus, along with affecting the severity of rheumatoid arthritis. Since this same CCR5 gene also is linked to memory suppression (plasticity), manipulation of the gene can increase learning, cognitive function, and increased memory.[19] That last possibility has the potential to become the *real* goal, which has captured the attention of ethicists. But here again, even with that increased cognitive and memory capacity, there arises the unintentional side effects of virus and bone density

17. Greely, "CRISPR'd Babies," para 11.

18. Yang, "CRISPR Scientist Still Hopeful," para. 8.

19. See Necula, "Roles of CCR5."

issues. They become calculated risks that one generation will knowingly or unwittingly impose on another generation.

Again, recall the evolution of ethical toleration, where the novel becomes customary, the customary becomes expected, and the expected can form into a cultural mandate. The author C. S. Lewis (d. 1963) warned that as human communities gain the technological power to make other humans into what is desirable, what really forms is the power of *some* humans over *other* humans. This carries with it the very real potential to devolve into manipulating those less powerful into becoming what the more powerful desire. That may be accepted as a dire warning—but, to be clear, it is not intended to dismiss the creativity of noteworthy technological advances that have enveloped society. It should be clear that the imposition of technology on some for the benefit of others (present or future) is a concern of dignity, and dignity is pinned to personhood. In this attempt to narrow the focus of the public abortion dialogue to personhood, it should now be evident that the pro-life and the pro-choice monikers are woefully inadequate, as the ethical issues encompassing the selections for potential humans and future offspring do not align by default with either stance. The future human concerns far transcend the concept of "sides." The point is simple: technology and society are intricately connected. But as stated at the onset of this section, technology is not self-directing. Without explicitly stated and knowable goals, any ontological appraisal of the human person as the central and foundational issue for the abortion conversation gives sway to utilitarian ethical progress that will govern the public climate. The technological goals and subsequent effects, which are never isolated from each other, require dialectical and sincerely respectful exchange.

FUTURE HUMAN WOMBS

If it is true that the ideas of *potential humans* and *future offspring* are rarely part of the public abortion dialogue or, worse yet, thought peripheral, then the idea of *future human wombs* is even less considered, though perhaps more consequential. Picture in the future a technologically orchestrated, prenatal nursery. Imagine it as a scene where schoolchildren are on a field trip to one of the decanting rooms, where cloned fetuses are gestating in rows of clear, womb-like containers. The decanters are periodically shaken to simulate human movement. Like all humans within the city, each embryo, fetus, and individual is genetically fitted to its prescribed role. So along with psychological conditioning, one's physical and mental abilities are engineered to conform to specific duties, designed to match their assigned tasks. The purpose for all this would be to offer each of the inhabitants the greatest happiness in life because each person's social stability is grounded in their community identity. Some people are scientifically predestined as leaders, and some as mechanics, while others are to be sewage workers. Each would be content. The rationale is that a person with a high IQ doing menial labor would be in a position of unimaginable discontent, required to repeat mundane, laborious tasks that utilize just a small portion of their mental capacity. The converse would be equally true for those of lower IQ, who would go mad if required to perform responsibilities above their cognitive level. Furthermore, the people who must do the unskilled or repetitive tasks are glad they have limited responsibility. It seems proper that they do not have to "think" as hard as the leaders. So, technological progress has allowed persons to be *engineered* into distinct levels of intelligence, to form a perfect social structure. This *future* scene is a paraphrase from the fictional account of Aldous Huxley, who in 1932 authored the dystopian novel *Brave New World.*

But back to the field trip . . . in the book, the children heard the Director of Hatcheries and Conditioning (DHC) use the term "parents," sending the young ones into an "uneasy silence." "One, at last, had the courage to raise a hand, asking if it is true that humans used to be viviparous"—that is, carrying developing babies inside the body of the female. But unfamiliar with any other term, they further asked how the babies were decanted from the body. "Born" came the correction. The Director explained that the parents were father and mother, terms that had become smut words.[20] Such language was relegated to a less advanced era, along with the notion that women would get pregnant from having sex in marriage, and couples within marriage only having sex with each other. For Huxley, this was a critique of the overreliance on scientific technology, which was grounded in the misplaced optimism he experienced in the culture of his time. He did not encounter the technological ability to clone children and dismantle the familial family structure, but was familiar with the goal of fitness through breeding. Huxley later thought this troubled future of *scientific futurism*, where technological progress

20. Huxley, *Brave New World*, 19.

was favored over human development, was happening sooner than expected. In 1958 he published an updated edition titled *Brave New World Revisited*, where the themes he perceived as no longer fiction were identified as threatening the onset of a technological dictatorship, reducing the human person as the means to societal progress.

Huxley's central concern was that the government would use technological advances in the form of *progress* to control society. The decanting and conditioning were simply a scientific means to that progress, which would thwart cultural development. In the discipline of philosophy (if it can truly be a separate discipline), the distinction is made between *progress* and *development*. Etymologically, the term *progress* holds the connotation of *moving forward* and is ethically neutral. The term *development* has the implied notion of cultivation, employing some internal process. Development requires reflection, while progress is doing the next step. Think of what one must go through to develop personal character, or what is necessary to form (develop) one's own conscience. Progress, on the other hand, does not contain that sense of *possibility* stemming from intention. Progress is like historical time; it marches on. Unlike incremental time, though, it does try to enhance what is presently available. But progress can imply the enhancement as a reaction, accepting something *different* as progress. In this way, it falls short of development. The concept of development is like ethical maturity, while progress is more like technological improvement. By definition, development exceeds being a mere reaction to what is presently available, as it moves toward an intentional, identifiable good of the human person. As both progress and technology can be employed devoid of their effect, development speaks to not just better technology (the newest phone), but to the use of technology (disciplined use). Progress, when left unchecked, actually devolves development, as in Huxley's novel. Progress considers what one *could* do, while development reflects on what one *should* do. Technology reaches for what is possible; it progresses, while development sorts out what is good in technology for the human person and society. This distinction is not merely pedantic and can be confusing because many people use terms haphazardly. Think in terms of personal relationships. One might frame the reconciliation of differences as making progress, but it would only be possible to the extent each person is developing personal skills and maturing in respect for the other as a person. Individuals—and, for that matter, society at large—exist in relation to technology. The reality is that even when one could achieve certain goals and thus refer to it as progress, individuals must ascertain what should be achieved, as the technology is utilized to develop the societal ethos as the collective character of the present. Without intentionality (technological progress), any effects of technology, both known and unknown, become situated within the cultural ethos and, once embedded, become difficult to undo. Again, this was Huxley's foreboding, and the truth nested in his fiction.

But an underlying concern by pairing technology with development as opposed to progress is that, except for a few powerful innovators, the average individual is limited in controlling technological progress. Think in terms of genetic engineering, where the power to determine technology's application in regard to "happiness for all" resides with certain entities, occupied by political and capital influence. Individual citizens become receivers and ultimately, as consumers, are unable to regulate the industry. Individuals possess neither the authority nor the ability to control what *could* be done, only whether or not they themselves *should* participate; but, again, this power can be subtle and the distinction between needs and wants can be confused. That is neither a minor nor an insignificant fact. Individuals do have the potential to develop their own character, with virtue theory, for instance, or the degree to which one conforms to utilitarian principles, or even perhaps in consideration of the application of Natural Law. And hopefully, through individual development, societal behavior ethically develops; but as argued previously, unless one's judgments are intentional, societal influence is a force not easily discerned.

But individual ethics has a much different dynamic collectively. And perhaps more importantly, technological advances often form as isolated powers determined by the ethical character of the few. The influence of these few, who are both powerful and rightly situated, can quickly morph into societal and State goals that are at odds with individually held ethical stances. That was Niebuhr's point with his *dualistic ethic*, where the dichotomy between moral individuals and immoral society is often paradoxically contradictory. So, if *happiness* (which is a vague term) is the governing factor for what is *good* for society, then in terms of technological progress, utility and availability may prove to govern or control the means to achieve that *good*. The distinction between what each individual strives for may very well have negligible effect at the societal level. There is no clear answer on how to ebb this tide; as to how such influence has played out historically, technological progress has proven difficult to discern from authentic societal development, and vice versa.

This section, then, will first look at where technology presently stands concerning *artificial wombs*, along with its likely *progression*. And finally, there will be some brief points offering insight into how the development of the artificial womb will affect the abortion dialogue in the future. As for where the present technology resides concerning artificial wombs, two significant scientific advancements are already a reality. First, it must be realized that the technology, in regard to human use of artificial wombs, is in its infancy. No pun is intended. Fetal lambs have successfully been gestated for weeks in an artificial womb referred to as a *biobag*. Another term used for the artificial womb is *ectogenesis* ("born outside"), which actually was coined prior to Huxley's novel. So, it is safe to assume his *decanting* idea for the novel was not entirely original, but obviously appears to be predictive. Others refer to the artificial womb as an *exowomb* (the prefix *ex-* again from the Greek *ektós* or the Latin *extra*, both meaning "outside"). Simply stated, the goal is an artificial environment "outside of the female body" that can sustain a fetus, serving as a substitute for the female's womb, placenta, blood supply, and so forth. The present goal of the scientific technology of artificial wombs is to allow human fetuses prior to or at viability the opportunity to continue maturation in a sustainable environment *outside* of the female's body. Presently, any child born prior to 37 gestational weeks is considered premature and is susceptible to health issues,[21] which likely include respiratory and heart conditions due to insufficient development. The survival rate is even lower for infants near viability but still pre-viable, where their organs are significantly underdeveloped. Presently, a fetus outside the womb at less than 22 gestational weeks may result in comfort care. The hope, then, and the application of such technology for human progress is that an artificial womb would allow the still developing child to be *transferred* to a sterile and controlled environment. The artificial womb is then a substitute for the female's womb that can continue providing nutrition and oxygen, while removing waste material. The artificial womb, which Huxley dubbed a decanter, can rightly be thought of as a neonatal incubator or an amniotic tank.

The artificial womb will be a lifesaving technological development. It is important to note that presently no researchers working on this

21. See Centers for Disease Control and Prevention, "Preterm Birth," para. 3.

practical application have expressed the intention of using this technology to begin the artificial process with an implanted embryo, as in Huxley's vision. Yet, most sensibly recognize that the technology may progress to that goal. To accomplish implantation of an embryo in an artificial womb, the female's endometrial cells would have to be successfully harvested and formed into an artificial placenta, which at some future time conjoined with the artificial womb *may* theoretically allow the unborn living human to gestate in this *future womb*, from fertilization to live birth. What term, other than *being born,* might catch hold is a curious thought, although the notion of to bear (*borne*) is to sustain, so perhaps it will remain appropriate. Nonetheless, the *prediction* for the artificial womb to become lifesaving for living fetal humans is near. By contrast, the forecast of such a *future womb* being used from the point of embryo implantation has many obstacles, but decades to come *will* find this technology exponentially closer to reality. It will progress, until such applied technology is something that *could* be done, and then the ethicists will debate to what extent it *should* be used in human reproductive applications, and how and if it can contribute to societal development. The general population, and the culture at large, reside somewhere between those two influences of "how" and "if," where allegiance to the "if" will increase steadily latent to the technological advances introduced by the "how" into society.

In terms of human sexuality (reproduction) and human sex (male/female), such fertility and reproduction have always been *outside* for the male. The male's sperm is necessary for fertilization, and the female's ovum is also necessary for fertilization, but the female body is presently necessary for gestation. To understand this *outside* relation to reproduction for the male, consider the term *semen.* It is a cognate term, meaning that the term shares the same meaning colloquially in English as it did in its ancestral language: the etymological source of *semen* in both Latin and English means "seed." That is a key point to recall in understanding how the male's role in reproduction was understood, prior to the discovery of the female gamete (ovum) in the nineteenth century. The general idea was that the male's *seed* contained all of the "material" of human life for reproduction. It was concluded that when the male placed his seed in the female's womb during intercourse, it was the female who then nurtured and brought this seed (material of human life) to birth. So, for the female, fertility and reproduction were always internal, and for the male, fertility and reproduction were always external. Although beyond the scope of this section, the sociological and psychological implications for both responsibility and participation in the pregnancy have been influenced by this notion.

But technology has changed the reality of the male being the sole sex excluded from fertilization. Initially, technological progress has permitted the male to be physically removed from the sexual act through sperm donation, and thus the female can become *pregnant* via artificial insemination. Still, the male's sperm was necessary for fertilization—but research is promising that soon sperm cells will be artificially engineered from embryonic stem cells rather than the testes. In fact, to preserve genetic material, some scientists envision deriving the cell line for artificial sperm from the female's bone marrow. If achieved, then the male will be removed as necessary for both fertility *and* reproduction. As to the female's necessary role in fertilization, decades earlier the first *test tube* baby was fertilized by what is now known as the IVF process. The discovery of the IVF process, developed by British physiologist Robert Edwards (d. 2013), was motivated by his early interest in the origins and transmission of genetic diseases during egg maturation.[22] But that process in the 1970s included harvesting sperm *directly* from adult males by ejaculation and by *harvesting* the ovum from females during naturally occurring cycles. Concerning technological progress with female gametes, now in tandem with the research toward artificial sperm, scientists are also investigating the means to grow a human ovum artificially from human tissue. In fact, mouse embryos have been created without the use of either sperm or ovum and then gestated in an artificial womb. That may not be possible with humans (yet), but it is predictive. So, where IVF was once the reproduction frontier, technological progress is on the brink of *gametogenesis*, a term referring to producing artificial sperm and ovum from the reprogrammed cells of a single adult of either the female *or* male sex. Theoretically, this removes the physical necessity of the female's gametic contribution (not necessary for fertilization). Coupled with the future success of the artificial womb, at that point fertilization will progress to also being *outside* the female's body, as it has historically been for the male. It might not be a matter of *if*, but *when*, gestation as well as fertilization is possible *outside* the female's body. In near-future hope, Dr. Zhang Qifeng of Kaiwa Technology has speculative plans of an artificial womb in humanoid form. The concept is relayed as a treatment

22. Johnson, "Path to IVF," para. 1.

for issues of fertility, but the practical and even time-saving applications are not lost on the potential for such surrogacy. At that point, *neither* sex would be necessary for fertilization or gestation. That would mirror the society portrayed by Huxley's "brave new world," with a surprising twist.

To be clear, these new biological technologies are not without regulation, though geo-political conditions vary. There are enforced time limits in which gestation is permitted to proceed only so far (embryos not permitted to the fetal stage). There is also regulation limited to data gathering (not for gestation), along with other various concerns on many ethicists' radar. But what was once impossible has become possible, and now ethicists are struggling to align technological *progress* with ethical *development*. In short, there are *moon shots* occurring within sexual reproduction technologies.

Here is the ethical dilemma and a concern that transcends the "sides" of the abortion dialogue. History has shown that what is thought possible is at some point attempted. Then when what is attempted becomes achievable, it is typically considered progress. What is achievable will at some point be accomplished. Then as what is accomplished becomes accepted, it will at some point be routine. Once such progress becomes routine or no longer novel in its use, it will then become customary. This can all happen without direct ethical development and easily within the time frame of a generation. In short, historically the segue for technology is from what is possible to achievable, and from what is novel to eventually becoming customary. Further, and more concerning, is that technological progress does not require ethical development to reach an achievement. Reflection on what should be done is the only safeguard to ensure that progress yields to development, in alignment with an authentic human good.

To that point, consider how few people question the use of IVF as a means for human reproduction (fertilization) now. The ethical evaluation of IVF has gained widespread approval, evidenced by the fact that whatever resistance Edwards might have faced in the 1970s with his research on IVF and human reproduction, by 2010 he was awarded the Nobel Prize for his efforts. It is safe to assume that continued acceptance of other currently novel forms of progress in fertility reproduction will parallel that strengthened support. Then the present novel applications themselves will become customary for subsequent generations; and like the ethical evolution of IVF, as these applications become customary, they also will be accepted as progress. Here is a syllogism to illustrate that claim.

P1 Technological advances inherited from past generations are acceptable in the present, because of familiarity stemming from their availability and common use.

P2 Those in the future who have access to customary technological fertility treatments will accept such present technological advances inherited from past generations.

C Therefore, those in the future who have access to customary technological fertility treatments will not likely question their use because of the present familiarity stemming from their availability and common use.

One should keep in mind that progress in fertility may seem value-neutral, but that value neutrality cannot apply to unforeseen effects that may disrupt ethical development. By definition, what is unforeseen is not identified in the present and consequently can be ethically judged only *after* the technological use has become customary. At that point, the original position (the elements weighed in the ethical evaluation) will have evaporated; and if the ethical effect is deleterious to human development, society can only seek to mitigate the undesired effects. There is typically some good in all advances, even if the ethical weight leans against those goods. Furthermore, it becomes difficult, if not impossible, to reject present technology once its use has been embedded in the culture. This reality itself is evidenced by the onset of regulations that crop up as the misuse of technology becomes apparent, but the utilitarian benefit, which is obvious, creates ethical tension against the undesirable effects. In short, it is often too late, as the imposition of one generation's technological progress on subsequent generations takes the form of customary use.

Relative to artificial wombs, what then is at stake for the public abortion dialogue? First, consider how entrenched female *bodily autonomy* is for an ethical judgment on abortion. It is so central for some that it has formed into the substance behind the pro-choice slogan. If female bodily autonomy is removed from the ethical calculus, then so too is the merit of the associated stance. Since the goal of this text is to position the abortion issue justly in relation to personhood as an ontological grounding, it logically follows that if the abortion dialogue is not about when life begins or the primacy of the female's bodily autonomy, then the idea of personhood and its subsequent value will be the only concept enduring into the future. Again, for many, bodily autonomy is *the issue* that determines the ethics of abortion. But bodily autonomy cannot retain its centrality or even its connection to abortion if (and when?) the female's womb is no longer required for gestation. At that point, since presently the female's body is not required for fertilization, gestation as necessarily involving the female will, as the last horizon, have evaporated. And the effect will appear even prior to that, for when artificial womb technology achieves even the ability to gestate infants post-viability, then any who have been holding onto fetus viability as the criterion will find it can no longer be held as the marker for an ethical evaluation. The consideration of assigning moral value will become tethered to the technological capabilities of the artificial womb, mirroring what some consider living human nonpersons in utero. But assigning moral value as the substitute for personhood as the source of dignity will simply rephrase the prime argument from *either all living humans are persons, or some living humans are persons* to *either some living humans have moral value, or all living humans have moral value*. If the immediate retort is that unlike personhood, moral value can be determined by degree, it does not resolve the criteria used or who determines such criteria relative to moral value. In short, the form of the argument will change, but not the substance.

So as to not overstate the concern of this technological progress as a threat, it should be made clear that simply because something is possible, customary, and even utilized, that does not imply that all utilize it, even those who have access and the means. The point is that even as IVF is presently acceptable, it is not presently universally used, so great caution should be taken before one imposes Huxley's vision as some universal scenario in the foreseeable future. For illustration, it is reported that only a third of couples utilize fertility treatment; perhaps 3 percent or fewer of children born were fertilized via IVF.[23] Percentages are helpful for perspective, meaning here that those 3 percent of children born translates to more than three million IVF cycles performed annually in the United States and thirteen million brought to birth worldwide since the original "test tube" baby was born in 1978.[24] The growing use is among those who are forty years of age or older. From that rising age

23. American Society for Reproductive Medicine, "US IVF Usage," para. 3.

24. Cassella, "How Many IVF Babies," para 1–2.

bracket, other elements present themselves also for consideration. So, accepting the conservative estimate of 3 percent of annual live births from IVF, and considering that the onset of delayed family planning is likely to increase, the concern of any effect from artificial wombs may be low but not insignificant and likely to increase in the near future. The point, stated simply with this introduction of technological advances, is not to predict a dystopian future and thus dismiss authentic developments from technological advances in sexual reproduction, but instead to offer a concrete example to serve the premise of this text, that *personhood* alone is the foundational element in the public abortion dialogue. To restate for emphasis, as bodily autonomy fades—and it eventually will—and abortion is not judged ethically by when life begins, the issue of personhood alone will persist. At some distant future point, as the availability of artificial wombs will be a feasible alternative, the ethical dilemma of abortion may (will?) necessarily adapt. At that point, on account of the customary technological advances, the focus will not reside with whether or not a female has bodily autonomy, but whether or not the fetus in the artificial womb, determined by some criteria, is deemed fit and, if not considered an ethical burden, is "born" into society.

If autonomy focuses on preserving what is deemed proper to the person, then rather than arguing over bodily rights determining the ethical judgment of an abortion in the future, some equivalent will likely arise in the abortion dialogue. What is now proposed as a *bodily rights argument* will morph into a *property rights argument*, meaning that there will be a legal claim to the artificially gestating, undecanted living human (post-birth fetus?), for those who do not hold that all living humans are persons. It will have to be articulated that the unborn in the exowomb may be discarded for reasons X or Y, in the same manner that one can legally dispose of owned property. In fact, by definition, something that is one's own property is determined not simply by possessing it, but by being able to legally dispose of it. So, in summation, now that artificial womb technology is presently *possible* and perhaps soon *achievable*, as it remains *novel* to the present generation, it will eventually become *customary* to those generations in the distant future. In the same way an adult today would not be surprised to learn that a female can presently become pregnant without sexual intercourse, future generations of adults may very well ask, "How were children gestated in the old days?" and be surprised to learn in reply, "They were gestated in the pelvic cavity of a female." Here is a syllogism to sum up these points and the thesis of this section.

P1 When artificial wombs in the future become customary as IVF is in the present, then only what constitutes personhood determined by value, capacity, or nature will persist in the abortion conversation.

P2 Female bodily autonomy will wane as gestation becomes external for the female, when artificial wombs in the future become customary as IVF is in the present.

C Therefore, female bodily autonomy will wane as gestation becomes external for the female; then only what constitutes personhood determined by value, capacity, or nature will persist in the abortion conversation.

So, regardless of how or when this reproductive technology *progresses*, only the idea of personhood, intentionally determined as the source of dignity, will permit the authentic application of technology to human *development*. Personhood alone will endure as the central and key element in the ethical analysis of the public abortion dialogue. For those who assert that every living human is a person, personhood will be attached to the embryo, fetus, newborn, and even those lacking consciousness, whether inside the female's womb or externally sustained in an artificial womb. For those who assert that some living humans are persons, the ethical assigning of personhood by Capacity X or Value Y will continue in tandem with assigning moral value, regardless of the location of the gestating living human.

8

For Consideration

Silence is one of the great arts of conversation.
—Marcus Tullius Cicero

A conversation is a dialogue, not a monologue. That's why there are so few good conversations: due to scarcity, two intelligent talkers seldom meet.
—Truman Capote

A single conversation across the table with a wise man is better than ten years mere study of books. —Henry Wadsworth Longfellow

OFTENTIMES PEOPLE WHO ARE conflicted with their stance or position on abortion feel a sense of hypocrisy if they question what is thought to be an associated fundamental tenet. One's affiliation to their political party, expression of dogmatic belief, and even social ideology are important aspects of the human person but, too often, are mistakenly the sole lens by which one views issues. Yet, in those intellectually lucid moments when what is argued by the "opposition" in an abortion conversation is recognized as reasonable or even perhaps agreeable, it is best to consider it rather than summarily dismiss it. But again, both to oneself and other fellow advocates, this becomes a perceived conflict of loyalty and an abandonment of one's identity with the associated position. At times, it appears as a matter of loyalty; since the stance is likely held with those one trusts, it seems both just and right to stand consistently with like minds. After all, loyalty is a virtue. A virtue can be defined as a developed disposition of the mind that leads to passion; formed as a habit, it genuinely leads one closer to perfection of character and truth. So, if this "habit forming" surfaces as loyalty solely to party, faith, and ideology, it is misguided. The virtue of loyalty requires an adherence first to truth, or it falls to mere sentiment and subjective ideology. In other words, no virtue is independent of another, and loyalty is to the pursuit of truth, which itself is a virtue destined to express one's held convictions. There is also the virtue of submitting to the prudence of those who share such a pursuit. Therefore, a pretentious loyalty is a false loyalty and thus not a loyalty at all. A false loyalty is a misplaced trust that actually disrespects both truth and other persons who aspire to such a pursuit. This fact, which should not be lobbed at the one who disagrees with a position considered sound (Bulverism fallacy), must form in respect, by way of engaging the other in an arena that offers the means to reconciling a position with an identified truth. There is neither loyalty nor truth-seeking in resisting growth, and no higher respect can be granted to oneself or another than to yield to a discovered truth, whether it alters one's stance or changes it entirely. Therefore, the aim of loyalty must always first be to truth, then to the expression of that truth; and being in the company of those who disagree (which is not giving comfort to the enemy) is the surest path to discover the veracity of one's own truth expression.

This was the very point made in *The Story of My Experiments with Truth*, an autobiography from Mahatma Gandhi, who did experience claims of disloyalty himself in the pursuit of truth. In the autobiography, he defended his singing of the British National Anthem while in Natal, South Africa.[1] Many questioned his national loyalty and wondered why he would participate in a symbol of an oppressor's national pride. It is obviously not because he supported the racial prejudice of British rule, but because he recognized prejudice (an ethical departure from truth) as a deviance that was both temporary (there were signs of growth) and local (it was not spread to all). He held that his love of truth was at the root of such loyalty, and he suffered from no pretense in recognizing truth wherever it exists, even in the stances of his so-called enemies. So then, with the public dialogue on abortion, if such a person adheres to a falsehood to avoid any sense of betrayal to their political party, belief expression, or social ideology, they have made loyalty to truth the actual enemy. But

1. Gandhi, *Story of My Experiments*, 172.

to address the sensing of an authentic conflict, in that political parties, belief expressions, and social ideologies are not monolithic (there may be nuanced positions, and not all aspects of the position are essential), it is not hypocrisy to continue even maintaining one's association, while the search for a deeper truth and clearer expression is underway. Each individual will have to determine if the position they are considering is a deal-breaker with the underlying or explicit tenets of the affiliated group. If one's newly discovered truth is in fundamental conflict with the group and the discord can only be alleviated by severing the association, then the severance (even if regrettable) points to a loyalty first to truth. But this need not be done to simply avoid the appearance of hypocrisy. People need to work out their own conflicting issues, and if one is honest as to where they are on their own journey, any sensible "opponent" will likely find that sensibly refreshing and intellectually honest. In fact, it may be that remaining in one's political party, belief expression, or social ideology is exactly what is needed to maintain the public dialogue, as the "outside" mentality often presents itself as a formidable obstacle. There is no neutral position, as one must reside where the truth finds them. In fact, truth itself does not have an isolated position "outside" of these relationships. An authentic loyalty may service the relation both to others within the affiliation and those not within the affiliation. Contrary to any appearance of hypocrisy or lack of loyalty, which is wisdom, one must find the means to remain within the dialogue, because oscillating public loyalties while one's reflection remains in flux signals both fickleness of character and unsteady reasoning.

REMAINING WITHIN THE DIALOGUE

An old English nursery rhyme speaks of being wise like an owl: the more the owl listened, the less the owl spoke; and the less the owl spoke, the more the owl listened. The straightforward logic it portrays is simple enough—in order to understand any truth, one must listen, understand, and then, if necessary, respond back in speech. Yet, this remains a rare commodity in the public abortion dialogue. It is more common for someone to listen for the first pause in speech, where the prepared counterpoint, which is typically a sound bite, is already loaded in one's mouth. But one must remain silent to listen, and one must listen to understand, and moreover, one must understand in order to respond and contribute to the abortion dialogue. Many people lack the acumen for critical thinking and, out of fear of being wrong, will display their conviction as proof in the confidence they hold. But this is a mask. It is not easy for any ego to accept correction, particularly in public. But this fear of being corrected publicly, and the penchant to double down, may come honestly because often the interlocutor will seize any pause or slip-up as an opportunity to thrust their ideology and partisan position as true by default. As a culture, people have not been conditioned to actively listen. Yet, silence is not always authentic listening, as *strategic silence* often is utilized to make the other unsteady. With those who seem to be gaining the upper hand in the argument, strategic silence can even be weaponized. People often feel the need to fill the gap of silence, and sometimes an inarticulate response made in haste will confirm the opponent's suspicion. It is also not charitable to allow the other person to flounder in their argument or persist in being inarticulate. Along with lacking charity, it demonstrates an intellectual disrespect on the part of the one posturing such feigned listening. Thus, conversation is an art. And the art of conversation requires listening and charity, along with intention and skill.

A requisite to entering into a public dialogue on the topic of abortion, or any contentious issue that is rightfully connected to deep-seated passions, is first to reform oneself. This will not appear pragmatic and is often found difficult—and because it is found difficult, it is left untried. But reform in this sense means to assess one's own conversational abilities and critical thinking skills. There is no upper limit to either, although good intentions in themselves offer no assurance that respectful dialogue will reach its mark. As important as it is to be willing to enter into a public dialogue on the topic of abortion, it is equally important to be willing to remain within that dialogue. The hope of remaining constructively engaged will diminish to the extent it becomes one's goal simply to win an argument or to reframe the conversation in a way thought advantageous for an individual's aligned position. Self-reform removes a stubborn obstacle, one's own ego, yet remains necessary for remaining within an authentic and constructive public dialogue on the topic of abortion.

THE GOAL OF DIALOGUING ON ABORTION

What, then, is the goal, if not to seek truth and, once truth is discovered and determined, to defend it against those who oppose such a logical approach to a rationally defendable stance? Recall how crucial it is to understand that the stances are not identifiable as sides, and to recognize the axiomatic claim that either *some living humans are persons, or all living humans are persons.* All of the many preliminary and foundational compositions offered in this treatise, along with the logical syllogisms, comparative examples, literary references, and reflective conversational insights, are designed to disclose and overcome the many errors of diversion and division that would otherwise frustrate the foundational claim and subsequently thwart the public abortion dialogue. Again, it is the common experience of most that demonstrating the ethical dilemmas of the abortion dialogue, which logically result from a poorly framed and inadequately understood argument, takes more time and explanation to unveil than simply asserting one's prepackaged point and aligning with an ideological or partisan stance. There is a reason such rational dialogue is rare. The willingness to listen and the principle of charity, in tandem with logic applied to critical thinking, cannot be constructive without an identified goal. It may sound like an oversimplification to assert, like Gandhi proposed, that truth is the goal. But that is not simply a visionary ideal. It is achieved with other like minds, who in respect and with loyalty to the pursuit of truth, are willing to listen, engage, and reflect.

The Socratic method (dialectic) requires questioning what another person claims to be true but also questioning what is thought to be true for oneself. In the abstract, most do accept "truth" as a primary goal, which is why stating it as a goal appears underwhelming and may even elicit indignation. But ideological loyalty is stubborn and has stymied the aspirations of many to reach such a truth, even when thinking one is in such pursuit. The issue, then, has not been identifying the goal, except for the uninformed and belligerent, but that the objectives to that goal are left untried and thus limit such achievement. Objectives are the path to a goal. If truth is the goal, then the objectives include the strategy and determination to make it to that goal. So, it may be more advantageous to speak here of those objectives—or, to be clear, what blocks the objectives en route to the goal toward truth. In fact, this section might have been more aptly titled "How not to argue" in order that by the process of negation (trimming away the illogical weeds) one discovers the path to dialogue properly. The most common and ineffectual path to the goal of truth is when either individuals or groups, unknowingly or overtly, engage in what is known as the *adversarial method.*

The term *adversary* properly invokes ideas of aggression in the form of a contest, with an opponent who must be beat. In every contest, it appears safe to assume that there are winners and losers. If that attitude is brought to the public abortion dialogue, it should be clear how it thwarts discussions. The adversarial method, which most are familiar with in civil disputes (battling lawyers), pits one disputer against another. The case is not decided by truth *per se*, but by how convincingly one can have their truth expressed to the ears of others who are often swayed more easily by crafty rhetoric. This has universally infiltrated the public abortion dialogue. When one becomes assured of the righteousness of their cause, it is considered just to use questionable tactics in order to "win" under the guise of defending one's position on abortion. This is how such adherence to a political party, belief expression, or social ideology feels right as a means to uphold one's position. The image of the *wise listening owl* is replaced by the *daft echoing parrot*. Admitted or not, this becomes a matter of disrespect, for other persons deserve not simply a thorough hearing but deferential consideration. Yet, it is important to insist that respect for the other person does not imply that one must remain silent while listening to an ideological diatribe. In the same way that one's autonomy stops at the threshold of another person, and one's rights end when another's rights are being infringed upon, so too does being disrespectful both solicit and deserve disengagement from the dialogue. But if the other person has critically thought out their position and is willing to both engage and listen, then respect demands reciprocation.

It may be psychologically agreeable to seek the company of like-minded individuals; but to reside within an echo chamber, in the public abortion dialogue, is a pretext to derail the objective of any dialectically oriented goal toward truth. In the public square, such a herd mentality has been inherited honestly from voices in entertainment news media, who know little of the substance of the abortion issue but never cease to share their distorted view with confidence. With such enterprises, the form of discussion rarely rises above the adversarial approach, resulting in discord. Politicians know even less about the issue and often employ deceptive tactics barely camouflaged by their theatrical delivery. Yet, in admitting such, if one seeks to be rational on the abortion issue, indicates a willingness to refrain from logical fallacies, and agrees to adhere to the method of critical thinking, there arises the temptation to think one is superior in being able to ferret out and thus recognize the other's errors. The individual who thinks they can always detect bullshit (which is a philosophical epistemology that some differentiate from lying as total disregard for the truth; to elucidate the distinction, the liar knows the truth and thus avoids it) may by that very pretense have fallen prey to such bullshit themselves. Humility is key—in fact, it is *the key*. In the same way that the proper use of logic and critical thinking does not make anyone "smarter" than another, it does make one's thinking clearer, and one's arguments sounder, which results in them being less apt to fallacious claims or patent rebuttals. Humility is not self-deprecation but an honest self-reflection, which requires the willingness to not simply be correct but also to accept correction.

To make the case then, the conversation must proceed in dialectical fashion, which is at once an admirable and possibly intimidating endeavor. The dialectical method is more cooperative and truth-driven than the adversarial method, which is both antagonistic and testimony-driven. By contrast, a dialectic requires rhetorical skills and a level of confidence that must be practiced and nurtured. More often than not in conversations, the expectation to have an ever-ready answer fosters the anxiety of an immediate response, as if there were an invisible game show buzzer nearing the allotted time. This has created the false expectation that no response, or a response given reservedly, is the equivalent of not knowing or of being wrong. Further, the perceived need for ready answers underlies the present trend of deferring to experts rather than offering one's own "amateur" judgments, which are thought too easy to dismiss. Quite frankly, it is why people seek books for better articulated arguments and videos to share in place of conversing, because it is thought the expert makes a better argument to support their "side" than they themselves could construct. By contrast, the focus of this treatise is not how to expertly present a side, but to distill the argument down to its essential premise and then encourage engaging dialectically in a good argument with truth as the goal. The sharing of an article or video cannot be interrogated directly and is therefore no substitute for an interlocutor and a live exchange. As to seeking the expert, since no single person can be an expert in all the fields and disciplines that intersect with the public abortion dialogue, any such attempt would become fragmented and thus unproductive. Once again, logic and critical thinking are of assistance here, as they each weigh the inferences and logical relations to detect unestablished or poorly aligned claims made in an argument. This is to mean that an "amateur," even in the presence of a panel of experts, only needs some semblance of logical relations to determine (1) in what manner a statement could be true or false in terms of its contingency of known factors and (2) at what point a statement presents a possible or necessary truth. And by understanding how to determine inferences and the relation of those expert claims, the truth value of their statements can be determined without knowing each of the facts separately that construct the proposed truth or falsehood.

In order to make that point clear as to how understanding inferential relations leads to knowledge, here is a joke that only logic professors may find humorous, but it will serve the present purpose. It begins, *Three guys walk into a bar. The bartender asks the first guy if everyone wants a beer; he says, "I do not know." The bartender asks the second guy if everyone wants a beer; he says, "I do not know." The bartender asks the third guy if everyone wants a beer; he says, "Yes."* That is the joke! Again, it is admittedly not funny except perhaps to logicians, but here it is explained. The inferences that can be made from each response, by understanding the logical relation to truth and falsehood, lead to the third guy knowing how to respond. The question to each guy was, "Does *everyone* want a beer?" So, the first and second guy could not say yes because even if they each took a beer themselves, the answer to the question remained only a possible truth, contingent on the next guy who had not yet responded. But when the third guy is asked the question, and he knows the previous two took a beer, and that he himself will take a beer, he could respond, "Yes." Unlike the first two guys, he is aware that each said yes. Therefore, what was only a *possible* truth for the first two guys (does everyone want a beer?) became actual when the third guy both wanted a beer and knew the first two guys received a beer. The bartender asked what is called a *contingent question*, which made it necessary for all three guys to receive a beer for his question if everyone wants a beer to be true. So, to turn this joke into a riddle, state the scenario and ask someone, "How many guys had a beer?" They will solve it, *if* they can consider the contingency of known factors in relation to what is a possible or necessary truth.

Now, to see how this logic joke applies to the premise of the text and this section in particular, suppose someone asks, "It is not even known exactly what it means to say when life begins, so how can anyone be certain an embryo is alive?" One need not be an expert biologist to answer that question; it is enough to know the embryo's relation to biological life as one of continuity, in that the living sperm and ovum fertilize into an embryo, and an embryo becomes a fetus, and a fetus becomes an infant, which no one denies is a living being. The issue is not really one of origins. Rather, the issue is relevant to whether an infant, as a living being, can come from anything that is not living—therefore, an embryo is biologically living. To the idea then of the embryo as a human being, one need not be an expert anthropologist to distinguish whether the embryo is a member of the species *Homo sapiens*. It is enough to know of the embryo's relation as belonging to the species of *Homo sapiens*, in that there is no neutral species that can become human at the infant stage (and no one argues an infant is not a human being). If only a human can form from a human, and the born infant is human, then the embryo that formed the infant is therefore also human. So with both cases, unless the biologist can empirically demonstrate that the origin of life begins with each new human offspring or the anthropologist empirically demonstrates that there is a "neutral species" that exists prior to the offspring being identified as *Homo sapiens*, their expert opinion on those matters is of little importance, because it is actually true that the embryo is both living and human by virtue of the logical relation to the living human species that propagated the embryo. That accepted, then, the relation of those empirically determined criteria of *life* and *human* is not something the pedestrian individual needs to concede to the experts, knowing the referential relations are sufficient. Then, specifically to the abortion topic, this reveals *personhood* as the logical focus of the public dialogue. This application of the inferential relation of human and life may not map the same way as the beers did to the initial question in the logic joke, but both fall within the parameters of logical relations understood in terms of modality.

It would be absurd to expect that the illustrations offered in the whole of this text could, or should, settle the public abortion dialogue, but they certainly can and do offer insight into how one may initiate, engage in, and sustain a potentially fruitful exchange. Yet, as one develops their own expression of an argument in support of their *either all or some* position, what the dialectical method ensures is not only self-correction, but charitable rebuffs offering the opportunity to amend and improve one's truth claims and thus the conclusion from the logical argument. If any logical controversy surrounding the ideas of the terms *living* and *human* can be set aside as sufficiently accepted empirically, then the errors will surface in dialoguing on the issue of personhood, which is in the realm of philosophy or theology. But both philosophical or theological expressions, along with their epistemological methods, must be held to the precision of logic and the rigor of critical thinking, which the dialectical method affords through corrections of propositional errors, argumentative form, and logical fallacies. But recognizing the presence or even persistence of potential errors does not dismiss what one *does know* with confidence, which lends itself toward an ethical evaluation. And any trepidation about the many errors one may or will make while in dialogue should be welcomed as an opportunity to articulate a held truth more accurately and thoroughly in the future. Though few of Epicurus's writings survive from the third century BC, his *Vatican Collection of Sayings* contains a list of numbered maxims, or bits of wisdom. His "Saying #74" reads, "In a philosophical dispute, he who is defeated gains the most, since he learns the most."[2] This is a rearticulation of what was shared in the first section of this text: if both the questioner and the interlocutor's goal is truth, regardless of the initial position, then making an error carries them one step closer toward the sought-after truth. One's goal should not be to "not make a mistake" but rather to "not make the same mistake twice." The strategy within the public abortion dialogue is to do more than just hold the appearance of being correct, which the adversarial method allows; the strategy is to *actually be* correct. This requires the sequence of ideas flowing from proposal to accepting the rebuttal, seeking a revision, reforming a proposition, and then each submitting to the unearthed truth. Those incremental ideas of the dialectic engagement are the *objectives* (steps) to the goal (purpose) of the sought-after truth. And if the objective toward a truth within the public abortion dialogue is centered on personhood, then it is important to keep in mind that the idea of personhood cannot be definitively settled or solved, but can be unraveled, with an increased depth of knowing. Contemplating the idea of personhood is a quest, and one which requires the participation of persons.

In that quest, individuals must seek to accept demonstrated certainty, which is good. But since with personhood, this cannot be empirical certainty (for Hume, such certainty referred to as facts can lead to skepticism), one must work toward assurances of credibility. For example, the rational argument for *all living humans are persons* or for *some living humans are persons* must make a credible claim that stands up to scrutiny, against the elements of critical thinking. This is to say, being *confident* that one is certain is not an *assurance of credibility* that one is certain. It is common to confuse certainty with confidence, which is not good. And though it is good to be certain, which would lead to confidence

2. Epicurus.info, "Vatican Sayings," #74.

of an established truth, the human person is easily self-deluded into thinking that what brings comfort can be true because of the comfort it brings. Sometimes what feels right *seems* right, but discernment is necessary for a well-placed confidence. Here is a literary example. The Lebanese-American poet Kahlil Gibran (d. 1931), in his book *The Prophet*, addresses in fable form various facets of discerning that which is good from that which is not good. It might help here to think of those ideas in terms of *good meaning true*, and *not good meaning false*. Gibran warns poetically that what is true will sometimes seek food in dark caves when hungry, and also sometimes drink from dead waters when thirsty. His point is that when confronted with a truth that threatens one's ego or foundational identity and thus jeopardizes one's comfort, the falsehoods presented as the "food in dark caves" and the "drink from dead waters"[3] bring satisfaction and confidence, but are deceptively received as a falsehood preferred over an uncomfortable truth. In brief, this is to mean that self-deception is the most difficult of weaknesses to uncover. Self-reflection is the necessary anecdote to overcome self-deception and unveil whether it is *the truth* or *the comfort* that affirms one's sense of credibility, and thus one's certainty. This is precisely why logic is both necessary but not sufficient in itself for the public abortion dialogue. Though a well-constructed syllogism offers both a succinct argument and the expression of how one's truth claims lead to a conclusion, the human person is not simply a digester of syllogisms. More is necessary to satisfy sufficiency in making a valid argument both digestible and convincing; otherwise, this entire book would have consisted of nothing but a series of syllogisms, sprinkled with facts and logical inferences. The human person is not just an intellect but a being of passions and appetites, and rightly seeks to have the sympathies of the heart's affections aligned with the credible claim.

Despite there always being some tension between what philosophers call the passions and reason, neither desires nor the intellect are necessarily in conflict, although one's desires can be irrational just as one's intellect can be deceived. Plato offered the allegory of the chariot while in dialectic on the use of rhetoric with his interlocutor, Phaedrus. The allegory, designed to illustrate the three aspects of the human psyche, is applied here in a slightly different manner but remains adequate to illustrate the point. For Plato, the human person, as the charioteer, is

3. Gibran, *Prophet*, 64.

pulled by two winged horses. One horse represents the *irrational desires* pulling the driver toward those immediate gratifications, which in the public abortion dialogue can be understood as seeking the appearance of *winning*. The other horse represents the *rational desires* pulling the driver toward those noble goals,[4] which in the public abortion dialogue can be understood as *certainty* and *credibility*. The human person in the abortion dialogue, like the charioteer using his reason as the reins, must not allow one horse to overtake the other. That would result in pulling the chariot off the path to truth. Stated another way, the human person has a mind and heart—but to appeal only to one's desires, as aligned with an identity or ideology, is akin to persuasion without logic and critical thinking. The goal traverses from seeking to be informed, and thus reformed, to mere manipulation of the conversation for the sake of one's own ego. But likewise, to appeal only to the intellect, mocking the passions and the rhetorical, will result in intellectual bullying, where success means sending the other cowering into submission or silencing them under the pretext of sounding correct.

This treatise has attempted to offer syllogistic reasoning, coupled with rhetoric, to offer an appeal to truth that satisfies the intellect and offers consideration to one's passions. To that end, what was offered in the text was purposefully peppered with anecdotes, explanations, and analogies, which are mere aids to help those logical syllogistic formations find a home in both the heart and mind. This text, to the degree it was possible to complete that task well, itself enters the public abortion dialogue. The hope is that, as a primer, this functions as a contribution to the public abortion dialogue. That is, in terms of substance it will contribute something for most, while in terms of benefit it may offer authentic development for all. The goal of *Autonomy, Consciousness, and Personhood* is to advance the rational public dialogue on abortion, by situating the premise that either *all living humans are persons, or some living humans are persons* as the central and sole tenet worthy of fruitful exchange.

4. Plato, *Phaedrus*, 250–51.

Bibliography

Alberts, Bruce, et al. *Essential Cell Biology, 4th ed.* New York: Garland Science, 2013.

American Society for Reproductive Medicine. "US IVF Usage Increases in 2023, Leads to over 95,000 Babies Born." ASRM.org. April 22, 2025. https://www.asrm.org/news-and-events/asrm-news/press-releasesbulletins/us-ivf-usage-increases-in-2023-leads-to-over-95000-babies-born/.

Aquinas, Thomas. *Summa Theologica*. Vol. 3. Translated by Fathers of the English Dominican Province. Notre Dame, IN: Christian Classics, 1981.

Arbesman, Samual. *The Half-Life of Facts*. New York: Penguin, 2013.

Aristotle. *Metaphysics*. In *The Complete Works of Aristotle: The Revised Oxford Translation*, edited by Jonathan Barnes, 1552–1728. Princeton: Princeton University Press, 1991.

———. *Physics*. In *The Complete Works of Aristotle: The Revised Oxford Translation*, edited by Jonathan Barnes, 315–446. Princeton: Princeton University Press, 1991.

———. *Politics*. In *The Complete Works of Aristotle: The Revised Oxford Translation*, edited by Jonathan Barnes, 1986–2129. Princeton: Princeton University Press, 1991.

Armstrong, Scott A., and Michael J. Herr. "Physiology, Nociception." National Library of Medicine. Treasure Island, FL: StatPearls, 2023. https://www.ncbi.nlm.nih.gov/books/NBK551562/.

Audi, Robert, ed. "Ship of Theseus." In *The Cambridge Dictionary of Philosophy*, 4th ed., 842. Cambridge: Cambridge University Press, 1999.

Bachrach, Susan. "Deadly Medicine: Creating the Master Race." U.S. Holocaust Memorial Museum. https://www.ushmm.org/exhibition/deadly-medicine/overview/.

Benner, Steven A. "Defining Life." *Astrobiology* 10 (2010) 1021–30. https://doi:10.1089/ast.2010.0524.

Berkeley, George. *A Treatise Concerning the Principles of Human Knowledge*. Edited by Colin M. Turbayne. New York: Liberal Arts, 1957.

Betz, Eric. "Pluto Has Likely Maintained an Underground Liquid Ocean for Billions of Years." *Astronomy*, June 23, 2020. https://www.astronomy.com/science/pluto-has-likely-maintained-an-underground-liquid-ocean-for-billions-of-years/.

Boethius. *Tractates, De Consolatione Philosophiae*. Translated by H. E. Stewart and F. K. Rand. Cambridge, MA: Harvard University Press, 1968.

Boyd, Richard. "Realism, Anti-Foundationalism and the Enthusiasm for Natural Kinds." *Philosophical Studies* 61 (1991) 127–48.

Buber, Martin. *I and Thou*. Translated by Walter Kaufmann. New York: Touchstone, 1996.

Bujo, Bénézet. *Foundations of an African Ethic: Beyond the Universal Claims of Western Morality*. Redwood City, CA: PublishDrive, 2001.

Carruthers, Peter. *Phenomenal Consciousness: A Naturalistic Theory*. 1st ed. New York: Cambridge University Press, 2000.

Cassella, Carly. "Study Reveals How Many IVF Babies Have Been Born Worldwide." ScienceAlert, August 4, 2025. https://www.sciencealert.com/study-reveals-how-many-ivf-babies-have-been-born-worldwide.

Centers for Disease Control and Prevention. "Preterm Birth." Maternal Infant Health, May 20, 2024. https://www.cdc.gov/maternal-infant-health/preterm-birth/index.html.

Chalmers, David. "Facing Up to the Problem of Consciousness." *Journal of Consciousness Studies* 2 (1995) 200–219.

———. *The Conscious Mind: In Search of a Fundamental Theory*. Oxford: Oxford University Press, 1996.

Chang, Iris. *The Rape of Nanking: The Forgotten Holocaust of World War II*. New York: Basic, 1997.

Chesterton, G. K. *The Illustrated London News*. Vol. 164, issue 4435 (April 19, 1924).

———. *What's Wrong with the World*. San Francisco: Ignatius, 1994.

Chung, Grace S., et al. "Obstetrician-Gynecologists' Beliefs About When Pregnancy Begins." *American Journal of Obstetrics and Gynecology* 206 (2012) 132.e1–132.e7. https://doi.org/10.1016/j.ajog.2011.10.877

Cicero, Marcus Tullius. *De Re Publica: Selections*. Edited by James E. G. Zetzel. Cambridge: Cambridge University Press, 1995.

Crane, Judith J. "On the Metaphysics of Species," *Philosophy of Science* 71 (2004) 156–73.

Crary, David, and Hannah Fingerhut. "AP-NORC Poll: Most Say Restrict Abortion After 1st Trimester." AP News, June 25, 2021. https://apnews.com/article/only-on-ap-us-supreme-court-abortion-religion-health-2c569aa7934233af8e00bef45 20a8fa8.

De Georgia, Michael A. "History of Brain Death as Death: 1968 to the Present." *Journal of Critical Care* 29 (2014) 673–78. https://doi.org/10.1016/j.jcrc.2014.04.015.

Dennett, Daniel. "Conditions of Personhood." In *What Is a Person?*, edited by M. R. Goodman, 145–67. New York: Springer, 1988. https://doi.org/10.1007/978-1-4612-3950-5_7.

———. *Consciousness Explained*. Boston: Little, Brown, 1991.

———. *Darwin's Dangerous Idea: Evolution and the Meanings of Life*. New York: Simon & Schuster, 1995.

Descartes, René. *Discourse on Method and Meditations on First Philosophy*. Translated by Donald A. Cress. 4th ed. Indianapolis: Hackett, 1998.

Dewey, John. "Psychology as Philosophic Method." *Mind* 11.42 (1886) 153–73. http://www.jstor.org/stable/2247469.

Didache, or the Teaching of the Twelve Apostles. In *Ancient Christian Writers*, edited by Johannes Quasten, 6:15–25. St. Louis, MO: Newman, 1948.

Doe v. Bolton. 410 U.S. 179 (1973). https://supreme.justia.com/cases/federal/us/410/179/.

Ellul, Jacques. *The Technological Society*. Translated by John Wilkinson. New York: Vintage, 1954. https://archive.org/details/JacquesEllulTheTechnologicalSociety/page/n1/mode/2up.

Epicurus.info (Epicurean Philosophy Online). "E-Texts: The Vatican Sayings (Unabridged)." Epicurism.info, 2025. https://www.epicurism.info/etexts/VS.html.

Frankfurt, Harry. "Freedom of the Will and the Concept of a Person." *Journal of Philosophy* 68 (1971) 5–20. https://doi.org/10.2307/2024717.

Fruhstorfer, Clark, et al. "Patient Experiences with Requests for Medical Assistance in Dying." *Canadian Family Physician* 70 (2024) 41–47. https://doi.org/10.46747/cfp.700141.

Galton, Francis. *Inquiries into Human Faculty and Its Development*. First electronic edition, 2001. Edited by Gavan Tredoux. Based on the 1907 Everyman Second Edition. https://galton.org/books/human-faculty/text/galton-1883-human-faculty-v4.pdf.

Gandhi, Mahatma. *The Story of My Experiments with Truth*. Translated by Mahadev Desai. Boston: Beacon, 1993.

Gibran, Kahlil. *The Prophet*. New York: Knopf, 1986.

Goff, Philip. "Are Electrons Conscious?" Oxford University Press's OUPblog, August 13, 2017. https://blog.oup.com/2017/08/electrons-consciousness-philosophy/.

———. *Consciousness and Fundamental Reality*. New York: Oxford University Press, 2017.

———. *Why? The Purpose of the Universe*. Oxford: Oxford University Press, 2023.

Gomez, Ivette, et al. "Abortions Later in Pregnancy in a Post-Dobbs Era." KFF, Feb. 21, 2024. https://www.kff.org/womens-health-policy/abortions-later-in-pregnancy-in-a-post-dobbs-era/.

Gómez-Márquez, Jaime. "What Is Life?" *Molecular Biology Reports* 48 (2021) 6223–30. https://doi.org/10.1007/s11033-021-06594-5.

Government of Iceland. "Facts about Down's Syndrome and Pre-Natal Screening in Iceland." Press release by the Embassy of Iceland in London, March 26, 2018. https://www.government.is/diplomatic-missions/embassy-article/2018/03/26/Facts-about-Downs-syndrome-and-pre-natal-screening-in-Iceland/.

Gramsci, Antonio. *Selections from the Prison Notebooks*. Translated by Quintin Hoare and Geoffrey Nowell Smith. New York: International, 1992.

Greely, Henry T. "CRISPR'd Babies: Human Germline Genome Editing in the 'He Jiankui Affair.'" *Journal of Law and the Biosciences* 6 (2019) 111–83. https://doi.org/10.1093/jlb/lsz010.

Harris, Sam. *Free Will*. New York: Free, 2012.

Hitchens, Christopher. "William Lane Craig vs. Christopher Hitchens." Transcript from 2009 debate. Accessed Feb. 28, 2022. https://christophererichitchens.com/william-lane-craig-does-god-exist/.

Hobbes, Thomas. *Leviathan: With Selected Variants from the Latin Edition of 1668*. Edited by Edwin Curley. Indianapolis: Hackett, 1994.

Hume, David. *An Enquiry Concerning Human Understanding, with A Letter from a Gentleman to His Friend in Edinburgh, and Hume's Abstract of A Treatise of Human Nature*. 2nd ed. Edited by Eric Steinberg. Indianapolis: Hackett, 1993.

Husserl, Edmund. *The Idea of Phenomenology*. Translated by William P. Alston and George Nakhnikian. The Hague: Martinus Nijhoff, 1964.

Huxley, Aldous. *Brave New World*. Garden City, NY: International Collectors Library, 1946.

James, William. "The Self." In *The Philosophy of William James*, edited by Horace M. Kallen, 124–57. New York: Modern Library, 1917.

Johnson, Martin H. "Robert Edwards: The Path to IVF." *Reproductive Biomedicine Online* 23 (2011) 245–62. https://doi.org/10.1016/j.rbmo.2011.04.010.

Kant, Immanuel. *Critique of Pure Reason*. Translated by J. M. D. Meiklejohn. New York: Prometheus, 1990.

———. *The Doctrine of Virtue*. Translated by Mary J. Gregor. San Francisco: Harper & Row, 1964.

———. *Grounding for the Metaphysics of Morals: On a Supposed Right to Lie Because of Philanthropic Concerns*. Translated by James W. Ellington. Indianapolis: Hackett, 1992.

Kastrup, Bernardo. *Brief Peeks Beyond: Critical Essay on Metaphysics, Neuroscience, Free Will, Skepticism and Culture*. Winchester, UK: Iff, 2015.

KFF. "What the Data Show: Abortions Later in Pregnancy." KFF news release, February 21, 2024. https://www.kff.org/womens-health-policy/what-the-data-show-abortions-later-in-pregnancy/.

King, Martin Luther, Jr. "Letter from Birmingham Jail." In *A Testament of Hope: The Essential Writings of Martin Luther King, Jr.*, edited by James Melvin Washington, 289–302. San Francisco: Harper & Row, 1986.

Kölle, Sabine. "Sperm-Oviduct Interactions: Key Factors for Sperm Survival and Maintenance of Sperm Fertilizing Capacity." *Andrology* 10 (2022) 837–43. https://doi.org/10.1111/andr.13179.

Lagercrantz, Hugo, and Jean-Pierre Changeux. "The Emergence of Human Consciousness: From Fetal to Neonatal Life." *Pediatric Research* 65 (2009) 255–60. https://doi: 10.1203/PDR.0b013e3181973b0d.

Lee, Iris T., and Kurt T. Barnhart. "What Is an Ectopic Pregnancy?" *Journal of the American Medical Association* 329 (2023) 434. https://doi.org/10.1001/jama.2022.22941.

Lewis, C. S. *The Abolition of Man*. San Francisco: HarperOne, 2000.

Libet, Benjamin. "Do We Have Free Will?" *Journal of Consciousness Studies*, 6.8–9 (1999) 47–57.

Lief, Jacob, and Andrea Thompson. *I Am Because You Are: How the Spirit of Ubuntu Inspired an Unlikely Friendship and Transformed a Community*. New York: Rodale, 2015.

Linde, Andrei. "Universe, Life, Consciousness." Excerpt from *Quantum Cosmology and the Nature of Consciousness* (n.d.), section 9. Accessed April 30, 2023. https://scienceandnonduality.com/article/universe-life-consciousness-by-andrei-linde/.

Locke, John. *An Essay Concerning Human Understanding*. Abridged and edited by Kenneth P. Winkler. Indianapolis: Hackett, 1996.

———. *Two Treatises of Government*. Reprint. Whitefish, MT: Kessinger, 1980.

Loseva, Polina A., and Vadim N. Gladyshev. "The Beginning of Becoming a Human." *Aging* 16 (2024) 8378–95. https://doi.org/10.18632/aging.205824.

Marcel, Gabriel. *The Mystery of Being (Gifford Lectures, 1949–1950)*. Vol. 1, *Reflection and Mystery*, translated by G. S. Fraser. South Bend, IN: St. Augustine's, 2001.

Mason, Rebecca. "The Metaphysics of Social Kinds." *Philosophy Compass* 11.12 (2016) 841–50. https://doi.org/10.1111/phc3.12381.

Meyer, Herbert H. "Max Scheler's Understanding of the Phenomenological Method." *International Studies in Philosophy* 19 (1987) 21–31. https://doi.org/10.5840/intstudphil19871913.

Mix, Lucas John. *Life Concepts from Aristotle to Darwin: On Vegetable Souls.* Cham, Switzerland: Springer, 2018.

Möhle, Hannes. "Scotus's Theory of Natural Law." In *The Cambridge Companion to Duns Scotus,* edited by Thomas Williams, 312–31. New York: Cambridge University Press, 2002.

Molefe, Motsamai. *An African Ethics of Personhood and Bioethics: A Reflection on Abortion and Euthanasia.* Cham, Switzerland: Palgrave Macmillan, 2020. https://doi.org/10.1007/978-3-030-46519-3.

Nagel, Thomas. "Panpsychism." In *Mortal Questions,* 181–95. New York: Cambridge University Press, 2012.

———. "What Is It Like to Be a Bat?" *Philosophical Review* 83 (1974) 435–50.

Necula, Deanna, et al. "Insight into the Roles of CCR5 in Learning and Memory in Normal and Disordered States." *Brain, Behavior, and Immunity* 92 (2021) 1–9. https://doi.org/10.1016/j.bbi.2020.11.037.

Niebuhr, Reinhold. *Moral Man and Immoral Society: A Study in Ethics and Politics.* New York: Scribner's Sons, 1960.

Nietzsche, Friederich. *On the Genealogy of Morals.* Translated by Walter Kaufmann. New York: Vintage, 1989.

Nucleus. "PGT-A Testing Accuracy for Sex Determination: A Complete Guide for IVF Patients." Mynucleus.com, 2025. https://mynucleus.com/blog/pgta-testing-gender-accuracy/.

Nwoye, Augustine. "An Africentric Theory of Human Personhood." *Psychology in Society* 54 (2017) 42–66. https://scielo.org.za/pdf/pins/n54/04.pdf.

Omni. "How Soon Can an Ultrasound Show a Baby's Heartbeat?" January 30, 2023. https://www.omnigynaecare.com.au/blog/how-soon-can-an-ultrasound-show-a-babys-heartbeat.

Petrina, Alessandra. "All Petrarch's Fault: The Idea of a Renaissance." *Padua Research Archive (University of Padua)* 6 (2020) 145–64. https://doi.org/10.13133/2283-8759/16405.

Plato. *Phaedo.* Translated by G. M. A. Grube. Indianapolis: Hackett, 1977.

———. *Phaedrus.* In *The Dialogues of Plato,* translated by Benjamin Jowett, 233–82. New York: Random House, 1937.

———. *The Republic.* In *The Dialogues of Plato,* translated by Benjamin Jowett, 591–879. New York: Random House, 1937.

Reid, Maddy. "The History of the Slave Trade." The Freedom Project, Aug. 22, 2022. https://www.thefreedomproject.org/blog/2022/8/22/history-of-the-slave-trade.

Reiman, Jeffrey. "Abortion, Infanticide, and the Asymmetric Value of Human Life." *Journal of Social Philosophy* 27 (1996) 181–200.

Revised Standard Version: Catholic Edition. *The Holy Bible.* San Francisco; Ignatius, 1965.

Riedinger, A. R. "Lexical Inequities in Marriage: Old English *Wif, Wer,* and *Husbonda.*" *Studia Neophilologica* 66 (1994) 3–14. https://doi.org/10.1080/00393279408588126.

Roe v. Wade. 410 U.S. 113, 114 (1973). https://www.loc.gov/item/usrep410113/.

Russell, Bertrand. *The Analysis of Mind*. Auckland, New Zealand: The Floating Press, 2009.

Salice, Alessandro, and Hans Bernhard Schmid, eds. *The Phenomenological Approach to Social Reality: History, Concepts, Problems*. Cham, Switzerland: Springer, 2016.

Sanger, Margaret, ed. "Birth Control Review, vol. 5, no. 11, Nov. 1921." *Birth Control Review*. Accessed April 30, 2023. https://birthcontrolreview.org/items/show/187.

Schechtman, Marya, "The Narrative Self." In *The Oxford Handbook of the Self*, edited by Shaun Gallagher (online edition, May 2, 2011). Oxford: Oxford Academic, 2011. https://doi.org/10.1093/oxfordhb/9780199548019.003.0018.

Schiller, Friedrich. *On the Aesthetic Education of Man*. Translated by Reginald Snell. Mineola, NY: Dover, 2004.

Schmal, Daniel. "Virtual Reflection: Antoine Arnauld on Descartes' Concept of *Conscientia*." *British Journal for the History of Philosophy* 28 (2019) 714–34. https://doi.org/10.1080/09608788.2019.1684238.

Scruton, Roger. *On Human Nature*. Princeton: Princeton University Press, 2017.

Searle, John. *The Rediscovery of the Mind (Representation and Mind)*. Cambridge, MA: Bradford, 1992.

Seneca the Younger (Seneca, Lucius Annaeus). *De Ira*. Translated by Robert A. Kaster (n.d.). https://ia804605.us.archive.org/33/items/seneca-on-anger-kaster/Seneca%20-%20%27%27On%20Anger%27%27%20%5Bkaster%5D.pdf.

Shelley, Mary. *The Essential Frankenstein: The Definitive, Annotated Edition of Mary Shelley's Classic Novel*. Edited by Leonard Wolf. New York: Plume, 1993.

Singer, Peter, ed. *Ethics*. New York: Oxford University Press, 1994.

———. *Rethinking Life and Death: The Collapse of Our Traditional Ethics*. New York: St. Martin's, 1995.

Tao, Mai. "Chinese Company Developing Humanoid Robot to Give Birth: Breakthrough or Dystopian Nightmare?" *Robotics & Automation News*, August 18, 2025. https://roboticsandautomationnews.com/2025/08/18/chinese-company-developing-humanoid-robot-to-give-birth-breakthrough-or-dystopian-nightmare/93760/.

Teague, Robin, and Ryan McRae. "Ancient DNA and Neanderthals." The Smithsonian Institution's Human Origins Program, June 14, 2012. https://humanorigins.si.edu/evidence/genetics/ancient-dna-and-neanderthals.

Tertullian. *Apologeticus*. In *Ante-Nicene Fathers*, edited by Alexander Roberts and James Donaldson, 3:17–55. Repr., Peabody, MA: Hendrickson, 2004.

Thomson, Judith Jarvis. "A Defense of Abortion." *Philosophy & Public Affairs* 1 (1971) 47–66.

Tooley, Michael. *Abortion and Infanticide*. New York: Oxford University Press, 1984.

Verhagen, Eduard, and John Lantos. "The Dutch Model for Regulating Paediatric Euthanasia." *Archives of Disease in Childhood* 110 (2024) e326998. https://doi.org/10.1136/archdischild-2024-326998.

Wayland, John Walter. "The True Gentleman." Originally published in *Baltimore Sun*, 1899. Accessed April 30, 2023. https://saepsu.org/about/the-true-gentleman/.

Weber, Bruce H. "Emergence of life." *Zygon* 42 (2007) 837–56.

WGBH Forum Network. "Christopher Hitchens and Rabbi David Wolpe: The Great God Debate; Harvard Book Store." March 23, 2010. Available at American Archive of Public Broadcasting, 2025. https://americanarchive.org/catalog/cpb-aacip-15-3n20c4sm15.

Wilkins, John S. *Species: The History of the Idea*. Berkeley: University of California Press, 2009.

Williams, Bernard. *Problems of the Self: Philosophical Papers 1956–1972*. Cambridge: Cambridge University Press, 1999.

Yang, Zeyi. "A Controversial Chinese CRISPR Scientist Is Still Hopeful about Embryo Gene Editing. Here's Why." MIT Technology Review, July 31, 2024. https://www.technologyreview.com/2024/07/31/1095509/he-jiankui-hopeful-gene-editing/.

Zhai, Xiaomei, et al. "Chinese Bioethicists Respond to the Case of He Jiankui." Hastings Center for Bioethics, Feb. 7, 2019. https://www.thehastingscenter.org/chinese-bioethicists-respond-case-jiankui/.

www.ingramcontent.com/pod-product-compliance
Lightning Source LLC
LaVergne TN
LVHW020532100826
845148LV00010B/1437

* 9 7 9 8 3 8 5 2 6 1 1 4 7 *